URBAN CONSUMPTION

For Ina
To Cecilie

URBAN CONSUMPTION

Tracing urbanity in the archaeological record of Aarhus c. AD 800-1800

Jette Linaa

With contributions by Lars Krants

Jutland Archaeological Society

Urban Consumption

Tracing urbanity in the archaeological record of Aarhus c. AD 800-1800

English revision: Anne Bloch and David Earle Robinson
Layout and cover: Jens Nygaard
Paper: Artic Volume 130 g
Fonts: Palatino, Futura
Printed by Narayana Press

ISBN: 978-87-93423-06-0
ISSN: 0107-2854

Jutland Archaeological Society Publications vol. 94

Published: Jutland Archaeological Society
Moesgaard
DK-8270 Højbjerg

Distribution: Aarhus University Press
Langelandsgade 177
DK-8200 Aarhus N

Published with financial support from:
Dronning Margrethe II's Arkæologiske Fond
Vilhelm Kiers Fond

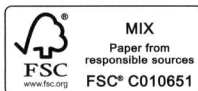

MIX
Paper from
responsible sources
FSC
www.fsc.org **FSC® C010651**

Cover: A poet drinks with his lady. 1305-1340©Heidelberg University Library, Große Heidelberger Liederhandschrift (Codex Manesse), 271r.

Contents

Preface

This book is the result of a research project funded by the Agency for Culture with the specific aim of activating Aarhus' exceedingly rich empirical archaeological record for research purposes. I offer my sincerest thanks to the Agency for Culture, Queen Margrethe II's Archaeological Foundation and Vilhelm Kier's Foundation for making the project and book possible.

To draw out human life from thousands of objects and numerous excavations is no easy task, and my heartfelt thanks goes out to the many people who have made the process easier. First and foremost, I would like to thank Director of Moesgaard Museum, Jan Skamby Madsen, and the Head of the Antiquarian Department, Mads Kähler Holst, for being supportive of this project and providing the best possible circumstances for its completion. I am also deeply indebted to Jens Christian Moesgaard, Søren Sindbæk and Hans Skov for making invaluable comments on relevant chapters and, last but not least, to Lars Krants for discussions during the course of the project. I would also like to thank the following, many of them my colleagues at Moesgaard Museum, for assistance, advice, information or comments that have made the process easier: Niels H. Andersen, Marianne H. Andreasen, Jens Andresen,

Michiel Bartels, Laurits Borbjerg, Rasmus Bretvad, Torbjörn Brorsson, Søren Bitsch Christensen, Axel Christophersen, Ole Degn, Renee Enevold, Lise Frost, J.H.M. Gawronski, Susanne Nissen Gram, Gitte Hansen, Connie Jantzen, Nina Linde Jaspers, Georg Haggren, Gitte Hansen, Rasmus Iversen, Ranjith Jayasena, Hanne Jeppesen, Jens Jeppesen, Sven Kalmring, Dorthe Haahr Kristiansen, Hans Krongaard Kristensen, Hans Jørgen Madsen, Per Mandrup, Peter Hambro Mikkelsen, Peter Mose Jensen, Ralf Mulsow, Magdalena Naum, Kirsten Nelleman Nielsen, Poul Nissen, Bjørn Poulsen, Karin Poulsen, Ib Radoor, Carsten Risager, Morten Søvsø, Torben Trier, Heiko Schäfer, Henrik Skousen, Claus Skriver, Susanne Østergaard and Jacob Westermann. My gratitude extends to Anne Bloch, Anne Lise Hansen, Louise Hilmar, Jesper Laursen, Jens Nygaard, Rógvi N. Johansen, David Earle Robinson and Casper Skaaning Andersen for their assistance in the publication of this book. Finally, I would like to thank an anonymous international referee for positive and helpful comments. Any errors or omissions are of course mine alone.

Jette Linaa
June 2016

Figure 1. *Archaeologists during their lunchbreak. Clockwise from left: Susanne Nissen Gram, Lene Mollerup, Karin Poulsen and Lars Krants. Photo: Moesgaard Museum.*

Figure 2. *Seven Works of Mercy, Master of Alkmaar, 1504 (detail). ©Rijksmuseum, Amsterdam.*

1 Introduction

This is a book about urban consumption. Much has already been written about the archaeology of Aarhus, based on the town as a place with its structures and institutions: A place where fortifications were made, streets laid out, churches constructed and houses built, rebuilt and demolished, all seemingly untouched by human hands. This book has a different agenda: It is written with humans in mind. The story of the Aarhus area that is unfolded in this study will be told not through the history of bricks and mortar, institutions and structures – but through the materiality of consumption. In this respect, consumption is perceived as a material social practice involving the utilisation of objects, also expressed as "the social process by which people construct the symbolically laden material worlds they inhabit and which, reciprocally, act back upon them in complex ways".[1] Consequently, consumption comprises foodways, as well as display, habits, rituals, language and drinking songs, while the material remains are ceramics, metal vessels, if we are lucky, wooden beakers and plates, and if we are even luckier, textiles and the like. I have done this because the project, which is concluded with this book, was financed by a research grant from the Danish Ministry of Culture, and the aim of the grant was to activate the archaeological record resulting from excavations carried out in Aarhus in current research. As my field of research is consumption studies, based primarily on materiality, I have chosen to fulfil this task by writing about urban consumption as a performance of urbanity.

Consumption-related studies are very topical at the moment. The archaeology of cultural meetings is on the ascent in historical archaeological circles in Scandinavia and beyond, and a number of publications speak of hybridisation, creolisation, ethnogenesis, acculturalisation etc., mostly in reference to studies of consumption.[2] Now it is time to explain the title of this book and the nature of urbanity: Why it can be complex, entangled and involved and why consumption matters. *Consumption* is defined here as the social contexts and processes surrounding the acquisition, preparation, storage, intake and disposal of food and drink. Consumption, in the broadest sense, has been chosen as the point of departure because ceramics, the most consumption-related of all artefacts, constitute the largest artefact group in almost all excavations, and the patterns of distribution we see are determined by consumption. According to Beaudry, ceramics are frequently seen as chronological tools or symbolic proxies for status and/or ethnicity, but in reality they are culinary utensils, which tell us about the role of the consumption of food in past societies. Consumption is an embodying activity, allowing not only nutrients, but also ideologies, to be literally integrated into, displayed upon, or acted out through the body, mediating and materialising social relationships in both real and ritual meals.[3] Consumption is viewed here as social practice mediated through the senses: touch, sight, smell and taste.[4] Moreover, the act of consumption lay at the centre of the Post-Medieval social world, where every transition in life was marked by a communal gathering with elaborate arrangements for seating, tableware, number of courses etc. This performance established order among the participants and marked inclusion and exclusion of individuals in the chosen collective.[5] This of course means that the practice of consumption played a central role in past societies in the form of feasts, banquets and daily meals; events we find reflected in our excavations.

Before I explain the nature of urbanity, I will first say a few words about the more familiar concept of *urbanisation*. Urbanisation is a hot topic in archaeology, with large, ambitious research projects focussed on urbanisation processes, linked to a sequence of building functions, institutions and activities. The frequent discussions on how towns can be defined have given rise to a series of urbanisation criteria: population density, structures, legal and physical demarcation and specific institutions, to mention but a few. Recently, the focus in urbanisation studies has shifted somewhat towards the people who lived in towns in the past. If looked for, a few of these inhabitants can be found referred to in wills, court rolls and town accounts, as is done in cultural history. But the actions of those humans, whose remains we discover, remains hidden: Their practices, their routinised actions, which are formed, performed and abandoned everywhere that humans interact with others, and with the materiality that surrounds them, are still invisible. The alternative term used here is urbanity, focused as it is on the human inhabitants of a town. The need to speak about human interactions may be perceived as more important by historical archaeologists than by archaeologists working with other periods, due to the formation in historical times of complex settlements, i.e. villages, and especially towns, cities and metropolises. This is because the dense population in towns facilitates human interactions, and the number of possible human actions rises exponentially. According to Wandschneider, a household with five members has ten possible interactions, and for a village of 100 people this number is 4950.[6] That means that the Viking Age town, with perhaps 300 people, may have hosted 45,000 potential interpersonal relations, while this number in Late Medieval Aarhus, with around 4000 inhabitants, is a staggering 8 million. Their sheer numbers alone are enough to convince us that we really need to take interpersonal relations seriously in historical archaeology. Furthermore, we are not alone – this basic condition is one we share with our colleagues who study complex prehistoric societies and societies in other parts of the world.

But first we must question the detailed nature of urbanity. In line with Axel Christophersen and Monica Smith, I understand urbanity as the urban ethos — *the urban communities´ shared horizon of understanding as a basis for the development of practice.* Consequently, urbanity comprises patterns of urban practice, created and developed through the town dwellers' shared experiences, competences, intentions and conceptions of many people living together in a dense and diverse community in interaction with the urban landscape.[7] In this definition of urbanity, consumption is a practice – one of many that can be formed, performed and abandoned. This will be dealt with in more detail later. There is nothing staged or theatrical about this performance, it simply means the distinction between being and performing. To be or to do, where being is static, while performing can be created and recreated in a social space, where countless practices are entangled in patterns, bundles and complexes, which combine to form a lifestyle.[8] Through social practices we understand routinised everyday actions – the actions we explore every day in our excavations. These social practices are much more than materiality – they encompass experience, insight and competence, and meanings, intentions, goals and expectations – formed by desires. This is a linear phenomenon: It opens up an entangled mess of unfulfilled promises, loose threads, dead ends and half-run courses, as well as the practice or practices actually followed through. This is human life as seen from the starting point, not from the final result as is usually the case. So social practices in towns, and the concept of urbanity, which includes the performance of social processes, practices and materiality, have led to perceptions of towns as not only bricks and mortar, but as complex and dynamic social spaces.[9] And one particular aspect of urbanity, the special pattern of practices that constitutes consumption, is the focus of this study. This urbanity can be described as entangled, a reference to the fact that the past is never clear-cut. Instead of black and white issues, we face myriads of actions, thoughts, meanings and lifestyles that are woven together into a complicated web, which at times feels more like a Gordian knot than a nicely ordered ball of string. Unwinding this web of practices is no easy task, and yet, as will be argued below, this deep entanglement might be the very point of it all.

If we look closer into what practice actually is, then it can be described as a routinised type of behaviour. The term "everyday" is frequently used to describe behaviour of this kind, but its use in archaeology can be problematic, given the fact that it is frequently undefined and not particularly applicable: What we find as archaeologists are not the products of specific everyday events, whatever those are, but the results of all kinds of events, both everyday and not: feast and famine, workday or Sunday. But if we address the concept of practice from a slightly different angle, as being the result of behaviour that has longevity and is repeated often enough to become routinised, its usefulness increases.[10] But first a few words on the more familiar concept of *urbanisation*. Urbanisation is a hot topic in archaeology, with large and ambitious research projects being undertaken on urbanisation processes linked to a sequence of buildings, functions, institutions and activities. The frequent discussions about how towns can be defined have given rise to a number of urbanisation criteria, including legal and physical demarcation and specific institutions, to mention but a few. But this frequently leads to a somewhat static image of towns and a reflection of them as being devoid of human life. Here, the term urbanity is used as an alternative, focused as it is on the human inhabitants of a town.

It is clear from the above that the focal point of this book lies firmly in the field of human agency and this work therefore perceives the town as not only a fixed geographical point, with walls and structures, but also as a sphere of interaction: An area for negotiation, transformation, mediation and materialisation; a place where human minds become fixed in matter through a perpetual meeting between agents; a nodal point of the mind. This study is therefore based on the materiality of the space of consumption and this materiality will, in turn, be compared and contrasted with the materiality of place, as well as with selected documentary evidence that provides us with names, dates and fates and an insight into what mostly the magistrate and the Crown thought was important. Although the title of this book is *Urban Consumption*, the only meaningful way to understand how consumption was performed or acted out in the town is to compare it with consumption in the areas that surround it: To transgress the urban-rural divide in the analysis, and not to reinforce it or to presume that it was impermeable in the past. This account will therefore unfold as a study of the differences and variations in consumption across the townscape and landscape; of fluctuations and movements of people and objects across the urban/rural and urban/urban boundaries that are embossed on present-day minds. This approach to urbanity gives rise to a series of research questions: What constitutes urban consumption and what leads to its development? At what point or time can we detect urbanity in consumption, if at all? Is urban consumption restricted to the area within the urban boundaries? Did all townspeople engage in urban consumption, and if not, which groups were excluded? Did people in rural areas participate in the performance of urbanity through consumption? And what about the people who did not? The aim of this book is to expand this field of study by addressing these topics in an attempt to examine the true nature of urban consumption. So how do we address the performance of urbanity in the material available for this study – the archaeological record? The answer is: By looking for patterns in the materiality. But do we see these patterns as reflections of economic development, traceable in monetarisation and the spread of coins? Do we see them as a consequence of trade and exchange with the outside world – exchange traceable here as the consumption of cloth and ceramics in the archaeological record and through evidence of foreign contacts, as documented in written records. Or do we see them as traces of age and gender? Or as a consequence of the transfer of urban culture from immigrants to urban dwellers. Or as materialisations of a social practice – a performance of urbanity? In my attempt to address these questions, I begin with portable artefacts and then continue on to the built environment and then to the texts. I have sought to document patterns of practice within my chosen field, embedding these patterns in structural developments and the historical context and, in the process, unravelling some of the ways in which humans negotiate their place in the world by socialising the goods that surround them.[11] This approach has determined the organisation of the analysis. The first part addresses patterns of human consumption, based on an analysis of excavation findings from 15 archaeological sites: eight in Aarhus and seven in the surrounding areas. The second part embeds these patterns of consumption in a wider comparative analysis involving other types of finds and other locations, in order to qualify the very large body of material. The third part examines these embedded patterns of consumption in the light of broader structural developments – it confronts urbanity with urbanisation – and the final part draws together conclusions on the performance of urbanity. From this disposition it follows that the relevant aspects of the archaeological record are presented in the first chapter, *Materiality*, together with reflections on sources, geographical scope and applied methodology. As ceramics constitute by far the largest group of consumption-related finds in Aarhus, the second chapter, *Phases*, focusses on the analysis of this particular artefact group. The third chapter, *Context*, embeds the information derived from the study of the ceramics in studies of the consumption of textiles and of published written sources relevant to the subject of consumption. Also included here are short sub-chapters dealing with specific processes especially relevant to consumption as a practice: monetarisation and immigration. The fourth chapter, *Horizons*, examines how consumption

interacts with structural developments in the sense of the town's physical layout and constructions, as I try to address the synchronous interaction between individuals, intent, material resources, space and time, rather than asking what happened before or after. All of this has been done in an attempt to establish the seven stages of urban consumption, all defined through the stabilisation of a new practice or practices and the destabilisation of another or others. The fifth chapter, *Conclusion*, revisits urban consumption as a reflection of the performance of urbanity. Consequently, readers seeking information on the excavations in Aarhus should read the first chapter, and those looking for information on urbanity should read the final chapter, whereas the second chapter is of greatest interest to those readers who are fond of artefact studies.

It is a characteristic of archaeology that our materiality grows constantly as new finds types are discovered and additional sites become available to researchers with every new excavation that is carried out, while archaeological methodology relating to recording, analysis and interpretation improves on a daily basis. This book cannot therefore be seen as the final statement on consumption, either in the urban or rural areas, but should be perceived in its proper context as a stepping stone on the way to an ever-improving insight into the lives of our predecessors. Furthermore, as this book deals primarily with specific aspects of the portable finds, each of the sites used cannot be said to have been fully investigated – the excavation records still hold valuable information on both structures and processes that deserves closer examination, and more material is uncovered every day. Consequently, a number of the excavations that have supplied material for this volume are currently undergoing publication in various forms under the auspices of other projects that focus on different aspects of Medieval and Post-Medieval life.[12]

As any archaeologist knows, however, context is everything. Exploring how consumption was performed in the town of Aarhus without taking account of the temporal/chronological and geographical context, i.e. what took place in the surrounding region, and with no clear understanding of the historical context, would result in in a study characterised by several major blind spots and deficiencies. Taking the human perspective into account means realising that we are dealing with people who lived on a very different temporal scale to ours, for whom the arc of human life did not extend from birth to death, but from Adam and Eve to Judgement Day. Not only their temporal references differed from ours: In a world where travelling was difficult, and where distant places, both at home or abroad, could be recreated, even integrated, through consumption, geographical scales were also very different. On our temporal scale, this study will concentrate on the period between the Viking Age and the Modern period, i.e. c. AD 800-1800. In addition, on a geographical scale, the study will address all levels of interactions – from meetings between urban inhabitants and people from rural areas to contacts with people of foreign origin and their integration into the community created by urban consumption.

Then we can consider Aarhus itself – how do we define the town as a meaningful geographical unit that can be distinguished from the surrounding area during the period from the Viking Age until today? My main definition is taken from historical sources: Aarhus received its town charter before 1317 and from this point onwards is considered a town with all its concomitant mercantile, economic and administrative privileges.[13] The legal status of the Viking and Early Medieval settlement is, however, as yet unknown, and to pursue this subject would demand resources far beyond those available for this study. Therefore, for purely practical reasons, the analysis of the pre-1317 situation employs a model whereby the settlement within the geographical boundaries of Aarhus before c. 1800 is targeted as a unit, which is then compared with the settlements outside these boundaries. Similar issues relate to the definition of the urban and rural population, with respect to the context of the materiality that forms the basis of this study. From historical sources, it is evident that a town was inhabited by citizens who had a defined legal status. However, there were also

several other groups – servants, apprentices, vagrants and many others – who were mostly included within a citizen's household. What we find archaeologically are the remains of these households but, as is evident from the above, a household was not a homogeneous unit, and only in very rare circumstances are we able to refer specific archaeological assemblages to specific members of the household. The fact that the analysis will be conducted on a household level is therefore not a choice, but dictated by the nature of the available evidence, i.e. the archaeological record. This means, furthermore, that we are only very rarely able to detect further social reactions, such as indications of dominance and resistance within a specific household. Although this may be achievable, it has not been possible within the economic framework of this study. Nevertheless, the data needed for such an analysis is already present in the database that forms the basis of this book, so this is one of the aspects I want to look into in the near future.

1.1 Inspiration

Consumption studies are, of course, nothing new. Consumption has been implicit in Danish archaeology for years, but it has largely been seen as the end result of production and distribution. Trade and social topography still constitute the focal points for many research projects, and the social processes embedded in consumption have been ignored in most studies and publications. Impulses from international research have opened up this field only recently. Internationally, the study of consumption is a large and rapidly developing research area within the disciplines of history and historical archaeology, and the flow of international research projects and publications has increased swiftly over the last decade. In these, consumption is recognised as a social and cultural practice that, according to Michael Dietler in his analysis of the history of consumption studies, must be studied and theorised as a discrete field of action.[14] International research has provided a wealth of information on food and drink and vessels and tableware, as well as on the social processes reflected in consumption. Historical and scientific studies have provided significant insight into consumption across broader sectors of Medieval society, both in other countries and in Denmark, as seen for example in the works of Sabine Karg and others.[15] The historian Peter Scholliers has been particularly active, along with a group of like-minded researchers who have made inspirational contributions to the field and directed us towards the special role of specific kinds of consumption. A classic example is the study of the role of the consumption of alcohol in social processes in Medieval society. [16] So we may speak of the conspicuous, conservative, aesthetic or sumptuous consumption of burghers, the conservative consumption of the nobility, the ascetic or restrained consumption of monasteries, the religious consumption of women or mystics and the sumptuous consumption displayed by princes, all of which is embedded in distinctive social processes.[17] I have previously reviewed Danish ceramics research c. 1950-2005, and this will not be repeated here.[18] International research has, until quite recently, generally had a minor impact on Danish historical archaeology, as most studies carried out by recent generations have been dominated by a strong empirical focus and an explicit interest in resources, economy, trade, exchange and social topography. Ceramics were largely seen as a dating tool and a low-value, purely functional commodity, and their distribution was at times said to be a function of two factors: People grabbing whatever they could get hold of at the cheapest price, or random souvenirs brought home by mad sailors. It goes without saying that any search for meaning behind material culture was met with suspicion, ceramics studies were marginalised and the material was seen as being secondary to textual sources or built structures. This was not only characteristic of Danish archaeology, the UK went through a similar phase.[19] Furthermore, few large-scale, comparative studies were published in a research field dominated by single-site publications, and in the one which did appear, consumption, and especially the interpretative framework surrounding it, played an insignificant part. Many publications therefore took as their starting point an analysis of the economy of the archaeological site in question, analysing the structures on site and placing emphasis on the biographies of artefacts and the origin of things. Small finds and ceramics thereby highlighted trade and exchange, markets and market networks and their role in the supply of goods. In these studies, "food culture" was studied through analyses of ecofacts and consumption studies, if present, were largely directed towards an examination of "lifestyle" with an emphasis on foreign contacts, frequently interpreted as evidence of trade. Two large but significantly different research projects, published in the 2000s, deserve to be highlighted as examples of this approach: *Tårnby – gård og landsby gennem 1000 år* (2005) edited by Mette Svart Kristiansen, and *Viborg Søndersø 1018-1030* (2006), edited by Charlie Christensen, Jesper Hjermind, Mette Iversen and David Earle Robinson. The Viborg Søndersø and Tårnby publications are both important interdisciplinary works that deal with their subjects in great depth and lead to significant insight, and yet they are very different in scope, means, scale and agenda. The excavation and subsequent publication of the Medieval farms at Tårnby constituted one of the largest research projects of its day, and the voluminous publication includes contributions by 18 authors.[20] The project was directed towards examining the economy of the farm, with excellent contributions on the environmental evidence (ecofacts) and a major chapter on the artefacts by multiple authors – including my own work on the ceramics. It is characteristic of this multi-disciplinary publication that the chapters dealing with the various disciplines were not integrated, i.e. inter-disciplinary, and discussions between the many specialists involved were largely absent. Furthermore, the framework did not allow for an in-depth analysis of consumption and the chapter on the artefacts therefore ends with a short conclusion, also in the case of my research, that only manages to draw brief and preliminary conclusions on the lifestyle on the farm contrasted with that in early urban Copenhagen. There is little doubt that the Tårnby material still holds vast potential for studies of how consumption was performed in rural areas, and much of the information can be found directly in the publication and the data-bases, and implemented in other projects. The Viborg Søndersø project was very different. It was aimed at the development of methodologies in urban archaeology, and was inter-disciplinary from the start resulting in many multiple-author chapters written by the project's 24 participants. The subject – the workshops of a blacksmith and a comb maker dated to 1018-1030 – was analysed from every angle, including application of the most advanced methodologies of the day, and the large publication remains a catalogue of modern archaeological and scientific approaches to archaeological excavation. The publication was naturally directed towards the main activities on the site – craft production, and consumption played a minor role: I wrote about the use of antler on site, and co-authored a chapter on the distribution of artefacts and waste with Jesper Hjermind, who wrote about the ceramics. Nevertheless, the subject was different, and there were many deliberations with respect to the definition and interpretation of contexts, and on preservation conditions, recovery and sampling strategies. Not least, there were several cases where scientists and archaeologists disagreed and discussed their disagreements in the publication. All of this has been very inspiring for my own approach to methodology and inter-disciplinary research, especially with regard to statistical analysis and representativity and, in recent years, the practising of social archaeology.[21]

Just as consumption studies were barely included in major Danish research projects, and where present largely constituted an extension of the chapters on the ceramics, this research field were virtually absent from a range of other large-scale publications. During the last decade or so, there have been several major research projects and subsequent publications directed specifically towards manors and castles. However, time-honoured perceptions of the value of ceramics still linger on, as consumption analysis is frequently lacking or underplayed in these works. Examples include *Gurre Slot, Kongeborg og Sagnskat* (2003) edited by Vivian Etting, *Borringholm – En østjysk træborg fra 1300-årene*

(2006), edited by Jan Kock and Else Roesdahl, *Kongens Borg – 123 års arkæologi på Vordingborg* (2014) by Dorthe Wille Jørgensen and *Nørre Vosborg – en herregård i tid og rum* (2005), edited by Anders Bøgh, Helle Henningsen and Kristian Dalsgaard. An exception to this is evident in the publication *Marsk Stig og de fredløse på Hjelm* (2002), edited by Pauline Asingh and Niels Engberg, where a chapter on zooarchaeology is directed towards the study of food, but a consumption analysis, encompassing the ceramics or other finds, is not included. That is why I made an effort to draw conclusions on the performance of consumption in an aristocratic setting in my own, non-project related, article of 2003.[22] The lack of consumption perspectives in these projects must be seen as a consequence of limited resources and a reflection of a limited research interest. If further aspects of consumption are to be investigated, this would require the development of a large dataset that permits comparative analysis of several sites. The development of methodologies enabling such comparisons, and gaining access to the relevant finds and the funding required to investigate and process them, puts a strain on both human and economic resources and, as a consequence, few such comparative studies have been published. However, an attempt was made in 2006 and further work is in progress as I write.[23] A book published in 2006, *Keramik, kultur & kontakter* (based on my own PhD thesis), was essentially a methodological research project directed towards the development of a series of tools that could make a cross-site consumption analysis possible on a limited budget. So far, the impact of this has been limited, but even so the methodologies live on in my other projects, including the present one. *Keramik, Kultur & Kontakter* was essentially a regional study of the use of ceramics in Jutland, based on statistical analysis of the relevant finds from 38 archaeological excavations in all parts of Jutland. In this, I introduced the methodologies that have been used in the current project. Most notably, I introduced the systematic comparison of ceramics across sites and, in so doing, I introduced correspondence analysis (CA) to Danish Medieval archaeology. The main outcome of *Keramik, Kultur & Kontakter* was the demonstration of increasing variety in the ceramics inventory from the 14th to the 17th century. This diversity was a general phenomenon, as more types were being introduced. Even more interestingly, the ceramics showed that rural sites and sites located on the periphery of towns had a greater relative amount of blackware than manors and sites in urban centres, and that this difference increased rapidly in the early 16th century. I interpreted this as evidence of an increasing social and cultural differentiation across urban-rural boundaries in Late Medieval and Early Modern Denmark. My research work since then has been dominated by efforts to examine this differentiation at different scales and on different interpretative levels.

The early 2000s was a challenging time. The perception of consumption-related objects as randomly distributed low-value commodities of limited research value lingered on, giving rise to a paradox: In order to give Danish consumption studies a voice internationally, it was necessary to follow an international research agenda that was met with scepticism at home. A research area solely dependent on external funding and/or rescue excavations is vulnerable to conjunctures and challenged by changing institutional affiliations and interests. My own strategy during this period was to build "big data": To continue the use of a strict British-inspired methodology that fell well within the narrow limitations for what is possible in rescue excavations, but still allowed for comparisons between sites. The prime inspiration came from the many ceramics specialists working in the UK. Working as an ad hoc ceramics consultant on various excavations did not, or only very rarely so, allow research. Nevertheless, it was possible within that narrow framework to record basic information regarding contexts, quantities and ware types, that would allow for comparative analyses to be carried out on many scales if it proved possible to activate the material in research at a later date. As Moesgaard Museum began employing me as a ceramics consultant back in 1995, much of the work I have done for the museum has been drawn upon in this book. At the same time, I have had the good fortune to be employed on a series of research projects led by others. Examples of the results of this work include the reports for Øhavets middelalderlige borge og voldsteder (2005) by Jørgen Skaarup and my paper in Glargårde. Dansk glasfremstilling i Renæssancen (2015) by Jens N. Nielsen, written in 2010. The papers on Sønderside (1999, 2005), the paper "Mester Trebing fra Hessen" from 2010 and the paper "Mad i Krig og Krise: Konsumption på tre af 1300-tallets borge" in Danish History of Food (2014) are based on a mixture of my own research and consultancy work. Later in the 2000s, however, Danish researchers became integrated into national and international research collaborations and networks within the field, also those involving researchers based in ethnology and history, especially at other museums. Among the long-time participants was archaeologist and leading expert on historical food, the late Bi Skaarup, member of the Danish Academy for Gastronomy and author of several volumes on Medieval and Early Modern food and consumption, including Renæssancemad. Opskrifter og køkkenhistorier fra Chr. IV´s tid (2006). These industry/museum/university-crossover collaborations between archaeology, history and ethnology have given, and continue to give, much-needed inspiration to the field. At this point there is every reason to highlight the work of the Danish National Museum and Den Gamle By in Aarhus, exemplified in Mikkel Venborg Pedersen's monograph Luksus. Forbrug og kolonier i det 18. århundrede (2013), and Anette Hoff´s volumes on coffee and tea: Den Danske Kaffehistorie and Den Danske Tehistorie (both published in 2015). Both institutions are active in the networks and in producing publications that will doubtless have an impact on not only historical but also archaeological consumption research.

These developments have had a profound effect on Danish research in this area. Participation in the Medieval Pottery Research Group and the Society of Post-Medieval Archaeology provided a gateway to international research. A similar function was performed by the Early Modern Town network, initiated by Per Cornell, of the University of Gothenburg, who gathered researchers, including consumption specialists, from all over Europe and beyond for the seminars. The same can be said of Jonas Nordin and Magdalena Naum's Glob-Arc-network, which acts as an inter-disciplinary forum for globalisation studies and has introduced perspectives from colonial studies into Scandinavian archaeology, with very promising results.[24] In recent years, the EAA – European Association of Archaeologists, has developed into quite a forum for inter-disciplinary consumption studies. The same is the case for the Nordic TAG, and many researchers, especially the younger generation, are quite active, forming networks, holding discussions and giving papers at the annual congresses. Involvement in the Society of Post-Medieval Archaeology, The Medieval Pottery Research Group and its German counterpart Internationales Keramiksymposium, as well as many other organisations, has raised the bar significantly in Danish research. And a promising collaboration is now evolving with the Australian Research Council Centre of Excellence for the History of Emotions, as well as with the newly-founded Centre for Urban Network Evolutions (UrbNet) and the very new network Science and Technology in Archaeological Research (STAR), both affiliated to the University of Aarhus. Through participation in these and other networks, what began as the involvement of individuals is developing into a large-scale movement towards international consumption research. The increasing national and international openness towards Danish consumption research has had profound effects on the scale and ambitions, as well as on the perceived relevance, of Danish Medieval and Post-Medieval consumption studies to other disciplines and society as a whole. This has led to several Danish or Danish-based research projects in the field receiving substantial public funding in recent years; among them the present project and also the consumption-based Urban Diaspora – Diaspora communities and Materiality in Early Modern Urban Centres, funded by the Danish Council for Independent Research/Humanities. What characterises these projects, and consumption studies in general in Danish historical archaeology, is that they are run primarily by museum employees as joint

museum/university initiatives, frequently in an integrated inter-disciplinary collaboration that may include not only scientific disciplines and historical studies, but also anthropology, art history, literature, media studies and cross-cultural studies. This approach has led to a continuous widening of the archaeological approach, as demonstrated by recent and ongoing publications and projects focused not only on consumption and identity, but also on aspects such as consumption and the sensuous experience and consumption and emotions.[25] But as a specific Danish voice is now gaining recognition in the field of archaeological consumption, we still face some challenges. One of these related to communication. As consumption research outside historical archaeology is mainly anchored in a university environment, the lines of communication between universities and museums are crucial. We need to work on communication outside of the circle of contributors to our own projects, to make researchers from other disciplines, especially at universities, aware of the quality of our research and our relevance for ongoing and future projects. But the growing collaboration with researchers at universities, the increased international attention and, not least, the substantial Danish research grants directed towards our research in recent years, indicate that we are reaching the tipping point. I am therefore in no doubt that consumption studies will spread rapidly within Danish archaeology in the coming years.

After these general remarks on the recent history of Danish consumption research in archaeology, I will present a few reflections on the publications and research topics that have inspired the present study. An obvious source of inspiration was provided by the work of researchers affiliated to the Medieval Ceramics Research Group. Of these, Per Kristian Madsen, with his studies of ceramics from Ribe in the 1990s, was very influential in Danish ceramics research.[26] Another major figure is David Gaimster, and his publications on the spread of Hanseatic material culture have also had a huge influence. David Gaimster's models of cultural transfer and resistance in identity formation in Hanseatic Medieval and Early Modern towns are among the most influential and inspirational in the field of consumption studies today. Gaimster works in the field of negotiating identities and considers that the spread of stoneware and stove tiles constitutes a marker for the transfer of Hanseatic culture relating to dining and domestic comfort among dispersed and heterogeneous communities. He even interprets the use of wooden vessels in Novgorod as evidence of resistance against Hanseatic dominance.[27] The most directly relevant model in this respect is to be found in Duncan Brown´s account of the ceramics of Medieval Southampton.[28] Brown's book combines a thorough analysis of the Medieval ceramics and their contexts with evidence from the very rich documentary record that is characteristic of British ceramics research. I have aspired to a similar approach in the present volume, although the dissimilar contexts mean that different time spans and methodologies have been applied. A more recent source of inspiration is Ben Jervis´s *Pottery and Social Life in Medieval England* (2014) and "Cuisine and Urban Identities in Medieval England" (2012) in which Jervis presents ceramics studies from a British perspective, advocating a relational approach, where human-object interactions are in focus along the entire chaîne opératoire. Jervis' approach provides insight into urban and rural identities from a consumption perspective, drawing upon ceramics studies, written texts and science.[29] Dutch archaeology has also provided important inspiration through the reference works of researchers such as Michiel Bartels and Jerzy Gawronski and, most recently, a range of specialist studies on for example Italian and Dutch majolica and porcelain, including those of Nina Linde Jaspers and Sebastiaan Ostkamp. These books, which deal with both dating and consumption patterns, are invaluable to anyone working on the identification and precise dating of ceramics.[30] The important German ceramics types have been presented by David Gaimster in his previously mentioned volume from 1997, and later works. Recently, Marion Roehmer has published several studies of Siegburger stoneware and other stoneware types, concentrating on functional types, ware types and decoration. As for ceramics from the Baltic area, which are very important for this study, I want to highlight the numerous works of Heiko Schäfer on ceramics from Mecklenburg-Vorpommern – especially those from Rostock and Greifswald, many of which are very precisely dated and with known users. While Hans-Georg Stephan has written standard works on the later northern German ceramics tradition and the ceramics from affiliated areas with special attention to decoration and form types.[31] While these European ceramic studies are invaluable, a great deal of the mental fuel for the present and previous works comes from other sources. One special area is American historical archaeology. This is because analysis of very recent 18th and 19th century consumption frequently addresses assemblages with known owners and the results can be deeply thought provoking and inspiring. Studies of consumption have therefore a huge role to play in the study of colonialism. With a primary starting point in American archaeology, this sub-discipline has raised important questions regarding cultural processes such as cultural transfer, hybridisation, creolisation and so on. Within the framework of a study of the Aarhus region, the direct parallels to colonialism are less relevant. Nevertheless, some of the approaches to dominance and resistance, especially regarding the way local consumers actively negotiate their relationship to a dominant culture, are fruitful. In recent years, the study of colonialism has reached Scandinavia, for example in archaeologist Jonas Nordin's ongoing study of the indigenous population of northern Sweden and parallels between the organisation of Swedish factories and the plantation system in the colonies. Similarly, Magdalena Naum is presently conducting an inspirational study on the materiality of Swedish settlers in New Sweden, USA.[32] An approach of this kind is productive in relation to for example the study of the mechanisms of the dominant Hanseatic mercantile and cultural power in the later Middle Ages. I have derived much of my own inspiration from Swedish archaeology, where theoretically conscious Swedish colleagues have involved themselves in studies of consumption or consumption-related materials in the materiality of cultural meetings. The works of Mats Roslund and Magdalena Naum has been especially important for my research: Mats Roslund because, as early as in 2001, he demonstrated the validity of studying cultural meeting through consumption, arriving at far-reaching conclusions on the social standing of potters (Roslund 2001), and Magdalena Naum because she has carried out several research projects focussing on cultural meetings, especially those between locals and Hanseatic merchants in Late Medieval towns (Naum 2012, 2013, 2014, 2015a+b). Naum's works in particular deserves special mention, because her analyses are clearly inspired by postcolonial theory. Specifically, she discusses the role of material culture in the formation of ethnic and social groups in two very different Baltic towns: Kalmar and Tallin. Her work demonstrates the potential of such analyses, i.e. combing historical records relating to the relationship between groups in the ethnically diverse towns in the eastern Baltic. These provide evidence on the translocal practices of the immigrants, all of which is correlated with materiality from archaeological excavations of town plots. Here, she focusses particularly on ceramics in her analysis of group identification and group formation.[33] However, as striking as the parallels between Naum's work and the present study may seem, the differences are numerous. First and foremost, cultural meetings are highly situational: There are vast historical and political differences between the town of Aarhus in the strong state of Denmark and the towns in the colonised areas of the eastern Baltic. Being able to explore the materiality of the meeting between coloniser and colonised is of course what interests Naum, who has also done valuable research in the Swedish colony of New Sweden in Delaware, USA. Furthermore, Naum takes as her starting point artefacts from excavations in quarters historically known to be dominated by different ethnic groups. This approach puts emphasis on basic data generation related to plot ownership, waste disposal patterns, household composition and relative abundance of pottery. Furthermore, the frequent use of the term "diaspora" in Naum's work and that of others underlines a need to clarify and nuance the term, examining the various strategies employed by trade diasporas, work diasporas and so on. Terminology aside, the main obstacle in this approach is that the selected historical sources lead to an a priori conclusion of ethnicity being the main factor behind group formation and interaction in the town. This official discourse may blur or redirect attention from underlying social processes, not necessarily ethnic in nature, in the towns in question. The question is whether a bottom-up approach involving multi-disciplinary analysis of materiality would reveal patterns of practice that provided deeper insight into the formation and interaction of social or ethnic groups. Such analysis could then be compared with the historical events and records. Instead of asking how we can detect and identify ethnic groups in the towns, we could ask whether ethnicity was the most important or only factor in group formation and interaction. Archaeologist Visa Immonen has carried out a similar thought-provoking study of cultural meetings in Medieval Turku[34] and Vesa-Pekka Herva has similarly studied the boundaries of materiality in the Finnish town of Tornio.[35] What characterises these studies is their focus on the immense degree of entanglement between groups in the towns in question. Here we do not find the clear-cut otherness that characterises studies in the colonies. Instead we see overlapping communities of different groups in dynamic social exchange. The applicability of the approach is underlined by a series of recent analyses focussing on the consumption of members of diaspora communities in Scandinavia. A community of German industrial workers in the Swedish town of Norrköping, who demonstrate strong material ties with their homeland, has been presented by Pär Karlsson and Göran Tagesson.[36] As in many recent immigrant quarters, this was identified using written records and maps. This clearly vastly improves the value of the archaeological remains recovered from these settlements, since we know that the families there were of foreign descent and are consequently able to draw somewhat reliable conclusions with respect to the consumption of these groups. It is no coincidence that these ideas have gained a foothold in Sweden, given the tradition of interpretative archaeology that is prevalent there.

Swedish archaeology has a long tradition of interpretative studies with special focus on questions of identity and Anders Andrén, Peter Carelli and Mats Roslund, in particular, have all contributed significantly to the field.[37] Roslund has already been mentioned above. Peter Carelli´s book *En Kapitalistisk Anda* (2001) is a tour de force in the study of Early Medieval society, with special emphasis on urbanisation, power and religion. The chapter on urbanisation is especially impressive in its analysis of the built environment, town plots, trades and crafts and monetarisation. Carelli takes his starting point not in legal boundaries or institutions but in urban living and points at the dialectics between life and town, urbanity and urbanisation. Consequently, this book is indebted to Carelli, as his approach has been one of my own personal sources of inspirations. Inspiration from more recent Swedish research is evident in a study of the identity of King Frederik II's master glassmaker Liboris Trebing, who originated in Hessen.[38] Here we have the advantage that Trebing's personal history is known and we have the correspondence between the king and his officials, so the interpretation of Trebing´s consumption is fairly straightforward. These analyses reveal a complex pattern of consumption incorporating both local and foreign elements. They thereby indicate the possibility of the formation of several overlapping communities within the urban space, but with all of these operating in very specific social, historical, political and cultural contexts.[39]

History has been important, not least in the many studies carried out by Bjørn Poulsen, which concentrate on identities in the Medieval town: Studies that form part of an international trend within the field of historical research that focuses on urban identities.[40] Poulsen analyses the rural-urban divide in the Late Medieval period and identifies an immense diversity, characterised by conflicts and large differences in wealth. As a consequence, he concludes that the differences in identity, which developed through the constant battle

for urban rights, together with urban duties, may have played a major role in the formation and continuation of a common identity in Danish Medieval towns. Poulsen also stresses the importance of guilds, the the theatre, religious practice and town histories for the formation and maintenance of urban identities. As this volume is based on the archaeological record, the materials and methodologies are different, but Poulsen's thoughts on the differentiated town-housing complex identities have, even so, been deeply inspiring for this study, and not least for my considerations of the different communities in the town, including those which crossed the urban-rural divide.

Another source of ideas lies outside archaeology and the related area of historical studies, in the fields of literature and anthropology. Carolyn Dinshaw´s *Getting medieval: Sexualities and Communities, Pre- and Postmodern* (1999) has been inspirational because it demonstrates how current issues can gain a perspective through investigations into Medieval and Early Modern societies. Moreover, it shows how the range of questions we can ask in relation to Pre-Modern societies is absolutely vast: Much greater than previously thought in the tradition in which I was educated. While Dinshaw's book deals with the queer, a kindred spirit is found in anthropologist Hans Peter Duerr´s book *Naktheid und Schamm* (1988), which writes the history of shame. Shame has since developed into a research field of its own. In this book I study neither shame nor queer specifically, but nevertheless I strongly feel the influence of these works. Both made me realise, from an early point in my career – around 2000 – that analyses of perceptions of cultural purity and impurity, pride and shame, norm and transgressions of norms are difficult, but nevertheless of great value in consumption studies. Consequently, I could see that the research area that constitutes archaeology is wider, much wider, than the archaeology I saw conducted in Denmark at that time. I also saw that studies on past communities such as these lead us into the realm of groups that are notoriously under-researched in Danish archaeology. I will not even begin to claim that my own research, in the form of this book, has brought me close to these groups, although I do hope to have approached them in some way. Dinshaw and Duerr's work has been a great inspiration in my own ongoing efforts to give a voice to the voiceless in our past – the people living on the margins of society: the poor, beggars, outcasts, strangers and, in my latest project, immigrants.

The final source of inspiration comes from studies of matter itself, transmitted through involvement in the *Saturated Sensorium* project, the results of which have been recently published.[41] Consumption lay at the very heart of Medieval sensorial perception, and many sensuous experiences were expressed in consummative terms: Christ was the fruit of the Tree of Life, his body was partaken of in the Eucharist, and his words were consumed during Mass. Every church and village or monastery and manor constituted an arena for the actual or ritualised consumption of food and drink, representing, as it were, processes of transformation, incarnation, embodiment and negotiation. This consumption balanced constantly on the edge between excess and repression, between gluttony and abstinence. At the very foundation of all these various forms of consumption were the senses. Involvement in this project opened my eyes, paradoxically, to the materiality of materiality – to the importance of sensuous experiences in the formation of past life. Due to this emphasis on the sensuous experiences connected with materiality, matter ceased to be a vessel for content and began instead to become an agent in its own right, through the stimulation of the senses it provided. It was via this project that I realised the importance of these sensuous experiences, which transformed food from simple bodily nourishment to a provider of food for the soul – from fulfilment of a physical need to a confirmation of order and an integration of the past into the present. This was the project that made me realise the importance of consumption in the order of things.

My final introductory remarks will address the frequently expressed claim that the value of archaeology lies in its ability to give a voice to the people not mentioned in historical records. This attitude is very relevant in a Danish context, where so-called ordinary people are virtually absent from written sources until well into

the 17th century. While I consider this to be a reasonable point of view, the above brief tour through my own sources of inspiration probably demonstrates that I find it somewhat lacking in ambition. Experience from American archaeology shows that materiality studies have the ability to shed light on the lives of not only the anonymous, but also of the well-known: The more we know about the society that surrounded the subject of our research, the more detailed and advanced the questions can we ask of its materiality. What I ultimately hope to achieve by presenting my sources of inspiration is to emphasise that, even though publication of source material is an important part of the inherent objective of this book, my primary aim is not to study types, dates or functions, but to dig deeper into the human mind.

1.2 Theoretical standpoint [42]

This is a book based on materiality, which leads to reflections on what this actually is, how it operates and performs, and how we can draw out the human aspect from the remains we find in archaeological excavations. In order to extract information on the research questions listed in the previous chapter, from the myriads of fragments and bits of information this study is based upon, we need appropriate, well-founded theory. To achieve this, I will use approaches from post-colonial studies, combined with social theory in the line of Pierre Bourdieu, as well as the Actor-Network Theory developed by Bruno Latour.[43]

First a word on the limitations with respect to theoretical approaches. This research project is mainly based on artefact studies, and I will refrain from using theory relating to buildings and monuments, such as empirical urban theory, which links the built environment to the actions of people within it. Not because the human-built environment is unimportant, but because such an analysis would go far beyond the scope of this book.

Returning to what I aim to do, I want to make it clear that I have taken my main theoretical approach from Pierre Bourdieu's influential thoughts on materiality as a non-speaking discourse: Developed, selected and used by specific groups in society to distinguish and dissociate themselves from other groups and to integrate, invent and reinvent traditions. This lead me to Latour's Actor-Network Theory, in which both objects and humans possess agency and are mutually entangled, together with other actors, in complicated shared networks that change over time as the objects and humans themselves change. Material culture is not only shaped by the user; the reverse is also true. Material culture also actively forms the user and forms his or her identity in a complex entanglement of humans and materiality that lies at the very heart of this study.[44] This leads us to question the nature of identity, and how it is reflected in our source material. In this study, identity express how people in the past positioned themselves within social, cultural and ethnic boundaries. Moreover, identity is not static, but fluent, constructed, relational and under constant change. The subject of this study is consequently consumption, because according to Emberling, the material culture related to consumption has huge potential for signalling and aiding the reproduction of identities.[45]

I also want to emphasise that identity should not be perceived as being static: It develops and changes through a human lifetime, which points towards what have been called "nested identities"; shifting identities in times of stress or challenge.[46] But in this study, focussed on a town and its surroundings, considerations of identity alone do not answer the question of how to bridge the gap between the materiality recovered from archaeological excavations and the development of urbanity. How do we activate artefacts into discussions of urbanity? This is where the social theory comes into play, because it adds a useful, practical model to the archaeological toolbox; a model that allows us to activate materiality in a study of *how* the materiality we find can be connected to human actions. However, we still need to interpret *why* this happened. Here we need to take a look at theories of cultural change.

Cultural change

In recent years, post-colonial theory has moved beyond its original colonial setting and is now being employed in a number of situations relating to European prehis-

tory and history. The advantage of this application is that the emphasis on the power relations in colonial theory sheds light on processes in cultural meetings that are otherwise difficult to grasp. The disadvantage is that the terms used in colonial theory become diluted or significantly altered when transported to a non-colonial context. One such example is given by Phillip Stockhammer regarding the term "hybridity", where Homi K. Bhabha's original definition as a strategy of the supressed against suppressors is transformed into a category of objects that resist classification within the usual taxonomy.[47] Stockhammer suggests using the term "entanglement" instead of hybridity as marker of the creation of something new.[48] Such shifting meanings risk undermining colonial theory and the colonial experience, and how it affects people even today. Nevertheless, consumption studies have a special role to play in colonial studies, given their emphasis on power relations and exploitation in a multi-cultural setting, and archaeology in non-colonial settings, i.e. outside the European colonies in Asia, Africa and the Americas, has much to learn. Culture is constructed through consumption. According to Michael Dietler, consumption is a process of structured improvisation that continually materialises cultural order by dealing with alien objects and practices through transformative appropriation, assimilation or rejection.[49] This is not something that only happens in colonial meetings, but the clear initial boundaries in the latter, and the power relations, make cultural processes initially less entangled and more clear-cut than in the processes operating in our part of the world. So culture is a transformative process, and colonial meetings place emphasis on multi-culturalism and ethnicity. Ethnicity is one of the most commonly employed concepts in archaeology today and its use has spread from the colonial context to studies of cultural encounters in our part of the world.[50] Perceptions of ethnic identity are an invention of sociology and anthropology through Fredrik Barth's *Ethnic Groups and Boundaries*" (1969), in which he states that all societies are poly-ethnic and ethnic groups internally heterogeneous, and that they develop when confronted with one other. This perception of ethnicity emphasis it as a process with three components: 1: How insiders view membership of their ethnic group. 2. How outsiders relate to and interact with insiders. And 3. How and why institutions draw boundaries around and classify people, and how these classifications are subsequently employed.[51] Furthermore, as pointed out by Di Hu, the sociologist Charles Tilly has defined a distinction between inscribed i.e. latent, social boundaries, and activated ones. To quote Tilly, after Di Hu "Inscription heightens the social relations and representations and comprises a particular boundary, while activation makes the same boundary more central to the organization of activity in its vicinity."[52] Activation takes place under duress, and it is this which leads to ethnogenesis: a creation of new cultures in a complex and multipolar web of interactions.

While scholars have questioned whether it is possible to identify ethnicity in Medieval archaeology,[53] there is little doubt that ethnic identity, reinforced or created through the "us and them" duality, becomes visible, especially through materiality and social behaviour, both of which are open to archaeological investigation. Speaking of ethnicity evokes unpleasant associations in Europe where the term has been abused in the recent past, but in the context employed here, it has nothing to do with nationalist propaganda, race or recent history.[54] Instead, it refers to the concept defined by Sian Jones as ethnic identity, ethnic group and ethnicity.[55] Ethnicity is consequently a cultural construct – a "consciousness of difference" and a process: A process that involves the formation of ethnic identities, and their maintenance and disappearance.[56] The focus here with respect to ethnicity is on the ethnic group, which thereby represents a community of people with a shared social practice in terms of their perceived cultural differentiation, which sets them apart from other groups. It goes almost without saying that this focus on ethnicity could tone down other equally socially constructed identity practices, whether linked to social differences, differences in age, gender, institutional affiliation, networks or a mixture of all of these. The Swedish archaeologist Mats Roslund has con-

ducted an influential study, published in 2001, on cultural transfer in Early Medieval Sweden, based on a reorientation of Fredrik Barth's principles. Recent research in ethnicity takes its starting point in post-colonial theory, where research on immigration, diaspora communities and questions relating to processes such as assimilation, segregation or integration are in focus. Much of this research is based on living communities and centres on the perceived common origin of the community, including the perceptions of home-lands and host lands so familiar to students of diasporic cultures. The extensive work of the Swedish archaeologist Magdalena Naum on cultural meetings in the Medieval town is a prime example of this approach.[57] In using concepts related to colonial and post-colonial studies, it is important to emphasise the profound difference between the colonial and post-colonial setting and Medieval and Early Modern Denmark, Scandinavia or Europe. To quote Barbara Voss, "Various models of cultural change – for example, acculturation, assimilation, bricolage, creolization […] foreground the dynamic and at times creative ways that colonised, captive, and subordinate populations engaged with newly imposed political systems and cultural influences."[58] This is the difference between the colonial experience, with its clear power relations and dated starting point on one side, and the immense entanglement created by thousands of years of varying contact that mostly characterises our part of the world. The exceptions are of course related to indigenous peoples like the Saami, a group investigated by for example Thomas Wallerström, and the colonisation of the eastern Baltic.[59] Nevertheless, speaking in colonial terms when describing people from neighbouring areas who have been in close contact and have moved back and forth for hundreds of years prior to the time in question, raise some questions about the general usefulness of such terms. However, instead of seeing this as a hindrance, I maintain that the deep entanglement which characterises our part of the world is a very valid study object. What we see here in our materiality can be interpreted as evidence of communities marked or separated by all kinds of differences, whether socially, gender, class, rank or ethnically related. The disentanglement of such a situation is no small task, and yet this deep entanglement might be the very point. This means of course that, although the concepts of hybridity, creolisation, ethnogenesis, syncretism and acculturalisation carry significant potentials, specifically in Scandinavia – and especially in the area dealt with in this book, these concepts must be used consciously and cautiously, as the situation here is very different from those, which these models were developed to address. Furthermore, in examining cultural encounters, not only cultural change but also cultural continuity should be considered, with an emphasis on which cultural traits are constant.

Social theory

The main inspiration for my own use of social theory comes from sociology, mainly Pierre Bourdieu's influential works *Outline of a Theory of Practice* (1977) and *Destinction: A social critique of judgement and taste* (1984). Further aspects of social theory are unfolded in *The Dynamics of Social Practice. Everyday Life and How It Changes* (2012) by sociologists Elisabeth Shove, Mika Pantzar and Matt Wilson: A book that I rely on in my own application of social theory, as will no doubt become apparent in the following, simply because I find the model presented here meaningful when translated from the present to the past. The specific use of this theory here is inspired by archaeologist Axel Christophersen's "Performing Towns. Steps towards an understanding of medieval urban communities as social praxis" (2015), with comments by Jeffrey Fleischer, Sven Kalmring, Ulrich Müller, LuAnn Wandsnider and Monica L. Smith.[60]

If we go deeper into social theory and try to clarify what practice actually is, then it can be described as a routinised type of behaviour, frequently described as "everyday". Use of the term "everyday" in archaeology can be problematic, given the fact that it is frequently undefined and not particularly applicable: What we find as archaeologists are not the products of specific everyday events, whatever those are, but the results of all kinds of events, both everyday and not: feast and famine, workday or Sunday. But if we address the concept of practice from a slightly different angle, as being the result of behaviour that has longevity and is repeated often enough to become routinised, its usefulness becomes obvious.[61]

If we look at what constitutes social practice according to Shove, Pantzar and Watson, we find it consists of three elements: material, meaning and knowledge. *Material elements* are the body and other physical objects, such as artefacts, infrastructure and so on – basically the physical objects and structures we find in excavations. *Meaning elements* are active and mental states, such as mood and intention and they represent the social and symbolic significance of participation in the practice. *Knowledge (or competence) elements* include skills and acquisition of knowledge. Patterns of practice then emerge when all three elements come together and are performed as stabilised or reproducible practice.

Before we examine patterns of practice in more detail, a few further words should be said about elements of practice in a specific archaeological context. Regarding the *material element* – normally referred to as "resources" in archaeology, it is obvious that access is very important, and that modes of transport, vehicles, vessels, roads and the like, play a crucial role. When dealing with *knowledge elements,* according to Elisabeth Shoves' analysis of competence, some everyday tasks are picked up easily, while others demand specialised long-term training, transferred via master-apprentice relationships, whether in craft workshops or in households. Others demand the circulation of competences between practices. This knowledge transfer is crucial.

In order to be transferred, the knowledge has first to be extracted from the practice in question – turned into conscious knowledge through decontextualisation and packaging (abstracting), then transported through some form of infrastructure. When it arrives, it needs to be reversed, in Shove's words, recontextualised, which means that someone at the receiving end has to have the practice and insight to decode it. In current social theory, "cosmopolitan knowledge" is frequently mentioned: A pool of already packed knowledge ready to use.[62] But the role of such a knowledge reservoir in the Middle Ages is doubtful, given that knowledge had to be transferred from person to person, simply because of the limited literacy. It was not until the 17th century that aids such as books containing recipes became widely used outside very specific circles. But if we accept that a reservoir of knowledge could exist in oral form, shared through personal contact, the concept is still useful. Furthermore, knowledge is not necessarily something that is transferred passively. Some form a bridge between practices by constituting, or even changing, the quality of the social fabric in which many such practices are rooted.[63] The German organisation of crafts is potentially a useful example of such a transfer.

The *meaning element* of social practice is more difficult to deal with, as interpretations or symbolic meanings can be debated and are relative and situated. But at the core of the matter is the notion that the status of the participants in the practice and the meaning of it are dynamic, and that such dynamics are central to the question of how social hierarchies are reproduced and sustained. As stated by Pierre Bourdieu, all cultural practice is "automatically classified and classifying, rank ordering and rank ordered", meaning that people position themselves within society by participating in some practices and not others, and in doing so reproduce specific structures of meaning and order.[64] It goes without saying that people sometimes position themselves in society not only by participating in some practices, but just as much by excluding other people from these practices. This is because practice requires monitoring, by the practitioners themselves or by someone outside, and this monitoring is, in its essence, a power relation.[65] The powerful members of society are therefore the ones who are able to define which social practices constitutes urbanity at any given time, and force others succumb to their practice and decide who is to participate and who is not. I will return to this point in my short analysis of urban outcasts in the end of this book. This takes us to the final point to be made here, on the link between social practice and social capital or, as expressed by Latour and Woolgar

"Cycles of credibility",[66] whereby a well-conducted social practice accumulates social capital or "honour", to use a Medieval term. This leads to increased prestige and inclusion in more practices, with new participants and an increase in social standing. Conversely, a failed practice leads to a downwards spiral of disrepute – expressed in Medieval sources as "evil housekeeping", and subsequent marginalisation and exclusion.

Returning to patterns of practice, we have seen that such a pattern is formed when materiality, meaning and knowledge/competence become intertwined. Before this happens, the practice exists as an inherent opportunity. When the practice is performed, it is stabilised, but when the link between the elements is dissolved, the practice become destabilised and ceases to exist (ex-practice) Practice can be adjusted along the way, and knowledge and meaning adjusted accordingly, or vice versa, but the link between them remains the same, meaning that the elements of practice shape one another.[67] If we look closer into the formation of practices, this usually takes place through the arrival of new elements and the subsequent breakdown of others in large and complex networks. This affects the performativity of the practice – it is no longer effective – and will weaken or dissolve the links between the elements of that practice. The elements can vanish, lie dormant or become integrated into new practices: so elements are quite stable, while practices are instable. The antiques, family heirlooms such as our grandmother's teapot, which many of us display in our homes, are actually residual elements of ex-practices, and are kept and integrated in a new one: The practice of display, because of the emotional values – the meaning – we remember through them.

Having examined the nature of practices it is time to focus on humans again – i.e. the carriers and executors of a practice. The question is how humans encounter practices, and how such practices spread through networks and communities. As already touched upon, according to Bourdieu, the chances of becoming a carrier of any one practice is closely related to the social and symbolic significance of participation, and to highly structured and vastly different opportunities to accumulate and amass the various types of capital required for, and generated through, participation. Furthermore, differences in participation accumulate over time, because experiences are important for access, and of course people can and will take up and abandon various practices through the course of their lifetimes.[68] If we then look at when and how humans are confronted with practices, recent social network analysis has demonstrated the importance of a closed circle with numerous actors, as it allows rapid interaction between members, who establish patterns of mutual obligation, and enables a productive concentration of energy and effort.[69] Such studies imply that new practices are formed in the footsteps of other, previous ones, exploiting connections created by them. These networks where meaning is shared between humans and humans/objects can be highly informal, cutting across institutions and daily roles – as seen in the informal networks in which my colleagues and I participate. The actors, whether humans or objects, can also transform and transfer meaning through these networks.[70] When such an informal network becomes a channel for the implementation or spread of new practices, it is because the members engage in many practices and, as such, belong to many communities at once, facilitating the spread of the new practice. When the practice has become established, the participant becomes committed and drawn in. As many people participate, some will be novices, other veterans in the practice. It is important to note that practice can diffuse through social hierarchies, for example as people emulate those of higher status, which leads to changes in the meaning of participation.[71] This is what we might see in the classic trickle-down movement of objects, with loss of status, that we know so well from archaeology. For example, porcelain that started out as very exclusive only to become quite widespread after some generations.

If we are to apply a preliminary model of cultural change, the relative amounts of local, regional and supraregional materials encountered in the settlements subjected to archaeological excavation will provide an indication of local, regional and supra-regional networks. The geographical distribution indicates the spread of practice relating to these, and the specific mixture of regional and supra-regional elements will point towards a cultural phenomenon such as hybridity or ethnogenesis. Consequently, a high percentage of foreign material culture indicates cultural hybridity, with the households in question being hybrids between foreign and local culture. While households with a low percentage of foreign material culture are rather unaffected and remain rooted in local culture. Regional material culture cuts across both of these categories. Following this, specific timeslots when new regional or supra-regional materials are introduced will be interpreted as innovative phases or phases with wide-scale changes in social practice. Of course, all of this took place within a specific historical context, which is why these materially-defined horizons will be contrasted and correlated with structural developments, such as trade and monetarisation, and with the built environment and the layout of streets, town quarters and harbours. We will note that chronological developments within each settlement are of less importance in this model than the inter-site comparisons within the same time-slot or horizon. This concurs with the notion that towns do not undergo a linear development, with the one step following the other, but proceed through different stages where many developments are possible. This entanglement mirrors rather nicely the development of urbanity.

1.3 The history of Aarhus and its archaeological practice

This study is, like all studies, limited by the nature of the available sources and by the availability of resources for its completion.[72] This chapter on sources will therefore begin start with a short survey of the history of the archaeology of Aarhus and the major, relevant publications.

The earliest archaeological investigation in Aarhus took place around 1900, and in the first half of the 20th century the town's archaeology was primarily in the hands of librarian Eilar Haugsted and later curator Gunnar Rasmussen from Den Gamle By open-air museum. Since the 1960s, Moesgaard Museum has been responsible for the town's archaeology and, as in many towns, the number of excavations multiplied through the late 20th century. The last two decades have been a busy time, with numerous large-scale excavations being undertaken within and outside the town centre, and many of these will be presented in this book. All in all, around 250 excavations have been conducted in the town during the last century, and many more in the areas around the town.

The most influential volume on the archaeology of the town is, of course, *Aarhus Søndervold*, published in 1971: "Of course" because this volume is one of the most famous publications in Danish Medieval archaeology, as it significantly raised the bar for the archaeological publications of its time. Furthermore, its subject – a Viking Age settlement with fortifications and dwellings and evidence of battle, provided a valuable insight into a previously little-known aspect of the town's past.

The recently published *Middelalderbyen Aarhus* (2014) is an obvious starting point for anyone interested in the history of archaeology in Aarhus, and in the physical layout of the Medieval town and its streets, buildings, squares and ecclesial institutions.[73] This book provides an impressive overview of the physical remains of the town's dwellings, streets, fortifications, wells, market squares, harbour and much more, all based on the results of excavations conducted by Moesgaard Museum and its predecessor. It is the last in a series of volumes on various towns – the results of a project defined more than 35 years ago. It is therefore not surprising that *Middelalderbyen Aarhus* puts emphasis on the built environment and the town's institutions, while human activities play a subordinate role. In recent years, curator Hans Skov of Moesgaard Museum has produced a long series of publications on the development of the town, based on the many excavations, especially during the 1990s and 2000s. Among his works are papers on the infrastructure in Aarhus c. AD 900-1600, on the Viking Age town and

on wells in town, as well as several papers presenting the results of urban excavations.[74] Another valuable source is a published MA thesis by archaeologist Karin Poulsen of Moesgaard Museum, which summarises and interprets the many excavations carried out in the northern part of town: A work that the present volume draws upon where possible.[75] But regardless of how much has already been published, the continuing excavations in Aarhus mean that further publications are on the way as our insight into the town increases. Leaving archaeology, the discipline of history has fostered many volumes on Aarhus that are of great value to any archaeologist working in town. The history of research given here is not complete, but aims to address the publications that have been of the greatest value when writing this book. The first of these is the series *Aarhus gennem Tiderne*, where especially volume 1, by Jens Clausen and Ejler Haugsted, has proved a source of useful information, together with *Århus bys historie* (1985) by Helge Paludan and *Det ældste Århus* (1961) by Helge Søgaard. Anyone interested in the most recent development of the town can look to Jens Toftgaard Jensen and Jeppe Norskov´s *Købstadens Metamorfose. Byudvikling og byplanlægning i Århus 1800-1920* (2005).[76] Søren Bitsch Christensen has written a series of volumes relevant to Aarhus. Information on the (lack of) Early Modern fortification in Aarhus can be found in *Renæssancens befæstede byer* (2011) edited by Bitsch Christensen,[77] while *Danish Towns during Absolutism* (2008), *Den klassiske købstad* (2005) and *Århus i verden* (2006), contains a wealth of information for anyone interested in the economic and social life of the Early Modern town.[78] Broad aspects of the Medieval town, such as monetarisation, the poor and the town guilds, are addressed in the anthology *Middelalderbyen* (2008) edited by Bitsch Christensen. As the present analysis is focused on finding evidence relating to very local history, the work most frequently referred to here is *Aarhus Byens Historie* volumes 1 and 2, edited by Ib Gejl. In this, Ole Degn, in particular, describes life in the town in great detail and deals with economic aspects, social differences, urban prosperity and decline and many other relevant subjects.[79]

1.4 The landscape

Aarhus lies at a meeting place in the landscape: A meeting place between the sea and the interior, which extended to the north, south, east and west. Seen from the sea, early Aarhus nestled between steep, forested slopes of Risskov to the north and Moesgaard Strand to the south, on the accessible sheltered area formed at the mouth of the river Aarhus Å. If boats did not land here, they had to sail a further 6 km to the north, to Egå, or 15 km to the south, to Norsminde Fjord, to find a sheltered landing place on the coast. The town itself arose on a low sandy area at the mouth of Aarhus Å, bounded by the river to the south and surrounded by low, swampy or wet areas to the north and west. The river connected the coast with the interior via Brabrand Fjord, which stretched about 12 km inland, giving easy access to the coast from settlements around its shores. Several other fjords, such as Egå Fjord and Norsminde Fjord, also penetrated inland, but Brabrand Fjord was the largest and longest, providing the best opportunities for waterborne transport between coast and interior.[80] At the same time, the fjord and its surrounding wetlands acted as a natural barrier between north and south, forcing land traffic either far to the west in the direction of *Hærvejen* (literally "the Military Road", also known as the "Ox Road"), or out to the coast. It was here, on an unoccupied area located at a natural meeting point, where a ready access route between the coast and the interior crossed the north-south transport lines, that the first Aarhus was founded. Rows of Bronze Age barrows still dominate the forested areas south of Aarhus and these may mark an ancient route running southwards along the coast towards Norsminde and the resource areas beyond around Horsens Fjord. In the same forest, traces of ancient roads, so-called hollow ways, are also still visible in the landscape. These roads, which are of unknown date, lead towards the later urban area, i.e. the crossing point over Aarhus Å, along the coast from the south. They may have been linked to a traffic route leading south towards resource areas around present-day Odder. Somewhere along the way there may

also have been a connection to a road system running southwest in the direction of the royal centre of Jelling, which was established in the early 10th century.[81] On its way southwest, this road passed Viby, a place known to be the site of a royal residence in the 12th century, traces of which were found in 1916.[82] From here the road continued through the landscape, following the top of the plateau to the village of Hørning. The age of this village is unknown, but its name suggests that settlement in the area has its roots in the Late Iron Age, c. AD 400-800. A runestone – the Hørning Stone, with origins in the late 10th or early 11th century, may have marked the crossing of Aarhus Å at this point.[83] From here, the route ran north of the lakes of Solbjerg Sø and Skanderborg Sø and then wound its way towards Jelling. North of the crossing over Aarhus Å roads led to the northeast, towards Djursland, and to the north, towards Randers Fjord. Both routes had to pass the wetlands around the river Egå, located about 6 km to the north. Two runestones may have marked these crossings: One at Egå to the east, where the Djursland road crossed, and one to the west at Vejlby, where the road led up on to the plateau at Lisbjerg – later the site of a major Viking Age manor – and from there on towards Randers Fjord. All of these traffic routes crossed Aarhus Å at the point where Aarhus was later established.

Aarhus was founded in a landscape very different from that of today. Evidence from archaeological excavations of settlements and from place names (the suffixes -lev, -ing and -sted) indicates that the landscape in the vicinity of the later Aarhus was rather open in the Late Iron Age, c. AD 400-800, with expanses of agricultural land around Odder to the south, around Adslev and Framlev to the west and around Lisbjerg to the north. These areas can be seen as constituting a coherent settlement pattern in eastern Jutland, established at least by the Late Iron Age and connected by routes linking inland agricultural areas. From the ploughed infield, the traffic routes ran through vast stretches of outfields, cutting through forests and crossing wetlands and watercourses.[84] The extent of these outfields, especially the forested parts, should not be underestimated. Even on maps based on information from the early 19th century, the forest is still very visible as a resource, covering vast tracts of the central and southern parts of eastern Jutland, but with a deforested belt along the coast that may have been created as a form of supply zone hosting intensive arable agriculture near the town of Arhus.[85] If we look more closely at these various settlement areas, their names indicate that at least three, perhaps four of them, had been established by the beginning of the Viking Age: These are the settlements around Odder, Brabrand and Lisbjerg, all of which lie demarcated by typical outfields, i.e. watercourses and forested hilly terrain.

The settlement area around Odder is located on very fertile land and even today the villages here lie close together. Archaeological information on the situation in the Viking Age comes primarily from excavations at Randlev, which revealed remains of a Viking Age village dating from the 9th and 10th centuries.[86]

The settlement around Brabrand is not very well known archaeologically. A burial ground, the Voldbæk cemetery, dated to the Late Iron Age and Viking Age, has been found a few hundred metres east of Aarslev, a village name with an Iron Age suffix. A further 500 m to the east of the cemetery, traces of settlement, probably comprised of sunken-featured buildings, were found between the gardens and villas that now cover the area. The cemetery also lies just a few hundred metres west of the Medieval stronghold of Hougaard, located in the meadows bordering the present-day lake Brabrand Sø.[87] A preliminary excavation of this stronghold was carried out in the 1960s, but further excavations and research may well enable conclusions to be drawn about the relationship, perhaps even the continuity, between the manor, the Late Viking Age settlement and the cemetery.[88]

Lisbjerg is the archaeologically best-known of the Viking Age settlements near Aarhus. Remains of a structure interpreted as a magnate's farm have been dated to the Late Viking Age. Here were traces of bronze and silver casting, glass working and iron smithing with a range of provenances, demonstrating an extensive network of contacts emanating from the site.[89] Situated at the crossing of the river Egå near the coast, another settlement appears to have concentrated on meat production: Primarily pigs and cattle, as well as fishing and hunting, thereby exploiting the typical resources of the outfield.[90] The village functioned from the beginning of 9th to the middle of the 11th century. Between the settlements and their surrounding agricultural zones, tracts of outfield, forests and wetlands dominated the landscape. These were not simply wastelands, they were also a potential resource ready for exploitation: Timber for fencing, building materials, firewood and charcoal, leaves for cattle fodder, acorns as food for pigs and game for hunting. Wetlands and heaths supplied peat for use as manure and fuel and provided grazing for cattle and sheep, while the coast could also be grazed and gave access to important resources such as fish – both shallow- and deep-water species. During the Viking Age and Early Medieval period, expansion into the outfield resulted in the founding of a wealth of new settlements in previously forested areas, most of them identifiable by their place name suffixes of -by and -torp.[91] These settlements, or *thorps,* can be seen as the expansion of arable agriculture into the outfields of the earlier central settlements.[92] A possible Viking Age expansion into forested outfield areas is apparent from data from archaeological surveys and excavations of settlements, at least in the Aarhus area,[93] although there is little doubt that most of the conversion of the outfield into arable agricultural land took place later, in the Early Middle Ages.[94] It could well have been continuing exploitation of the available resources in the landscape, combined with the exchange of the agricultural surplus derived from these new settlements through maritime networks with the Baltic lands, that led to the founding of Aarhus and, subsequently, to the urban growth of the Middle Ages. This, in turn, formed the basis for the urban consumption that will be dealt with in the following chapters.[95]

1.5 The topography of Aarhus – a short survey

Before we address the subject of urban consumption, a brief history of Aarhus will be presented. Much of the information summarised here will be dealt with in greater detail later in this volume, but this summary is intended as a guide to the topography of the town and some of the topographical features that receive frequent reference here. Aarhus is mentioned for the first time in AD 948, as the seat of Bishop Reginbrand, who took part in a synod in the German imperial town of Ingelheim on the Rhine.[96] Apart from scattered evidence of settlement in the Stone Age and the Roman Iron Age, the earliest datable traces of occupation in the area later covered by Aarhus appear to be from the 8th or the 9th century AD, although their precise date remains unknown. This early settlement was surrounded by a narrow ditch, probably marking out the area as a special statutory entity. The settlement itself covered an area of approximately 11 ha and was located where the river, Aarhus Å, meets the coast. It was one of the few immediately coastal settlements in Denmark at this time. After some time, probably in the 10th century, the settlement was fortified. This lead to a contraction of the settlement, as sunken-feature buildings have been found below and beyond this fortification.

After a period of apparent vacancy, Aarhus was again designated an episcopal seat, and shortly after this the first cathedral was built west of the ramparts. Over the next century, further ecclesial institutions followed: The churches of Our Lady and St. Oluf are mentioned in 1203. The Church of Our Lady has not been encountered archaeologically, although the presence of graves points to a location west of the fortification. St. Oluf's Church was built very near the coast, to the north of the Viking Age rampart – a structure that was still very much a visible feature of the town. The church's graves date from the 13th century, but a grave found under its foundations indicates the existence of an earlier, as yet unknown, church on the site.[97] All these churches were built outside the Viking Age rampart. The area inside the rampart may have also have hosted a chapel: A chapel "by the sea" is mentioned in the middle of the 13th century, referring to the situation in the late 12th century.[98]

Aarhus housed other institutions too: Coins were minted in the city during the reign of Hardicanute (1035-1042): The mintmaster, Ciadwinw, must have been Anglo-Saxon, as must mintmaster Lifsig, who struck coins in the town under Hardeknud's successor, Magnus the Good (1042-47).[99] Not all encounters were peaceful: According to Adam of Bremen, Aarhus was attacked in 1050 by the Norwegian king Harald Hardrada and the church and unfortified parts of town burned to the ground.[100] The town may have had a military function: Saxo Grammaticus mentions that Prince Magnus used the harbour at Aarhus as naval base. He also states that Aarhus was attacked by Slavic Wends in 1158, but as yet we have no clear archaeological evidence of warfare in the city.[101]

In the 13th century, a new cathedral, St. Clement's, was constructed within the fortified area, beginning around 1200-1250, and probably on the site of an earlier chapel mentioned in 1191.[102] The former cathedral, St. Nicholas, was handed over to Dominican monks before 1245, the church was rebuilt and a convent was founded on the site. While the cathedral was being built, the spatial layout of Aarhus was altered. This reorganisation included refortification of the old rampart, clearing and laying out of a market square, Store Torv, breaching of the rampart to the west to create Borgporten, and laying out of Lille Torv, Immervad and Vestergade, in addition to many of the streets to the west and north of the fortification. A dendrochronological date from Lille Torv places its establishment between 1253 and 1268.[103] In the 14th century, Aarhus spread south of Aarhus Å along the road leading south, and in the 15th century, a new harbour was constructed along the south bank of the river. In the 15th century, a number of brick-built houses was constructed along the coast to the north of the rampart around the city. The cathedral and the monasteries were also rebuilt, and a new monastery was founded along the main road to the south. But

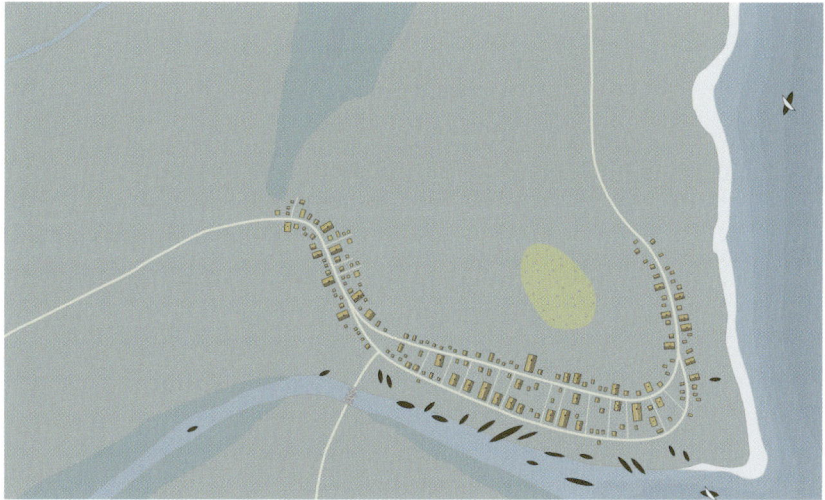

Figure 3. Earliest Aarhus – before the Viking Age fortification. The settlement follows roads running along the river, Aarhus Å, and the coast. Map: Graphics Department, Moesgaard Museum.

Figure 4. Fortified Aarhus in the 10th century. The earliest church is situated to the west, outside the fortifications. Map: Graphics Department, Moesgaard Museum.

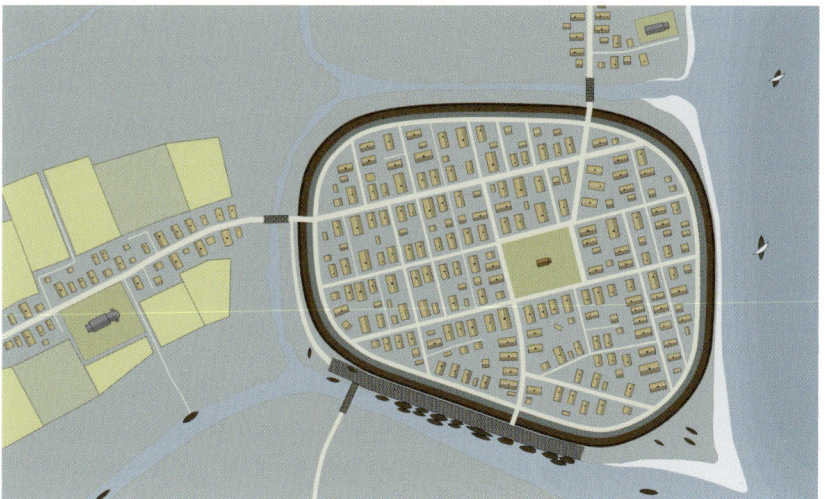

Figure 5. Aarhus at the end of the 13th century. St. Clement's cathedral is under construction in the middle of the fortified area and the market squares are being established. Map: Graphics Department, Moesgaard Museum.

33

in the 16th and 17th centuries, this newly founded monastery was demolished, as were all the churches, apart from the cathedral and the Church of Our Lady. These areas were rebuilt, but the topography of the town largely followed its Medieval layout.

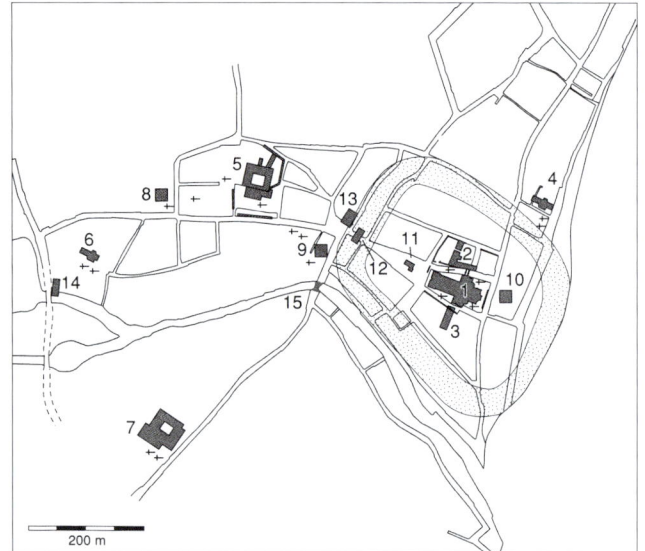

Figure 6. Aarhus. Map showing ecclesiastical institutions and the most important secular institutions in the Medieval town. 1. Cathedral. 2. Bishop´s residence. 3. Chapter House. 4. St. Oluf´s Church, 5. Dominican monastery, 6. St. Mary´s Church (Church of Our Lady), 7. Carmelite monastery, 8. Hospital of St. Catherine (Karen), 9. Hospital of the Holy Ghost, 10. Cathedral school, 11. Town Hall, 12. Borgporten (Town gate), 13. Bathhouse, 14. Watermill, 15. Immervad bridge. Drawing: S. Kaae.

Figure 7. Prospect of Aarhus c. 1640 in the collection of Den Gamle By. © Photo: Knud Nielsen.

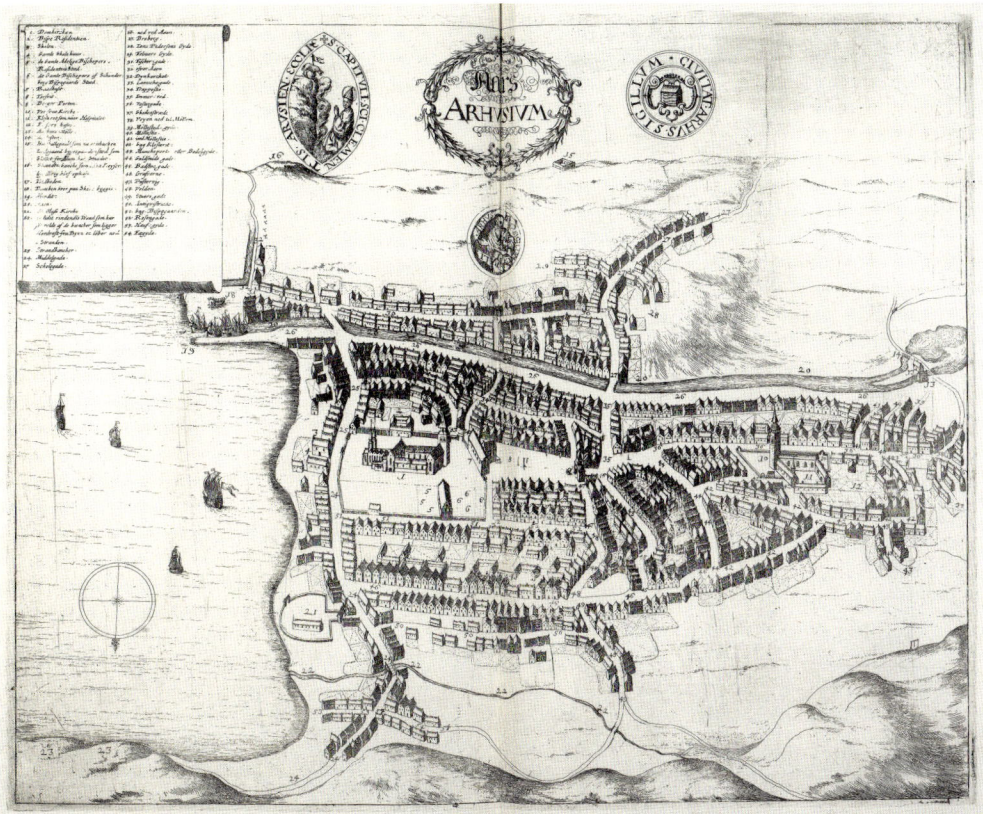

Figure 8. Aars Arusium: Prospect of Aarhus, 1677. © The Royal Library, Copenhagen.

Figure 9. Prospect of Aarhus from the south, Johan Jacob Bruun, 1755. © The Royal Library, Copenhagen.

Figure 10. *Emblematic Still Life with Flagon, Glass, Jug and Bridle, Johannes Torrentius, 1614. ©Rijksmuseum, Amsterdam.*

2 Materiality

Archaeology is cursed by an information gap arising from the patchy and inconsistent survival of its source material – the archaeological record. This means that the results of very few archaeological excavations constitute a direct reflection of what was originally left in the ground for us to find. Everything has been through a process of taphonomy, filtered through patterns of transformation and even destruction that affects different kinds of materiality in different ways. Metals were largely reused in the past and this means that the few fragments of iron, brass and pewter vessels we do find represent only the slight remnants of what was actually used, sifted by past practices of recycling, destruction and by decay. Organic materials, such as paper, wood, leather and textiles, rarely survive in the ground and archaeology is consequently left with virtually indestructible inorganic components – such as household ceramics. This means that aspects of consumption in which ceramics are brought into play are where the archaeological record survives best and the information gap can be effectively bridged. Numerically, ceramics represent by far the largest group of archaeological finds available to us for study. This is largely due to their widespread use and to prevailing preservation conditions, as mentioned above and dealt with in more detail below. The dominance of the archaeological record by ceramics does, however, lead to a corresponding dominance of this book by ceramics analysis. This was not intended, but is a consequence of the nature of the available sources. I therefore ask the forgiveness of the reader, who may find this kind of analysis heavy reading.

Furthermore, documentary information on consumption in urban and rural areas is sparse and much is unpublished. This study therefore aims to bridge the consequent information gap by employing an integrated approach which encompasses science and history – both disciplines that are embedded in the field of historical archaeology. However, although information from science and history is drawn upon here, the resources available for this research project did not permit the employment of either scientists, for new scientific analyses, or historians, for new studies of unpublished documentary material. These important tasks must await future research projects.

2.1 The geographical scope of this investigation

This project is based on archaeological material – the archaeological record – and for practical reasons the study area corresponds to Moesgaard Museum's area of archaeological responsibility as it was in 2013 (figure 11), i.e. the municipalities of Aarhus, Odder and Faurskov. The results of archaeological investigations and excavations carried out within this area constitute the primary source material. Present-day administrative boundaries may appear rather arbitrary relative to the situation in Medieval times, and so they are. Nevertheless, these three municipalities have their roots in the *herred*, or hundred, an administrative unit that extends back at least to the 11th century and which, in turn, reflects a resource area. As such,

Figure 11. *The study area for this project.*

this investigation covers the following hundreds in the vicinity of Aarhus: Hads, Ning, Hasle, Framlev, Lisbjerg, Sabro and Gjern, together with parts of Houbjerg, Galten and Øster Lisbjerg. This specific study area has, however, been deviated from in some instances, especially with regard to the historical sources on urban immigration, where exclusion of information from other areas would mean an unreasonable loss of readily available data. For the purposes of this investigation, the landscape has been divided up: The urban zone is the area within the town gates of Aarhus in 1800, corresponding approximately to the streets of Nørre Allé, Nørregade, Vester Allé and Sønder Allé, with areas outside this being considered as rural. The division of the landscape according to resources and use, i.e. agricultural land, heath, wood-

land etc., is based on the classification defined by the Forest and Nature Agency in 1997 and on information from the Royal Danish Society of Sciences and Letters' map, drawn up in the 1780s for the Aarhus area.[104] The coastal zone is less clearly demarcated, and for practical purposes it has been defined as extending 5 km inland from the maximum high-water mark.

2.2 The material

The material basis for this book is threefold, being comprised of an overview of finds of lead cloth seals, coins and ceramics. While the analyses of the lead cloth seals and coins found in the study area are fairly straightforward, as the numbers involved are modest: 24 lead cloth seals and fewer than 200 sin-

Figure 12. Locations of the selected rural sites around Aarhus.

gle finds of coins plus several hoards, all of which are published, the ceramics record is less manageable. In order to carry out a consumption analysis it was necessary to apply a research strategy that permitted a relational analysis of multiple features on several scales. I aimed at a form of recording that allowed analysis of spatial distribution, of the relative quantities of various types of ceramics and of the material and functions of the specific types of these. The number of ceramic sherds dating from the period AD 800-1800 recovered within the study area is unknown, and no counts and calculations have

been made in this respect. However, the total is very probably close to 500,000. It is therefore evident that a targeted research strategy was necessary in order for results to be achieved within a reasonable time-frame. Fifteen recent excavations of high technical quality and with detailed stratigraphic information were therefore chosen for individual analysis, eight in the town and the remainder in surrounding rural areas. In all cases, the ceramics assemblages have been fully recorded and analysed. An overview of the parameters recorded will be given later. In order to be able to discuss the distribution of the various types across a wider area, all ceramics available in Moesgaard Museum's collections have also been surveyed. The principles behind this survey will also be presented later. The analyses of coins and lead cloth seals will largely be presented in the form of maps, but finds of these from the selected sites will be discussed in the context of the individual excavations. There have been rather few excavations of Medieval and Post-Medieval rural settlements, and the material recovered from them is relatively sparse. The remains of many past villages lie beneath the present ones, and what extends outside these has been partially destroyed. This is due to preservation conditions: The fertile soil of eastern Jutland has been under agriculture for hundreds of years and, as a consequence, most settlements and their associated cultural layers containing archaeological finds were disturbed long ago, leaving only pits, wells and postholes with a sparse content of artefacts. Every available excavation of a rural site, large or small, has therefore been used in this investigation. The selection of urban excavations followed a rather different route. In the town we are spoilt for choice and many sites have been excavated during a century of archaeological investigations in Aarhus. Nevertheless, in order to ensure the best possible quality of the material evidence, the excavations selected here were mainly carried out during the last 15 years and targeted at larger areas, where major parts of the settlement were uncovered and numerous finds recovered. An attempt has also been made to include all quarters of the town.

These 15 excavations form the foundation for the chronology and the analyses of ceramics and other artefacts presented in this book. A few further words should be said about the selection of the basic material for this study. As previously stated, only larger excavations of high technical quality have been included. This high technical standard also applies to the excavation methodology. It is obvious that the excavation method is very significant when estimating the representativity of the recovered material. The use of sieving during excavation is an important factor relative to the composition of ceramics assemblages. Some ceramic fabrics break and fragment more readily than others and the sherds are therefore smaller, resulting in a potential loss of very small sherds if contexts are not sieved. On the other hand, coarseware sherds are generally larger, but as they are grey-brownish in colour, they may be more easily overlooked during excavation when sieving is not employed. Systematic sieving was introduced as part of the standard archaeological practice at Moesgaard Museum around 2002. For this reason, it would be advantageous to limit this investigation to post-2002 excavations. However, as some sites of great information potential with respect to consumption studies were excavated prior to 2002, their exclusion would lead to an unreasonable loss of otherwise valuable information. The representativity of the material has already been touched upon. As this analysis has its foundation in excavations of sites that include structures such as houses and so on, all of the ceramics have a context. We know where the material was deposited and we are able to deduce, or at least confidently presume, that the material in question was used and discarded on or very near the spot where it was found – in archaeological terms in primary and secondary deposits related to dwellings on the plots in question. No redeposited material, i.e. major areas of fill in individual plots, public refuse dumps or similar, has been included in this investigation – not because it lacks research potential, but because the information it is able to provide relates primarily to aspects of waste management and related topics and therefore lies outside the scope of this analysis. A waste management system was of course in operation during most of the time span analysed here, which means that we must expect some materials to have been transported away from the plots and therefore not included in this analysis. So what we are left with as a basis for this study are, so to say, the remains of the remains. However, these remains have a known, verifiable context and, as such, constitute a solid basis for a comparative analysis of consumption. The subject of this book is, however, urban consumption,

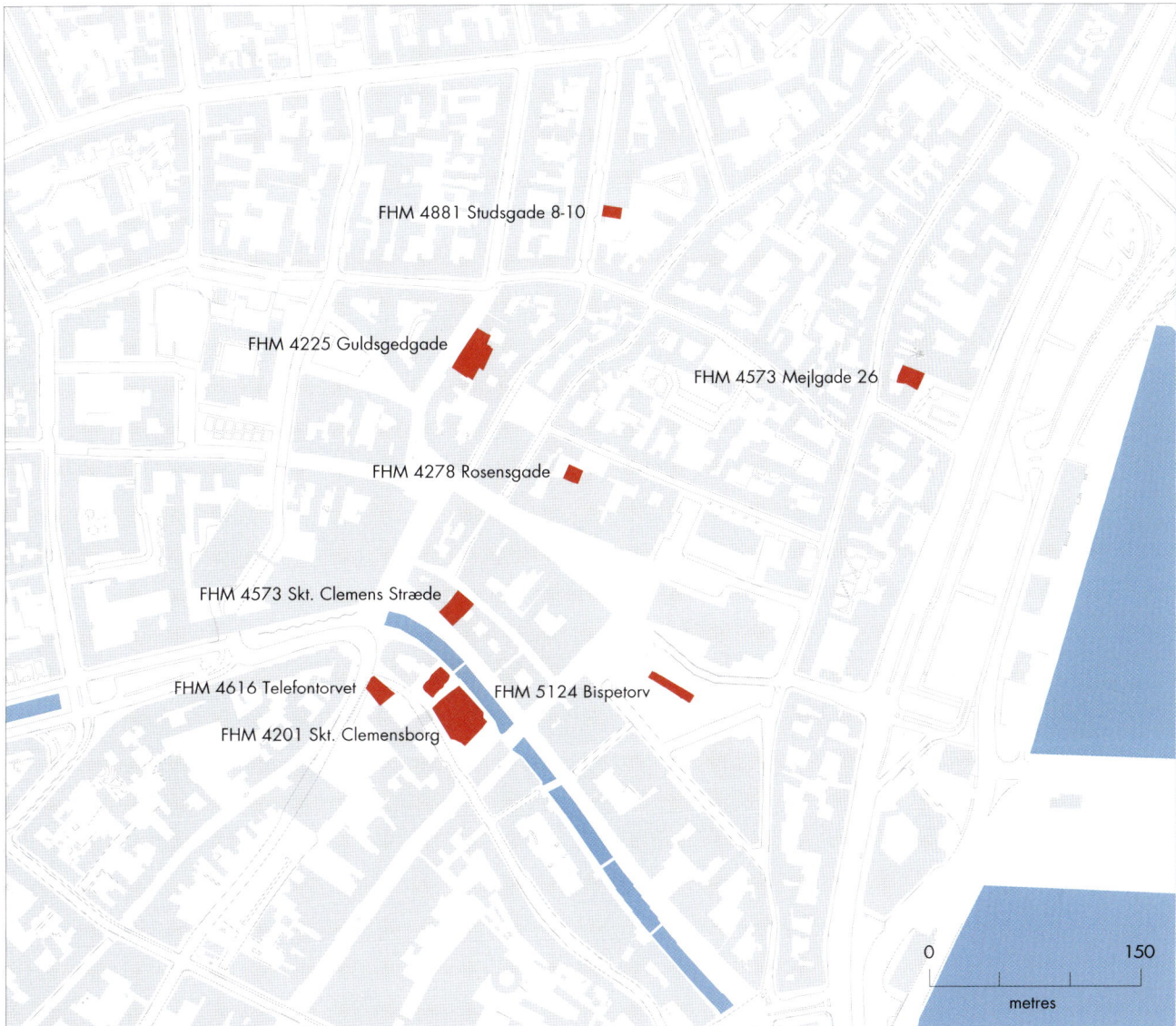

Figure 13. *Locations of the selected urban sites in Aarhus*

not consumption as reflected at a limited number of excavated sites. The 15 selected sites cannot be presumed to be representative of the study area as a whole, and recording has therefore been supplemented by a further survey carried out according to different principles and resulting in the production of a number of maps. This involved the examination of material from archaeological excavations carried out before 2014 within the boundaries of the urban area; 202 in total. In this secondary survey only the pres-

ence/absence of imported ceramics types has been noted. No attempt has been made at quantification or recording of local ceramics types as neither was an achievable task within the limits of this project. This two-pronged approach was adopted in order to put the detailed results from the 15 excavations in the context of the study area as a whole. It allows us to actually observe the distribution of for example specific imported types within the urban area, as reflected in the finds that have been recovered. The

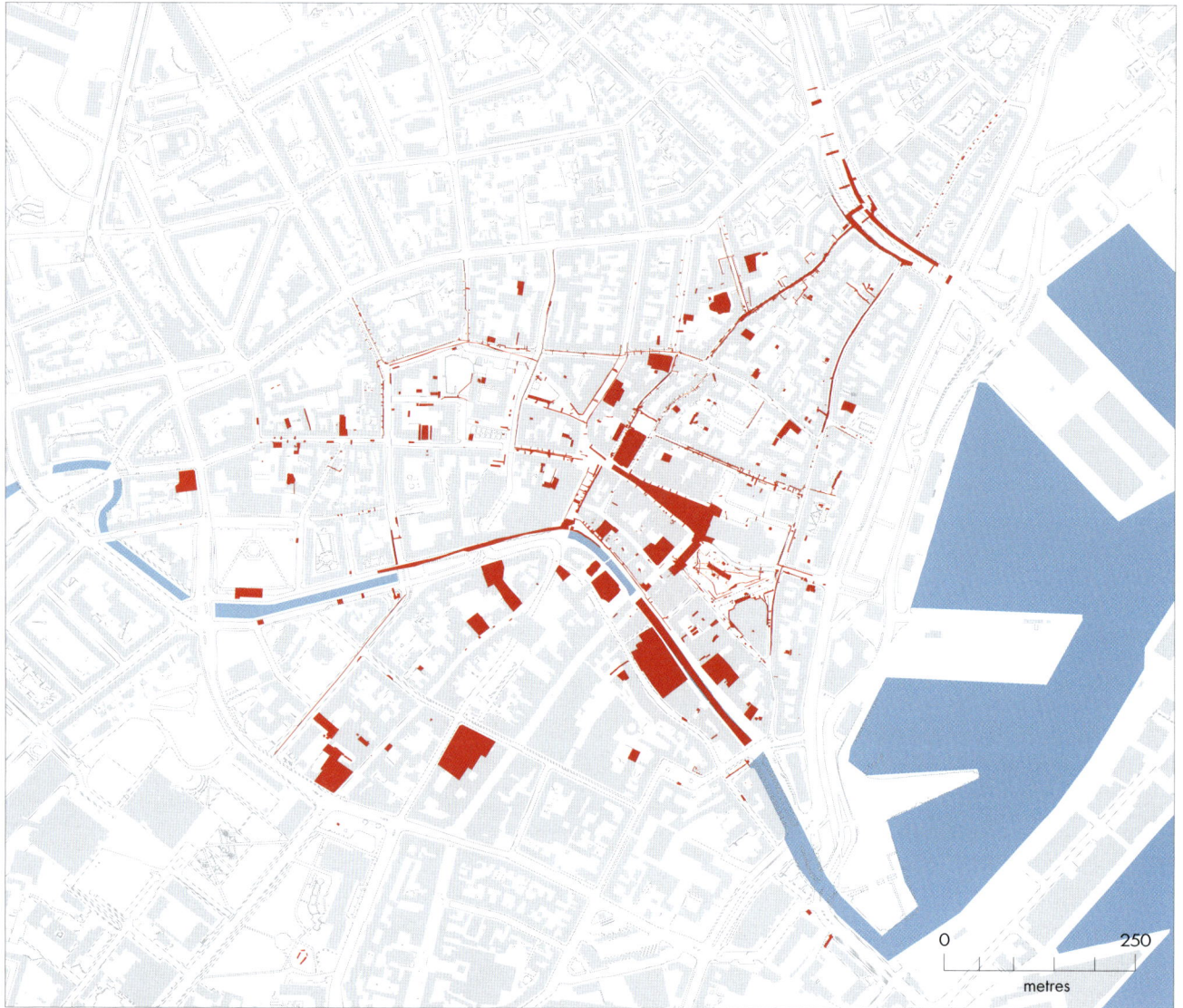

Figure 14. *Locations of the c. 200 archaeological excavations carried out in Aarhus.*

representativity of this material may still be questionable, as many of the finds were recovered in the early 20th century during construction work. Moreover, some parts of the town have not been subject to as much development and construction work as others, resulting in a limited number of finds from these parts. But even given these reservations, the detailed analysis of the basic material, coupled with the survey of the total assemblage of recovered finds, is probably as close to a representative overview of the urban consumption that it is presently possible to achieve.

2.3 Methodology and data collection

The methodology used in this study is threefold. Information on single finds of coins and coins recovered during excavations is mainly held in the archives of Moesgaard Museum, as is information on the lead cloth seals. The coin hoards have been subjected to analysis and are all published, while this only applies to a few of the lead cloth seals.[105] With some notable exceptions already mentioned above, the ceramics are, on the other hand, largely unpublished and only available in the museum's collections. The processing and examination of this material therefore followed principles that have been tried and tested in numerous previous works, and involved the characterisation of each individual sherd according to fabric and form.[106] By fabric I mean the material, i.e. the clay type with inclusions, from which the vessel was made. By form I mean the shape of the vessel or its components – rim, handle(s) or base. Accordingly, a fabric type series and a form type series constitute the basis for the identification of the ceramics from the study area. The fabric type series follows the principles outlined in my previous works and will only be briefly summarised here.[107] Fabric is the most specific definition, and each ceramic fabric has been described according to the character and quality of the clay and inclusions following the principles outlined by Clive Orton, Christopher Tyers and Alan Vince.[108] In this recording process, fabric colour at the core, margin and surface, hardness, type, size and distribution of inclusions, form technique, type and placing of surface treatment and mention of typical decorations were recorded, thereby forming the basis for a series of ware type definitions that are presented in the appendix section of this book. According to the character of the clay and inclusions, all fabrics have been classified according to a three-level system comprising: 1. ceramics group, 2. ceramics subgroup and 3. ware type, each of which is denoted by a combination of letters and numbers. This resulted in a list of ware types with a three-letter fabric code and an individual ware name that is referred to in the text (see table 33: ceramics classification, in the back of this book). For example, the local black-pot production known as Vorup has the letter code A for the ceramics group "greyware", 1 for the ceramics subgroup "soft-fired" and c for the specific ware type within the subgroup, as well as the ware name "black pot of Vorup type", in short A1c. The codes for the ceramics groups and subgroups are rarely mentioned in the text as these mainly serve an analytical function in the ordering of the type series and as input into the statistical analysis where a short

reference code is needed. Reference is most frequently made to the ware names in the text, e.g. "black pot of Vorup type" as a book filled with references to types A1c, B2c and so on would be very heavy reading indeed. Any reader familiar with the principles behind the recording and naming of ceramics in the tradition of the Medieval Pottery Research Group will now be aware of the differences between the two systems: The letter and number codings are different, as the system used here was developed within a research context originally based on a German tradition.[109] But it will hopefully also be clear that the fabric definition is transparent and that the principles behind it, and the ware nomenclature, are the same whatever system is employed. For example, Werra ware is the same wherever it is found, and non-Danish readers should therefore be perfectly able to study the distribution of this type in this book, and of other imports and even local wares, and integrate this information into their own studies. A few words should be said on the nature of the ware type names. Any geographical reference in a name should be understood in its broadest sense as an eponym, attached to a type that was either produced or found in larger quantities in that area. As in the example "Werra ware": This term is used here not in the sense of "ceramics produced in the exact location of Werra" – or in Raeren, Brugge, Saintonge or any other place that may be part of a ware name, but in the broader sense as "the type of ceramics that is commonly known as Werra ware" – or Saintonge or Brugge ware, or whatever we are dealing with.

2.4 Recording and quantification

Recording and quantification is a complex subject. In the recording process in this project, each context at the sites included in the basic material has been given a special sheet in a database containing information on the excavation number, site name, means of absolute dating in relation to the context (coins, associated dendrochronological dates, radiocarbon dates etc.), excavation phase, construction unit (of which the context is part), context number and the interpretation arrived at by the excavator: i.e. a structure such as a latrine or a cellar, a pit or a surface such as a floor in a building. The ceramics from each context were then sorted according to the attached finds numbers and each individual sherd was assigned a ware type and a form type and information was recorded on vessel type, vessel function and decoration techniques and special features such as misfiring or traces of use. In order to facilitate quantification, the rim percentage present (RP), weight (g) and number of sherds (Sherds) were recorded. This threefold quantification is very flexible and allows different methods of measuring the ceramics that are applicable for different purposes.[110] Most of the analyses in the following are based on rim percentages, followed by sherd counts in some cases, as fabrics present in small quantities do not always include rim sherds.[111] In the recording of the basic material, the ceramics from around 1000 contexts were recorded in a database with about 6000 individual posts referring to c. 25,000 individual sherds. In order to manage this material, fabric group and ware name abbreviations were added to the database, as were abbreviations that permitted rapid analysis of the ratio of for example local to imported wares or various form types. In the following, the quantitative ceramics data are presented in the form of tables and charts, primarily in the categories RP and Sherds. Each of the methods has its advantages and disadvantages, especially when making comparisons between different sites. A sherd count is easy to carry out, but differences in fragmentation between sites make direct comparison difficult: Coarse wares may fragment into larger sherds than thinner fabrics, leading to over-representation of the latter. Weight is also easy to use, but differences in weight between different fabrics (coarse greywares are generally thicker-walled and therefore heavier than finer fabrics) lead to potential under-representation of for example finer fabrics. RP is a measure that is independent of breakage and fabric thickness and many charts are therefore based primarily on this measurement. However, rarer fabrics are sometimes not represented in the rim sherds so another measurement has to be used in these cases.

Finally, it is important to state that ceramics constitute a material that was produced by humans in the past and which, regardless of the assistance provided by various data-processing tools, is analysed by humans in the present. Consequently, the factor of human subjectivity, human error even, has to be taken into account. Handmade vessels show slight variation, even when produced in series. Kilns fire differently according to where in them the vessels are stacked. Inclusions can be distributed unevenly during the mixing of the clay prior to forming the vessels, and it is the human eye, with its ability to distinguish around 2 million colours, and human touch, equally fine-tuned, that decide which fabric group any sherd should be assigned to. It is of course a human decision whether a slight variation, in for example the colour of a fabric, is distinctive enough to qualify it as being different, or whether this simply arises from unintentional variations in the kiln atmosphere. In this study, I have chosen to adopt a conservative approach, hoping to be able to trace changes in the ceramics that potters intended to make, and that consumers chose to acquire, rather than those which were the random results of factors beyond human control.[112]

2.5 Presentation of the sites

This chapter gives a brief outline of the 15 sites, including their location and size and the results obtained in their excavation. Each summary is followed by a presentation of the ceramics recovered from the site, arranged according to the stratigraphic phasing, followed by a discussion of contexts or structures of particular interest for the study of consumption on site, and the ceramics they contained. Please note this presentation of the excavations is based on information given in the excavation reports. This means that the definition of individual contexts and of stratigraphic phases and information on scientific dating of the phases was taken directly from these reports. The names of the contests and phases used, e.g. FHM 4226 phase 5, are as given in the excavation reports. When individual contexts are referred to, the principle is

All sites																
Sum of sherd counts																
Ware types	FHM 1978	FHM 3474	FHM 3731	FHM 4074	FHM 4201	FHM 4225	FHM 4278	FHM 4573	FHM 4587	FHM 4616	FHM 4730	FHM 4881	FHM 4999	FHM 5124	FHM 5419	Total
Andenne-type ware									2					2		4
Baltic blackware		20				108		16				46		53		243
Baltic burnished greyware				1		5	2		40	9				9		66
Black pot, early type						1560						341		65	83	2049
Black pot, Varde type	121				346	440	59		55					113		1134
Black pot, Vorup type	76	150														226
Brügge-type ware						1										1
Capuchin ware	6															
Cologne stoneware	151				5					4		7		1		168
Danish slipware	10				20	7	2		3					5		47
Frechen stoneware					5	7	1		1			1		1		16
Industrial ceramics	6	10			206	31	8			1		5		19		286
Langerwehe stoneware					1	5										6
Low Countries redware					1	2				1		10		5		19
Low Countries tin-glazed ware					1		1		1			3		4		10
Low Countries/ German Post-Medieval whiteware			17	193	12	1			35	7	4	9		75		353
Medieval low-fired coarseware						397	2					177	89	508		1173
Medieval well-fired coarseware		188	56	424	81	1011	320		193	551	119	259	82	825		4109
Medieval well-fired redware		20	4	176	43	351	53		53	269	2	15	4	126		1116
Other blackware		4		6	938	65			323	79		192		262		1869
Other porcelain	16				18	2			1					4		47
Pingsdorf-type ware														2		2
Post-Medieval redware	295	46		130	1981	636	94	47	412	116		1084	6	767	26	5640
Post-Medieval redware with slip decoration	463	5		7	108	33	2		12	7		303		13	22	975
Proto stoneware						5	5		3	6		1		5		25
Raeren stoneware		1		4	19	19	1		2	3				32		81
Rouen-type ware				1		2			2					4		9
Saintonge polychrome ware										1						1
Siegburg stoneware					7	32	4		11	7				3		64
Other tin-glazed wares	95				15	3	5		2					2		121
Viking Age low-fired coarseware						177	1833	1				432		2450		4893
Waldenburg stoneware							5									5
Werra ware												2				2
Weser ware				1	2	1										4
Westerwald stoneware	4				10	3	1		1					2		21
Total	**1243**	**444**	**60**	**766**	**4001**	**4738**	**743**	**1896**	**1151**	**1063**	**125**	**2887**	**181**	**5357**	**131**	**24786**

Table 1. Abundance of ware groups at the selected sites, based on sherd number.

Excavation number + Site name + Context name or number: For example, FHM 4225 Guldsmedgade A107, and then the ceramics from that specific context are referred to an object number which normally covers all the sherds of a specific ware type from a given context: e.g. X25. These numbers are taken from the museum recording system used in the excavation reports. The ware type and form type definitions cited in brackets, e.g. (rim type 308), refer to the appendix section of this volume, where form types like handles and rims are depicted and the ware types are defined. For practical reasons, the urban excavations will be dealt with first, followed by the rural sites. But before this, an overview of the ceramics is given in table 1.

2.6 The urban sites

As mentioned above, the entire corpus of about 200 archaeological investigations carried out by Moesgaard Museum in Aarhus prior to 2014 was surveyed in order to provide a reliable background relative to an assessment of the occurrence of ceramics and coins across the entire urban area. The location of these investigations is shown in figure 14.

From these, eight urban sites were selected for further analysis. The selection criteria have already been briefly outlined above, but only more recent excavations of high technical quality, covering larger areas with evidence of occupation over longer time spans, a well-defined stratigraphy and clear stratigraphic phasing, preferably relating to structures where dates other than those from ceramics could be applied, were chosen. Furthermore, representation of all parts of the town was prioritised. The excavations are analysed below and recorded according to archive no., site name, land registry title no., year of excavation, total area excavated and sources available, followed by a summary of the excavation, including the ceramics and datable finds, all classified according to occupational phases. All percentages are based on sherd numbers. All excavation reports and materials are located at Moesgaard Museum.

2.6.1 FHM 4201 Skt. Clemensborg (land registry title no. 166a) (with Lars Krants)

Excavated 2001. Total area c. 1300 m².
Sources: Excavation report; Krants 2005.

FHM 4201 Skt. Clemensborg comprises two adjoining areas in the southern part of the Early Medieval and Medieval town, just north of Fiskergade and immediately south of the river Aarhus Å. The site covers the southern bank of Aarhus Å, east of Immervad. During the excavation, six plots extending north-south between Fiskergade and the river were excavated. A series of river walls, 19 in all, built into the river bed,

were found in each plot; the earliest was constructed in 1443-52/53 and the latest in 1838. Each of these has been dendrochronologically dated, providing a solid and detailed chronology for the ceramics analysis covering the site's period of use. As an integral part of the construction of each river wall, fill material was placed behind the structure, keeping the horizontal branches and planks in place. This provides a very fine chronological framework for the deposition of ceramics and other small finds on the site and the date of a river wall is, accordingly, the date for the deposition of the fill behind it. This material therefore serves two purposes: It provides a fine chronological framework for the ceramics deposited in the fill, and it gives an overview of the consumption on each of the six plots. Furthermore, the construction and maintenance of the river walls was a private task in the hands of the owners and users of the plots leading down to the harbour – plots that were in the backyards of the farms or houses along Fiskergade, so it is clear that it was their waste that was used. This arrangement is mentioned 1627, when the town council requested that those people owning property bordering to the harbour carry out maintenance of the river walls. This request was repeated in 1665.[113]

River wall phase	Dendro date
2	After 1443 and before 1452/53
3	Winter 1452/53
4	1455-67
5	Winter 1456/57
6	1467-80
7	After 1467-80 and before 1499-1514
8	1499-1514
9	Winter 1512/13
10	Winter 1547/48
11	C. 1571
12	After 1571 and before 1651/52
13	Winter 1651/52
14	Winter 1772/73
15	1779/80
16	After 1779-94
17	After 1779-94 and before 1838
19	After 1838

Table 2. FHM 4201 Skt. Clemensborg: The river walls and their dates.

As the dendrochronologically-dated phases obviously form the backbone of a local ceramics chronology covering the Early Modern period, these will be outlined here. An overview of the dating of the phases is given in table 2. While an overview of the quantities of ceramics is given in table 3. I have chosen to present the material in a chronological sequence, with grouping of the phases in time slots to avoid detail overload.

C. 1450 (phases 1-5)	Sum of sherd counts	Sum of RP	Sum of weight (g)
Baltic burnished greyware	1		1
Black pot, early type	44	91	1170
Post-Medieval redware, early type	9	14	152
Dutch/German whiteware	3	20	72
Siegburg stoneware	2		16
Total	**59**	**125**	**1411**

Table 3. Ceramics from FHM 4201 Skt. Clemensborg c. 1450 (river wall phases 1-5). Note the presence of Post-Medieval redware, early type.

Around 1450 (phases 2-5: before 1452-53 to winter 1456/57) (table 3).

What characterises this phase is Post-Medieval redware, an early type used for cooking pots (rim type 1016), characterised by a glaze that is thin and patchy below the rim.

This type deserves special attention as the date for its introduction is interesting in a Danish context. The occurrence of Post-Medieval redware, early type, was only recently recognised and dated. So far, the earliest introduction of this type has been dated to before 1433, which seems to be in accordance with the other available dates and, as we have seen, this type was certainly present in Aarhus before 1453.[114] The rim type fits perfectly with other finds of this early date. Later in the 15th century the shapes changed, as we will see in the next phase. The imports at this time are obviously Baltic Burnished greywares, jugs of Siegburg stoneware and some whiteware, probably of German origin. The whiteware is thin-walled, buttery-yellow and of the same type as sherds found at FHM 5124 Bispetorv. Most of the material comprises black pots of early type, the form of shallow cooking pots (rim type 308).

C. 1475 (Phase 6+7)	Sum of sherd counts	Sum of RP	Sum of weight (g)
Black pot, Varde type	5	113	27
Medieval well-fired coarseware	24	408	33
Other blackware	113	3299	110
Dutch/German Post-Medieval whiteware	1	4	
Post-medieval redware	54	1000	88
Other	1	8	
Total	**198**	**4832**	**258**

Table 4. Ceramics from FHM 4201 Skt. Clemensborg, c. 1475 (river wall phases 6-7).

Around 1475 (phases 6-7: 1480 until before 1499-1514) (table 4).

At this point, the Baltic Burnished greyware is no longer evident, but the German/Dutch whiteware cooking pots and the Siegburg stoneware jugs are still present. The black pot, early type, is the dominant type, still in the form of cooking pots with partial burnishing (rim type 308) and some jugs. The defining form comprises cooking pots in Post-Medieval redware, early type (rim types 1016, 1017, 1005 and 1035). The handles are soft-formed (handle type 1048)

C. 1500 (phases 8-9)	Sum of sherd counts	Sum of RP	Sum of weight (g)
Black pot, early type	255	432	5972
Post-Medieval redware, early type	7	222	2313
Raeren-type stoneware	2		3
Siegburg stoneware	1		6
Total	**265**	**654**	**8294**

Table 5. Ceramics from FHM 4201 Skt. Clemensborg, c. 1500 (river wall phases 8-9).

Around 1500 (phases 8-9: 1499/1514 until winter 1512/13) (table 5).

The material from phases 8 and 9 was obviously deposited in the first decades of the 15th century. The imports represent a continuation of those of the previous phases: utilitarian stoneware of Rhenish provenance. The main body of the material still comprises black pots, early type cooking pots (rim type 308) and

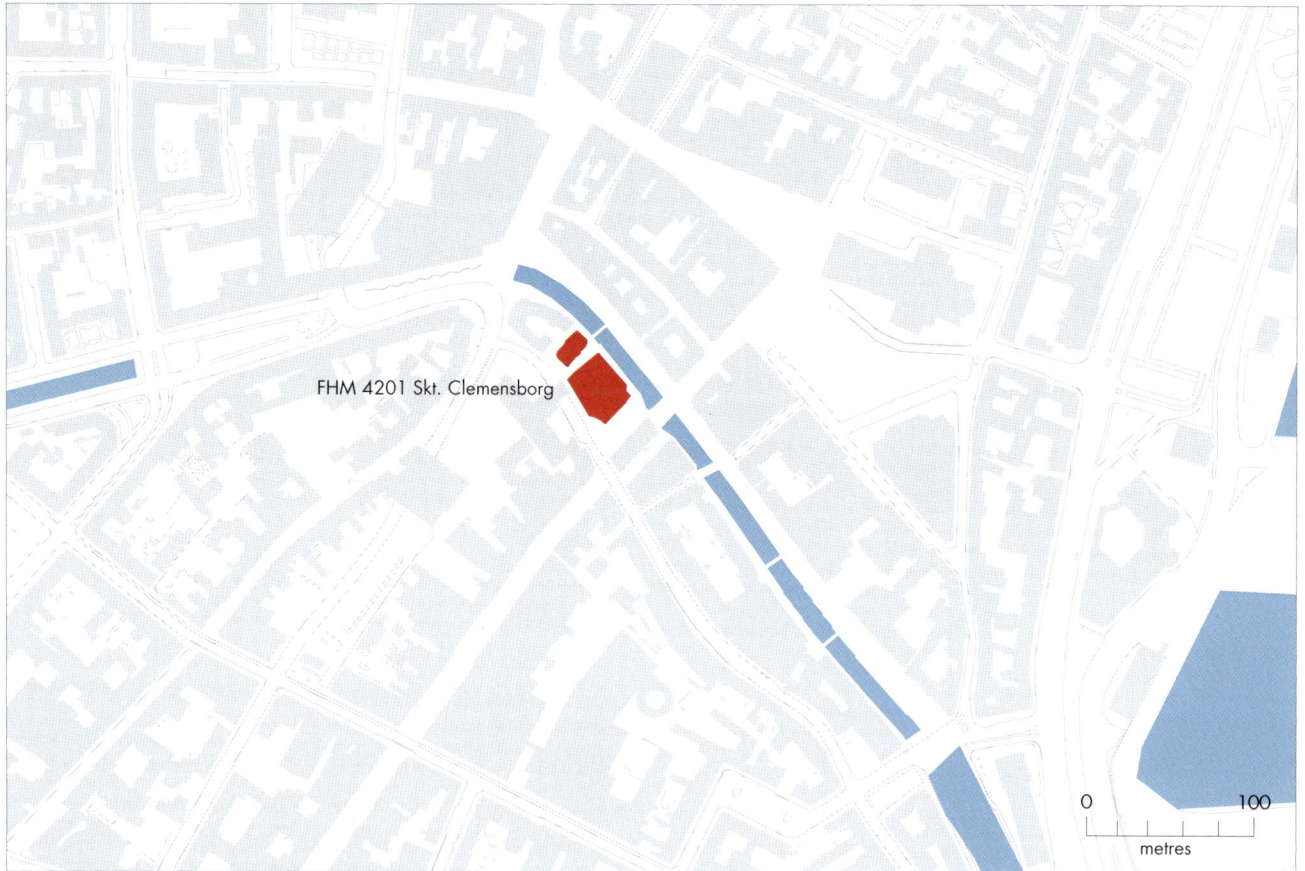

Figure 15. Location of the site FHM 4201 Skt. Clemensborg.

cooking pots in Post-Medieval redware, early type (rim types 1005, 1016, 1017 and 1035). The black pots, early type, are burnished on the rim and shoulder and some have stamped decoration below the rim in the form of crosses and stars.

C. 1550 (phase 10)	Sum of sherd counts	Sum of RP	Sum of weight (g)
Black pot, early type	129	200	3422
Black pot, Vorup type	3	45	234
Post-Medieval redware	65	182	1320
Dutch/German Post-Medieval whiteware	2		36
Total	**199**	**427**	**5012**

Table 6. Ceramics from FHM 4201 Skt. Clemensborg, c. 1550 (river wall phase 10).

C. 1550 (phase 10: winter 1547/48) (table 6).

The black pots, early type cooking pots still have stamped decoration below the rim (rim type 308), and a new type is introduced: the developed black pot, which we now meet in the form of a large cauldron with simple rim (rim type 302), 24-26 cm in diameter. It is the classic, best-known type of black pot which turns up at this point. The type has previously been dated to c. 1550, being found in a context sealed by a building constructed in 1550, and the Aarhus examples match this date perfectly.[115]

Post-Medieval redware, early type, is no longer present, only developed Post-Medieval redware; tripod pipkins constitute the dominant form (rim types 1017, 1035 and 1001 with handle 1043). These forms, especially rim type 1001, have previously been dated to the early part of the 16th century, and rim type 1004 to the mid- to late 16th century, but no precise date has so far been available, so the dated material from Aarhus is a welcome addition.[116]

C. 1571 (phase 11)	Sum of sherd counts	Sum of RP	Sum of weight (g)
Low Countries tin-glazed ware	2		7
Black pot, other type	730	1454	2245
Danish slipware	5	7	49
Post-Medieval redware	363	650	6446
Dutch/German Post-Medieval whiteware	7	20	84
Raeren-type stoneware	5		76
Siegburg stoneware	3		38
Total	**1115**	**2131**	**8945**

Table 7. Ceramics from FHM 4201 Skt. Clemensborg, c. 1571 (river wall phase 11).

Around 1575 (phase 11: c. 1571) (table 7).

The main characteristic of this phase is the introduction of a new type: slipware. The slipware fragments from this phase clearly come from a plate with concentric circles around the rim, so this type was introduced in Aarhus prior to 1571. It has previously been seen at a number of sites dated to the late 16th century, which concurs with dates from Lübeck, where the type was deposited prior to 1564.[117]

Imports are still dominated by utilitarian Siegburg stoneware and Raeren-type stoneware. The sherds of Low Countries tin-glazed ware are much fragmented, but appear to be from blue-painted plates that probably originated in the northern Netherlands. This is the earliest occurrence so far of this ware type in the area around Aarhus – the previously known sites are some decades later in date.[118] Low Countries/German Post-Medieval whiteware is used for tripod pipkins with either external and internal green glaze or green glaze on the outside and yellow glaze on the inside. The dominant types are still the black pot cauldron (rim type 302) and the tripod pipkin in Post-Medieval redware (rim types 1001, 1004, 1008, 1020, 1035). All these types have previously been recorded in similarly dated assemblages, most of them of type 1008, which is known from a tripod pipkin found in the foundations of a manor house constructed

in 1579.[119] A new vessel form is the pan (rim type 1028). The handles are angular (1043).

Between 1571 and 1651/52 (phase 12)	Sum of sherd counts	Sum of RP	Sum of weight (g)
Black pot, other type	9	17	248
Black pot of Vorup type	3		30
Danish slipware	5		40
Post-Medieval redware	65	41	1186
Dutch/German Post-Medieval whiteware	23	46	165
Total	**105**	**104**	**1669**

Table 8. Ceramics at FHM 4201 Skt. Clemensborg, after 1571 from before 1651/52 (river wall phase 12).

Between 1571 and 1651/52 (phase 12) (table 8).

This phase is not as precisely dated as the others and it contains significantly fewer sherds than the previous phase. Between 1571 and 1651/52, the cooking pots in the lead-glazed material become taller with more elaborate rims (rim types 1002, 1003 and 1006) and the handles have a rounded form (1046). The black pots are all developed cauldrons (rim type 302). The only imports are plates and cooking pots in whiteware (rim type 1425).

Winter 1651/52 (phase 13)	Sum of sherd counts	Sum of RP	Sum of weight (g)
Black pot, other type	6	20	144
Danish slipware	6	18	2
Post-Medieval redware	60	135	1105
Dutch/German Post-Medieval whiteware	2		12
Westerwald stoneware	1		1
Total	**75**	**173**	**1264**

Table 9. Ceramics from FHM 4201 Skt. Clemensborg, constructed in the winter 1651-52 (river wall phase 13).

Winter 1651/52 (river phase 13) (table 9).

The material deposited in the winter of 1651/52 is rather modest in extent. The Post-Medieval redware tripod pipkins become more elaborate and elongated, with decorated rims (rim types 1002, 1003, 1006, 1013 and 1019). The black pots are still variants of the cauldron (rim type 302) and the imports are still whiteware cooking pots, but a Westerwald stoneware mug or jug is evident in this phase, too. The local slipware

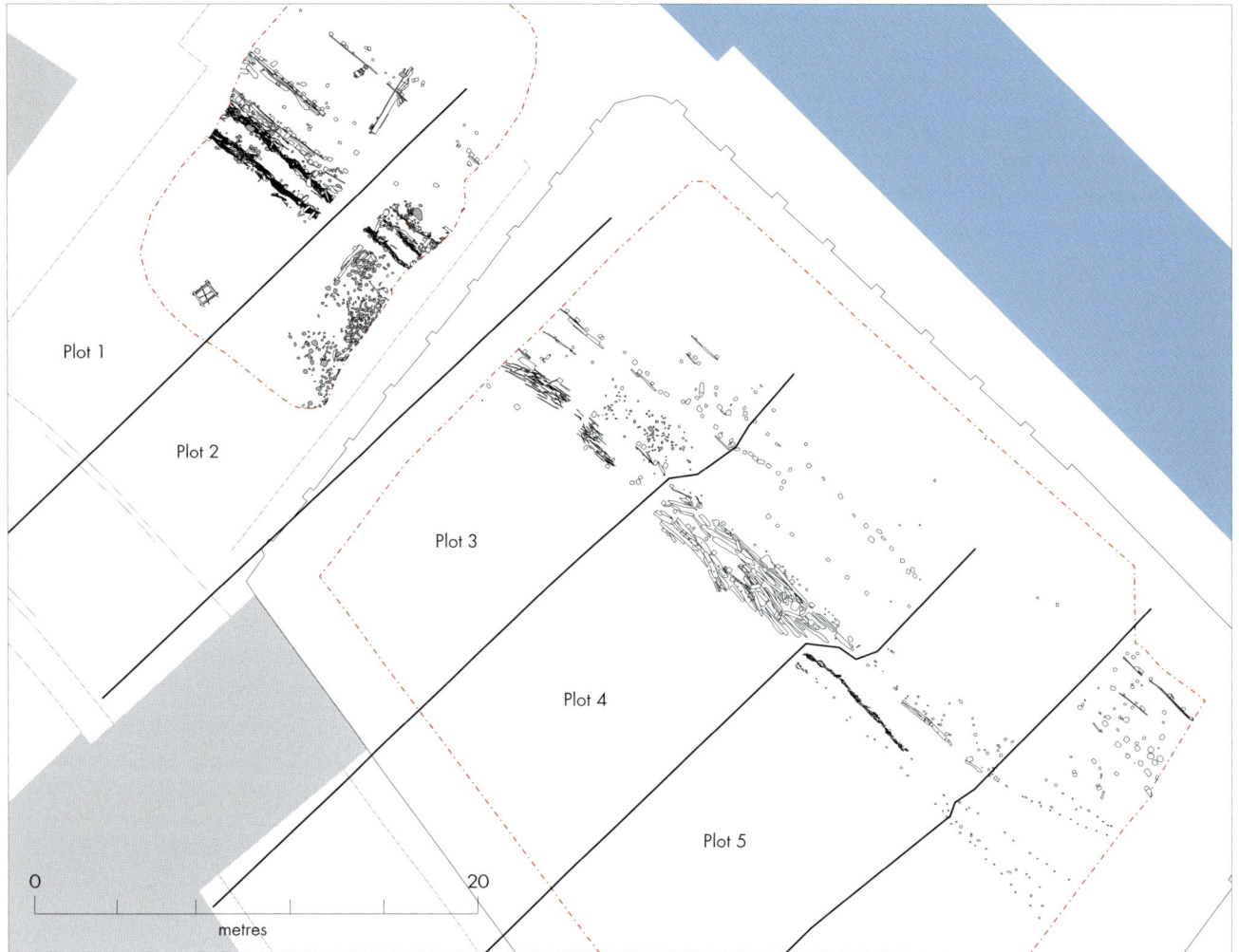

Figure 16. *The river walls at FHM 4201 Skt. Clemensborg. Western part of the excavated area. Drawing: Lars Krants/Moesgaard Museum.*

Around 1775 (Phase 14+15)	Sum of sherd counts	Sum of RP	Sum of weight (g)
Black pot, other type	129	316	4912
Low Countries redware	1		24
Black pot, Varde type	124	190	2875
Black pot, Vorup type	17	23	410
Cologne stoneware	2		10
Danish slipware	27	76	334
Post-Medieval Redware	632	1391	11526
Dutch/German Post-Medieval whiteware	56	121	982
Low Countries tin-glazed ware	1		6
Raeren-type stoneware	6	40	81
Total	**995**	**1628**	**21160**

Table 10. *Ceramics from FHM 4201 Skt. Clemensborg, c. 1775 (river wall phases 14-15).*

comprises the usual plates with concentric circles around the perimeter.

Around 1775 (phases 14 and 15: winters 1772/73 and 1779/80) (table 10).

The material from FHM 4201 Skt. Clemensborg shows a gap between 1651/52 and 1772/73: If river walls were built during this time-slot, traces of them were not preserved. If we compare the material deposited at the middle of the 17th century with that from phases 14 and 15, it is obvious that the consumption has changed significantly over the c. 120 years: The form

Figure 17. Plan of river walls with dendro dates. Drawing: Lars Krants/Moesgaard Museum.

A1=1600?

A3=1550?

A4=1500
A5=1452

A6=ca. 1450

A7=1448 +-5
A8=1440?

A9=omkring 1600

0   5
metres

Figure 18. Detail of river walls from the 15th century. Photo: Lars Krants/Moesgaard Museum.

Figure 19. River walls from the 15th and 16th centuries during excavation. Photo: Lars Krants/Moesgaard Museum.

Figure 20. *Detail of part of ship reused in the river walls. Photo: Lars Krants/ Moesgaard Museum.*

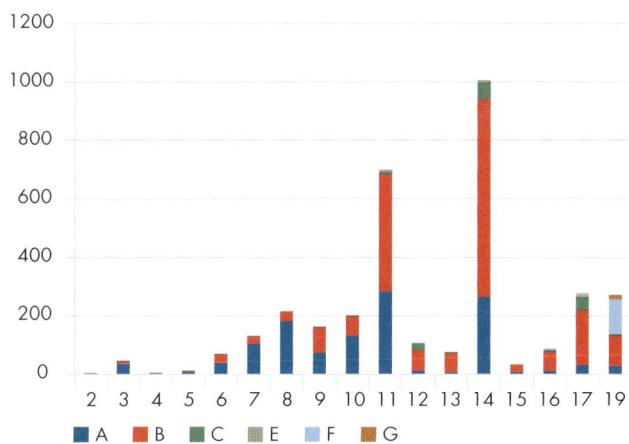

Figure 21. *Ware types in river wall phases in FHM 4201 Skt. Clemensborg, based on sherd count (No = 4001). Based on data shown in table 3-12. A = Greywares. B: Redwares. C: Whitewares. E: Stonewares. F: Majolicas. G: Porcelain.*

Figure 22. *Stoneware jug made at Waldenburg in Germany. National Museum acc. no. D1543_1975 ©Lennart Larsen Danish National Museum.*

Around 1800 (phase 16)	Sum of sherd counts	Sum of RP	Sum of weight (g)
Black pot, other type	3		165
Black pot, Varde type	7	23	294
Black pot, Vorup type	1	5	37
Tin-glazed ware	5	0	47
Danish Slipware	15	31	231
Dutch/German Post-Medieval whiteware	5	17	112
Raeren-type stoneware	2	0	26
Post-Medieval redware	42	36	500
Total	**80**	**112**	**1412**

Table 11. Ceramics from FHM 4201 Skt. Clemensborg, after 1794 (river wall phase 16).

and function types differ and new imports have been introduced. Several well-known types of black pots are now evident and must have been introduced in the preceding years. There are now both the exported Varde type and the local Vorup type, both of which are present in significant numbers. The Varde pots are the conventional, large burnished cooking cauldrons and jugs (rim types 302, 307, jug 309), while the Vorup forms are the just as conventional cauldrons and bowls (rim types 504, 505). Both the Varde and the Vorup productions are very well known from previous excavations, and the Varde type of black pot has been studied from both historical and ethnological perspectives.[120]

The imports are decorated utilitarian jugs of Raeren-type stoneware. The local slipware is now used for both tripod pipkins and plates. The slipware pipkin is a well-known type, but its first occurrence in Denmark is not well researched. So far, no finds have been located that are earlier than the mid-17th century, and the Aarhus examples clearly prove that these vessels were widespread in the late 18th century. The plates are richly decorated, with flowers, dots and so on. The local slipware cooking pots constitute a new type (rim type 1108). Their decoration consists either of waves on the rim or stripes on the body. The Post-Medieval redware tripod pipkins show a variety of rim types, but their basic shape remains the same: elongated bodies and rather narrow rims (rim types 1007, 1009, 1010, 1013, 1014, 1019 and 1020). The handles are trum-

pet-shaped. Pans are rather common. The whitewares are represented by cooking pots, plates and saucers. The vessels are lead-glazed in yellow or copper green. The stoneware is of Cologne or Raeren types, all of it utilitarian. A Low Countries tin-glazed ware plate is the only lead-glazed type at this time.

Around 1800 (phase 16: after 1779-94) (table 11).

The rather small body of material from around 1800 shows the introduction of a new type – industrial whiteware.

The wares here are decorated with transfer printing and take the form of plates and cups. They most likely originated in the United Kingdom, though there are no sherds with a manufacturer's mark among the finds. The stoneware comprises utilitarian Raeren-type storage vessels. The black pots are of Varde and Vorup types and the vessel forms are the same as in the previous phase. Local slipware plates and pots are still in use and now decorated with a ring of dots below the rim. The plates are decorated with zigzag lines and have elaborate rims. Whiteware plates are common – green-glazed. The Post-Medieval redware tripod pipkins all have ribbed rims.

After 1779-94 and before summer 1838 (phase 17)	Sum of sherd counts	Sum of RP	Sum of weight (g)
Black pot, other type	17	13	599
Tin-glazed ware	4	12	12
Black pot, Varde type	6	15	112
Black pot, Vorup type	8	34	196
Danish slipware	22	25	339
Post-Medieval redware	158	227	2592
Dutch/German Post-Medieval whiteware	42	37	330
Porcelain	2	7	60
Raeren-type stoneware	3	5	65
Westerwald stoneware	5		24
Total	**267**	**375**	**4329**

Table 12. Ceramics from FHM 4201 Skt. Clemensborg, c. 1800 (river wall phase 17).

Around 1825 (phase 17: after 1794 until before summer 1838) (table 12).

Figure 23. Post-Medieval redware, early type (rim type 1016), deposited c.1450 (FHM 4201 xZN). Diameter 18 cm. Photo: Moesgaard Photo/ Medialab.

Figure 24. Black pot, early type (rim type 308), dated to c. 1475. Photo: Moesgaard Photo/Medialab.

Figure 25. Ceramics deposited c. 1475-1500. Clockwise from left, rims of Post-Medieval redware, early type (rim types 1016 and 1005), a bowl (rim type 308) and a coarseware jug (FHM 4201 xAHE; xAHK; xCS) Photo: Moesgaard Photo/Medialab.

55

Figure 26. *Ceramics deposited 1547/48. Clockwise from left, handles and rims of Post-Medieval redware (rim types 1005a and 1017) and Black pot cauldrons (FHM 4201 xAVQ) Photo: Moesgaard Photo/Medialab.*

Figure 27. *Low Countries tin-glazed ware, Low Countries/German Post-Medieval whiteware and Raeren-type stoneware deposited c. 1571. (FHM 4201 xCN). Photo: Moesgaard Photo/ Medialab.*

Figure 28. Ceramics deposited 1651/52. Clockwise from left Post-medieval redware with slip decoration, Westerwald stoneware and two tall Post-Medieval redware tripod cooking pots with elaborate rims (rim type 1002) (FHM 4102 xABE). Photo: Moesgaard Photo/Medialab.

Figure 29. Ceramics deposited after 1794. From left Raeren-type stoneware, Post-Medieval redware with slip decoration and Danish slipware plates. (FHM 4201 xAMY). Photo: Moesgaard Photo/Medialab.

The final phase, around 1825, contains a variety of types. The Varde black pots are now densely burnished, and on one the burnish forms circular patterns – the first occurrence of this kind of decoration. The Vorup pots are all of standardised shape (rim type 501) with incised wavy patterns. A new type comprises European porcelain: a cup with a dark-brown exterior and flowers on the inside – also the earliest occurrence of this type. Faience is represented by a blue-fluted porcelain plate. The stoneware is utilitarian Raeren type and Westerwald. Whiteware is used for plates and bowls – yellow-glazed with simple rims and some with floral decoration. The cooking pots in Post-Medieval redware have simple upright rims (rim type 1014). The glaze is now very dense and shiny and the plates have roulette or incised decoration. All these shapes and types have parallels in the region – a well-dated example is provided by material from a cellar in the Vilhelmsborg manor, south of Aarhus, dated to the final decades of the 18th century.[121]

Figure 30. Transfer printed industrial ceramics deposited after 1794 (FHM 4201 xAMY). Photo: Moesgaard Photo/Medielab.

Figure 31. Slip decorated redware pots and a Black pot of Varde-type with burnished pattern, deposited c. 1825 (FHM 4201 xADK). Photo: Moesgaard Photo/Medialab

2.6.2 FHM 4225 Guldsmedgade (land registry title no. 633)

Excavated 2000-01. Total area 345 m².
Sources: Excavation report; Franciere 2002; Høyem Andresen; Linaa & Skov 2003.

FHM 4225 Guldsmedgade was excavated in the winter of 2000-01. The site is situated in the northwestern part of town, immediately outside the location of the Viking Age/Medieval town rampart, but well within the boundaries of the Medieval town. The street of Guldsmedgade has been dated to the 14th century and may be even earlier, being possibly laid out when Lilletorv was constructed between 1253 and 1258.[122] Four urban plots were excavated on the area, extending east-west from the street Guldsmedgade and eastwards to the edge of the rampart. The western half of the two southern plots, the parts nearest to the street, had been destroyed by later building activities, but the rear parts were intact, as were the two northern plots, in their entirety. Although these latter plots were fully preserved, only some of the rear parts could be fully excavated because the surrounding standing buildings were unstable. FHM 4225 Guldsmedgade was a complicated site where the excavation uncovered built remains dating from c. 1100 to c. 1700. Among the structures exposed were the remains of at least eight town houses facing the street. The backyard area contained traces of at least two stables and a large number of latrines with their contents intact. The excavated structures were divided into ten stratigraphic phases as part of the recording process (Table 13).

The excavation
In the earliest occupational phase, phase 2, the only structure preserved comprised postholes from a building aligned NE-SW, with a lightly-constructed fence to the west. No cultural layers or pits were evident and the house had been disturbed prior to later building activities on the site. There then appears to be a gap in the material – the area apparently having lain derelict for a while, until the beginning of phase 3, when another

Sum of sherd counts

Ware type	Phase 1	Phase 2	Phase 3	Phase 4	Phase 5	Phase 6	Phase 7	Phase 8	Phase 9	Phase 10	No-Phase	Total
Baltic blackware		97		8		2					1	108
Baltic burnished greyware					1	2			2			5
Black pot, early type				24	28	205	330	185	656	72	60	1560
Black pot, Varde type						19	65		138	82	136	440
Brügge-type ware					1							1
Danish slipware										3	4	7
Frechen stoneware									7			7
Industrial ware									1	20	10	31
Langerwehe stoneware					3	1			1			5
Low Countries redware									1	1		2
Medieval low-fired coarseware	50	228	84	2	28		5					397
Medieval well-fired coarseware		42	41	62	382	353	33	29	28	8	33	1011
Medieval well-fired redware		10	13	35	110	124	19	8	8	3	21	351
Other blackware						5	5	1	3	44	7	65
Other whiteware							2	1	6	1	2	12
Porcelain										1	1	2
Post-Medieval redware			1	24	2	107	50	37	224	75	116	636
Post-Medieval redware with slip decoration									9	12	12	33
Proto stoneware				2	3							5
Raeren stoneware						3	1	1	1	8	5	19
Rouen-type ware					1						1	2
Siegburg stoneware				2	15	3	2		4	5	1	32
Tin-glazed ware											3	3
Weser ware											1	1
Westerwald stoneware									1		2	3
Total	50	377	139	157	573	827	512	262	1090	335	416	4738

Table 13. FHM 4225 Guldsmedgade. Ware types and number of sherds in stratigraphic phases.

house was built in the northern part of the area (house 13). The subsequent phase, phase 4, saw the digging of pits and latrines on the plots. The latrines were lined with wooden planks and were primarily sited on what is interpreted as the back of the plots, closest to the town rampart.

Phase 5 sees the construction of yet another house (house 6), measuring c. 5 x 13 m, and this time oriented towards the street, with associated wells, latrines and pits. The house had a large bread oven that was replaced and repaired several times over a short period. The repairs were prompted by stability problems, as the oven was constructed over a recently-filled pit containing organic material. This led to frequent renewal of the subsiding oven and, subsequently, of the floor in the house. A coin minted in 1310-20 was found on the latest floor in the house.

In phase 6, the house was demolished and a replacement built on exactly the same site (house 5), as well as two stables/workshops, houses 2 and 4, on the back of the plot (figure 33-35). The paved courtyard was preserved, as were at least three floor layers, one of them a layer of mortar, showing traces left by benches along the south and north walls of the living room. A room was separated off towards the gable facing the street, possibly a small shop. A number

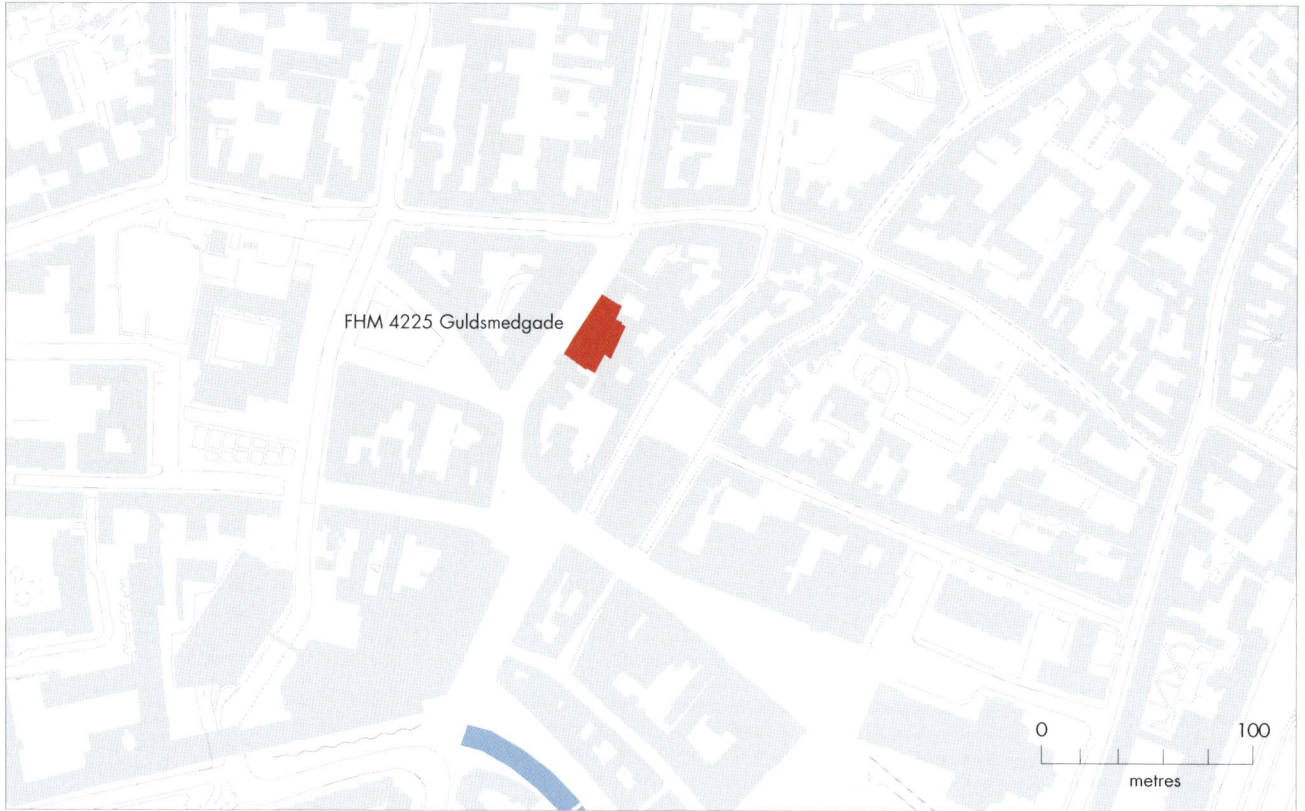

Figure 32. Location of the site FHM 4225 Guldsmedgade.

Figure 33. HM 4225 Guldsmedgade. Section through floors in house 6 (bottom) and house 5 (top floors). Photo: Moesgaard Museum.

of latrines and pits were also dug to the rear of the plot near the stables. Several were cut through thick layers of manure spread out from the stables into the moat. Phase 7 sees the demolition of house 5 and the construction of houses 15 and 10. These are less well-preserved houses with partly paved floors and some rubbish pits at the rear.

Phase 8 sees the construction of two new buildings, houses 9 and 3, replacing houses 10 and 15. House 3 was poorly preserved, but the adjoining house 9 survived much better. This was a smithy, and a coin minted in 1444-40 was found on the floor, which was covered in thick layers of charcoal and slag. The house showed evidence of at least two chambers: the smithy facing the street and possibly a kitchen to the rear; here were traces of the fireplace – a paved structure facing the wall (figure 36).

Phase 9 is very extensive and dominated by material related to the continued use of the smithy in house 9,

Figure 34. The excavation at FHM 4225 Guldsmedgade. House 5 seen from the west. 14th century. Photo: Moesgaard Museum.

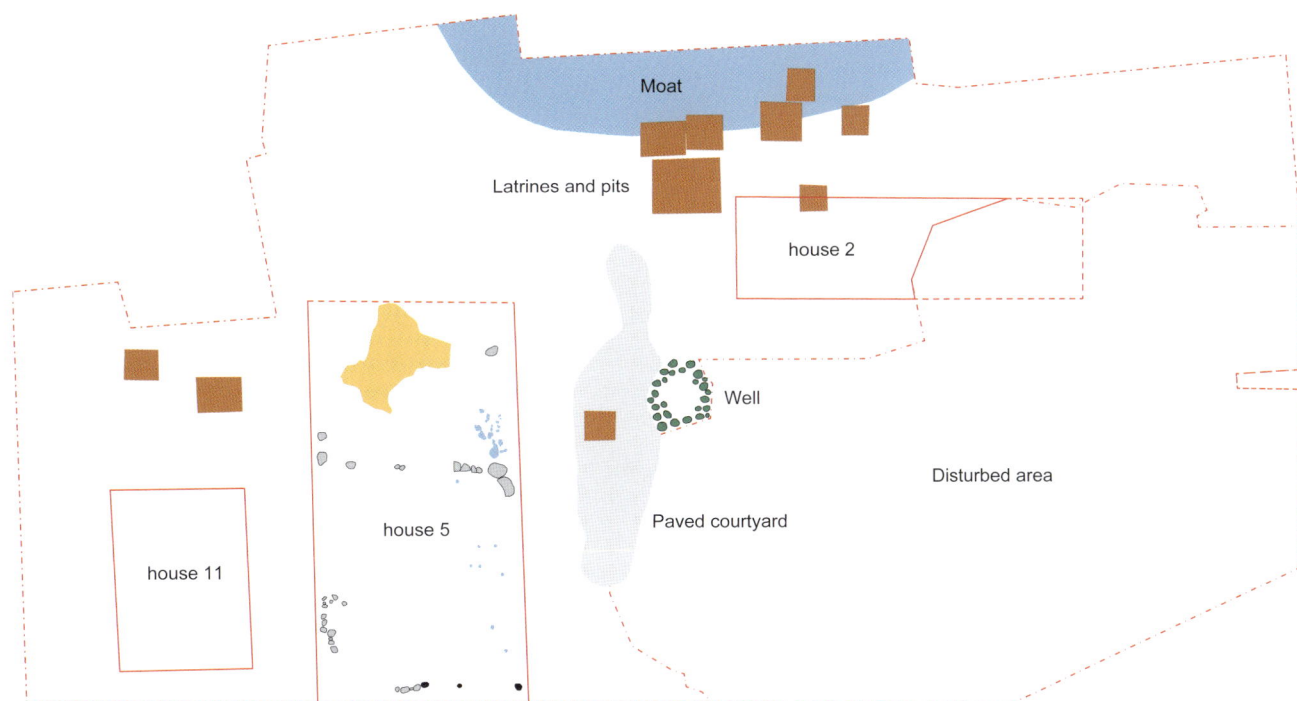

Figure 35. Plan of FHM 4225 Guldsmedgade phase 6.

Figure 36. 15th century smithy (house 9) during excavation. Photo: Moesgaard Museum.

as well as the construction of a new house, house 1, on the plot to the south. This latter house was less well preserved due to later disturbances; only traces of a wall and some clay floors were found. At the end of this phase the smithy appears to have burnt down and the house was demolished.

Phase 10 consists of fills of mixed composition as well as the poorly preserved remains of one building (house 12).

Figure 37. Early medieval greyware pot from the earliest phase at Guldsmedgade, 11th- or 12th century (FHM 4225 xMY). Rim diameter 16 cm. Photo: Moesgaard Museum.

Any later remains had been disturbed by Early Modern or Modern building activity on the site. The detailed internal stratigraphy provides us with the foundation for obtaining a varied and detailed insight into the shifting consumption on the site.

An overview of the ceramics is given in figure 39 and 40. It is obvious that this material is much more fragmented than that from FHM 4201 Skt. Clemensborg, with an average sherd weight of 15 g as opposed to 20.5 g. This is most likely the result of the Guldsmedgade sherds from primary and secondary contexts being more prone to breakage than those from the deposits at Skt. Clemensborg. The majority of the material came from pits, structures and surfaces, while a smaller amount was recovered from cultural layers. The fine relative stratigraphy of the FHM 4225 Guldsmedgade site allows detailed discussion of the occurrence of fabric and form types.

In the earliest phase, phase 2, only sherds of greyware cooking pots and Baltic Blackware rims were found. There then seems to be a gap in the material – the area appears to have lain derelict for a while – until the beginning of phase 3, when house 13 was built.

Figure 38. Baltic blackware pot found in posthole in building in phase 2. From FHM 4225 Guldsmedgade (FHM 4225 xVQ). Photo: Moesgaard Museum.

A mixture of Medieval well-fired redware jugs and Medieval low- and well-fired coarseware were found in this building. The rims are simple and out-turned (rim type 601) and the jug is red-glazed and shows manganese streaks. The following phase, phase 4, contains conventional Medieval well-fired coarseware cooking

pots of a conventional, hard-fired type that is known from numerous sites in Aarhus. The rims are all simple and out-turned. The Medieval well-fired redware jugs are red or green, decorated with scales – either in white firing clay or painted black. The only imported type is a Siegburg stoneware jug. These jugs are normally used as a dating tool – a function they do not have in this analysis. A large amount of material relating to phase 5 was recovered from house 6. The sherds were found on the floors and the vessels were probably destroyed during demolition of the house. Included among the material are the earliest black pots, early type: pots or bowls (rim type 608) with light burnishing on the rim and shoulder. The imports are of varied types: Rhenish Siegburg jugs, jugs of Rouen-type ware and Low Countries highly-decorated redware, as well as a jug of Baltic well-fired, burnished ware. The Medieval well-fired redware jugs are still red or green with applied decoration (pellets in white clay, flowers etc.), and some with rows of stabs around the neck. The Medieval well-fired coarseware comprises cooking pots (rim types 605 and 606), sometimes decorated with sloppy furrows, and large bowls (611). Phase 6 sees the construction of house 5, on the floors of which Rheinish stoneware, mainly Siegburg type, and Baltic burnished greywares

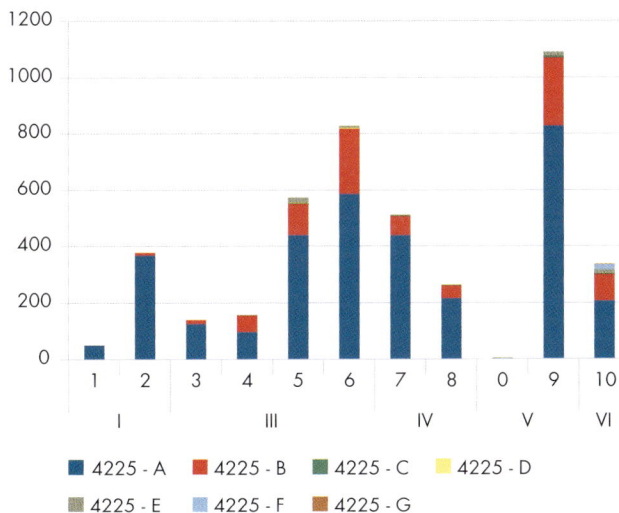

Figure 39. Ware types in stratigraphic phases in FHM 4225 Guldsmedgade, based on sherd count (No=4738). Based on data shown in table 13. A = Greywares. B: Redwares. C: Whitewares. D: Proto stonewares. E: Stonewares. F: Majolicas. G: Porcelain.

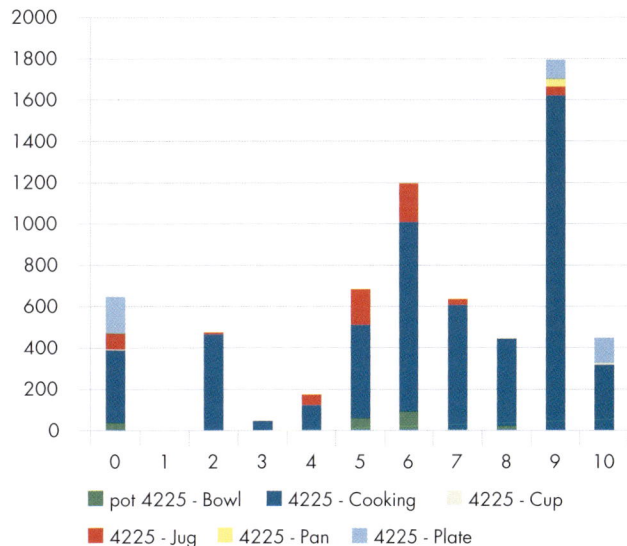

Figure 40. Functional types/Stratigraphic phases in FHM 4225 Guldsmedgade based om rim percentages (No=6539).

Figure 41. Ceramics from house 5 at FHM 4225 Guldsmedgade. Left: Medieval well-fired redware jugs. Right, from top to bottom: Rouen-type ware, Medieval well-fired redware handle and Siegburg stoneware jug (FHM 4225 xAFV; xAFK). Photo: Moesgaard Photo/Medialab.

were found. The cooking pots are of Medieval well-fired coarseware with simple (rim type 601) or more elaborate rims (rim type 605), as well as large bowls (rim type 611). The Medieval well-fired redware jugs are still lead-glazed, red or green, somewhat careless in execution, and decorated with applied strips, painted black. The earliest black pots are common in this phase, still shaped like shallow bowls (608); one of them has a row of stamped decoration below the rim. In this phase we see the earliest Post-Medieval redware, early type. A rather large accumulation of ceramics was found on the latest floor in the building: Medieval well-fired redware jugs, Medieval well-fired coarseware cooking pots with simple rims (rim types 601, 608), early black pots and fragments of a pot, possibly a tripod pipkin in Post-Medieval redware, early type. The latter pot is characteristically glazed and has a simple rim (rim type 1017). There is no doubt that these types were used in the house during the relatively short time span

when this particular floor was walked upon. In phase 7, the stratigraphically earliest contexts contain the same types as seen in phase 6. These are mainly early black pots and cooking pots in Post-Medieval redware, early type, with a few sherds of Medieval well-fired coarseware and Medieval well-fired redware jugs – red or green. However, in the stratigraphically later part of the phase, Medieval well-fired coarseware and the Medieval well-fired redware jugs are absent. Now the material is dominated by black pots, early type, and Post-Medieval redware, early type (rim types 1017, 1005). The imports are Siegburg stoneware jugs and a new type attributed to Low Countries/German Post-Medieval whiteware: very thin-walled vessels with yellow glaze. A similar type has been found in Horsens, where it is dated to the 15th century.[123] From the floor in the smithy in phase 8 there are fragments of lead-glazed jugs, as well as jugs of Raeren-type stoneware, whiteware vessels of the same type as in the previous

Figure 42. Late 14th and early 15th century ceramics from FHM 4225 Guldsmedgade. Two Post-Medieval well-fired redware early type pots (rim 1005) and three Black pot early type bowls (rim 308) from phase 7 (FHM 4225 xZZ; xJT; xAJB). Photo: Moesgaard Photo/Medielab.

phase and tripod pipkins of Post-Medieval redware, early type (rim types 1005, 1017). The dominant type comprises early black-pot bowls of well-known type (rim type 608); one with perfectly stamped decoration below the rim and a high foot. Burnishing is now common on this type. The ceramics assemblage from phase 9 is very large and dominated by bowls of blackware (rim type 608) as well as cauldrons of black pot, Vorup type (rim types 501, 504). Post-Medieval well-fired redware, developed type, tripod pipkins are frequent (rim types 1001, 1004). Pans are a newly introduced type. The imports are utility jugs of Siegburg and Raeren-type stoneware and pots and plates in Low Countries/German whiteware. A fragment of a plate with traces of incised decoration is possibly of Low Countries redware – this piece is awaiting inductively coupled plasma (ICP) analysis. Curiously, the pans were found in the same house as this plate. Phase 10 consists of fills of mixed composition and the sparse ceramics are dominated by black pots of Vorup type, Post-Medieval redware (rim type 1013) and Raeren-type stoneware utilitarian wares as well as local slipware plates. If we take a preliminary look at the composition of the ceramic assemblage in relation to functional types, the results can be seen below.

The dominance of cooking pots is hardly surprising, given the predominance of the coarsewares in the material. But jugs and bowls are prominent in the earlier phases, only to disappear later. The general traits will be discussed in the inter-site analysis presented later in this volume.

Figure 43. *Location of the site FHM 4278 Rosensgade.*

2.6.3 FHM 4278 Rosensgade (land registry title no. 733a)

Excavated 2001. Total area 100 m².
Sources: Excavation Report.

FHM 4278 Rosensgade was excavated in winter 2001. The site is situated in the northwestern part of the inner town centre, well within the Viking Age and Medieval rampart enclosing the inner town and immediately south of the Medieval street of Rosensgade. This is one of the oldest streets in town and it appears to have been laid out in the 12th century.[124] The excavation was situated in a backyard, so only the rear part of at least one urban plot facing Rosensgade was investigated. The excavators identified four activity phases: The earliest

structures on the site comprised traces of four sunken-featured buildings (phase 1) (houses I-IV, with III being stratigraphically the earliest) with an associated well and several pits and postholes.

A gap in activity is then evident, probably or perhaps the result of a break in settlement and/or removal of deposits, and a pit is the only trace from this phase. In the following phase (phase 3), a house (house III) is constructed and a well is dug beside it. The house was only partially excavated – only the eastern wall with adjoining clay floors was uncovered – but the excavators concludes that this building had its gable facing the street, as most of it lay outside the boundaries of the site. A coin – a copper sterling minted under Erik of Pomerania (1420-40) – was found on the floor in the house. After

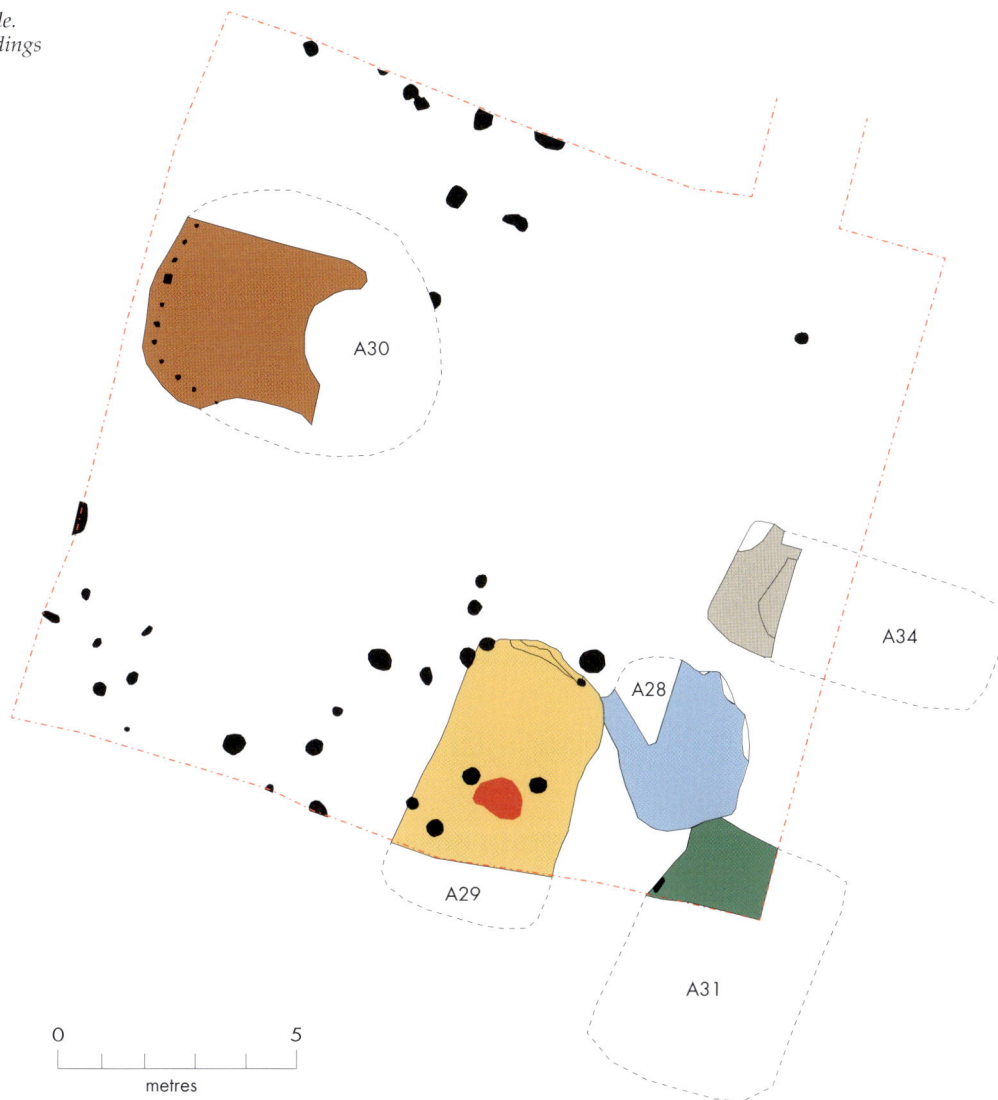

Figure 44. FHM 4278 Rosensgade. Viking Age sunken-featured buildings in phase 1. Plan: Lars Krants/ Moesgaard Museum.

A30

A34

A28

A29

A31

0   5

metres

a further clearance of the site, another house was built (house 1a) (phase 4). This was a half-timbered building, constructed over a stone-built cellar. The back-filling of this cellar is the latest activity identified at the site.

According to 17th century taxation records, Rosensgade was one of the poorer areas of town and this aspect will be discussed later.[125]

An overview of the material is given below.

The material from phase I comprises ordinary local Viking Age ceramics with no imports being detected. The vessel forms are cooking pots (rim types 1a, 1c, 1e), and it is clear that the ceramics within this small assemblage are not very varied. The material relating to phase II contains Rhenish proto-stoneware jugs

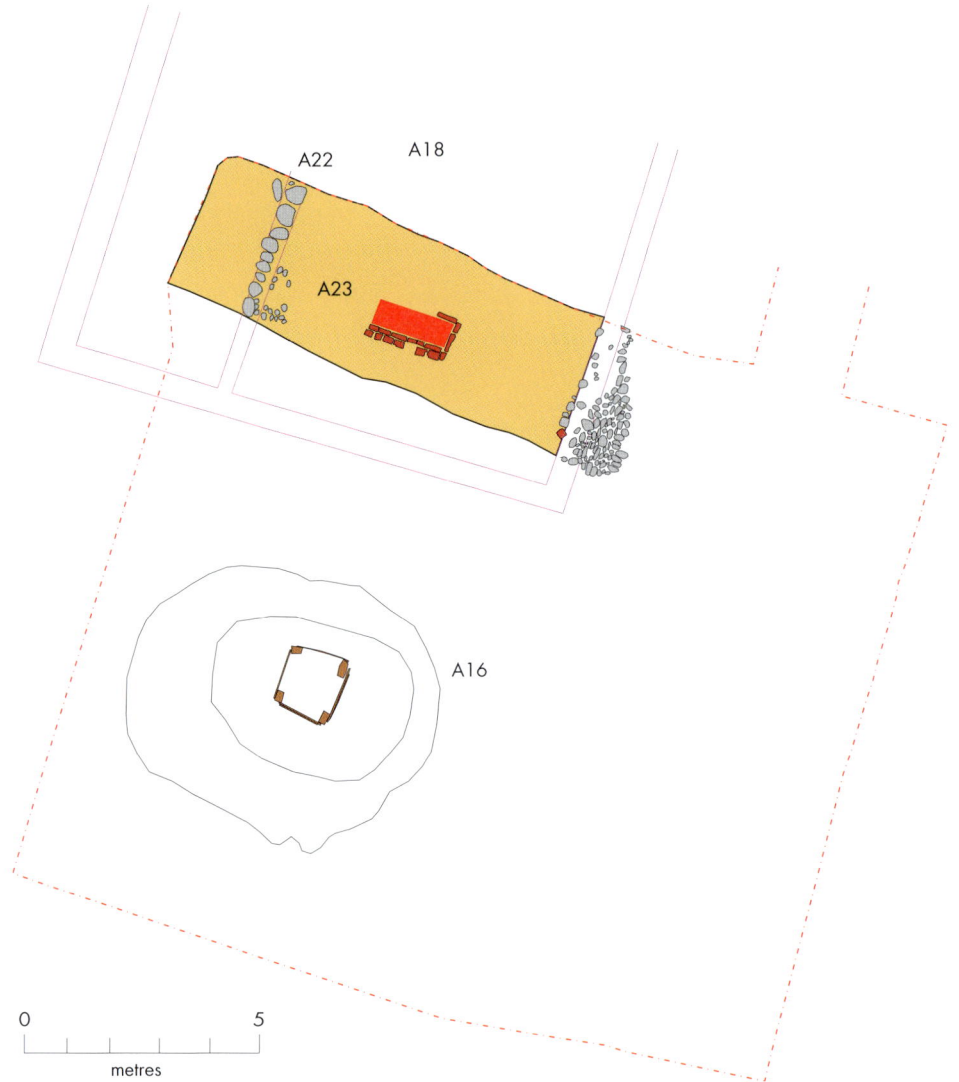

Figure 45. Well and house remains in phase 3, dated to the 15ᵗʰ century. Plan: Lars Krants/Moesgaard Museum.

and fragments of Medieval well-fired coarseware cooking pots. There is a larger amount of material from phase III: Several sherds of the same Waldenburg stoneware jug were found trodden into the floor of house III (A18), as was sherds of bowls/cooking pots in Medieval well-fired coarseware (rim type 608).

The material is quite sparse as only the eastern part of the house was excavated. All the material in phase V was found in the cellar and was deposited as the cellar was filled in. Represented in the sherd assemblage are cauldrons, in the form of black pots of Vorup type (rim type 501), Post-Medieval redware tripod pipkins (rim types 1004, 1009) and Post-Medieval redware plates (rim type 1024). The only decorated tableware comprises sherds of local slipware plates. The imports in this phase are a Raeren utilitarian stoneware vessel and small fragments of Low Countries tin-glazed ware plate.

Figure 46. Remains of house III in phase 3, dated to the 15ᵗʰ century. Photo: Moesgaard Museum.

Figure 47. House Ia (phase 4) with cellar during excavation, 16ᵗʰ century. FHM 4278 Rosensgade. Photo: Moesgaard Museum.

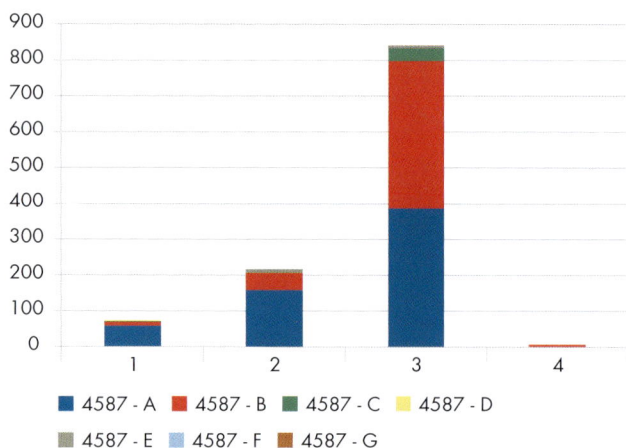

Figure 48. Ceramics from FHM 4278 Rosensgade, based on number of sherds in stratigraphic phases (No= 743). Based on data shown in table 14. Note the rather large amount of redware in the later phase.
A = Greywares. B: Redwares. C: Whitewares. D: Proto stonewares.
E: Stonewares. F: Majolicas. G: Porcelain.

FHM 4278 Rosensgade						
Sum of sherd counts						
Ware types	**Phase 1**	**Phase 2**	**Phase 3**	**Phase 5**	**No phase**	**Total**
Baltic burnished greyware					2	2
Black pot, Varde type				9	50	59
Danish slipware					2	2
Frechen stoneware				1		1
Industrial ware				7	1	8
Low Countries tin-glazed ware				1		1
Medieval low-fired coarseware					2	2
Medieval well-fired coarseware	1	8	48	1	262	320
Medieval well-fired redware					53	53
Near-stoneware		1				1
Near-stoneware		1			3	4
Other whiteware					1	1
Post-Medieval well-fired redware				22	72	94
Post-Medieval well-fired redware with slip decoration				1	1	2
Raeren stoneware					1	1
Siegburg stoneware					4	4
Tin-glazed wares					5	5
Viking Age low-fired coarseware	88				89	177
Waldenburg stoneware			4		1	5
Westerwald stoneware					1	1
Total	**89**	**10**	**52**	**42**	**550**	**743**

Table 14. FHM 4278 Rosensgade. Ware types and number of sherds in stratigraphic phases.

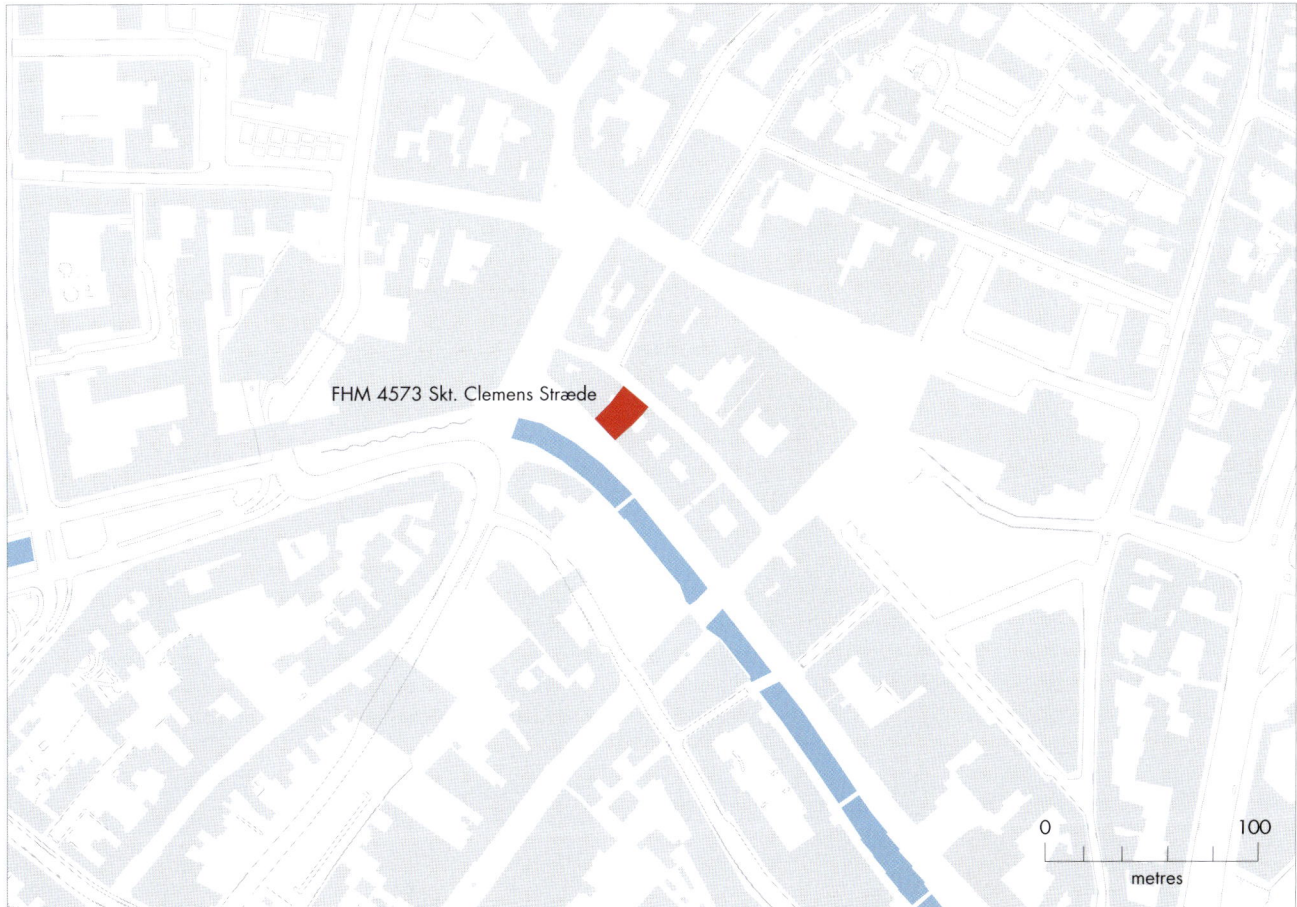

Figure 49. *Location of the site FHM 4573 Skt. Clemens Stræde.*

2.6.4 FHM 4573 Skt. Clemens Stræde (land registry title no. 766) (with Lars Krants)

Excavated 2005. Total area 100 m².
Sources: Excavation Report.

The excavation of FHM 4573 Skt. Clemens Stræde is currently undergoing publication and it will therefore only be summarised briefly here. The excavation took place about 100 m west of the large, well-known site of Aarhus Søndervold, published in 1971,[126] which uncovered remains of an extensive Viking Age settlement. Settlement appears, accordingly, to have been very intensive at this time in the Store Torv area, south of the present St. Clement's Cathedral and close to the river.[127] The excavated area is located on the site of the Viking Age rampart which encircled the town, and the excavation cut through this, exposing remains of a Viking Age settlement below the rampart. This settlement was clearly demolished prior to the construction of the earliest rampart. The precise date of the latter is not yet known – analyses are underway – but it seems very likely that it lies in the early 10th century.

The earliest feature on the site was a shallow ditch that became filled in with domestic waste from a settlement that lay outside the boundaries of the excavation. After the ditch was filled in, a succession of sunken-featured buildings were built on the site, one after the other, before they were replaced by a post-built house. This house was then demolished immediately prior to construction of the rampart. The excavated structures were

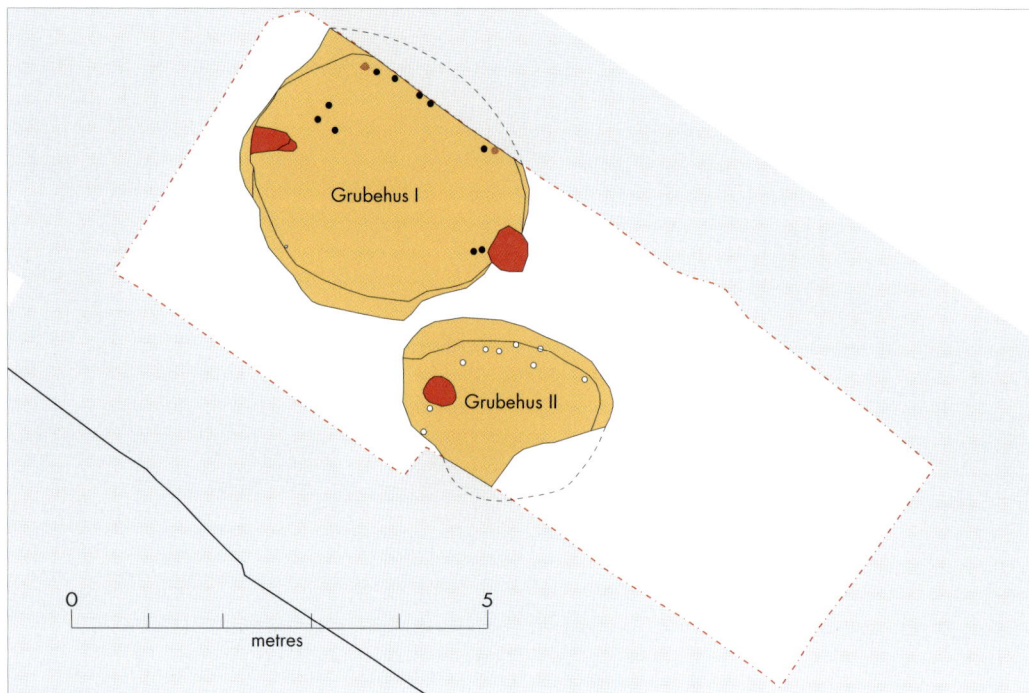

Figure 50. Sunken-featured buildings in FHM 4573 Skt. Clemens Stræde, both excavated below the Viking Age fortification around the town. North is up. Plan: Lars Krants/Moesgaard Museum.

Figure 51. Post-built houses at FHM 4573 Skt. Clemens Stræde below the Viking Age fortification around town. North is up. Plan: Lars Krants/Moesgaard Museum.

Figure 52. Sunken-featured building I during excavation. FHM 4573 Skt. Clemens Stræde. Photo: Moesgaard Museum.

Figure 53. Pot in Baltic ware, so-called Feldberger type, found in FHM 4573 Skt. Clemens Stræde (FHM 4573 x861). Diameter 20 cm. Photo: Moesgaard Museum.

FHM 4573 Skt. Clemens Stræde										
Sum of sherd counts										
Ware types	**Phase 3**	**Phase 4**	**Phase 7**	**Phase 8**	**Phase 10**	**Phase 6**	**Phase 5b**	**Phase 9**	**No Phase**	**Sum**
Baltic blackware						26			13	39
Viking Age low-fired coarseware	6	79	172	81	14	432	39	8	979	1810
Medieval well-fired redware								13	34	47
Total	**6**	**79**	**179**	**81**	**20**	**458**	**39**	**8**	**1026**	**1896**

Table 15. FHM 4573 Skt. Clemens Stræde. Ware types and number of sherds in stratigraphic phases.

grouped into 15 stratigraphic phases, two of which relate to the pre-rampart settlement. It must be stressed that the relative stratigraphic dating of the material is good and the phasing is detailed. However, an absolute dating of the phases has not yet been established, as the excavation is still undergoing analysis as part of another project. The ceramics from this excavation will be analysed in detail as part of that project and will therefore only be summarised here.

FHM 4573 Skt. Clemens Stræde has yielded one of the larger ceramics assemblages, including 1896 sherds of Viking Age pottery: Of the total assemblage, 97% comprises Viking Age low-fired coarseware of uniform type with only a few Medieval and Post-Medieval sherds from later structures, which explains why the ceramics content of the stratigraphic phases is not presented here. Most of the material is fairly uniform, comprising coarse, thick-walled cooking pots with a rounded corpus and an upright rim, 11.4-18 cm in diameter; only a small proportion of the sherds show any decoration. This situation is fairly typical for Viking Age material from Aarhus.[128] The later post-built house contained a small, but remarkable, collection of imported sherds of Feldberger type, as well as a pan of Frisian type. As the excavation is presently undergoing further analysis as part of a larger study of Aarhus in the Viking Age, more detailed analysis of the stratigraphy and interpretation of the occupation will be left to this publication. Furthermore, the assemblage is very uniform and shows no clear chronological development at this, apart from its content of imported ceramics, and is almost exclusively related to the Viking Age. As the

settlement was cleared prior to the construction of the Viking Age rampart, this site shows no continuity into the Middle Ages.

2.6.5 FHM 4587 Mejlgade 26 (land registry title no. 869a)

Excavated 2004. Excavated area 400 m².
Sources: Excavation report.

This excavation was situated very near the former coastline, immediately north of St. Oluf's Church, on the east side of Mejlgade. It lies to the north of the Viking Age rampart which encircled the town centre, but still well within the boundaries of the Medieval and Post-Medieval town. In the Middle Ages, and up into recent times, Mejlgade was the main thoroughfare leading from the town centre to the north gate and the route to the northern part of the region therefore passed by here. The area as a whole is remarkable because it contains remains of a number of Medieval cellars of fairly early date. This particular excavation revealed traces of a cellar from the 14th century, and a very similar cellar was found a little to the south, beneath Skolebakken 11-15, in 1914.[129] The latter is undated, but a nearby well was dated to the 14th century, so it may have been of approximately same age as the cellar located at FHM 4587 Mejlgade 26. In 1922, the remains of a brick building, dated to the middle of the 14th century, were found further to the south at Mejlgade 8, while a vaulted cellar from the later Middle Ages was seen at Mejlgade 24 in 1908.[130]The most noticeable feature here is that the large, well-built

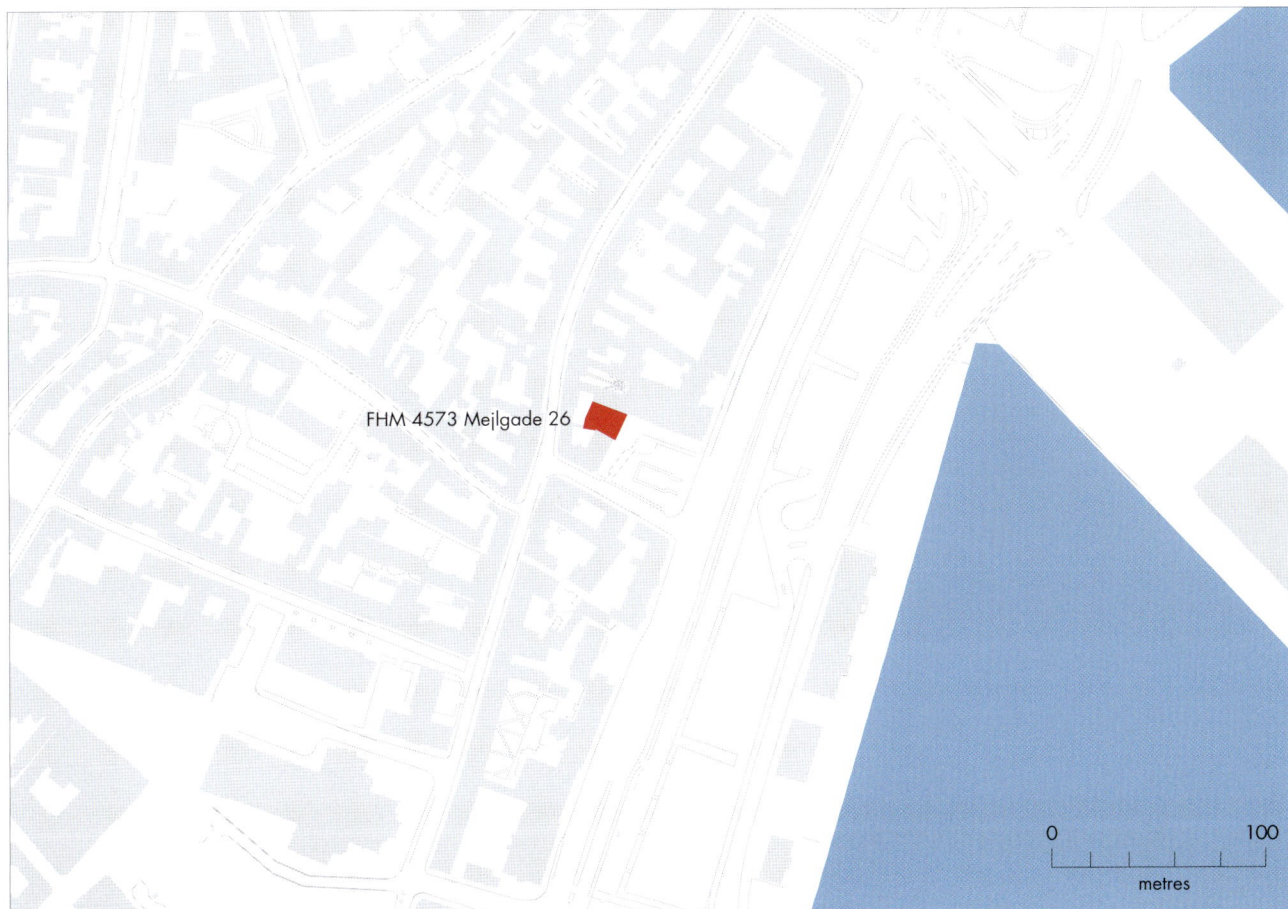

Figure 54. Location of the site FHM 4587 Mejlgade 26 on a modern map.

houses with cellars in this area differ significantly from the simpler, smaller cellar-less houses seen at FHM 4225 Guldsmedgade and at FHM 4616 Telefontorvet. All the cellars have been encountered in the eastern part of Mejlgade, located between what was the coast at that time and the road. They obviously indicate a requirement for safe storage of bulk wares, and one may wonder, encouraged by the traces of lightly-constructed buildings found between the large houses and the road, whether these houses were intended for use by merchants or other people with a surplus for storage and easy access to the coast. Unfortunately, no excavations have been able to reveal the position of the Medieval coastline here. If we look further into this particular site, remains of at least six houses and a road were found, dating from c. 1250 to c. 1750. The

excavators divided the activities on the site into three stratigraphic phases. In the earliest phase, phase 1, a paved road was constructed east-west, leading from the shore to Mejlgade, and a house (house 1) was built on the plot. The paved street closely resembled the earliest phase of Mejlgade, remains of which have been recorded several times, and may have been constructed at the same time, i.e. at some point in the 13th century.[131] A coin dated to the 1260s was found on the floor in the building and three coins from the early 14th century were found in culture layers related to the house and probably date its use.

In the second phase (phase 2), a large half-timbered house was built (house A125). The building was oriented with its gable facing Mejlgade. Its length is

75

Figure 55. The 13th century street running from the harbour to Mejlgade, beside the cellar at FHM 4587 Mejlgade. Photo: Moesgaard Museum.

unknown, but it was at least 7 m wide. It had a very solid stone- and brick-built cellar and a very well-built staircase with brick details. The robust foundations indicate that the building had several storeys. The road leading to the beach was renewed and the entrance to the cellar faced on to this road, giving easy access. A lightly-constructed building was erected between the road and the south wall of the house; this is interpreted as a booth by the excavators. The road was repaired several times during the period when this building was in use. A coin from the early 14th century was found in one of the later phases.

In phase 3, three further houses (houses 2, A140 and 50), all of them half-timbered, were built in rapid succession on the site. Using the remains of these houses, the excavator divided phase 3 into three sub-phases: phase 3.1 (house 2 and related features), phase 3.2 (house A140 and related features) and phase 3.3

Figure 56. The cellar at FHM 4587 Mejlgade, dated to the early 14th century (house A125). Note the fine staircase with brick details. Photo: Moesgaard Museum.

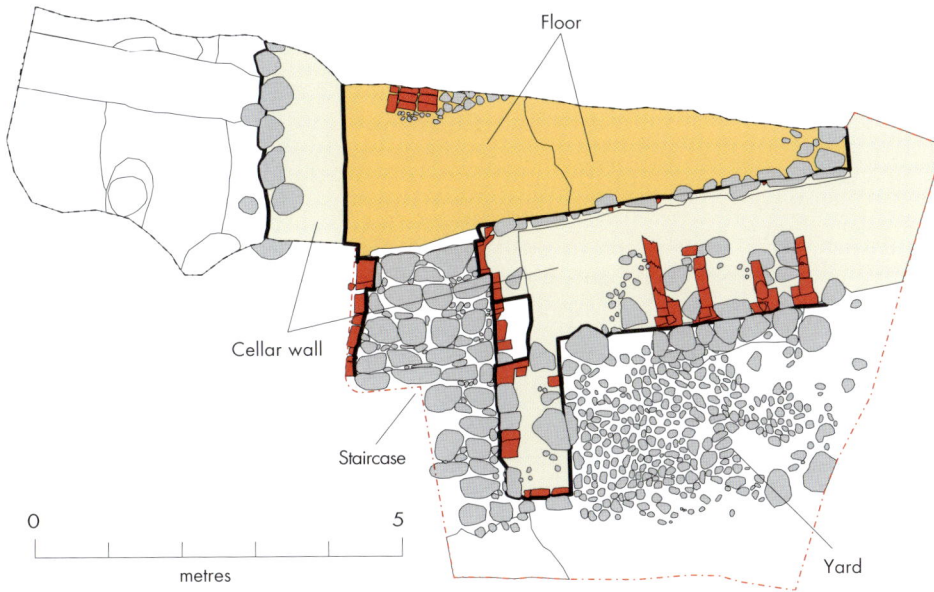

Figure 57. Plan of the early 14th century cellar (FHM 4587 Mejlgade) with staircase and part of the floor made of bricks and clay. North is up. Note the well-constructed staircase and the remains of a pavement in the yard in front of the house.

(house 50 and related features). Houses 2 and A140 both contained coins that were probably minted in 1420-40. House 50, which replaced house A140, contained a coin minted in 1445-1520.

Most of the ceramics from this site were found in cultural layers, with a significant amount from structures, mainly the cellars, and surfaces, i.e. the floors in the houses and the roads.

An overview of the material is given in table 16.

75% of the ceramics from this site are Post-Medieval, reflecting the later phase 3, with the remainder being Medieval. Of the Medieval material, 24% comprises redware and 12% imports. These are second highest proportions of both of these ware types found in any of the excavations in Aarhus, only matched by FHM 4616

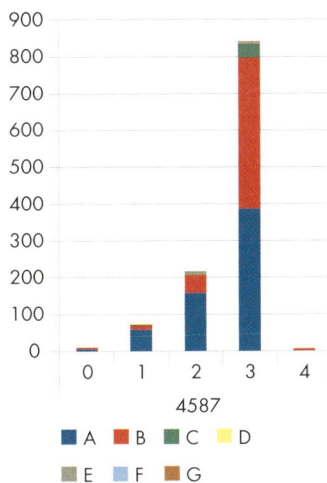

Figure 58. Ceramics from FHM 4587 Mejlgade, based on number of sherds in stratigraphic phases (No= 1151). Based on data shown in table 16. Note the rather large amount of redware in the later phase. A = Greywares. B: Redwares. C: Whitewares. D: Proto stonewares. E: Stonewares. F: Majolicas. G: Porcelain.

Figure 59. Siegburg jugs from the cellar (house A125) at FHM 4587 Mejlgad (FHM 4587 x343). Photo: Moesgaard Photo/Medialab.

FHM 4587 Mejlgade						
Sum of sherd counts						
Ware types	**Phase 1**	**Phase 2**	**Phase 3**	**Phase4**	**No Phase**	**Total**
Andenne-type ware	2					2
Baltic burnished greyware		40				40
Black pot, Varde type			55			55
Danish slipware			3			3
Frechen stoneware		1				1
Low Countries tin-glazed ware			1			1
Medieval well-fired coarseware	59	98	32		4	193
Medieval well-fired redware	7	38	6	1	1	53
Other blackware		20	300	1	2	323
Other whiteware			35			35
Porcelain			1			1
Post-Medieval well-fired redware	4	10	390	5	3	412
Post-Medieval well-fired redware with slip decoration			12			12
Proto stoneware	2	1				3
Raeren stoneware			2			2
Siegburg stoneware		9	2			11
Tin-glazed ware			2			2
Westerwald stoneware			1			1
Viking Age Low-fired coarseware					1	1
Total	**74**	**217**	**842**	**7**	**11**	**1151**

Table 16. FHM 4587 Mejlgade. Ware types and number of sherds in stratigraphic phases.

Figure 60. Baltic burnished greyware jugs from the cellar (house A125) at FHM 4587 Mejlgade (FHM 4587 x242). Photo: Moesgaard Photo/Medialab.

Telefontorvet. The Post-Medieval material includes more moderate amounts of imports and redware: 4% and 52%, respectively. Quite a few sherds were found associated with the coin-dated structures. Jugs of Rouen- type and of Rhenish proto stoneware were found on the road, together with the afore-mentioned coin from the early 14th century, as were jugs of Medieval well-fired redware, both red and green, with round handles. Remains of bowls and cooking pots in Medieval well-fired coarseware were recovered too (rim types 611 and 605). The floors in the house (house 1) contained fragments of a jug of Andenne-type ware, as well as jugs in Medieval well-fired redware, and cooking pots and bowls in Medieval well-fired coarseware (rim types 606, 611).

Most of the material from phase 2 was found in the fill of the cellar of house 125 and must have been deposited here during the demolition of the building. A small quantity of ceramics was found in the con-struction layers relating to the building of the cellar. These contained fragments of Medieval well-fired redware jugs, as well as bowls in Medieval well-fired coarseware (rim type 611). On the road that passed by the building were some sherds of imported ceramics, most notably from of a Baltic burnished greyware jug and a Siegburg stoneware jug.

This relates neatly to the earliest cellar floor, where sherds of the same types were found, i.e. Siegburg jugs and Baltic burnished greyware jugs, as well as jugs in Medieval well-fired redware. These jugs were clearly bell-shaped with a wide base, well-formed and well-glazed with red glaze and decorated with applied flowers in white clay. The Medieval well-fired coarseware cooking pots had elaborate rims (rim type 606). The fill of the cellar contained the same types: Siegburg jugs and quite a large amount of Baltic bur-nished greyware, Medieval well-fired redware jugs and cooking pots in Medieval well-fired coarseware (rim type 605). The latest road in this phase only contained a Medieval well-fired coarseware pot, but its rim was of a type new to this site (rim type 608).

In phase 3, the earliest house, house 2, only con-tained Medieval well-fired coarseware, while the con-struction layers for house A140 contained Medieval well-fired redware. On the floor in house A140, and probably relating to its demolition, was a collection of Post-Medieval redware, early type tripod pipkins (rim types 1005, 1004) and some plates, as well as black pot, early type cooking pots (rim type 608), some local slipware plates and some sherds of utility Raeren-type stoneware jugs. The stratigraphically latest house in this phase contained cauldrons of black pot Vorup type (rim type 502), some local slipware and Post-Medieval redware tripod pipkins. In conclusion, the most notable features of this excavation are the rather well-dated earliest phases and the varied collection of imports relating to the use of the site. The latest phase is of rather extended duration compared to the earlier ones.

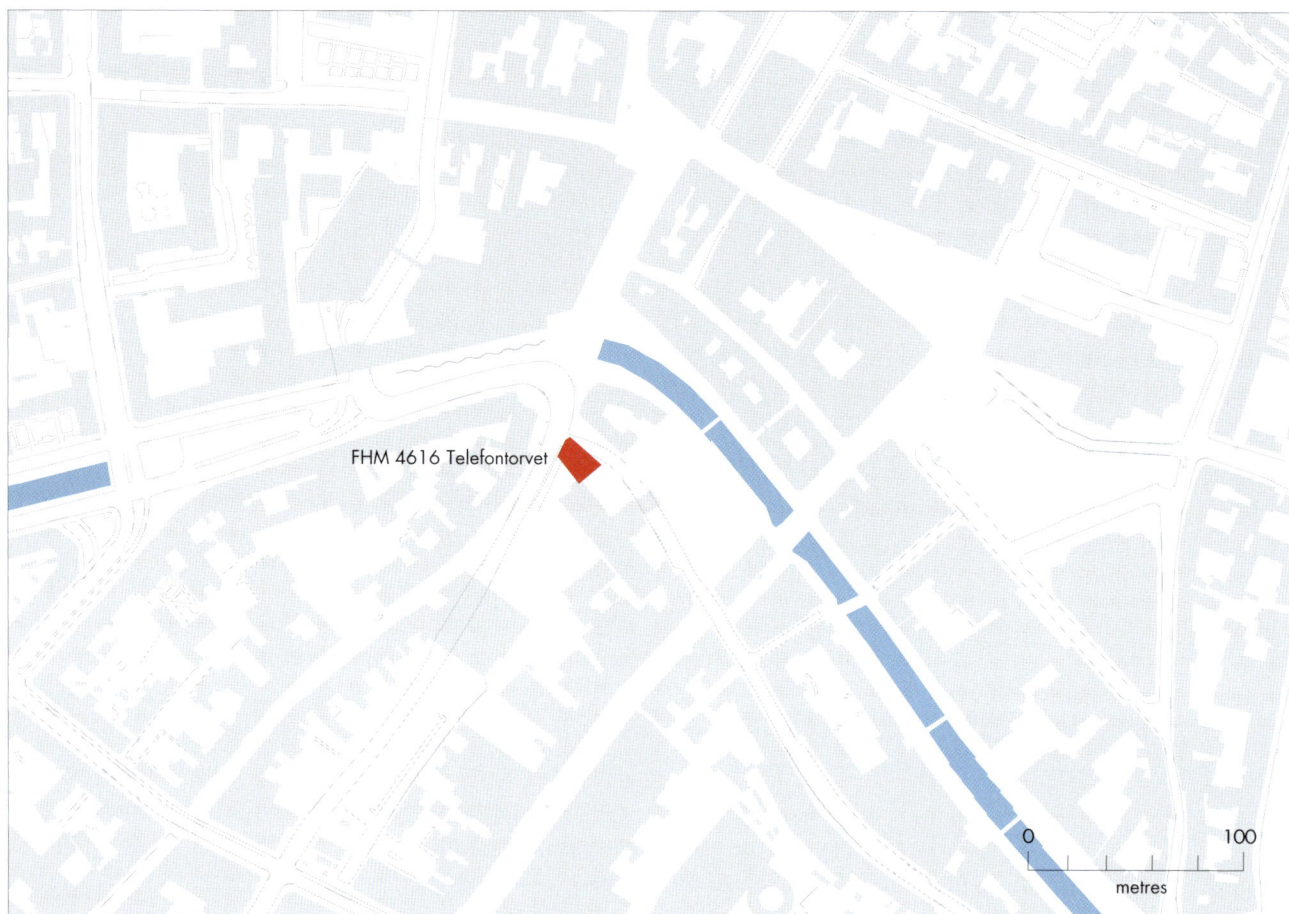

Figure 61. Location of the site FHM 4616 Telefontorvet on a modern map.

2.6.6 FHM 4616 Telefontorvet (land registry title no. 217b)

Excavated 2005. Excavated area 150 m².
Sources: Excavation Report.

The site is situated centrally in the Medieval town on the south bank of the river Aarhus Å, close to Immervad. It bordered Frederiksgade, the main southern thoroughfare leading from the crossing over Aarhus Å, Immervad, to the southern gate and onwards into the southern part of the region. The excavation uncovered the remains of a town house with a gable facing the street. It was rebuilt repeatedly over a short period of time due to stability problems arising from local ground conditions; it was partly constructed on fill layers in the river basin. A post in the fill layers beneath the house has been dendrochronologically dated to the 13th century, providing a post quem date for the construction of the house. The house itself was built facing east-west as a half-timbered construction resting on a sill. It was 5 m wide and its length exceeded 11 m; the exact length could not be determined because its western gable had been disturbed by later building activities. The house remains could be divided into five stratigraphic phases.

Phase 1 relates to its construction and earliest use. Marks in the floors indicate that the house was fitted with wall benches and had internal walls that separated off rooms to the east and west. The western room, facing the street, was used as a smithy.

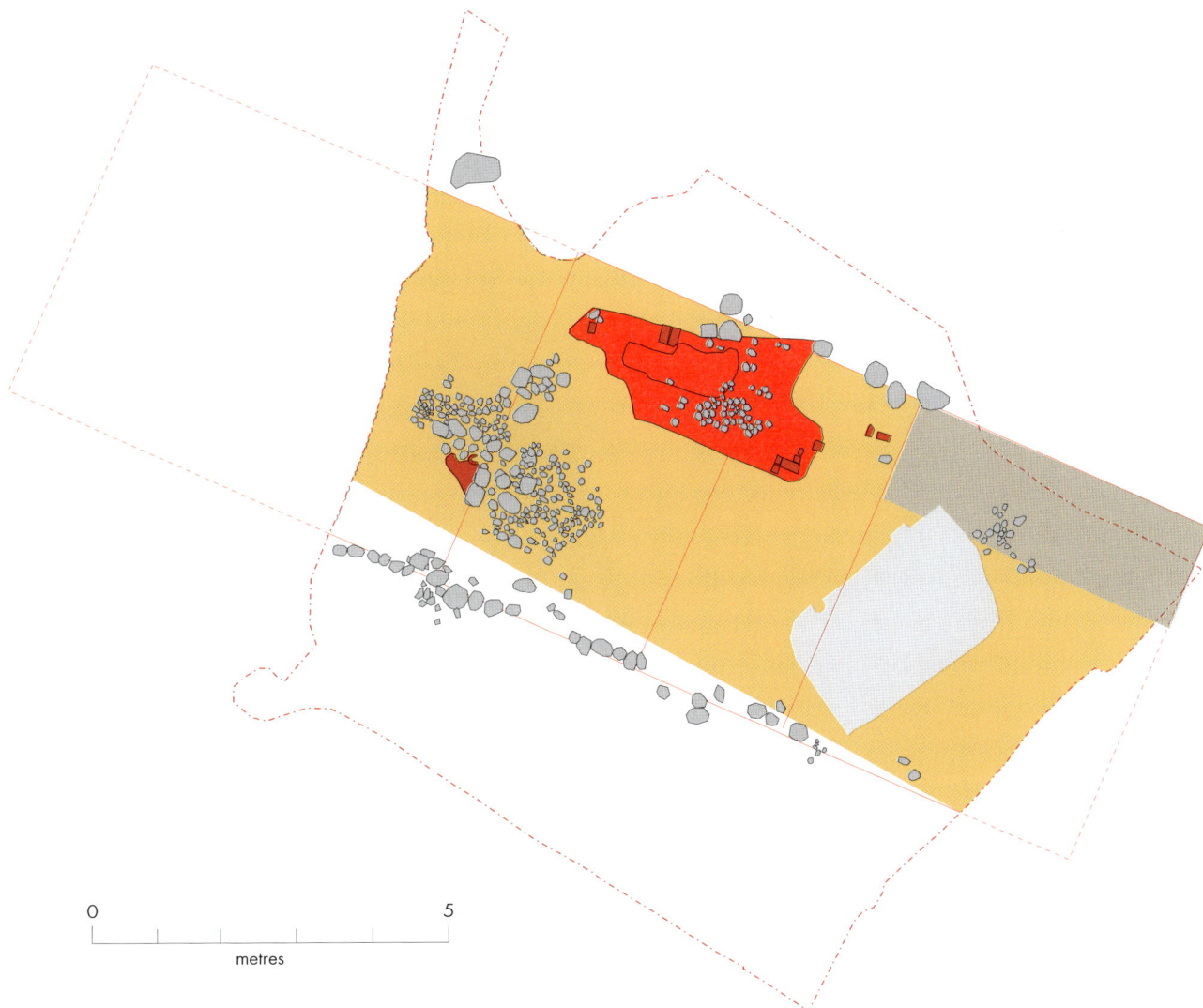

Figure 62. FHM 4616 Telefontorvet phase 1. A house, 11 x 5 m, constructed on the river bank in c. 1300. Plan: Lars Krants/Moesgaard Museum.

In phase 2, the house was given new floors and the internal walls were replaced. A post in a new wall has been dendrochronologically dated to after 1335.

In phase 3, the floors were renewed and the internal walls moved yet again.

In phase 4, the latest phase, the floors were again renewed and a new smithy and oven were built. After this the house was demolished and layers of refuse were dumped, perhaps as a foundation for later buildings that have not been preserved (phase 5). The ceramics from the house have been analysed in relation to the stratigraphic phases described in the excavation report. An overview of main ware types and functional types is given in table 17.

30% of the ceramic assemblage is Medieval well-fired redware – the highest percentage of this ware type yet found in Aarhus. The percentage of imports is lower,

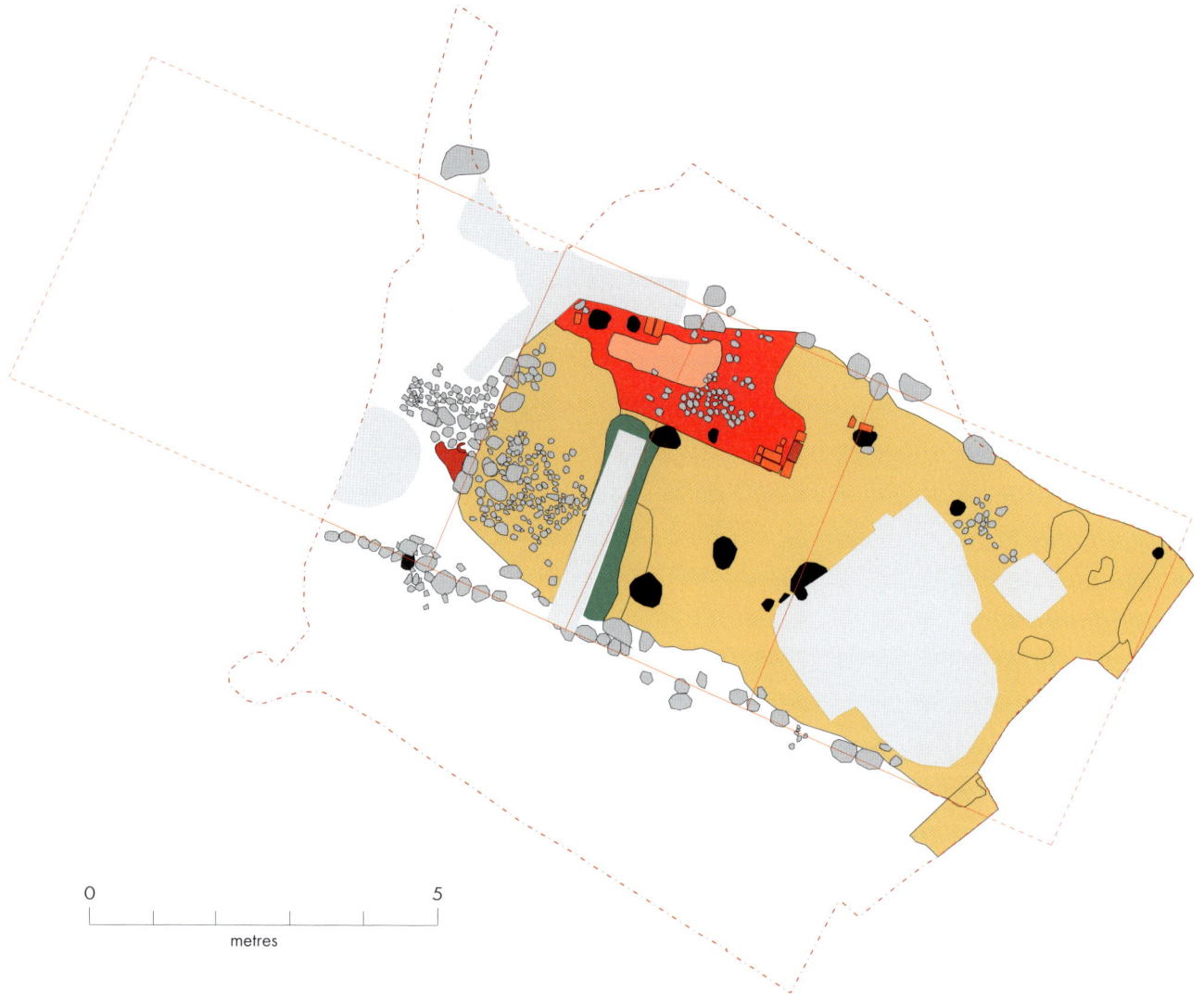

Figure 63. FHM 4616 Telefontorvet phase 2. The rebuilt house, dated to after 1335. Plan: Lars Krants/Moesgaard Museum.

only 3%, but the material is very varied. Most of the ceramics were found on surfaces, mainly house floors, and in layers related to the use of the house. The assemblage is one of the smaller examples from Aarhus, a function of the short time span of the structure and the relatively limited excavated area. Nevertheless, the detailed stratigraphic phasing gives this excavation potential in relation to consumption studies.

Phase 1 contains imports: Siegburg stoneware and a Rouen-type ware jug were found on the earliest floor, so there is no doubt that these were used in the house. Also from the house are cooking pots in Medieval well-fired coarseware. No rim-sherds were present.

The majority of the material is Medieval well-fired redware, of rather coarse fabric and with red glaze.

Figure 64. *FHM 4616 Telefontorvet phase 3. Rebuilt house with oven. Plan: Lars Krants/Moesgaard Museum.*

Phase 2 contains sherds of the same type: Medieval well-fired coarseware cooking pots (rim types 601, 606, 607 and 623) and bowls (rim type 611) as well as Medieval well-fired redware jugs: red-glazed with dark manganese streaks or green-glazed.

The handles are strap-shaped with three furrows, which is fairly typical for Aarhus. The imports are varied: A beautiful Rouen-type ware jug, a Saintonge polychrome ware jug and a jug of Baltic burnished hard Greyware were found on the floor together with local coarsewares and redwares.

This is the only example of Saintonge polychrome ware found in the Aarhus area. The smaller amount of material from phase 3 contains no imports apart from the Baltic well-fired burnished ware. The local types are the usual Medieval well-fired redware jugs, green

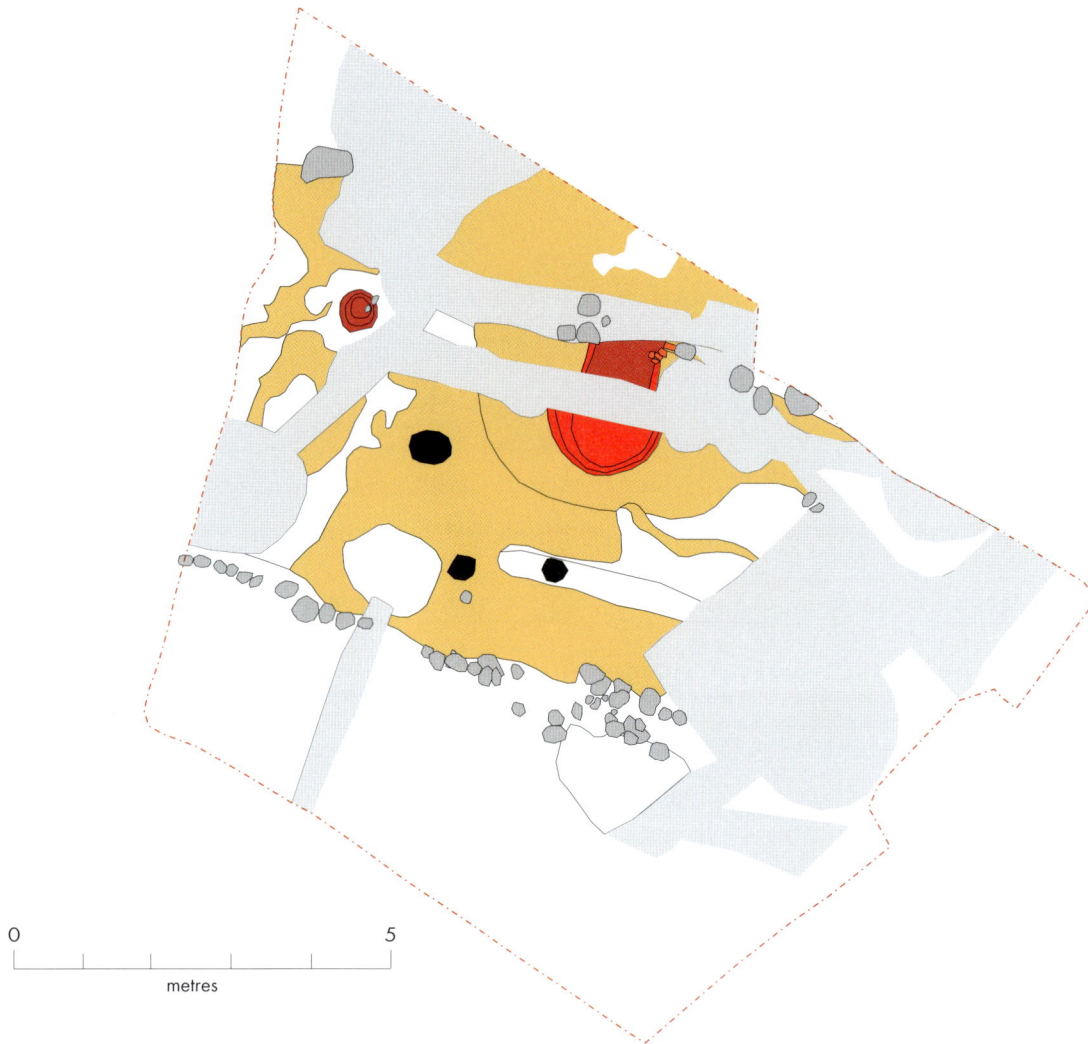

Figure 65. FHM Telefontorvet 4616 phase 4. Rebuilt house with new floors, new oven. Plan: Lars Krants/Moesgaard Museum.

and red, with rather thin glaze, and Medieval well-fired coarseware cooking pots with rather simple out-turned rims (rim types 601, 602). In the latest phase, phase 4, we still see burnished Baltic ware jugs, Medieval well-fired coarseware and Medieval well-fired redware jugs used in the house. The Medieval well-fired redware jugs are all red or green and thinly glazed. One is decorated with black streaks and another has black, applied flower decoration. Fragments of at least one beaker and a jug of Siegburg stoneware were also found. In conclusion, it is worth noting how the proportion of redware/blackware is relatively high at this site throughout all its phases. The imports are rather varied in the early phases 1 and 2, but from phase 3 onwards only the stoneware and the Baltic well-fired burnished wares are seen; French imports are not evident.

Figure 66. FHM 4616 Telefontorvet phase 4 during excavation. Archaeologists Lene Mollerup, Stine Højbjerg and Birka Bitsch mark wall posts in the south wall. The circular construction in the section is one of the ovens. Photo: Lars Krants/Moesgaard Museum.

Figure 67. Kiln (phase 3) from FHM 4616 Telefontorvet. Photo: Lars Krants/Moesgaard Museum.

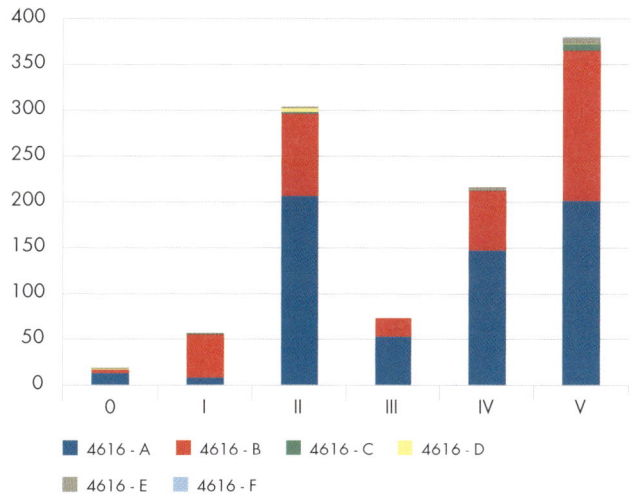

Figure 68. Overview of the ceramics from FHM 4616, based on stratigraphic phases (No. of sherds= 1063). Based on data shown in table 17. A = Greywares. B: Redwares. C: Whitewares. D: Proto stonewares. E: Stonewares. F: Majolicas.

FHM 4616 Telefontorvet							
Sum of sherd counts							
Ware types	**Phase I**	**Phase II**	**Phase III**	**Phase IV**	**Phase V**	**No Phase**	**Total**
Baltic burnished greyware		2	3	3	1		9
Cologne stoneware					4		4
Dutch redware					1		1
Industrial ware					1		1
Medieval well-fired coarseware	8	204	50	144	125	20	551
Medieval well-fired redware	47	90	20	65	42	5	269
Other blackware					75	4	79
Other whiteware					7		7
Post-Medieval well-fired redware					114	2	116
Post-Medieval well-fired redware with slip decoration					7		7
Proto stoneware		4			1	1	6
Raeren stoneware		1		2			3
Rouen-type ware	1	1					2
Saintonge polychrome ware		1					1
Siegburg stoneware	1	1		2	2	1	7
Total	**57**	**304**	**73**	**216**	**380**	**33**	**1063**

Table 17. FHM 4616 Telefontorvet. Ware types and number of sherds in stratigraphic phases.

Figure 69. Rim-sherd of Medieval glazed redware jug, found on the floor in the house that was rebuilt after 1335 (phase II). (FHM 4616 (x556). Rim diameter 10 cm. Photo: Lars Krants/Moesgaard Museum.

Figure 70. Rim-sherd of Rouen-type ware jug, decorated with applied pellet. Found on the floor in the house that was rebuilt after 1335 (phase II). (FHM 4616 x559). Rim diameter 12 cm. Photo: Moesgaard Museum.

Figure 71. Sherd of large Medieval coarseware bowl (x550) (rim type 611) found on the floor in the house that was rebuilt after 133 (phase II). (FHM 4616 x550). Large bowls such as this example, which is 28 cm in diameter, are very typical for Aarhus. Photo: Moesgaard Museum.

Figure 73. Base of Baltic burnished greyware jug (x334), found on floor in the house in phase II, dated after 1335 (FHM 4616 x334). Photo: Moesgaard Museum.

Figure 72. Sherd of Saintonge ware jug found on the floor in the house in phase II, dated to after 1335. (FHM 4616 x445). Photo: Moesgaard Museum.

Figure 74. Siegburg stoneware jug (FHM 4616 x124) phase 4, 15th century. Photo: Lars Krants/Moesgaard Museum.

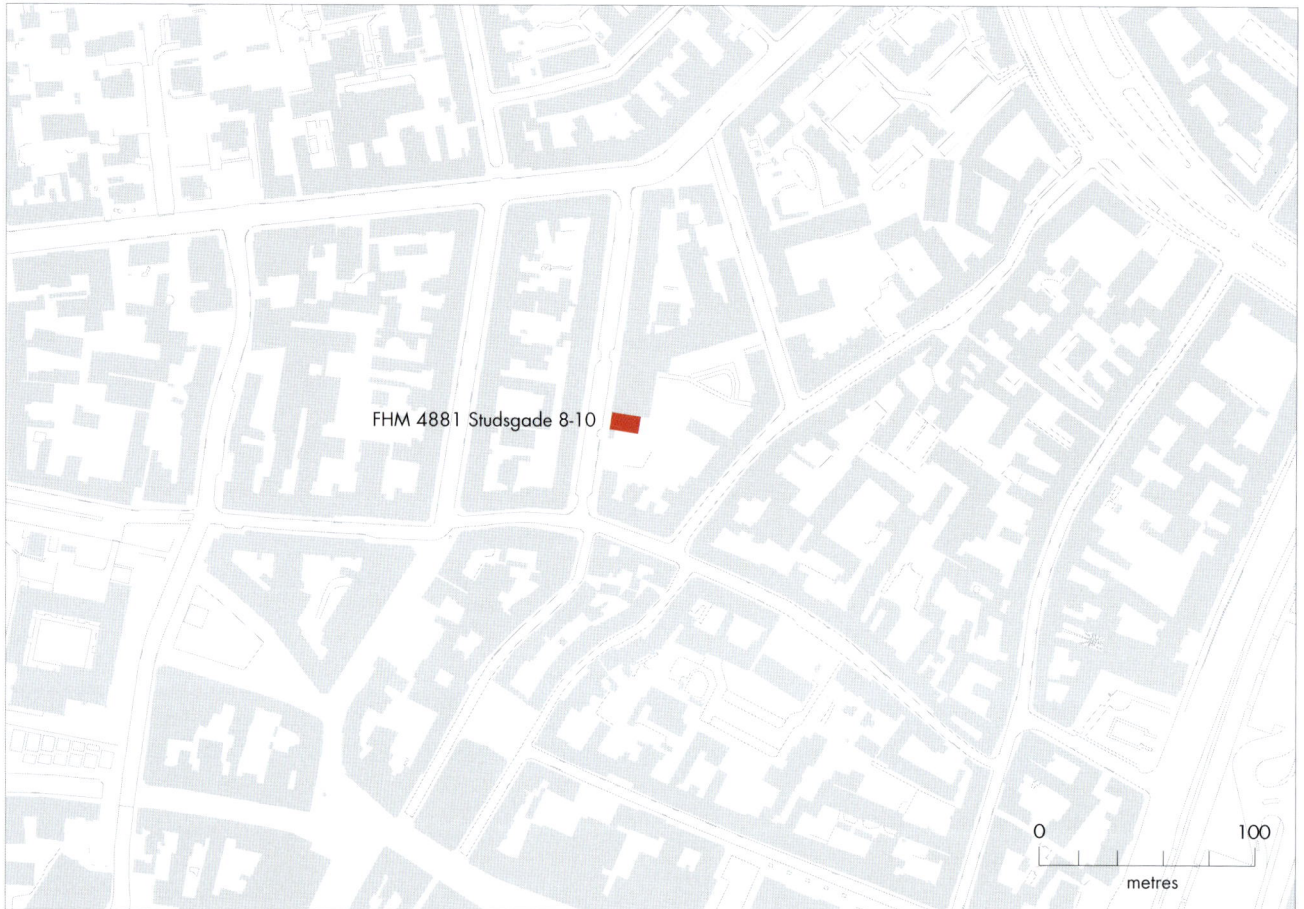

Figure 75. Location of the site FHM 4881 Studsgade 8-10.

2.6.7 FHM 4881 Studsgade 8-10 (land registry title no. 1046c)

Excavated 2007. Excavated area 200 m².
Sources: Excavation Report.

The site lies in the northwestern part of Aarhus, close to the main thoroughfare leading from the town centre to the northwest. It is located outside the rampart that encircled the inner town centre, but well within the boundaries of the Medieval town. The inner part of the street Studsgade is Medieval and appears to have been laid out in the 13th or perhaps even the 12th century.[132] The excavation revealed remains of Viking Age, Medieval and Early Modern settlement, but no traces of Early Medieval settlement were located. The

on-site activities were assigned to seven stratigraphic phases. In the earliest phase, phase 1, two typical Viking Age sunken-featured buildings were found (A1 and A510).

A post-built house (phase 2) is stratigraphically later than one of these sunken-featured buildings (A510). A similar pattern was evident during excavations further north, at Studsgade 32-36, and beneath Studsgade itself, so settlement here does appear to have been somewhat intensive.[133] Following demolition of the Viking Age settlement, the area appears to have lain open. The next activity (phase 3) was the construction of a stable (A83). Traces of dwelling houses were not found, but as the excavated area was situated in a back yard, the dwelling house may well have faced on to the

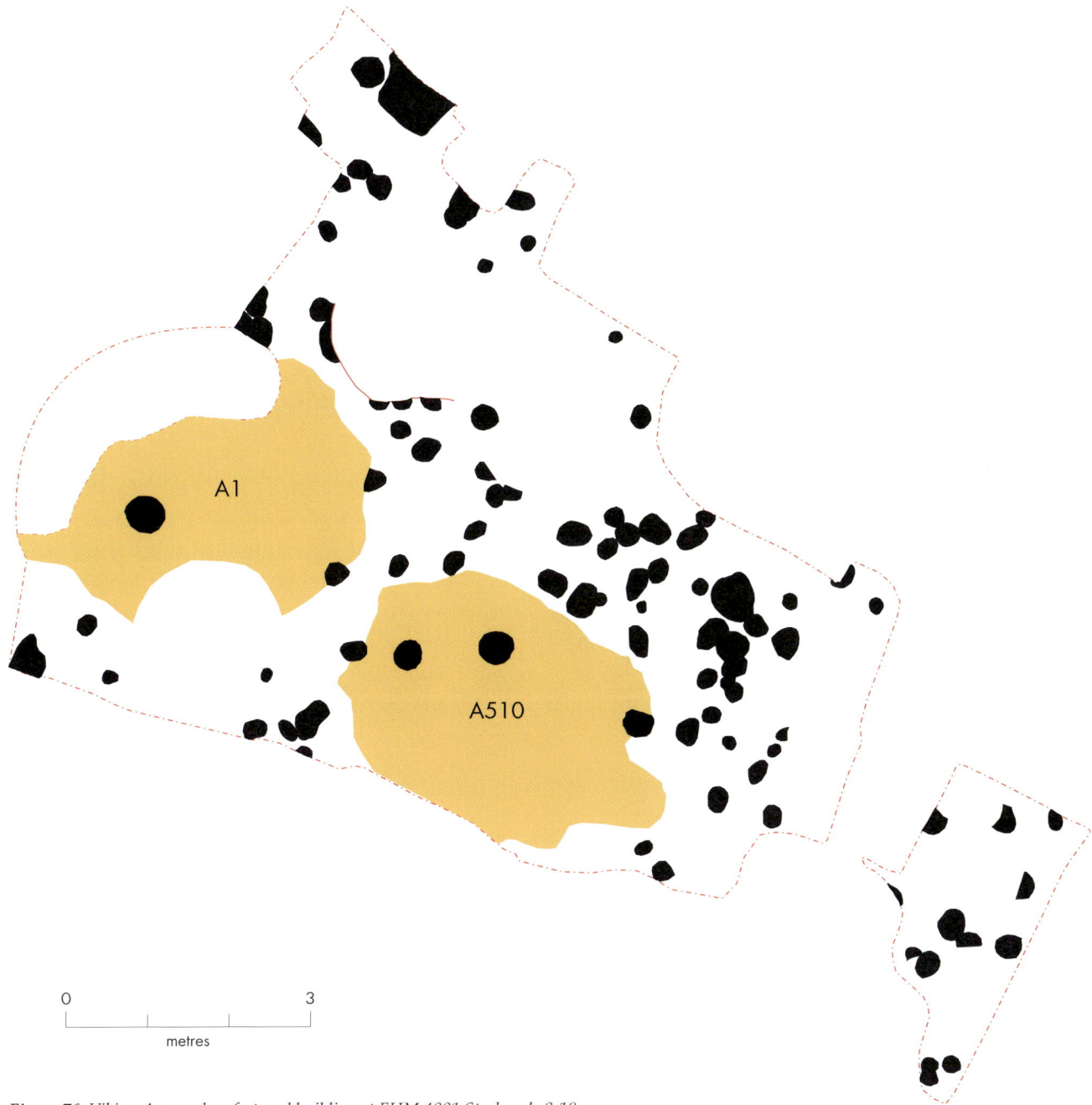

Figure 76. Viking Age sunken-featured building at FHM 4881 Studsgade 8-10.

street, being located in the same position as the present houses on Studsgade. At some point the stable was demolished and a dwelling house (house IV) was constructed on the spot (phase 4). A sequence of floors shows that this house was rebuilt several times before being destroyed in a fire and then demolished. In phase 5, several large wooden barrels and a well were positioned in the yard. This was probably as part of some industrial activity, possibly the production of ceramics or tiles nearby. Shortly after the fire, the house in phase 4 was replaced (phase 6). The walls of the new house extended outside the excavated area, so its size

Figure 77. FHM 4881 Studsgade 8-10 during excavation. Photo: Moesgaard Museum.

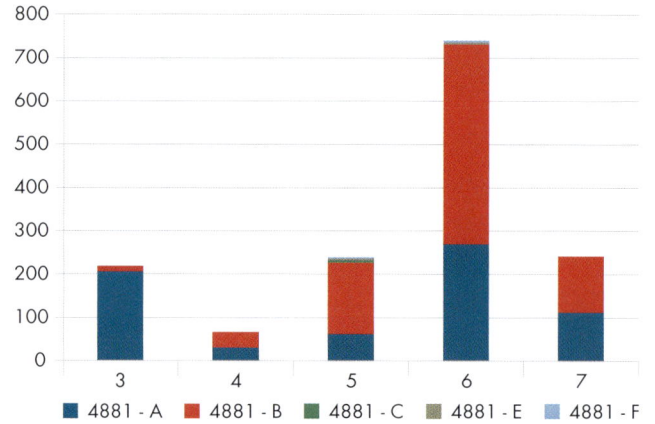

Figure 78. Overview of the ceramics from FHM 4881 Studsgade based on stratigraphic phases (No = 2323). Based on data shown in table 18. A = Greywares. B: Redwares. C: Whitewares. D: Proto stonewares. E: Stonewares. F: Majolicas.

and orientation are unknown. However, the evidence suggests it was rebuilt several times.

An overview of the ceramics is given in table 18. The material from this site reflect its long time span: Viking Age low-fired coarseware makes up 10% of the assemblage, with only 3% low-fired coarseware,

reflecting the lack of settlement structures from the Early Medieval period. 10% of the material is Medieval, but the major part is Post-Medieval. 85% of the Medieval ceramics comprise coarseware and the remainder Medieval well-fired redware. No Medieval imports were identified. The majority (71%) of the Post-Medieval ceramics comprise redware, with very

FHM 4881 Studsgade 8-10								
Sum of sherd counts								
Ware types	**Phase 1**	**Phase 3**	**Phase 4**	**Phase 5**	**Phase 6**	**Phase 7**	**No phase**	**Hoved-total**
Baltic blackware	40				1		5	46
Black pot, early type	7	10	4	28	162	93	37	341
Cologne stoneware				3	4			7
Dutch redware					10			10
Frechen stoneware				1				1
Industrial ware				3			2	5
Low Countries tin-glazed ware					2		1	3
Medieval low-fired coarseware	151	1	2		16		7	177
Medieval well-fired coarseware	2	186	2	27	14	6	22	259
Medieval well-fired redware		8	1	2	2	2		15
Other blackware		4	22	8	49	14	95	192
Other whiteware				5			4	9
Post-Medieval redware	1	5	34	154	427	125	338	1084
Post-Medieval redware with slip decoration			2	7	24	3	267	303
Proto stoneware	1							1
Viking Age low-fired coarseware	392	6	1		29		4	432
Werra ware				2				2
Total	**594**	**220**	**68**	**240**	**740**	**243**	**782**	**2887**

Table 18. FHM 4881 Studsgade. Ware types and number of sherds in stratigraphic phases.

Figure 79. Viking Age ware with stamped decoration found in a Viking Age sunken-featured building (A1) at FHM 4881 Studsgade 8-10 (FHM 4881 x336). Photo: Moesgaard Photo/Medialab.

Figure 81. Cologne stoneware jug found on floor in the 16th century house at FHM 4881 Studsgade 8-10. Late 16th century. Photo: Moesgaard Museum.

few imports. The assemblage includes a great amount of ceramics waste, i.e. misfired ceramics, which will be dealt with in a later project.

The sunken-featured buildings contained ceramics of Viking Age type, as well as loom weights, spin-

Figure 80. Baltic blackware-inspired local ceramics from a Viking Age sunken-featured building (A1) at FHM 4881 Studsgade 8-10 (FHM 4881 x1354) Photo: Moesgaard Photo/Medialab.

dle whorls and fragments of soapstone vessels – all typical of Viking Age Aarhus. The Viking Age type ceramics are notable due to two sherds decorated with stamped decoration. Sherds with exactly the same decoration were found at FHM 4573 Skt. Clemens Stræde. The post-built house contained Viking Age low-fired coarseware of a type with typical linear patterns of incised decoration. Following the demolition of the Viking Age settlement, the area seems to have lain open during phase 2, from which only a few sherds were found. Sherds of Medieval well-fired redware jugs, all green-glazed, and Medieval well-fired coarseware cooking pots were frequent in the layers related to phase 3. The ceramics are sparse in phase 4, but the floors of the presumed stable contained fragments of black pot, early type cooking pots (rim type 308) and fragments of Post-Medieval redware, early type tripod pipkins (rim type 1005 and handle 1048). The barrels and the well of the industrial phase 5 contained misfired ceramics and it seems likely that these were related to the production of ceramics or tiles nearby (see below). The barrels also contained fragments of black pots, early type, and tripod pipkins in Post-Medieval redware (rim type 1004). The

Figure 82. Post-Medieval redware plates with slipware decoration (Found at FHM 4881 Studsgade 8-10. Late 16th century. Photo: Moesgaard Photo/ Medialab.

newly constructed dwelling house in phase 6 was rebuilt several times. The house floors and the culture layers related to its function contained a wide variety of ceramics types. Most notable are fragments of a mug of Cologne stoneware, a Low Countries redware plate and fragments of Low Countries tin-glazed ware: a plate with blue and yellow decoration and an apothecary vessel.

The majority of the material therefore comprises Post-Medieval redware tripod pipkins (rim types 1005, 1017 and 1004) and black pots, early type (rim type 308). Pans are also present (rim type 1028). The heavily disturbed phase 7 contained Post-Medieval redware tripod pipkins with elaborate rims (rim types 1009, 1013). The rear of the yard contained several pits filled with ceramics production waste. It is therefore obvious that this dwelling was associated with a ceramics workshop. As a consequence, the waste, which primarily consisted of tiles, will not be analysed in this study of consumption, but awaits a forthcoming analysis of ceramics production in the town.

Figure 83. Clockwise from top left, Low Countries majolic plate, Cologne stoneware mug and Low Countries redware plate found in the Renaissance house iin FHM 4881 Studsgade 8-10 (FHM4881 x476; x1156; x70; x115). Photo: Moesgaard Photo/Medialab.

Figure 84. Ceramics en masse. Late 16th century waste from FHM 4881 Studsgade 8-10 during excavation. Photo: Moesgaard Museum.

Figure 86. Dish with Pomegranates, Anonymous, c. 1620 – c. 1635. ©Rijksmuseum, Amsterdam.

Figure 85. Low Countries tin-glazed majolica plate, found at FHM 4881 Studsgade 8-10. 16th century (FHM 4881 x476). Photo: Moesgaard Museum.

Figure 87. Stoneware jug with applied decoration produced in Cologne c. 1520-45. Height 14.2 cm. British Museum inv. 1887, 0211.10 © The Trustees of the British Museum.

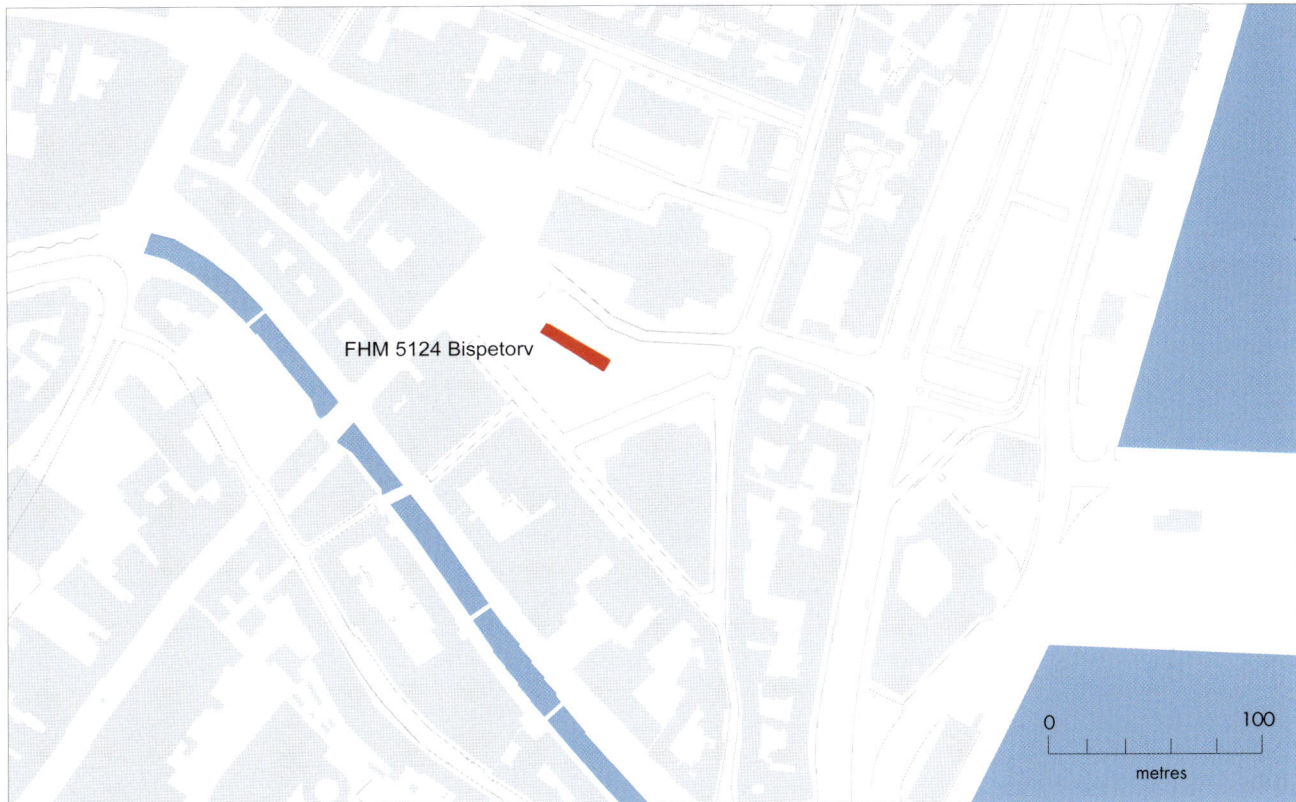

Figure 88. Location of the site FHM 5124 Bispetorv.

2.68   FHM 5124 Bispetorv
(land registry title no. 7000ac)

Excavated 2009. Excavated area 250 m².
Sources: Excavation report.

The Bispetorv site was investigated in 2011 as a research excavation on the site of the former chapter house of St. Clement's Cathedral. The location of the site is shown below: It lies in the centre of the town, immediately south of the cathedral, on the low sandy hill by the river mouth on which the earliest Aarhus was founded.

Brick houses are mentioned in the area in 1286 and 1298, so it was expected to find remains of these. Furthermore, remains of Medieval brick buildings were demolished during large-scale construction work in 1921.[134] The excavation revealed traces of Viking Age, Medieval and Post-Medieval settlement,[135] i.e. built remains from a very long time span, including substantial traces of Viking Age occupation. The site is characterised by its large size, complicated stratigraphy and phasing (more than 400 individual contexts contained ceramics), the numerous built remains and the intense building activity in the Late Middle Ages and Early Modern period.

Because of the long time span and the size of the material, a detailed overview will be given below.

Viking Age and Early Middle Ages 800-1200
As stated above, evidence relating to the Viking Age and Early Medieval occupations has been heavily disturbed by later building activity. Nevertheless, the excavation provides valuable information on consumption during the Viking Age and Early Medieval period via the remains associated with a series of houses. The earliest structures on the site comprise the remains of at least

Figure 89. Chapter House A22 and adjoining buildings. Plan: Lars Krants/Moesgaard Museum.

seven sunken-featured buildings and a well (figure 91): This settlement awaits scientific dating. One of the sunken-featured buildings was provisionally dated to the 10th century by the excavators on the basis of a piece of jewellery, but it is clear that several phases are represented (sunken-featured buildings A831, A334, A685, A707, A850, A952 and A958). The sunken-featured building settlement appears to have been replaced with post-built houses by the 11th century at the latest, in what may be a parallel situation to that evident at FHM 4573 Skt. Clemens Stræde and FHM 4881 Studsgade 8-10.

Phases II and III c. 1200-1400

The remains from phases II and III are slight and disturbed by later building activity. What remained comprised largely pits and layers (pits A20, a272, a490, a495, a576 and floor A575). There do not appear to be remains of larger structures on the site, with the exception of a

kiln (A582) and the floor of a workshop, probably a smithy (A291).

Phases IV and V. c. 1400-1700

In phases IV and V, intense building activity resulted in the construction of three buildings: the so-called Monk's House (A22/A93), the Chapter House (A245) and a stone-built cellar (A5309).

The Monk's House A22/A93 was a well-built brick building, from which the cellar with a sequence of floors was preserved. The southern end of the house was excavated: This was a brick building, 9 m wide, with paved cellar floors in several phases and, according to the excavators, dated from the 15th century. The foundations indicate that the building had several storeys. It was demolished and the cellar filled in during the 16th century (figure 92).

Figure 90. Sunken-featured building A334 during excavation at FHM 5124 Bispetorv. Photo: Moesgaard Museum.

The Chapter House A245 was an equally well-built brick building with a preserved construction layer, floors and fills. This building was encountered in 1921 and was found then to measure 36 x 19 m. Only a minor part of the eastern part of the house lay within the area of the recent excavation. The foundations and parts of the cellar floor were preserved. While the house originated from the 15th century, the cellar floors were renewed later. Like the Monk's House, the Chapter House was demolished prior to the construction of the Post-Medieval episcopal residence on the site. The latter construction was removed by subsequent activities here.

A small cellar (A503) located between the two areas was the latest structure on the site. This cellar was demolished at the same time as the other buildings. The brick buildings on FHM 5124 Bispetorv are not unique, but were succeeded by a number of other brick buildings

encountered in excavations and construction works in the area. Medieval brick houses have been seen to the east of Bispetorv, to the west at Clemens Torv and to the north of the cathedral, too. We must therefore envisage a complex of brick-built houses surrounding the cathedral during the later Middle Ages.[136]

Ceramics

The material from FHM 5124 Bispetorv is clearly associated with built remains: 32% of the material was recovered from contexts related to structures – mostly cellars, 28% from surfaces such as floors and pavements, 10% from pits; 20% is from layers, and the rest has not yet been functionally defined. The intense building activity on the site has disturbed the remains of earlier settlement, as is evident in the rather high degree of residuality in the material found in layers and, especially, in pits. These residual types cannot

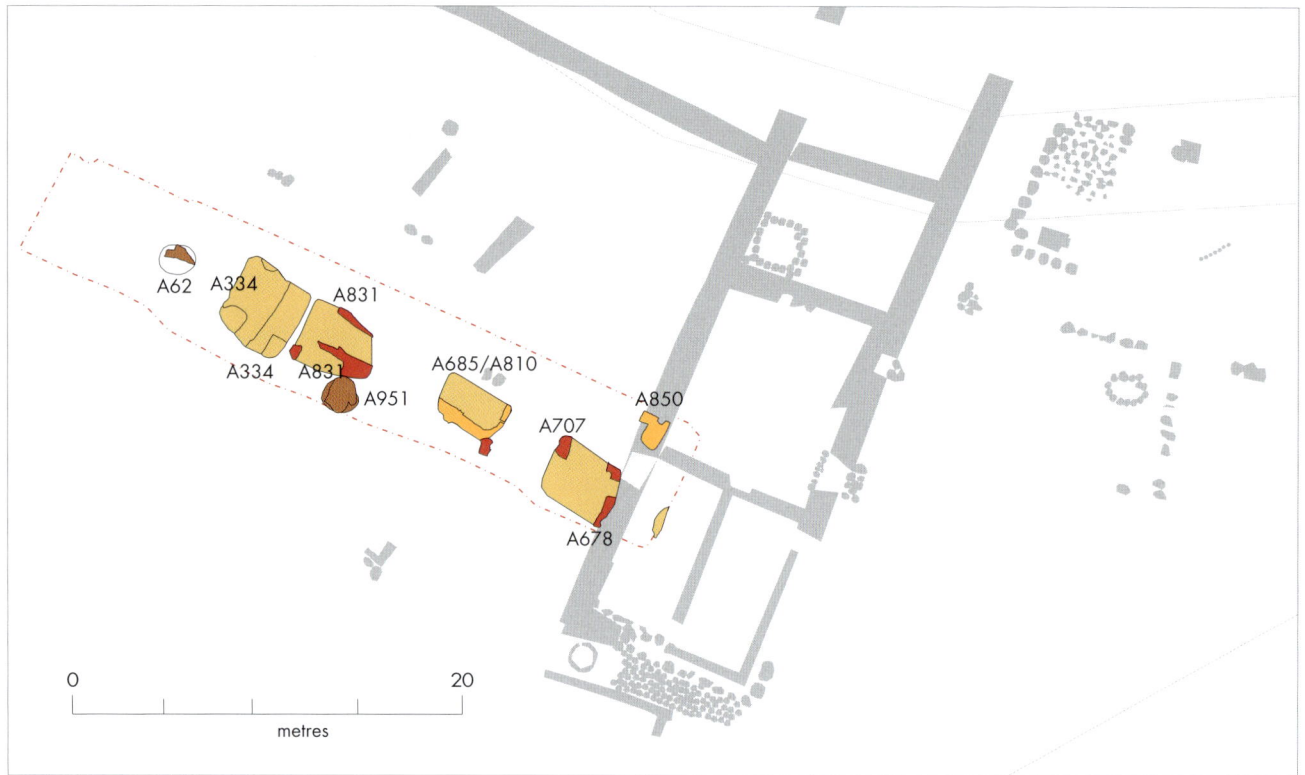

Figure 91. *Sunken-featured buildings from the Viking Age at FHM 5124 Bispetorv. Plan: Lars Krants/Moesgaard Museum.*

be included in the consumption analysis, but must be extracted beforehand.

Ware types

If we look at the numbers (table 19), it is clear that the Viking Age presence is massive: 33% of the material is Viking Age low-fired coarseware, 6% is Early Medieval, 17% is Medieval and 44% is Post-Medieval. Except for a few imported sherds, all the Viking Age material is local, i.e. Viking Age low-fired coarseware. Imports are similarly not visible in the Early Medieval material. The Medieval material consists of 6% Medieval well-fired redware and 2% imports, but the proportions are very much dependent on the context type. Surfaces, especially the floors in the Chapter House and Monk's House, yielded much higher percentages, up to 36% redware and 12% imports, while the later material is dominated by Post-Medieval redware. It must be noted that, as a

consequence of the ongoing analysis of this site, the stratigraphic phasing is less clear at present for some parts of the assemblage. The consumption analysis is therefore based on material recovered primarily from the structures. In particular, some cellars have provided valuable information. If we compare the contents of the phases it is clear that coarseware dominates and that glazed, primarily domestic, wares constitute an increasing part of the material from the 13th century onwards, and that their abundance increases rapidly from the 14th century – the same time as the imported wares make up a larger part of the assemblage (figure 94).

If we study the consumption through the successive phases, these differences become more nuanced. In terms of shape and form, it is clear that the variation in form types increases over time. Cooking pots and bowls dominate, but jugs are present from the 13th century onwards, while a wider variety of function

Figure 92. Monk´s House A22 during excavation at FHM 5124 Bispetorv. Photo: Moesgaard Museum.

types appears from the 16th century onwards (figure 95).

The Viking Age and Early Middle Ages (phase I)
Bispetorv yielded the largest Viking Age and Early Medieval assemblage of all the excavations. As stated earlier, the Viking Age and Early Medieval occupation deposits have been heavily disturbed by later building activity. Nevertheless, the excavation provides valuable information on consumption during the Viking Age and the Early Medieval period, through a succession of houses.

The floor of sunken-featured building A831 contained only Viking Age ceramics, pots with in-turned rims, while its fill contained Viking Age types with out-turned rims, a Viking Age type handled vessel and a miniature vessel. A burnt sunken-featured building, A334, contained Viking Age types and a

miniature vessel was found on the floor. Sunken-featured buildings A685, A707, A850, A952 and A958 contained Viking Age ceramics of local types only: All the rims are in-turned. A stratigraphically later post-built house, A566, is dated to the 11th century: It is later than one of the sunken-featured buildings and earlier than a construction from the 12th century. The house contained a small collection of Viking Age low-fired coarseware, some Medieval low-fired coarseware with Baltic-inspired ornamentation (figure 96) – all with rims turned outwards and some of the earliest imports in the town: sherds of Pingsdorf type. Two sherds of lead-glazed ceramic were found on the floor. The sherds are very coarse and grey in colour and their glaze is yellow; they are very different from the usual Medieval well-fired redware. Since the stratigraphy indicates a date in the 11th century, it is suggested that these sherds were either imported or

Figure 93. *The Chapter House was previously recorded in the 1920s. The recorded remains are marked in grey. Plan: Lars Krants/Moesgaard Museum.*

are of the same type as the lead-glazed ware produced in the 11th century in Dalby and Lund.[137]

The High Middle Ages (phases II and III)

The material from the phases II and III is fairly limited and most was found in pits and cultural layers (pits A20, A 272, A490, A576 and floor A575). There do not seem to be remains of larger structures on the site, apart from a kiln (A582) and the floor of a workshop (A291). Most of the material comprises Medieval well-fired coarseware cooking pots and bowls (rim types 606, 605, 611), but almost a fifth consists of Medieval well-fired redware jugs, which is quite a significant proportion for Aarhus. It amounts to 17% of the assemblage according to the number of sherds and 30% according to rim percentages: The latter are probably a fairer reflection of the on-site consumption (measured on 493 sherds). The jugs are well-shaped,

well-fired and decorated with applied decoration, which typically takes the form of scales in white clay and applied dots or strips of black-painted clay. The only imported ceramic is a piece of Rheinish proto stoneware, found in a pit.

The Late Middle Ages and Early Modern period (phases IV and V)

The Late Medieval material is quite substantial, representing 40% of the total assemblage from the excavation, and this is a reflection of the increased activity on the site at this time. Three buildings provide information on on-site consumption: the Monk's House (A22/A793), the Chapter House (A245) and a stone-built cellar (A5309).

The Monk's House A22/A93 reflects consumption during the mid-15th century. A large assemblage of

FHM 5124 Bispetorv											
Sum of sherd counts										Phase	
Ware types	**Phase 1**	**Phase 2**	**Phase 3**	**Phase 4**	**Phase 5**	**Phase 6**	**Phase 7**	**Phase 8**	**Phase 9**	**No Phase**	**Total**
Andenne					1		1				2
Baltic blackware	4	16	11		2	8	1		4	7	53
Baltic burnished greyware					4	1		2		2	9
Black pot, early type			6		16	39	2	1	1		65
Black pot, Varde type					14	65	19	4	6	5	113
Cologne stoneware						1					1
Danish slipware						2	1		2		5
Frechen stoneware					1						1
Industrial ware					1	1	3	6	8		19
Low Countries redware						2	1			2	5
Low Countries tin-glazed ware					2	1			1		4
Medieval low-fired coarseware	28	238	165	4	12	32	10			19	508
Medieval well-fired coarseware	28	18	289	96	132	153	30	58	14	7	825
Medieval well-fired redware		2	69	9	12	5	2		4	23	126
Other blackware	1		15	1	11	166	30	18	15	5	262
Other whiteware					14	40	16	3		2	75
Pingsdorf-type ware		2									2
Porcelain						1			1	2	4
Post-Medieval redware	6			1	167	320	94	106	21	52	767
Post-Medieval redware with slip decoration						5	4		2	2	13
Proto stoneware					2	1				2	5
Raeren stoneware				1	3	15	8	2	1	2	32
Rouen-type ware					4						4
Siegburg stoneware					2	1					3
Tin-glazed ware								1	1		2
Viking Age low-fired coarseware	1695	238	209	41	32	132				103	2450
Westerwald stoneware							2				2
Total	**1762**	**514**	**764**	**153**	**432**	**991**	**224**	**201**	**81**	**235**	**5357**

Table 19. FHM 5124 Bispetorv. Ware types and number of sherds in stratigraphic phases.

Siegburg- and Raeren-type stoneware was found on the floor in the cellar and this probably relates to the function of the house. Remains of barrels tell

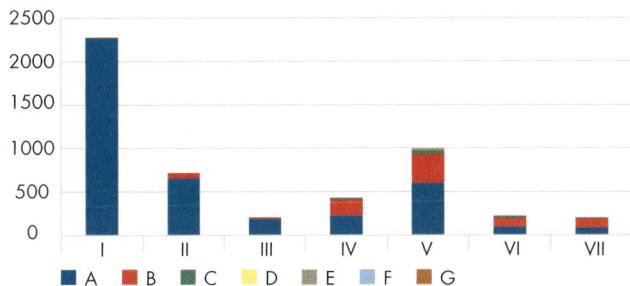

Figure 94. Overview of the ceramics in stratigraphic phases at FHM 5124 Bispetorv based on sherds (No = 5357). Based on data shown in table 19. A = Greywares. B: Redwares. C: Whitewares. D: Proto stonewares. E: Stonewares. F: Majolicas.

the same story. The stratigraphically earliest layer (A815) in the sequence of cellar floor layers provides a more detailed insight into consumption here, with the sherds being found trodden into the floor. Here was a collection of Medieval well-fired coarseware pots with out-turned rims (rim type 608), black pots, early type, and a Medieval well-fired redware jug, at least two jugs of Siegburg stoneware and two of Baltic burnished blackware, at least one pot in Post-Medieval redware and a Rouen-type ware jug. Among the rarer ware types is a Low Countries tin-glazed ware vessel with parallels in Amsterdam.[138] The stoneware in this phase is remarkable: Small apothecary vessels were found on floor A22 in the Chapter House, while the rest of the stoneware comprises decorated tableware.

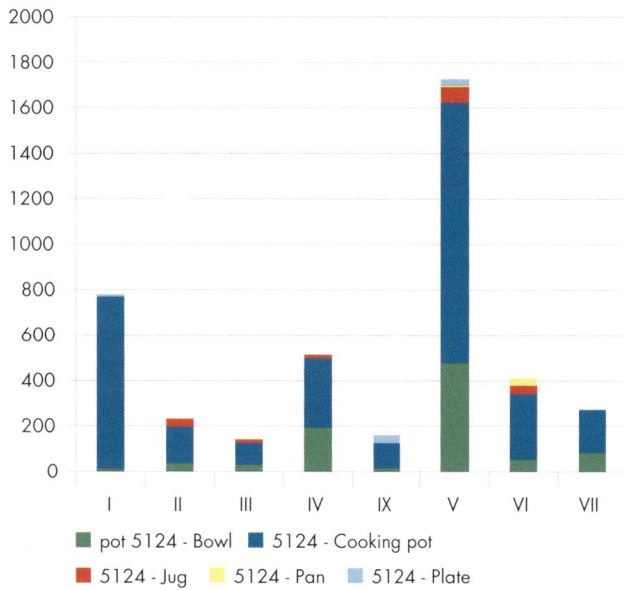

Figure 95. *Overview of functional types at FHM 5124 Bispetorv (No= 4253 RP).*

Figure 96. *Baltic Blackware-inspired pots from from the earliest phase at Bispetorv, 11ᵗʰ or 12ᵗʰ century (FHM 5124 x1229; x3677). Photo: Moesgaard Photo/Medialab.*

A large tankard of Siegburg stoneware was probably produced in the workshop of Hans Hilgers. It was found in cellar A530, together with another two tankards and at least two plates in whiteware. The most remarkable vessel from this phase is a tankard of Cologne stoneware bearing the portraits of princes. This vessel was recovered from the floor of the Chapter House, together with at least two jugs of utilitarian stoneware. Similar pieces are dated to 1530-41.[139] All the fragments were found on the same floor and the vessels were presumably dropped and broken during a relatively short period in the mid-15ᵗʰ century. The French jug was probably quite old when it was broken. In the 16ᵗʰ century, the building was demolished and the cellar filled in. The fill was found to contain a Low Countries tin-glazed ware plate and the handle of a Low Countries tin-glazed ware. A strainer in Low Countries redware was found in cultural layers related to this building phase.

The Chapter House A245 has yielded material from a construction layer, floor layers and fills. On the stratigraphically earliest floor were fragments of proto stoneware and hard, Medieval well-fired coarse-

ware. The later floors contained fragments of jugs of Raeren-type stoneware, some black pots, early type, Low Countries/German whitewares and a piece of a Danish slipware plate that, as previously argued, dates the floor to the mid-16ᵗʰ century.

Cellar A503 contained only sherds from the fills of the buildings, not from actual use. These included a rich selection of black pots of several types (early type and Vorup type), local slipware plates and Low Countries/German whitewares, Post-Medieval redware tripod pipkins, an apothecary jug, two tankards and one

Figure 97. *Andenne-type ware found at Bispetorv (FHM 5124 x520). Photo: Moesgaard Museum.*

barrel of Raeren-type stoneware, a Siegburg stoneware jug and at least one jug in Baltic burnished greyware. The vessels represented include four tankards, one of them manufactured by the Rhenish master Jan Beldam in c. 1620. Display vessels include another Raeren-type stoneware jug with relief decoration of Justitia, dated 1583 (figure 100). Fragments of a jug bearing the coat of arms of Julich-Kleve-Berg also belong to this phase, as does a Low Countries redware strainer: Low Countries redware is rather rare in Aarhus, but does occasionally occur. A sherd of a so-called "Malling jug", a tankard in Low Countries tin-glazed ware, is

Figure 98. Low-fired Greyware pot (FHM nr. 8151). Photo: Moesgaard Photo/Medielab.

Figure 99. Complete Medieval Redware jug discovered in the sea off Endelave near Horsens (FHM 1621A). Photo: Moesgaard Photo/Medialab.

Figure 100. *Clockwise from top left, Westerwald stoneware, Raeren stoneware mug/tankard with princes, Raeren jug with Justitia, Siegburg tankard from the workshop of Hans Hilgers, Raeren jug with coat-of-arms and whiteware bowl (FHM 5124 x559; x3203; x558; x986; x972; x1101). Photo: Moesgaard Photo/Medialab.*

the only sherd of its kind in Aarhus (figure 104). It was found in fill that was disturbed during demolitions in the early 20th century, but there is no doubt that it originally belonged to the 16th century phase on the site.[140] If we look at the total picture, there is about 10% imported ceramics in the later phases. The

imports in the later contexts are varied with a wide range of provenances: Rouen-type ware jugs and jugs of Siegburg stoneware, Raeren-type stoneware, Frechen stoneware and burnished greyware jugs from the Baltic. A small element of Low Countries redware is also present: a chafing dish. In the 16th century con-

Figure 101. Stoneware tankard with the arms of Jülich-Kleve-Berg. Produced in Siegburg 1572. Height 25 cm. British Museum inv. 1855,1201.175© The Trustees of the British Museum.

Figure 103. Silver-mounted tin-glazed jug, socalled Malling jug produced in Antwerp c. 1550. Height 15.5 cm. British Museum inv. AF3137© The Trustees of the British Museum.

Figure 102. Tin-glazed jug produced in Faenza in the late 15th century. Height 18 cm. British Museum inv. 1898, 1019.© The Trustees of the British Museum.

Figure 104. Clockwise from the left, Low Countries tin-glazed jug (Malling jug), Low Countries tin-glazed jug and Low Countries redware strainer from FHM 5124 Bispetov (FHM 5124 x442; x335; x1254). Photo: Moesgaard Photo/Medialab.

Figure 105. *Stoneware jug decorated with armorial medaillions. Produced in Raeren 1592. Height 18 cm. British Museum inv. 1855, 1201.188 © The Trustees of the British Museum.*

texts, the imports are similar: jugs of Raeren-type stoneware and Frechen stoneware, Low Countries/German whiteware plates and a jug in Low Countries tin-glazed ware. If we look at the material recovered from the houses as a whole, it is evident that Medieval well-fired redware is almost as common on the site as Medieval well-fired coarseware: The Chapter House presumably reflects the consumption of the clergy, and the ceramics from here include a wide variety of imports, mostly intended for use at the table as drinking or pouring vessels.

2.7 The rural sites

In order to be able to compare urban and rural consumption, a number of rural sites were chosen for analysis following the principles outlined in the previous chapter. Here the analysis was concentrated on larger excavations of settlements dated to between c. 1200 and 1800 with a reasonable number of artefacts, i.e. more than 100 sherds that can be linked to features such as cultural layers, floors, postholes, pits and wells. Three excavations of Medieval settlements with small numbers of artefacts: The Early Medieval settlement FHM 5177 Houvej in Voldby and the 13th century settlement FHM 4679 in Harlev have not been quantified, but are mentioned in the text where relevant, as are older collections and artefacts recovered during excavations of other features.

2.7.1 FHM 1978 Vilhelmsborg

Excavated 1978-79. Excavated area 500 m².
Sources: Excavation Report; Madsen 1991; Linaa 2006.

Vilhelmsborg is located south of Aarhus. The manor itself goes back to the middle of the 16th century, being owned by the noble families of Ulfeldt and later Friis. In 1673 Vilhelmsborg was given to the Güldenkrone family, who owned the manor until 1923. The present manor house was constructed in 1842-43 on the site of an earlier manor house of unknown construction date. However, an inventory from the year of the sale in 1673 shows this to have been a large timber-framed house with two adjoining wings, one to the north and one to the south. This manor house was demolished prior to 1817, perhaps shortly after 1780, when the owners moved their residence further north to Moesgaard manor. During the excavation, cellars and sills were encountered and the cultural layers and the fill in the cellar contained a large number of finds. An overview of the material is given in table 20.

Of primary importance for this work are the ceramics contents of a refuse pits, pit V, and the fill in the cellar, T, which must have been discarded immediately after the abandonment of the house. Pit V, a refuse pit, was stratigraphically linked to the earlier occupation phase. The pit contained 560 potsherds, the majority of which are Post-Medieval redware tripod pipkins (76%) and Vorup-type blackware cauldrons (23%) with a few sherds of Westerwald stoneware mugs and jugs. The Post-Medieval redware consists of a majority of tripod pipkins (rim types 1002, 2007, 1009, 1010) and a few fragments of redware plates (rim types 1024, 1025, 1026, 1031). The blackware is of Vorup type and consists of large cauldrons, 24-28 cm in diameter (rim type 501) (figure 107-109). The pit contained no coins, but a few stems of clay pipes were found, dating it securely to after 1600. The fill in cellar T had a very different composition. The date of deposition must be prior to 1817, by which time we know the manor house had been demolished, and probably after 1780. The fill contained 563 potsherds. The blackware is all large cauldrons of Vorup type with tall rims (rim type 504) The dominant type is slipware pipkins with the same rim type as the comparative phase in FHM 4201 Skt. Clemensborg (rim type 1108), decorated with waves on the rim and/or stripes, dots or spirals on the body. Slipware plates with dots or spirals on the rims are rather common. The Post-Medieval redware tripod pipkins display elongated bodies and rather narrow rims (rim types 1007, 1009, 1020) Their handles are trumpet-shaped. The Low Countries/German Post-Medieval whitewares are yellow- or copper-green glazed, and the functional types are cooking pots, plates and saucers.

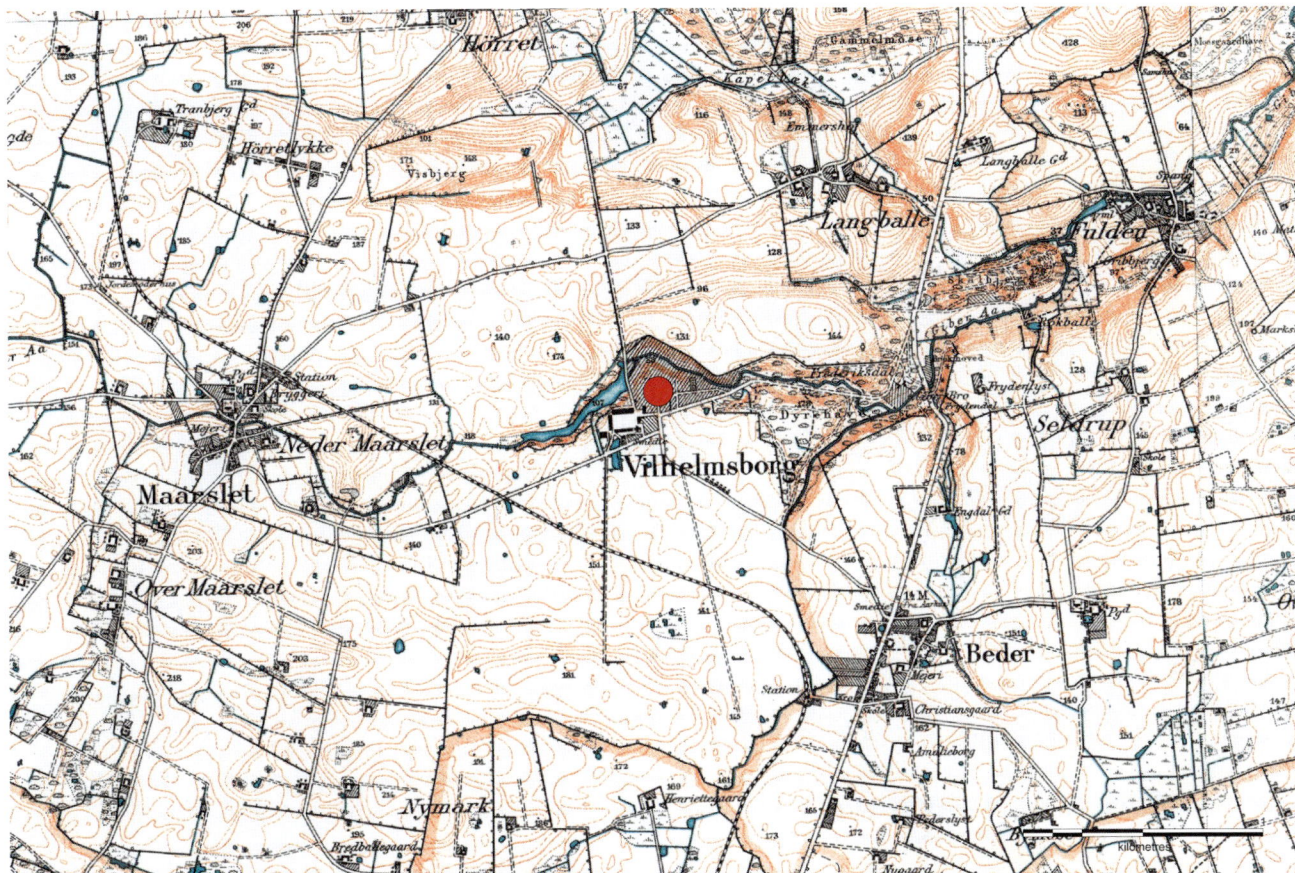

Figure 106. Location of the site FHM 1978 Vilhelmsborg.

A plate is dated 1764. The stoneware is of Cologne type, used for water bottles with a maker's mark, all of it utilitarian (figure 111). A capuchin-ware porcelain plate was found in the cellar (figure 113).

In the assemblage from the cellar is a range of rather unusual faiences: mainly octagonal plates that were produced at a factory in Store Kongensgade, Copenhagen, where production started in 1722 (figure 114). Porcelain is represented by cups of so-called capuchin ware with a brown exterior and blue-white interior. A collection of industrial ceramics from Staffordshire, England, all salt-glazed and probably datable to the late 18th century, is a very unusual component of the cellar finds (figure 112).[141]

FHM 1978 Vilhelmsborg	
Sum of sherd count	
Ware types	**Total**
Black pot, Varde type	121
Black pot, Vorup type	76
Cologne stoneware	151
Danish slipware	10
Industrial ware	6
Porcelain	22
Post-Medieval redware	295
Post-Medieval redware with slip decoration	463
Tin-glazed ware	95
Westerwald stoneware	4
Total	**1243**

Table 20. FHM 1978 Vilhelmsborg. Ware types and number of sherds in stratigraphic phases.

Figure 107. *Ceramics from Vilhelmsborg, 17ᵗʰ century. Post-Medieval well-fired redware and black pots of Varde type (FHM1978 xV). Photo: Moesgaard Photo/Medialab.*

Figure 108 Post-medieval well-fired redware plate with incised
decoration from Vilhelmsborg, 17th century (FHM 1978xV).
Photo: Moesgaard Photo/Medielab.

Figure 109. Black pot cauldron of Vorup-type, 17th century. Notice the
incised decoration (FHM 1978xV). Photo: Moesgaard Photo/Medielab.

Figure 110. Ceramics from
Vilhelmsborg, late 18th century.
Slip-decorated pots and black pot
of Vorup type (FHM 1978 xT).
Photo: Moesgaard Photo/Medialab.

111

Figure 111. Late 18th century Cologne stoneware bottles found at FHM 1978 Vilhelmsborg (1978xT). Photo: Moesgaard Photo/Medialab.

Figure 112. Lid from butter-dish in salt-glazed stoneware produced in Staffordshire c. 1765, found at FHM 1978 Vilhelmsborg (FHM1978xT). Photo: Moesgaard Photo/Medielab.

Figure 113. Capuchin ware (porcelain) plate found at FHM 1978 Vilhelmsborg (FHM1978xT). Photo: Moesgaard Photo/Medielab.

Figure 114. Late 18th century faiances ound at FHM 1978 Vilhelmsborg, manufactured in Store Kongensgade in Copenhagen. (1978xT). Photo: Moesgaard Photo/Medialab.

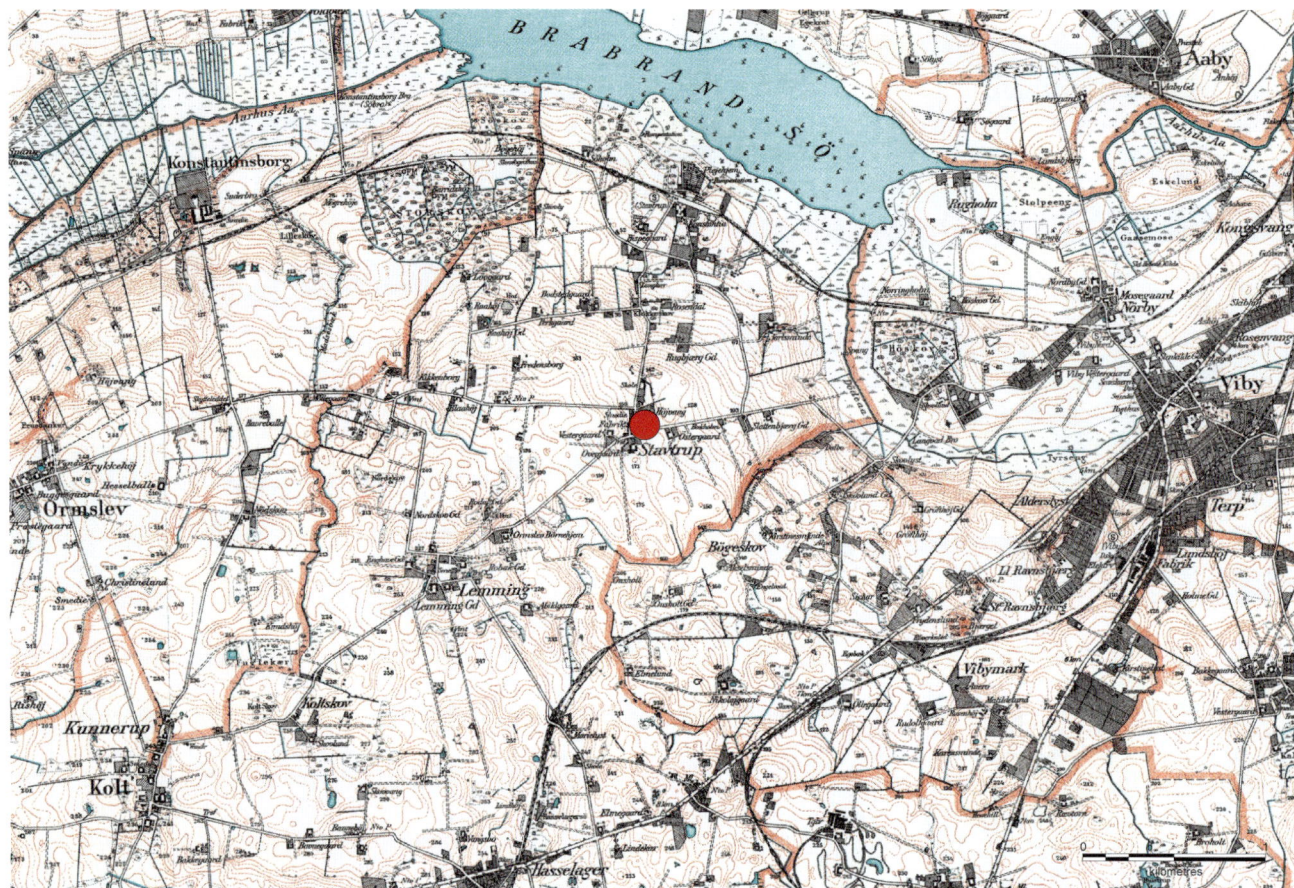

Figure 115. *Location of the site FHM 3474 Stavtrup.*

2.7.2 FHM 3474 Stavtrup

Excavated 1992. Excavated area 380 m².
Sources: Excavation report.

The site of FHM 3474 Stavtrup was excavated in 1992. It lies just northeast of the present-day village of Stavtrup, immediately south of the lake Brabrand Sø. The area is hilly and was probably forested in the Viking Age and Early Middle Ages, as place names with references to woods are frequent in the area (see the chapter: Landscape). The excavation revealed traces of what must have been a Medieval settlement with a house, pits and an associated well (phase 1)

The cultural layers from the settlement were not well-preserved, but remains of a post-built house

(house P), measuring 15 x 5 m, were recorded (figure 116). The ceramics were recovered from the house's postholes, a number of pits, the remains of cultural layers and the destruction layer and from the nearby well. The well was dendrochronologically dated to 1321, thereby providing a date for the construction of this short-lived settlement. Scattered remains of a significantly later settlement were also found, including a possible cellar and a few postholes (phase 2). Due to the limited size of the excavation, it is likely that further remains of the latter settlement are to be found outside the excavated area. No dendrochronological dates or dates of other kinds can be linked to this phase.

The assemblage from FHM 3474 Stavtrup is predominantly Medieval.

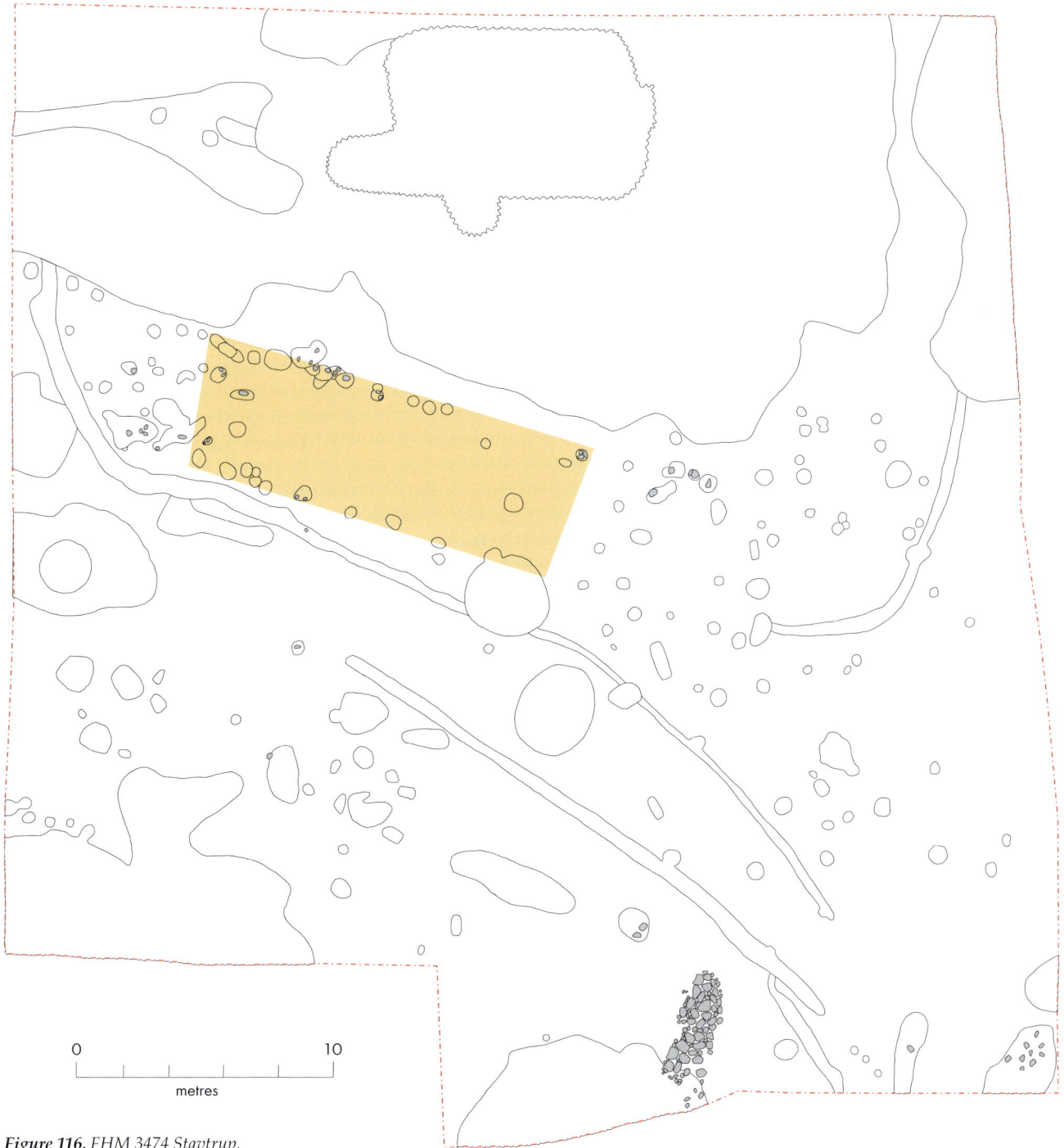

Figure 116. FHM 3474 Stavtrup.

No Medieval imports were, however, identified and 80% of the Medieval material is coarseware. The ceramics from the earlier settlement phase consist largely of Medieval well-fired coarseware cooking pots (rim types 606 and 608).

FHM 3474 Stavtrup					
Sum of sherd counts					
Ware types	**Phase 1**	**Phase 2**	**Phase 3**	**No Phase**	**Total**
Baltic blackware	1		2	17	20
Black pot, Vorup type		108	42		150
Industrial ware			10		10
Medieval well-fired coarseware	161	9	18		188
Medieval well-fired redware	15		5		20
Other blackware	1		3		4
Post-Medieval well-fired redware		28	18		46
Post-Medieval well-fired redware with slip decoration		4	1		5
Raeren stoneware			1		1
Total	**178**	**149**	**100**	**17**	**444**

Table 21. *FHM 3474 Stavtrup. Ware types and number of sherds in stratigraphic phases.*

Figure 117. *Greyware and misfired glazed redware jugs found in well dated to 1321 at FHM 3474 Stavtrup (FHM 3473 xBG) Photo: Moesgaard Photo/Medialab.*

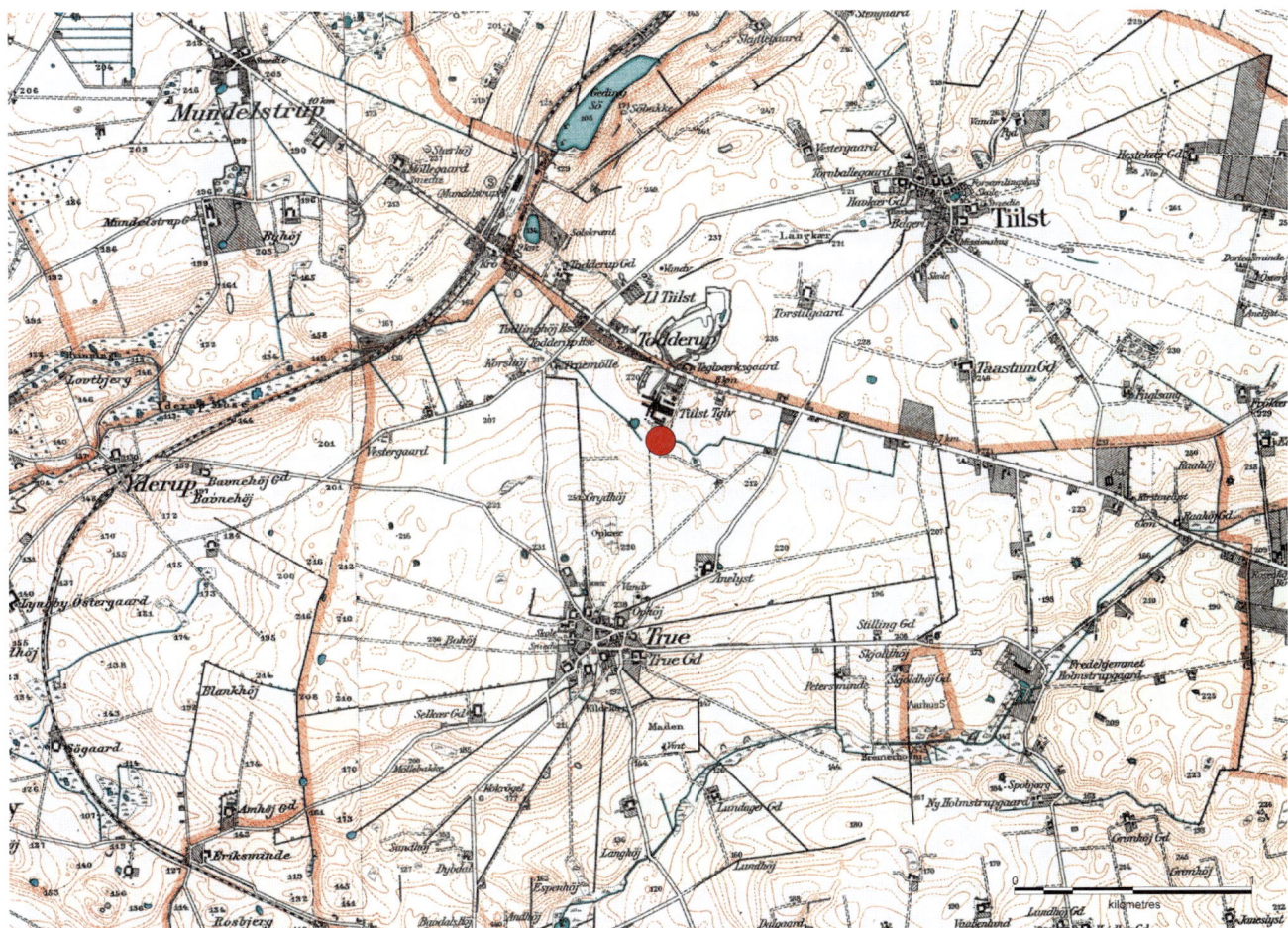

Figure 118. Location of the site FHM 3731 Todderup.

The two almost complete jugs from the dendrochronologically-dated well are the most interesting finds (figure 117): One is a Medieval well-fired coarseware jug, which is 27 cm tall with a strap-shaped handle and a flat base. It is decorated with a double row of incised dots. This jug is completely handmade, not wheel-thrown. The Medieval well-fired redware jug is wheel-thrown and has a patchy red glaze. The handle is strap-shaped with three furrows. As the well was dendrochronologically dated to 1321, this gives a post quem date for the deposition of the jugs. The material from the later, less well-preserved settlement shows greater variation. The cellar was found to contain remains of local slipware plates, black pots (rim type 308) and Post-Medieval redware tripod pipkins and plates. The majority of the material consists of burnished cooking pots in local

blackware. Due to the location of the excavated area near to the village, it seems likely that this cellar belonged to a farm situated to the south.

2.7.3 FHM 3731 Todderup

Excavated 1991. Excavated 500 m².
Sources: Excavation Report; Hoff 1991; Jeppesen 1992; Hoff & Jeppesen 1992.

The abandoned village of Todderup, located about 7 km west of Aarhus, was excavated in 1991 by Moesgaard Museum. The area is wet and low-lying and the local place names indicate poor, stony soil. During the excavation, remains of two houses, a barn, two wells and a shallow ditch, probably marking a boundary

Figure 119. Plan of FHM 3731 Todderup.

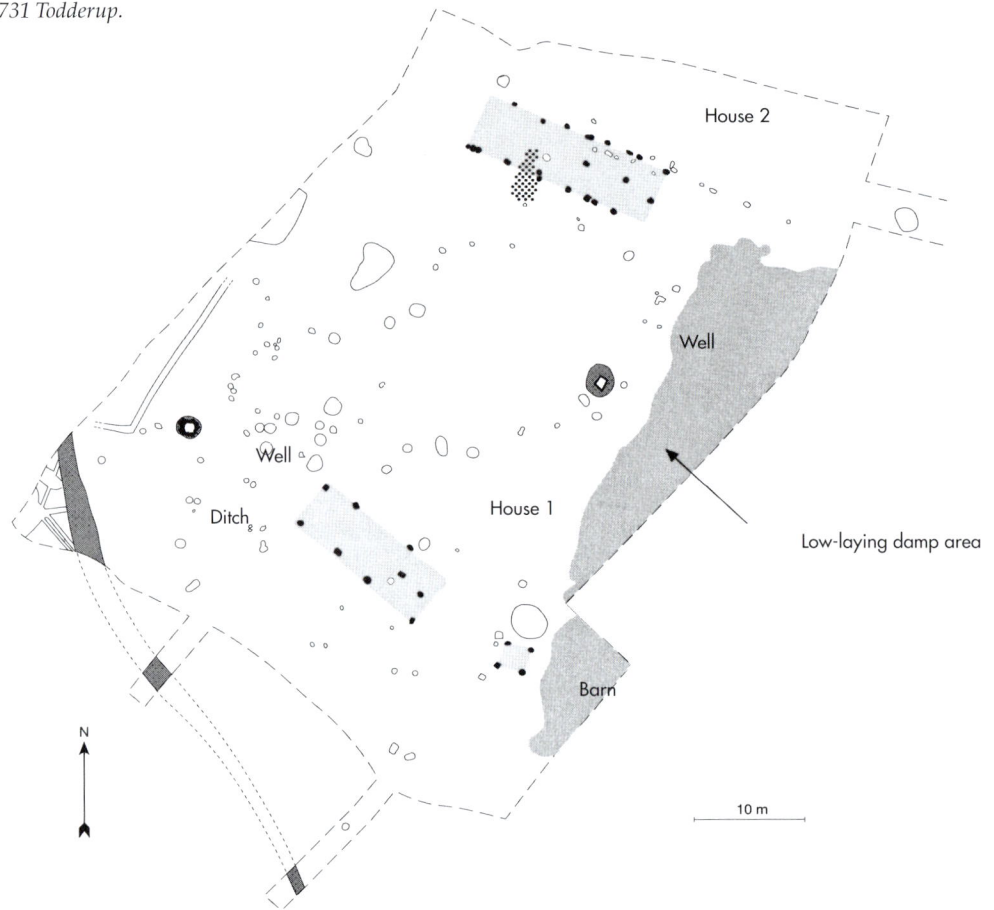

House 2

Well

Low-laying damp area

Well

Ditch

House 1

Barn

N

10 m

Figure 120. Greyware bowl and pot found in well at FHM 3731 Todderup, abandoned in 1313 (FHM 3731 x6). Photo: Moesgaard Photo/ Medialab.

between settlement and fields, were found (figure 119). The area was naturally delimited by low-lying, damp areas to the south, east and west, and no further settlement traces were found, showing that Todderup was a very small hamlet of only one, perhaps two farms. The settlement had two phases: One house had burnt down and the excavators concluded that another building, further to the north, was constructed as a replacement.[142]

Two wells were excavated, one was dendrochronologically dated to 1230, giving a post quem date for the settlement. This well belongs to the earliest settlement phase and the farm may have functioned for some time after this date. As the farm(s) and the finds have been published previously, the material will only be summarised here.

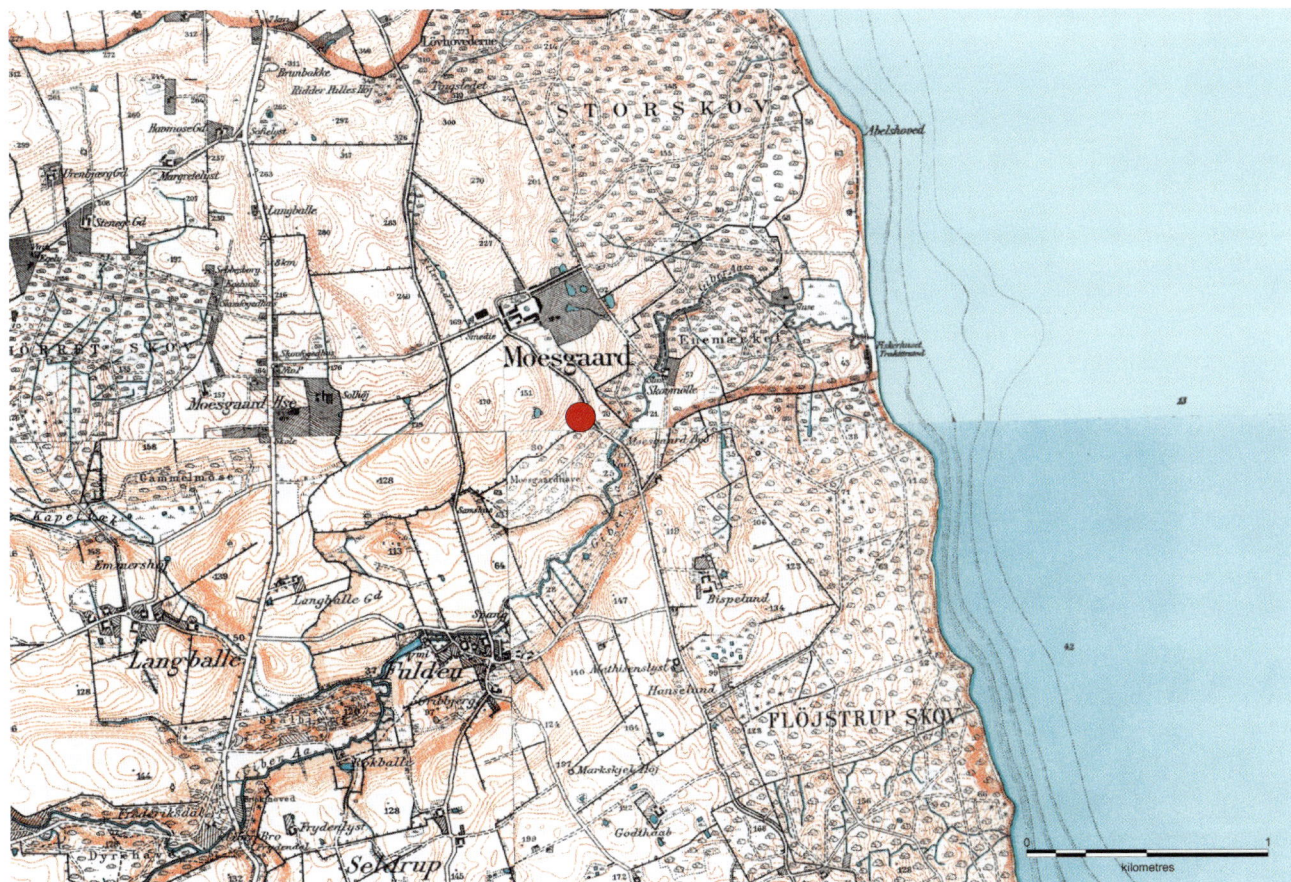

Figure 121. Location of the site FHM 4074 Gammel Moesgaard.

The ceramics material relating to the settlement was very limited: only 60 potsherds with a weight of 778 g. The remaining finds are bricks, fragments of iron, horse shoes and a spindle whorl. Most of the ceramics, 56 sherds, are Medieval well-fired coarseware, with only 5% Medieval well-fired redware. The material was found in the well (A8), the houses (A4, A11, A13, A15, A17, A26), the pits (A3, A7, A30), the cultural layers (A1, A18) and the ditch (A29). The material derives from at least two Medieval well-fired redware jugs, one with a dark green glaze and one red-glazed with black decoration. Medieval well-fired coarseware bowls (rim type 611) and cooking pots (rim types 601, 606, 608) dominate the material. The rather sparse assemblage probably reflects, in part, the spreading of waste from the farms on to the fields during the lifetime of the settlement, as well as post-depositional

processes associated with later agricultural activities on the site. Nevertheless, the stone well belonging to the later phase of the occupation contained remains of the red-glazed, dark-decorated jug as well as two cooking pots – objects that may have been thrown into the well as the settlement was abandoned prior to 1313. No traces of imports were evident in the assemblage.

2.7.4 FHM 4074 Gammel Moesgaard

Excavated 1989-99. Excavated area 175 m^2.
Sources: Excavation Report; Ceramics report by Jette Linaa 1999; Skriver 2001 pp. 11-15.

Gammel Moesgaard was excavated in 1998-99.[143] The site is situated in the coastal zone about 15 km

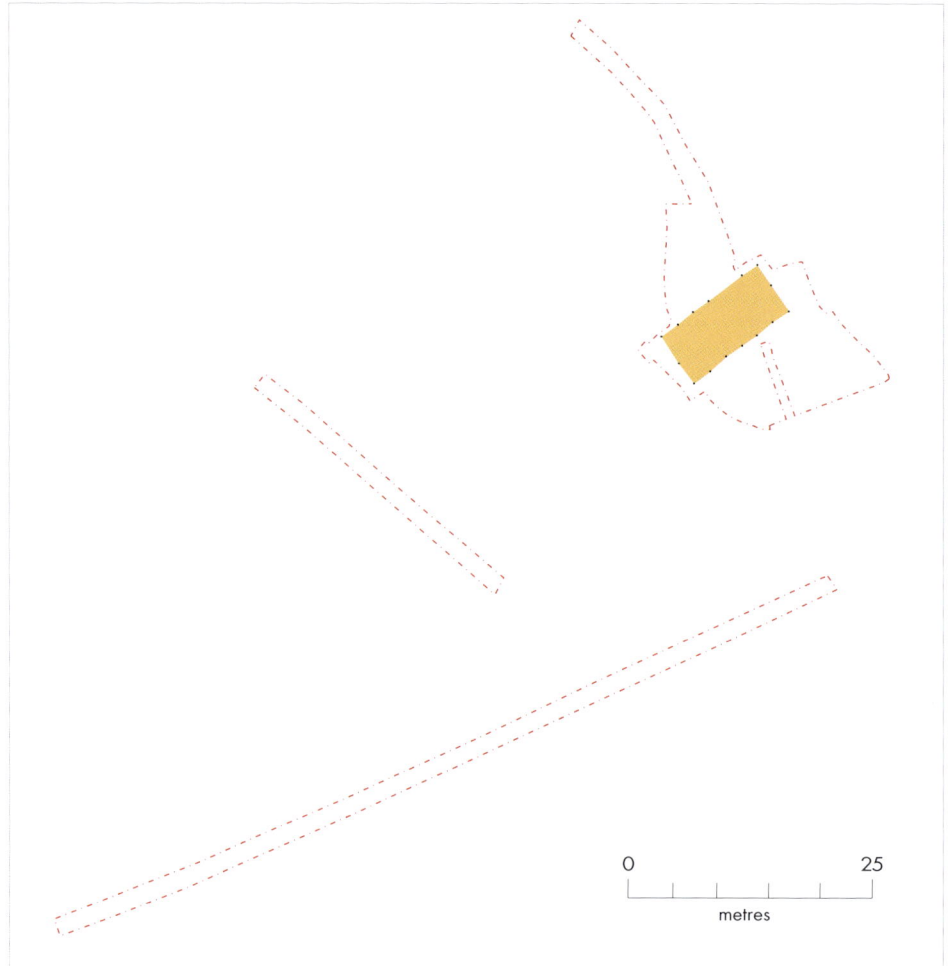

Figure 122. Plan of FHM 4074 Gammel Moesgaard.

0   25

metres

south of present-day Aarhus. The area is densely forested and the site lies on a hill, surrounded by wet, boggy areas. A field name of Gammel Moesgaard (Old Moesgaard), mentioned in 1783, indicates that the structures investigated represent a precursor of the present-day Moesgaard manor. During the excavation in 1999, a building measuring 12 x 6 m was uncovered (figure 122).

Its wall posts were rammed as much as 2 m into the subsoil, indicating a building with several storeys. The posts were dendrochronologically dated to the winter of 1395/96, thereby dating this house and giving a post quem date for the deposition of the ceramics material.

Only pits and postholes were found, as all remains above subsoil level were disturbed, probably due to clearance of the area in 1840, when a large number of boulders were removed. It therefore seems likely that several other buildings of later date were destroyed at this time, if not before, and that these must be seen in relation to the Post-Medieval material recovered from the site. Of the total ceramics assemblage, only material from the pits and cultural layers associated with the dendrochronologically-dated post-built house has been included in this investigation (table 22).

The assemblage includes imports: a Raeren-type stoneware jug and Rouen-type ware jugs. Most of the

120

FHM 4074 Gammel Moesgaard				
Sum of sherd count				
Ware types	Phase 1	Phase 2	Phase 5	Total
Medieval well-fired coarseware	424			424
Medieval well-fired redware	168	8		176
Other blackware		6		6
Other whiteware		17		17
Post-Medieval well-fired redware	1	129		130
Post-Medieval well-fired redware with slip decoration		7		7
Raeren stoneware	3		1	4
Rouen-type ware	1			1
Weser ware		1		1
Total	**597**	**168**	**1**	**766**

Table 22. FHM 4074 Gammel Moesgaard. Ware types and number of sherds in stratigraphic phases.

material is Medieval well-fired coarseware: cooking pots and bowls (rim types 608, 606, 605 and 611) and Medieval well-fired redware jugs and bowls. Some of the jugs are decorated with very small applied motifs and others show streaks of black paint beneath a thin green glaze (figure 124). It is worth noting that the proportion of Medieval well-fired redware vessels (36%) is greater here than at the other rural sites, and that the assemblage is also much larger, partly due to the preservation of cultural layers at this site. Numerous metal finds were recovered by metal detector both prior to and during the excavation. These include a number of horseshoes of Medieval types, other horse equipment (harness components), fragments of chain mail, a strap fitting shaped like a shield and seven coins of civil war type. The Post-Medieval material was primarily found in contexts that were disturbed during clearance of the site in the 19th century, thereby demonstrating that it was occupied over a longer time span.

Figure 123. Timber post from FHM 4074 Gammel Moesgaard. Photo Hans Skov/Moesgaard Museum.

Figure 124. Glazed redware jug from Gammel Moesgaard, deposited after 1397 (FHM 3474 xDZ). Photo: Moesgaard Photo/Medialab.

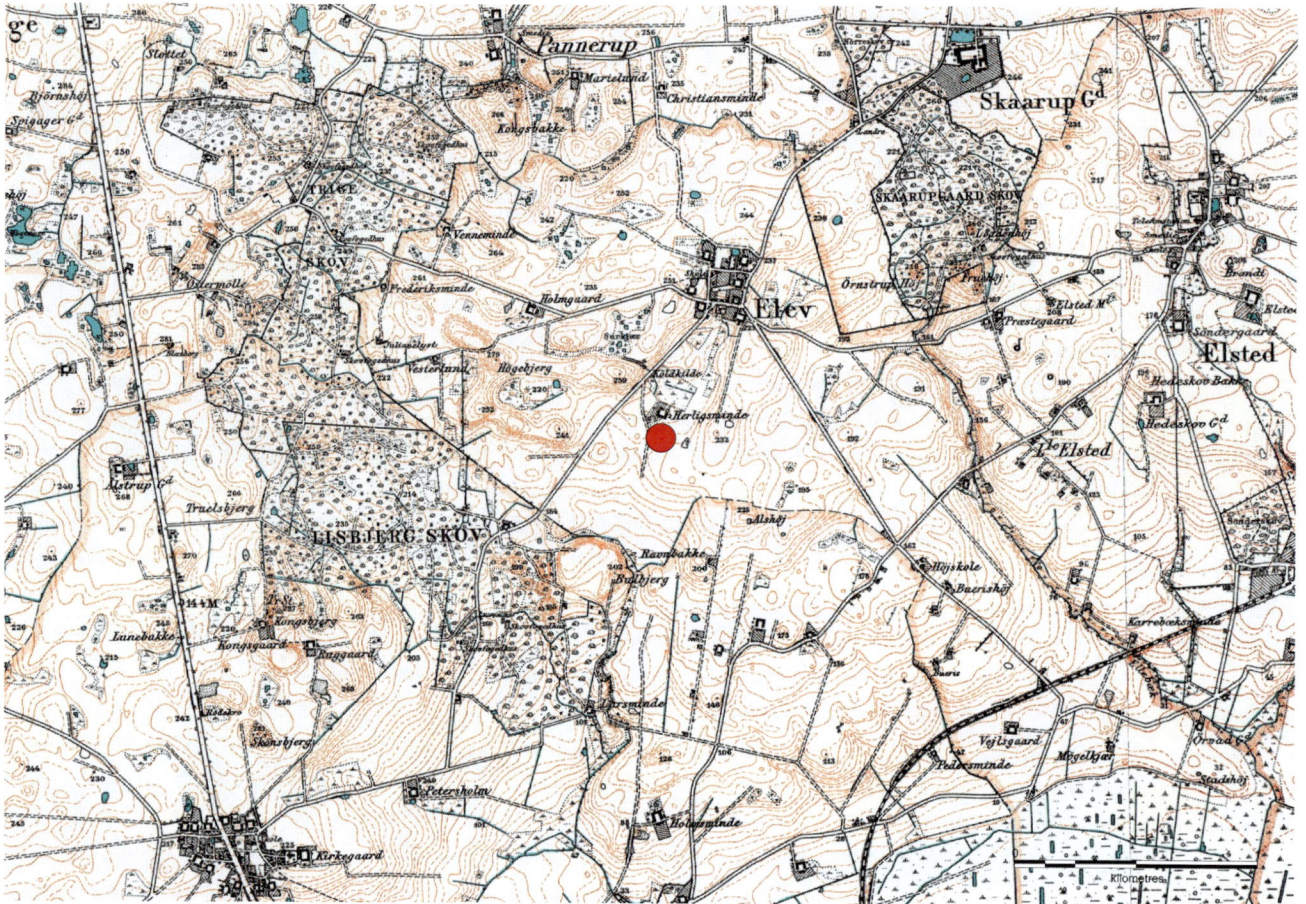

Figure 125. Location of the site FHM 4730 Elev.

2.7.5 FHM 4730 Elev

Excavated 2003. Excavated area 6000 m².
Sources: Excavation Report.

The site FHM 4730 Elev was excavated in 2003.[144] It is situated outside the present-day village of Elev, in a hilly area with wetlands to the north of Aarhus, about 3 km from the coast. The area is still forested today. The main features uncovered in the excavation were the remains of Iron Age and Viking Age settlements, but traces of a Medieval settlement were found too. The latter is as yet undated by coins or dendrochronology. No cultural layers were preserved, but the remains of a post-built house with a low cellar (EQ) were excavated (figure 126). The cellar measured 5.5 x 5 m and extended 70 cm into the subsoil. In the Aarhus area, Late Medieval and Post-Medieval rural buildings rest on sill stones and are very prone to destruction as a consequence of long-term agriculture. A somewhat unusual piece of jewellery – a gilt bird – was found in the cellar (figure 127).

The cellar contained a small quantity of ceramics (125 sherds) totally dominated by Medieval well-fired coarse-ware (119 sherds) with a few sherds of Medieval well-fired redware jugs and tripods. The glazed jug was misfired, with damaged glaze. The Medieval well-fired coarseware cooking pots (rim type 620), bowls (rim type 611) and jugs were of exactly the same type as the sherds from FHM 3437 Stavtrup.

122

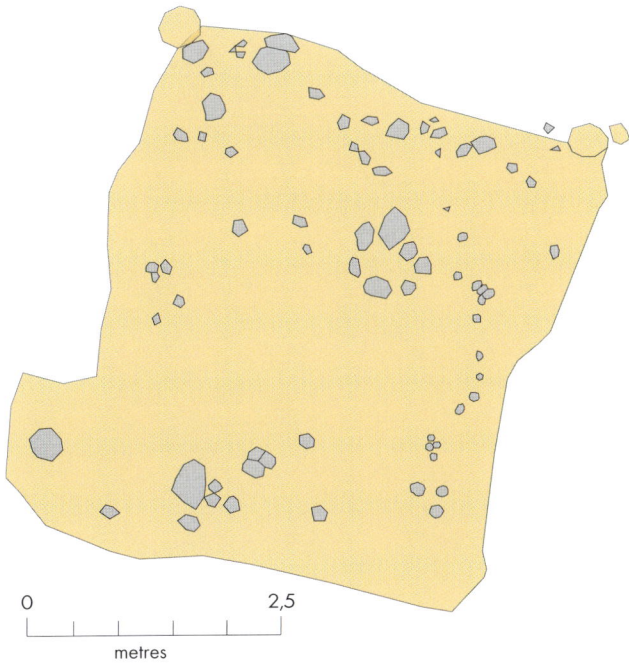

Figure 126. *Plan of FHM 4730 Elev.*

0   2,5

metres

Figure 137. *Gilt bronze ornament found at FHM 4730 Elev (FHM 4738 x48) Photo: Moesgaard Museum.*

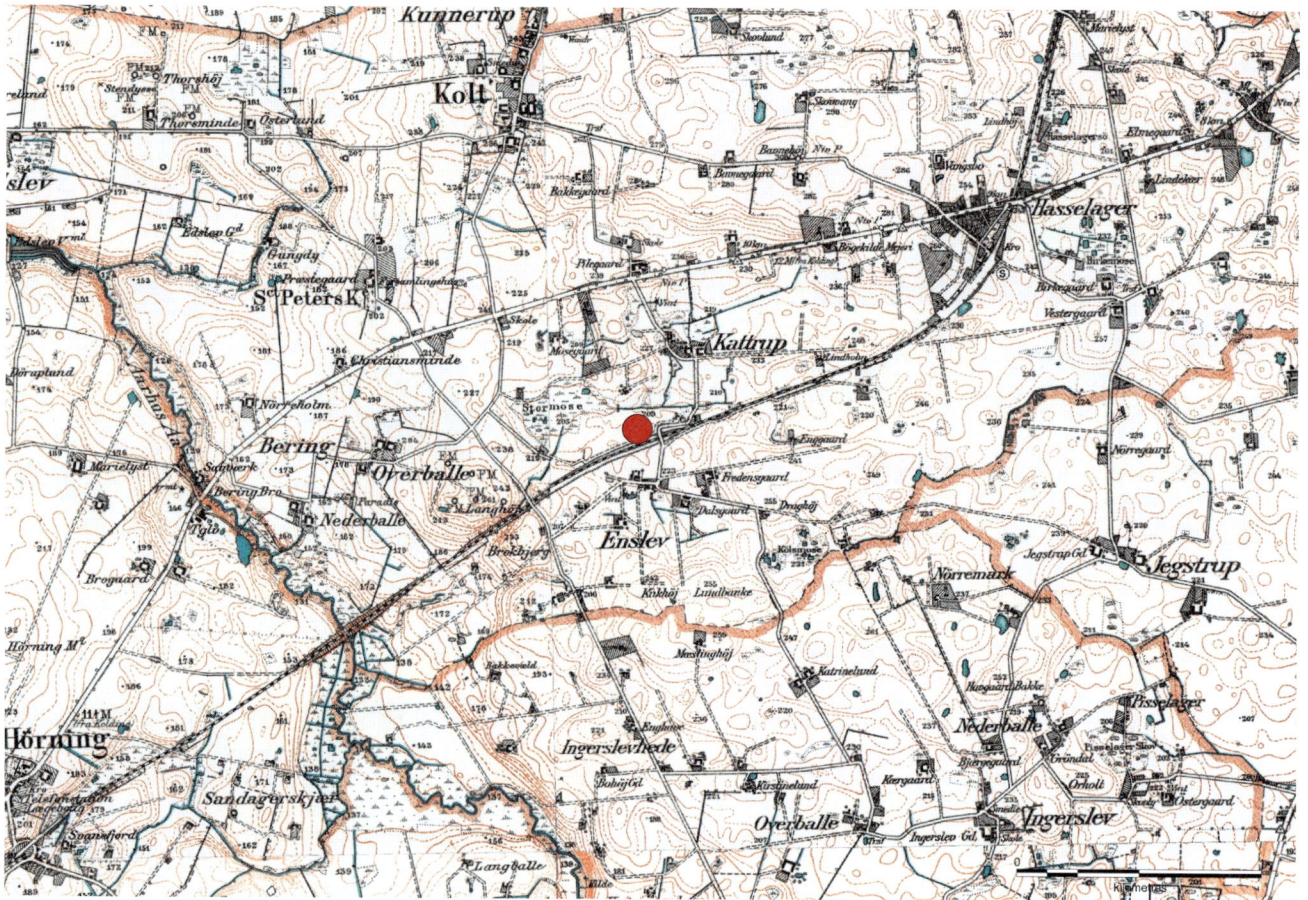

Figure 128. Location of the site FHM 4999 Kattrup.

2.7.6 FHM 4999 Kattrup

Excavated 2011. Excavated area: 2500 m².
Sources: Excavation report.

The site of FHM 4999 Kattrup was excavated in 2011.[145] The area, south of Aarhus, is hilly with many small lakes and wetlands – a typical expansion area. Two farmsteads were excavated, one with a large main dwelling house (A1250) and an adjoining building or outhouse (A1251), the other with the remains of two buildings (A1252 and A1253) (figure 129).

No cultural layers were preserved and the majority of the material was found during excavation of the main dwelling house (A1250), which was quite large,

measuring 18 x 6 m. The house did not rest on a sill, but was constructed with wall posts and internal roof-bearing posts; its construction was very sturdy with deep postholes. Most of the ceramics were found in these postholes (table 23).

The majority of the small ceramics assemblage (181 sherds) is Medieval in type, with some Medieval low-fired coarseware as well. The latter was found in separate pits and may represent traces of other, less well-preserved, settlement phases. The ceramics from this farm comprise Medieval well-fired coarseware cooking pots and jugs – the majority with burnishing, as well as cooking pots in later lead-glazed ware and a jug in Medieval well-fired redware. The greyware is varied, with several varieties of Medieval well-fired

124

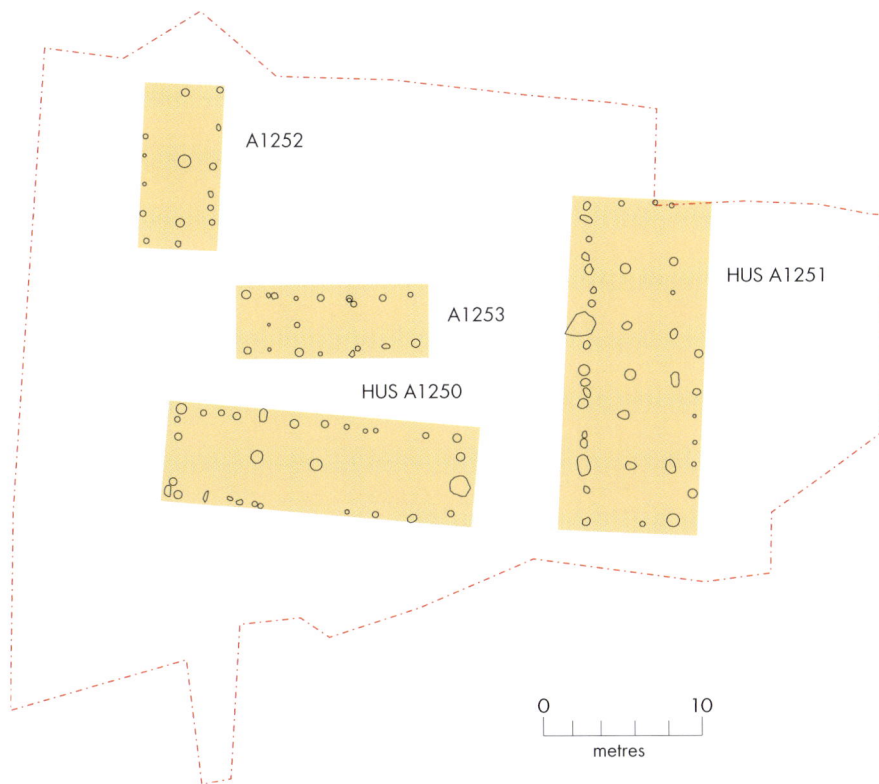

Figure 129. Plan of FHM 4999 Kattrup.

FHM 4999 Kattrup	
Sum of sherd counts	
Ware types	**Total**
Medieval low-fired coarseware	89
Medieval well-fired coarseware	82
Medieval well-fired redware	4
Post-Medieval well-fired redware	6
Total	**181**

Table 23. *FHM 4999 Kattrup. Ware types and number of sherds in stratigraphic phases.*

Figure 130. *FHM 4999 Kattrup during excavation.. Photo: Moesgaard Museum.*

coarseware represented, but the shapes are fairly uniform: shallow cooking pots/bowls (rim type 608) with a burnished rim and outer surfaces. A worn Medieval well-fired redware jug is the only example of this type, with red glaze and a red margin bordering a grey core. The handle is strap-shaped. The tripod pipkin in Post-Medieval redware, early type, is a type known from other sites, including the very well-dated FHM 4201 Skt. Clemensborg (rim type 1017). Medieval well-fired coarseware cooking pots with burnishing are also present. No dating evidence is available, apart from that provided by the ceramics.

Figure 131. *Location of the site FHM 5419 Damagervej 2.*

2.7.7 FHM 5419 Damagervej 2, Viby

Excavated 2013. Excavated area: 400 m².
Sources: Excavation report.

The site of FHM 5419 Damagervej 2, south of Aarhus, is in a former village, close to the oldest house in Viby, which was built in the 16th century. During the excavation, badly preserved remains of a Post-Medieval dwelling house, c. 15 x 7 m (A18, A32) were found (figure 132).

The house was built on a sill and only remains of floors, fireplaces, an oven and some pits were preserved.

The very small assemblage is shown in table 25.

The sherds that can be related to the house were found in remains of floors and in pits and postholes. The stratigraphically latest floor contained a clay pipe, which dates the demolition of the house to post-1600. The majority of the small assemblage comprises early blackware pots with low rims (308), combined with sherds of Post-Medieval redware, early type (rim type 1035). An outhouse or utility building contained mainly slipware plates and sherds of tripod pipkins (handle type 1045 and rouletted rim type 1013).

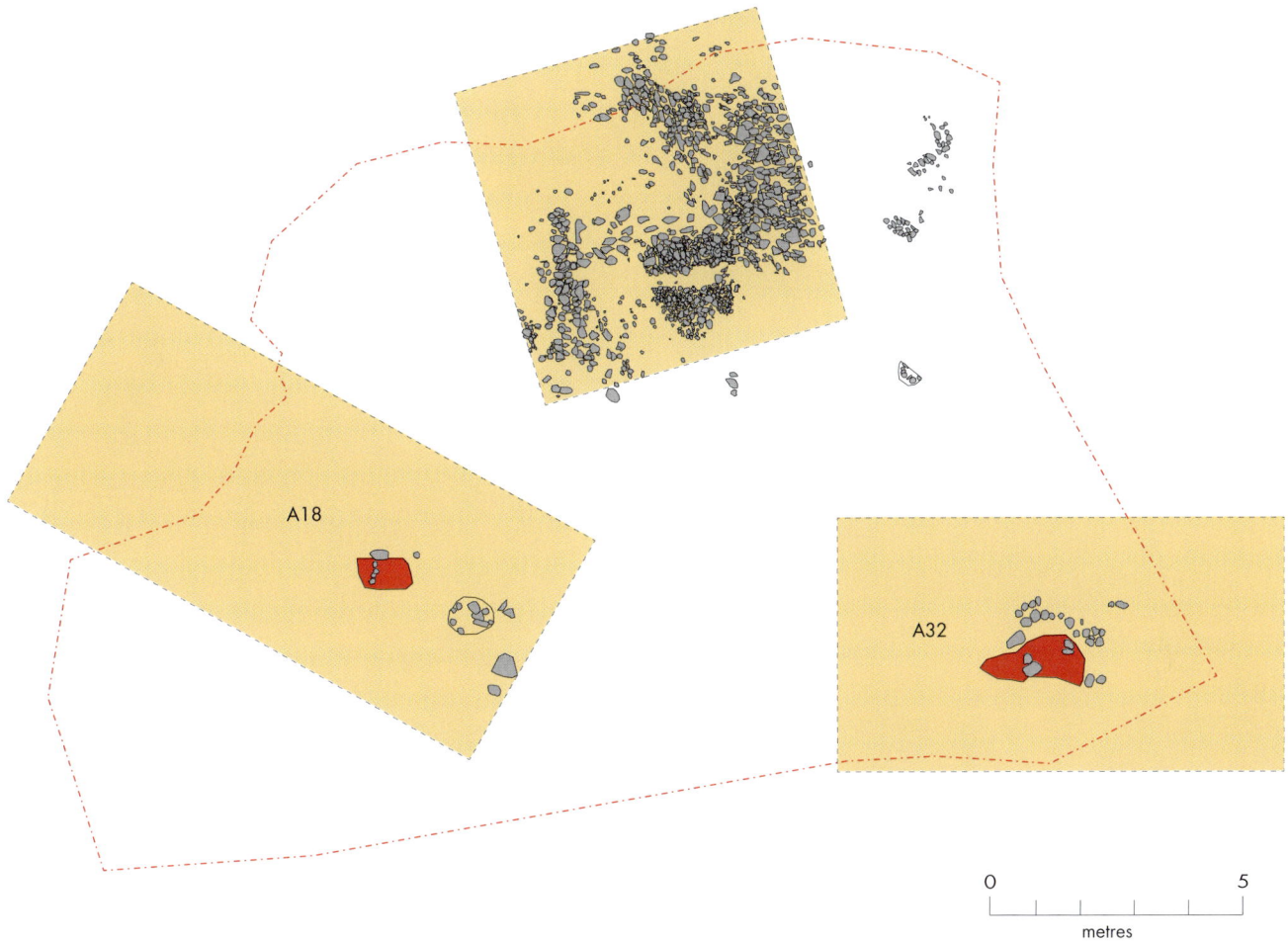

Figure 132. Plan of FHM 5419 Damagervej 2.

FHM 5419 Damagervej	
Sum of sherd counts	
Ware types	**Total**
Black pot, early type	83
Post-Medieval redware	26
Post-Medieval redware with slip decoration	22
Total	**131**

Table 24. FHM 5419 Damagervej. Ware types and number of sherds.

3 Phases

In the following chapter, a chronological analysis will be carried out on the basis of the material recovered during the various excavations.[146] In a later chapter, the results from this will be used to present an overview of the consumption in the urban landscape as a whole, relative to a series of urban (town) phases with contemporary material from several excavations; phases that will be established below. This project is based on a study of the material culture of several sites and this brings with it a special set of problems that must be solved in order for any analysis to be valid. The chronological sequencing of the sites is obviously of the utmost importance if comparative studies of consumption, or any other aspect of the sites, are be undertaken. The main question then is how to do this? Consumption analysis within the individual sites is relatively unproblematic as their stratigraphy has been analysed and a relative chronology of contexts defined through the excavation: A relative site chronology, indicating which contexts are relatively earlier or later than others, has been produced by the excavators as part of the archaeological excavation report. The relative chronology for the finds that results from this can be dated by various means, typically dendrochronological or radiocarbon dating, or sometimes using numismatic evidence or other means. Basing a study of consumption on a chronological framework of this kind is relatively unproblematic given that we are able to distinguish between those contexts that were formed through activities on the site, and therefore contain ceramics used there, and those representing levelling layers and the like, where the ceramics and other artefacts could have been deposited from elsewhere and are therefore irrelevant to consumption on this particular site. However, comparison of material from several or many sites is

rather more difficult. We not only have to establish a relative chronology for one site, but for many sites, and then place them in an overall chronological sequence. The most precise way of achieving this is to employ scientific dating throughout. But it is extremely rare that an entire site can be dated by such means: FHM 4201 Skt. Clemensborg is one of the few examples. The most typical situation for sites in Aarhus is that each of them has only one or a few scientific dates available for absolute dating of a stratigraphic sequence spanning centuries. In order to overcome this problem, we need a dating tool that covers a long period (i.e. spans centuries), is found everywhere and has a high resolution over time. The tool of this kind available in the study area is the ceramics record. However, a paradoxical situation then arises whereby ceramics constitute both the subject of the consumption studies and the provider of the dating framework for these studies. The chronological sequencing of the sites has had to be based on the ceramics because it is, unfortunately, very rare for all the phases of the sites in an investigation to be datable by way of dendrochronology, written sources or date-conferring artefacts other than ceramics. We therefore run the risk of basing a comparative study of consumption patterns on a chronology that is shaped by – consumption patterns. It was crucially important to ensure that the chronology was not based on material that would be targeted in the consumption studies, for example the presence of imported ceramics. This problem can be addressed in various ways depending on which tradition of ceramics study is followed.[147] In this case, the rims and handles of locally produced ceramics were chosen as the basis for the chronology, because these features can be assumed to show the greatest degree of variability over time and the lowest degree of consumer choice dependence, thereby resulting in the least possible bias in the result. The method selected here involved multivariate statistical analysis of the occurrence and frequency of rims and handles in local ware types (Medieval low-fired coarseware, Medieval well-fired coarseware, Medieval well-fired redware, Post-Medieval redware and black pots of all types) using a method first applied to Danish Medieval and Post-Medieval ceramics by the author in 2000. The basis for this particular use of the analysis has been dealt with at length previously and will only be summarised in the following:[148] The ceramics from primary and secondary deposits at the sites have been recorded with reference to ware type and rim and handle types, and all related to individual contexts and stratigraphic phases, as defined in the excavation report. The excavation sites had been divided into between one and 19 stratigraphic phases by the excavators as part of the excavation process, resulting in a grand total of 83 stratigraphic phases defined in this way. During the analysis undertaken here, a datasheet with the numbers of specific rim and handle types in each of the stratigraphic phases at the individual sites, e.g. 14 rim type 1001 from FHM 4225 Guldsmedgade stratigraphic phase 10, was fed into a statistical analysis program.[149] In order to facilitate the construction of an appropriate chronology, the rim and handle types of the aforementioned wares were recorded during the data-gathering process for the present study. There were c. 250 different types in c. 3000 contexts, and these had, in turn, been grouped together by the excavators of the individual sites into between one and 20 stratigraphic phases. The overall result was a data matrix containing 83 stratigraphic units in the horizontal rows and 50 form types (rims and handles in local ceramics types) in the vertical columns.

The analysis sorts both units (in this case the stratigraphic phases) and variables (in this case the rim and handle types) in such a way that units with a similar content of variables are grouped in clusters in a multidimensional grid. The advantage of the analysis is that the results are depicted in a visually clear way.

If the variables (here rim and handle types) and units (here stratigraphic phases) are depicted as a parabola, then there is a structure, i.e. a sequence, present in the material. This sequence can represent a number of things, like a geographical distribution or a chronology. It is worth stressing yet again that the sequencing here is based on rim and handle types on locally produced ceramics, found in contexts related to stratigraphic phases, that are a stratigraphically sequenced in the individual excavations as defined by the excavators. It is worth repeating that, while the form types of rims and handles were defined by me, the link between the sherds and the contexts, the definition of the contexts in which they were found, and the ordering of these contexts into stratigraphic units/phases, were all defined by the individual excavators in the site excavation reports, i.e. before I obtained access to the material and as such I have had absolutely no influence on this aspect. Returning to the analysis, whether or not the sequence actually does represent a chronology can then be tested by the ordering of the relative stratigraphic phases at the individual sites. If the chronology is reliable, then the order of the stratigraphic phases at each site as reflected in the analysis must follow this in reality: i.e. as established in the excavation. If the latest stratigraphic phases defined in the excavation comes out as being the earliest in the analysis, or if the order of the stratigraphic phases is random throughout the analysis, then the seriation that is produced by the analysis does not represent a true chronology, but something else. If, on the other hand, the stratigraphic phases from the individual excavations are plotted in correct stratigraphic order in the seriation, the resulting relative chronology can then be rendered absolute by way of the numismatically- or dendrochronologically-dated stratigraphic phases. The outcome is shown in figure 134.

The resulting sequence shows that the stratigraphic phases are plotted in order from right to left according to their relative age. For example, FHM 4616 Telefontorvet phase 1 is stratigraphically earlier than phase 2 in the same excavation and we can see how phase 2 is,

Objects and variables on the 1st and 2nd principal axes

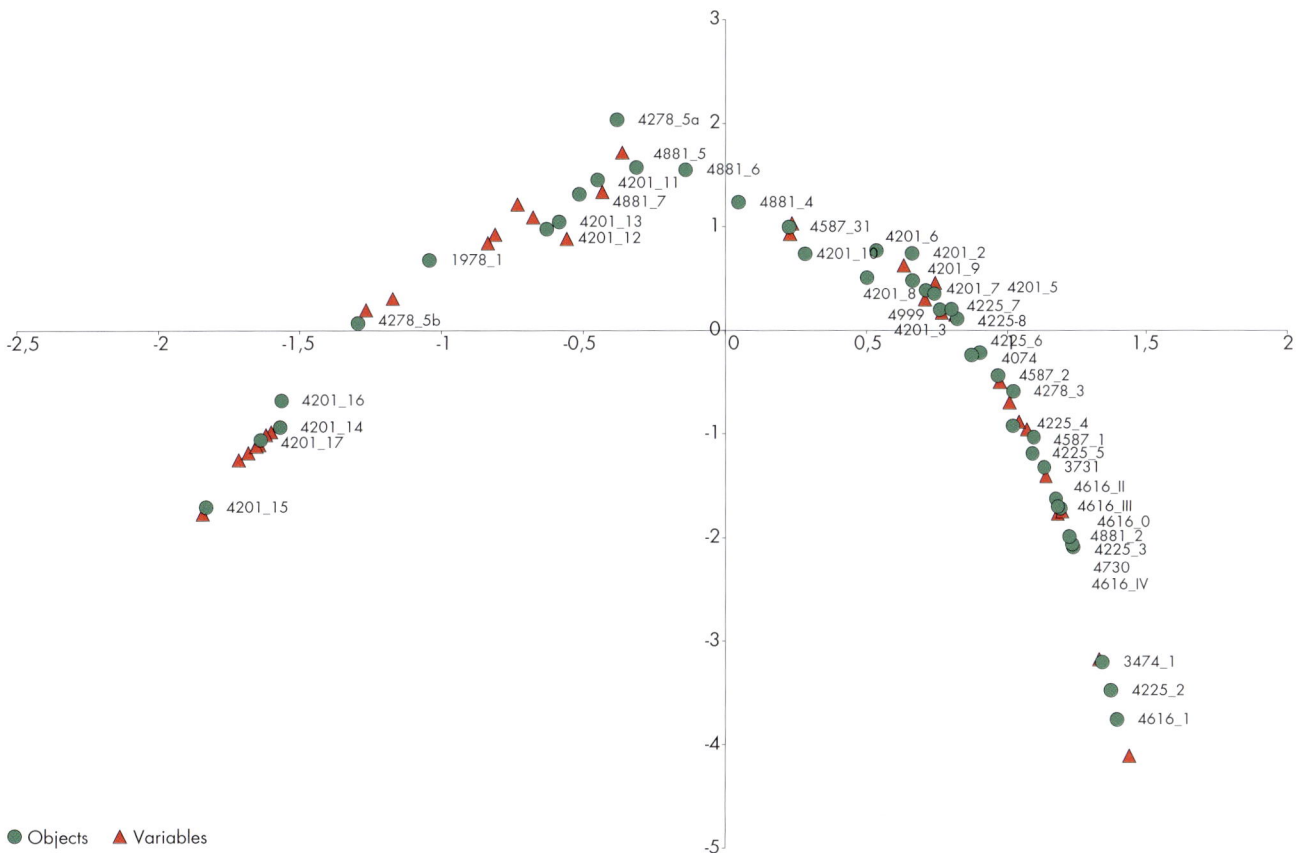

Figure 134. Correspondence analysis of rim and handle types in local wares: 39 rim and handle types in 42 stratigraphic phases. Note how the stratigraphic phases are sequenced in correct stratigraphic order from earliest on the right to latest on the left, as demonstrated by the ordering of for example FHM 4616 Telefontorvet phases 1-2, FHM 4225 Guldsmedgade phases 2-11 and FHM 4201 Skt. Clemensborg phases 2-17 and FHM 4587 Mejlgade 26 phases 1-5.

correctly, plotted after phase 1 in the sequence. The same is true for a number of the other stratigraphically sequenced excavations, where the stratigraphical phases are plotted in correct order in the seriation. For example, FHM 4587 Mejlgade 26 phases 1-3 and FHM 4278 Rosensgade phases 3 and 5. It appears that the analysis has established a seriation, which seems to be a relative chronology for the stratigraphic phases at all the excavation sites. Or, in other words, the analysis has established an ordering of rims and handles on local wares that seems to concur with the stratigraphic evidence and thereby appears to be a chronology. This relative chronology can then be rendered absolute because 32 of the stratigraphic phases have numismatic dating

evidence or dendrochronological dates. But it is worth noticing that the stratigraphic units represent a time span, no matter how short, and that the vessels have had a life span too that could vary between ware types, just like some rim types, for example in blackwares, have a tendency to be used over a longer time span than others. Attaching the dating evidence from both coins and dendrochronological analyses is no easy task. Coins have a period of circulation, just as ceramics have a temporal use span, and the link between objects, fills and the feature that has been dendrochronologically dated is not always straightforward.[150] However, these obstacles apply to any artefact study, and if we put them aside for now and plot in the absolute dates for

Objects and variables on the 1ˢᵗ and 2ⁿᵈ principal axes

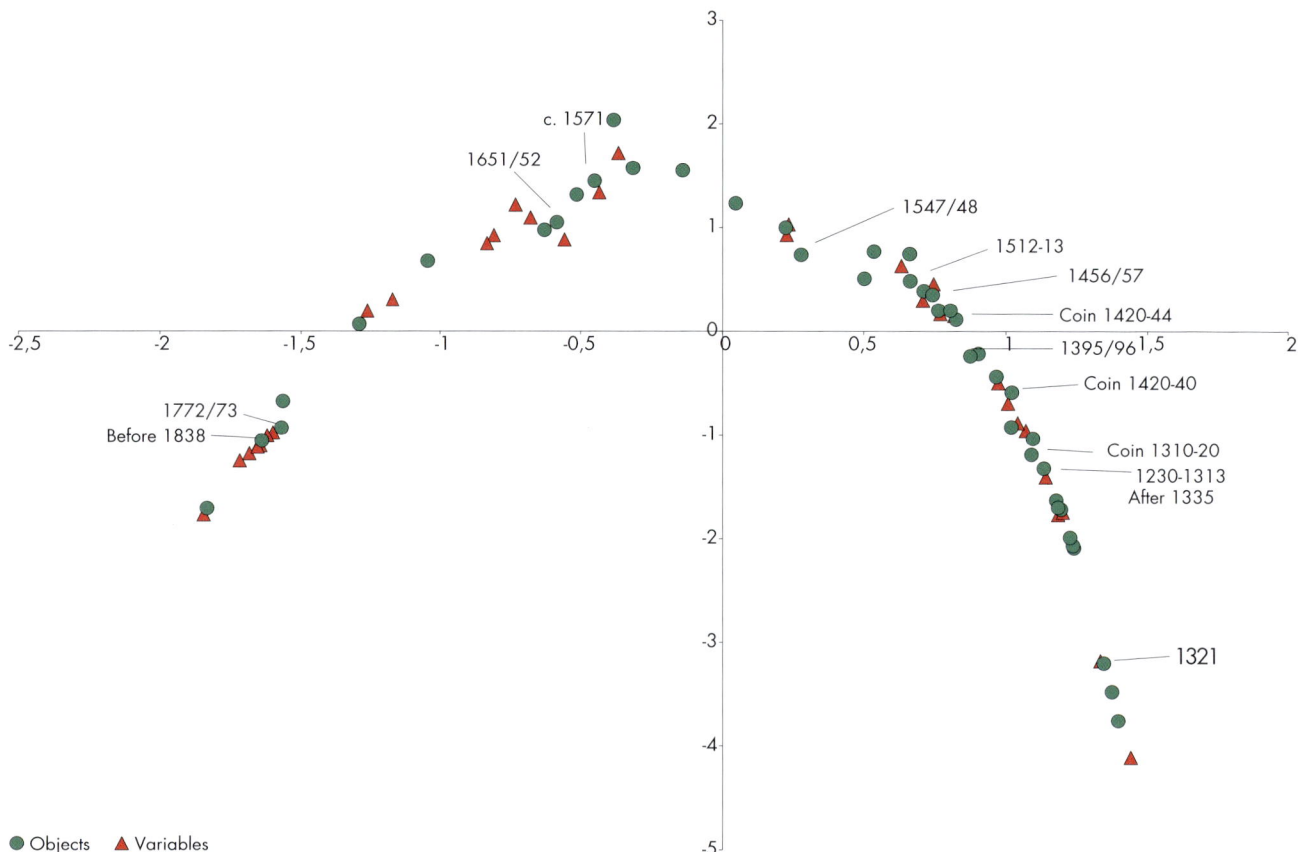

Figure 135. *Correspondence analysis of rim and handle types in local wares: 39 rim and handle types in 42 stratigraphic phases. Absolute dates are plotted. Note how for example the dendro-dated phases from FHM 3747 and FHM 4616 are plotted to the left in the diagram and the phases from FHM 4201 to the middle and right, in order.*

the stratigraphic units in the sequencing, the result are shown in figure 135. The most significant rim and handle types are added in figure 136.

In the figure, most of the stratigraphic sequences are plotted in the correct order. But the varying amounts of ceramics in the units influence the results, as do the factors regarding use span and the relationship between the ceramics and the dated features mentioned above. This is very obvious in the dendrochronologi-cally-dated material from FHM 4102 Skt. Clemensborg, where phases 2-9 are dated to the period from post-1443 to winter 1512/13. The phase – the stratigraphically earliest phase – with only one rim type present, is plotted after phase 9, which contains a large number

of rim types. The same phenomenon is seen in the later phases 15-16 at the same site, dated to 1778-94. Here, phase 15, which only contains few sherds, is plotted after the stratigraphically later phase 16.

The chronology established by these means can then be tested by comparing precisely dated material from the same area: For example, the ceramics from Hjelm, dated to 1292-1305, and the material from Stenhule, dated to 1604-10.[151] The rims from Stenhule (rim types 1002, 1009, 1013 and 1009) fit nicely into the later phases and correspond particularly well to FHM 4201 Skt. Clemensborg phase 12. The types from Hjelm (rim types 605, 611, 606 and 601) fit well into the beginning of the sequence from Aarhus. Another chronologi-

Objects and variables on the 1st and 2nd principal axes

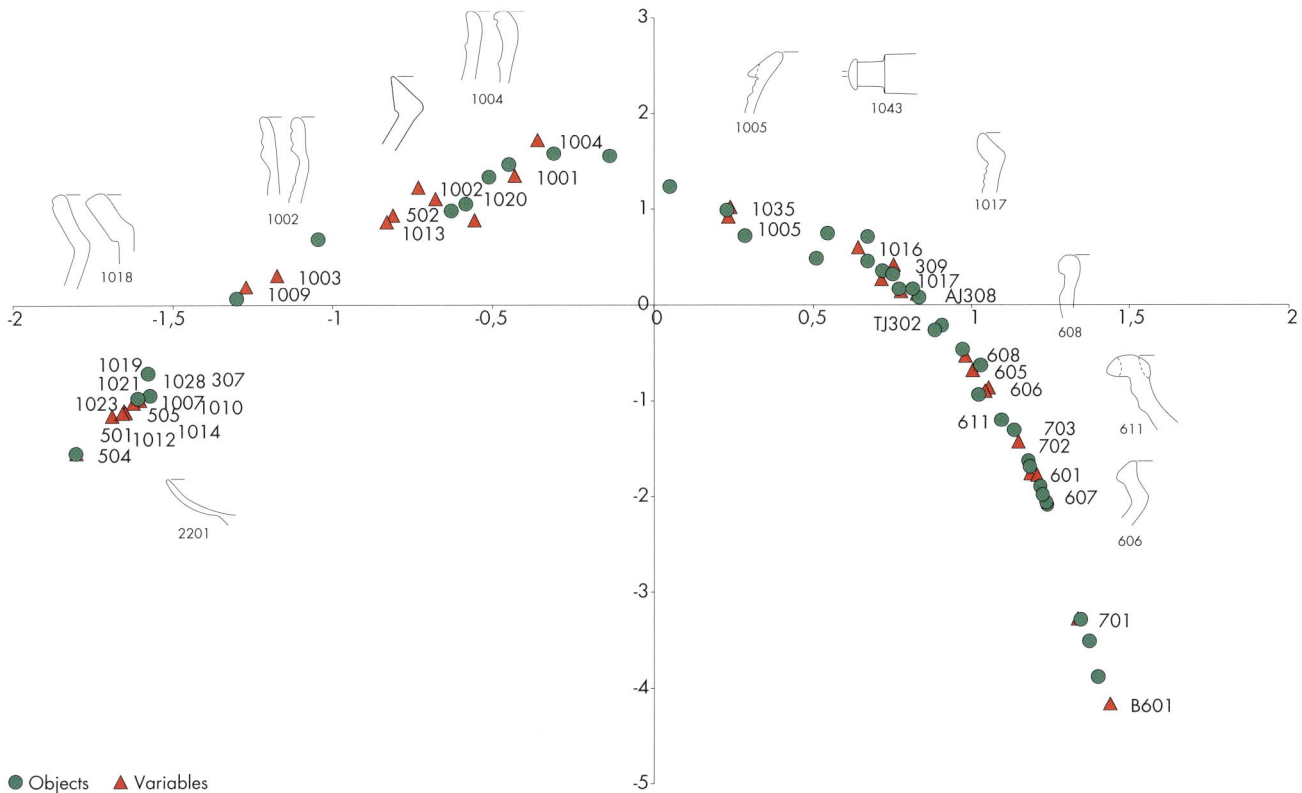

Figure 136. Correspondence analysis of rim and handle types in local wares: 39 types in 42 stratigraphic phases. Rim types plotted.

cal parallel is evident in the ceramics from the town square in Horsens, where later lead-glazed redware of rim type 1017 was deposited prior to 1433. This corresponds to the time when it appears in the Aarhus material, according to dendrochronologically-dated phases at FHM 4201 Skt. Clemensborg.[152] The Aarhus chronology can, furthermore, be compared to a similar chronology for local wares, constructed using the same methodology, and published in 2006.[153] This chronology, based on sites from all over Jutland, refers to the period 1350-1650, while the Aarhus chronology covers a longer time span, from the mid-13th to the mid-19th century. No site, except FHM 1978 Vilhelmsborg, features in both chronologies, so they are independent, but the results are, nevertheless, remarkably similar. Comparison of the two chronologies reveals a considerable concurrence, but it is not surprising that the longer Aarhus chronology provides more information on the

introduction and the disappearance of the various rim and handle types.

This established chronology for rim and handle types in local wares can be used for dating purposes in other areas or applied in future work. When doing so, however, it is advisable to have as large an assemblage of material as possible at hand, and to be very conscious about possible local differences in the use span and occurrence of types and the site formation processes at the site. A combination with scientific dating is always preferable, but not always possible for practical or economic reasons. If we return to consumption history, we need a larger-scale framework that enables comparison between stratigraphic unites in appropriate time slots: i.e. town phases. The plot of the absolute dates renders the relative sequencing of the stratigraphic phases absolute, enabling us to define town phases of

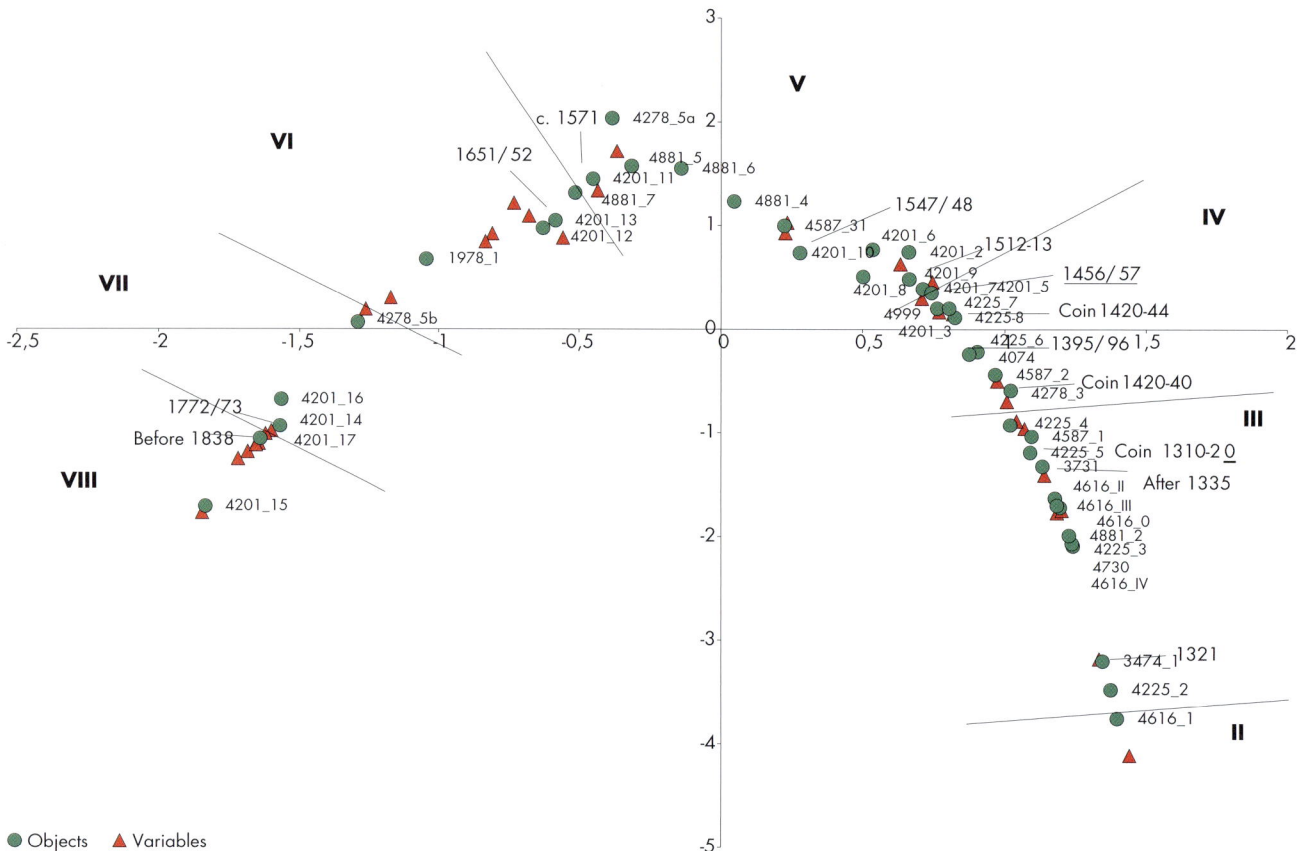

Figure 137. Correspondence analysis of rim and handle types in local wares: 39 types in 42 stratigraphic phases. Town phases plotted and marked with lines. Phase II: 13ᵗʰ century. Phase III: 13ᵗʰ century. Phase IV: 15ᵗʰ century. Phase V: 16ᵗʰ century. Phase VI: 17ᵗʰ century. Phase VI: 18ᵗʰ century.

about a century each, guided by the absolute dates. Each of the town phases thereby contains a number of stratigraphic phases – some are dendro- or coin-dated, some not – from a number of excavations: The results are shown in figure 135.

Despite the name, each town phase contains stratigraphic phases from both urban and rural areas – the name simply reflects the fact that the bulk of the material was excavated within the urban boundaries. If we unfold the chronology and attempt to order the archaeological excavations with all their stratigraphic phases according to their absolute dates and the order established in the multivariate analysis, the results are seen in figure 137. Figure 137 is then unfolded in

figures 138 and 139. As stressed above, the result is a graphical representation of how the stratigraphical units are grouped together in time slots/town phases, and we have to exercise some leeway in the interpretation of the figure. For example, FHM 4225 Guldsmedgade phase 8 does not necessarily start precisely in calendar year 1450 or end in calendar year 1500, and activity on site may not have been equally intense during all of the 15ᵗʰ century. Nevertheless, figures 138 and 139 may be helpful when reading the following chapters.

These figures should not be interpreted too rigidly, as the length of the phases, especially those with no dendrochronological or other absolute dates, varies. For now, the analysis has arranged the material from

Town phase	I				II	III
Century	9th	10th	11th	12th	13th	14th
FHM 4573 Skt. Clemens Stræde	1 2 3	4 5				
FHM 4881 Studsgade 8-10		1			2	
FHM 5124 Bispetorv		1	2	3	4	5
FHM 4278 Rosensgade		1				2
FHM 4225 Guldsmedgade			1		2	3 4 5F 6
FHM 3474 Stavtrup					1 C	
FHM 3731 Todderup						1 AH
FHM 4616 Telefontorvet						1 D 2 3
FHM 4578 Mejlgade						1BE 2
FHM 4730 Elev					1	
FHM 4074 Gl. Moesgaard						1 G
FHM 4999 Kattrup						
FHM 4201 Skt. Clemensborg						
FHM 1978 Vilhelmsborg						
FHM 5419 Damagervej 2						

Figure 138. Seriation of the excavations from the Viking Age to the 15th century (Town phases I-III) based on the multivariate analysis (figs. 135-137). Numbers refer to stratigraphic phase numbers in the excavation reports. Capital letters in the figure (A, B…) refer to absolute dates available from for example coins and dendro-dated structures: A is a coin dated 1230-1313; B a coin dated 1260; C. Dendro-date 1320s; D. Dendro-dated 1335; E. Coin dated 1320-29; F. Coin dated 1310-1320; G. Dendro-date 1396. H. Lay waste 1313 (Historical date).

Town phase	IV	V	VI	VII	IX
Century	15th	16th	17th	18th	19th
FHM 4573 Skt. Clemens Stræde					
FHM 4881 Studsgade 8-10		4 5 6 7			
FHM 5124 Bispetorv	6	7	8	9	
FHM 4278 Rosensgade	3 I		5		
FHM 4225 Guldsmedgade	6 7 8 J	9	10		
FHM 3474 Stavtrup		2			
FHM 3731 Todderup		2			
FHM 4616 Telefontorvet	4				
FHM 4578 Mejlgade		3 K	4		
FHM 4730 Elev					
FHM 4074 Gl. Moesgaard					
FHM 4999 Kattrup	1 L				
FHM 4201 Skt. Clemensborg	2 Q 3 R 4 S 5 T 6 U 7 V	8 W 9 X 10 Y 11 Z	12 AA 13 AB	14 AC 15 AD 16 AE 17 AF	19 AG
FHM 1978 Vilhelmsborg			1 M	2 N O	
FHM 5419 Damagervej 2					

Figure 147. Seriation of the excavations from the 15th to the 19th century (Town phases IV-VIII) based on the multivariate analysis (figure 135-137). Numbers refer to stratigraphic phase numbers in the excavation reports. Capital letters refer to absolute dates available as above. Absolute date plotted in relevant phases: I. Coin 1422-1440; J. Coin 1422-1440; K. Coin 1422-1440. L: Dendro-date 1396. M: Post quem datable artefact. N: Post quem datable artefact. All the stratigraphic phases in the excavation FHM 4201 Skt. Clemensborg (Matr. nr. 166a) are dendro-dated. O: Historical date. P: Post-quem datable artefact.

the sites into eight phases and these phases will act as the backbone for the following study of the consumption in town.

If we look at the composition of the total material, some obvious chronological traits become evident. It is very clear that the consumption of different ware types varies over time and it is precisely this pattern that will be investigated further in the study of consumption in the landscape. If we look at the quantities of ceramics recovered by the excavations, phase by phase, some characteristics become apparent (table 25).

First and foremost, the aforementioned sparseness in phases II, VIII and IX is obvious. There is simply not very much material available for these phases, as most sites lay waste at this time or have had any relevant settlement evidence removed by later building activities. Phase I is dominated by FHM 5124 Bispetorv, FHM 4573 Skt. Clemens Stræde and FHM 4881 Studsgade 8-10, while phase III is dominated by FHM 4225 Guldsmedgade, but is represented at all the sites, with the exception of FHM 4201 Skt. Clemensborg. Phase V is generally rich in material, while phase VI is sparse, as the later phases are dominated by FHM 4021 Skt. Clemensborg.

Because this investigation is based on finds from both urban and rural settings, a little should be said about this situation. In total, 94% of the basic material is from excavations carried out within the boundaries of Aarhus as they were in about 1800. This figure is not surprising, given the different character of the sites and, especially, the different conditions for the preservation of the archaeological record. If we look more closely at the rural material, it is evident that the major part of it can be related to phase III, probably representing deserted Medieval villages.

The contents of the individual town phases will be dealt with in the following. As this is a study of consumption, it is of interest to compare the relative abundance of the different ware groups and functional types present in the phases. This is done in figures 140 and 141.

Town phase	Sum of sherd counts	Sum of RP	Sum of weight (g)
0	1666	3461	27032
I	5245	2611	48164
II	946	348	7186
III	3998	4006	54621
IV	2607	3024	36247
V	5100	7579	85938
VI	1950	3859	21513
VII	2476	5418	37692
VIII	718	1278	10169
IX	80	163	1588
Total	**24786**	**31747**	**330150**

Table 25. Ceramics (sherds) in the town phases from all sites combined.

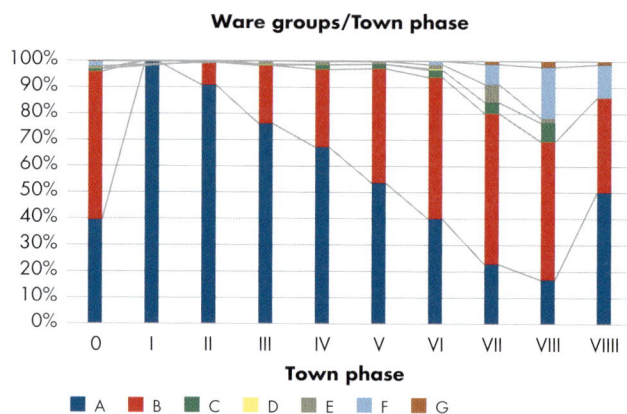

Figure 140. Relative amounts of ware groups in town phases (No= 24786 sherds)

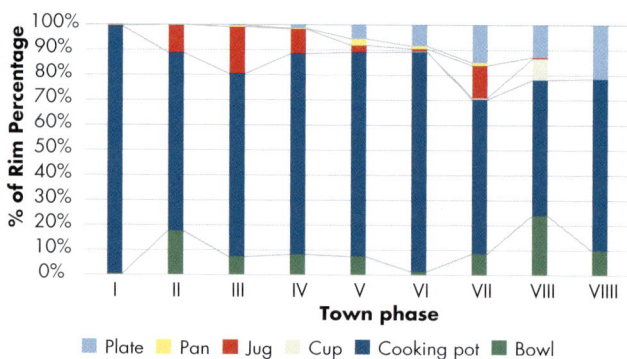

Figure 141. Relative amounts of functional types in town phases (No =27802 rim percentages)

If we go deeper into the material and compare the relative amounts of ceramics across the urban/rural boundary and through time from the 13th to the 18th century, we see a clear chronological development

Objects and variables on the 1ˢᵗ and 2ⁿᵈ principal axes

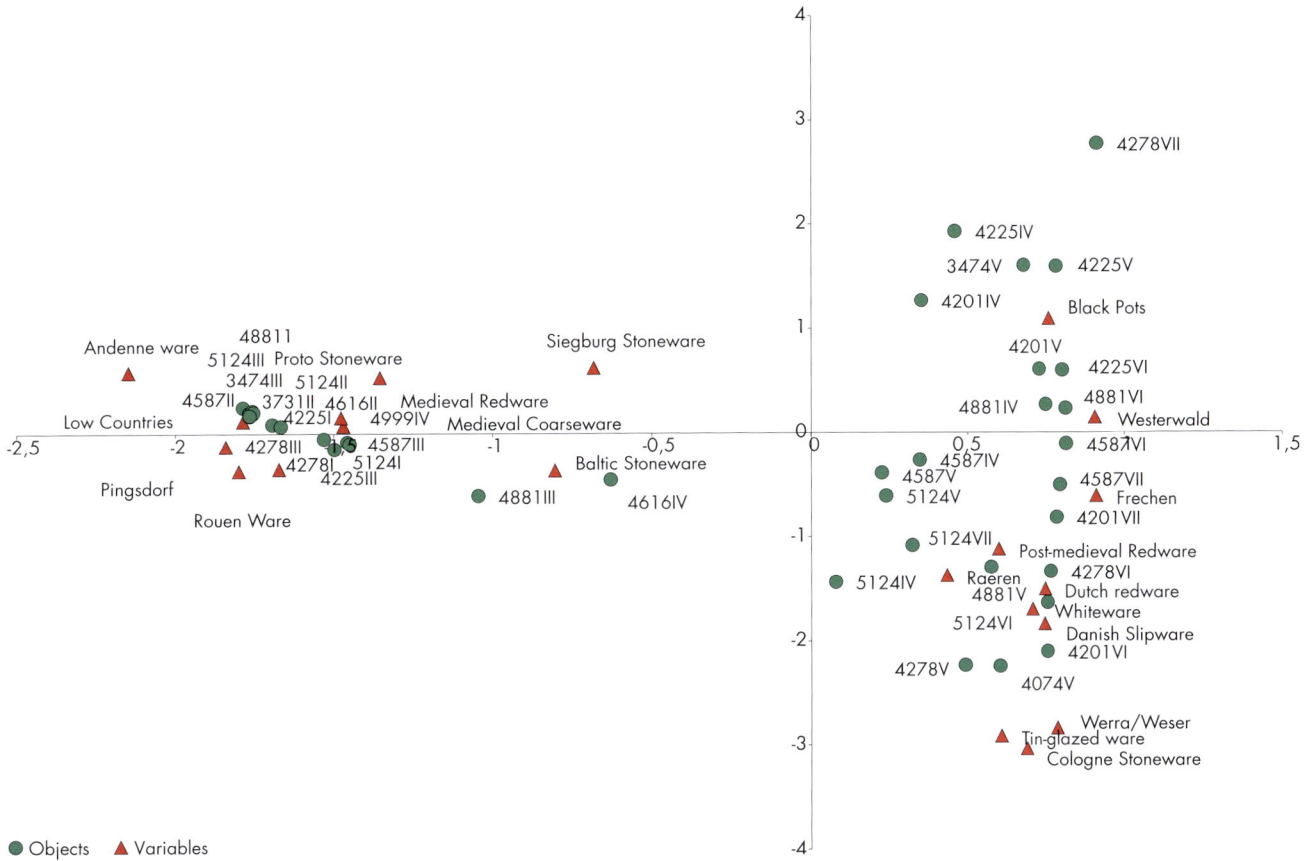

Figure 142. Correspondence analysis of the relative amounts of ware groups from the 12ᵗʰ to the 18ᵗʰ century (39 sites/phases, and nine main ware types (no. = 25570; rim percentages)). Note how time is expressed on the x-axis, while variation is expressed in the y-axis. It is obvious how the variation in the ceramics inventory increases rapidly from the 15ᵗʰ and 16ᵗʰ centuries onwards.

from the Early Middle Ages until the 18ᵗʰ century. See figure 142.

Most notable is the break that occurs as the Medieval ware types, Medieval well-fired redware and coarsewares, are replaced by the Post-Medieval redwares and blackwares, and at the same time the variation in ceramics content between sites increases This rapid development or break has been seen before and interpreted as a marked shift in ceramics consumption around 1400, combined with an increasing differentiation in consumption between various social groups from the 16ᵗʰ century onwards.[154] This development and its implications will be analysed phase by phase in the following chapters.

3.1 Phase I: The Viking Age and Early Medieval material c. 800-1200 (With Lars Krants)

If we compare the relative abundance of the ware groups in the town phases, there seems to be very little Early Medieval material.[155] All the Viking Age sites are similar and there is not much difference in their ceramics inventories. All are dominated by Viking Age low-fired coarseware, except for FHM 4573 Skt. Clemens Stræde, which has a small quantity of Baltic types. As stated above, there are no major imported wares, i.e. no Tating ware or similar. The conclusion from this is that if there were significant differences in consumption between these sites, these are not immediately visible or

137

even expressed in the ceramics. The exception is FHM 4335 Skt. Clemens Stræde, which stands out as having a special status or function in Aarhus due to the Baltic blackware found there. However, as this latter site is currently under publication as part of another project, its special status and function will not be investigated further in this volume.[156] Accordingly, a major investigation of the archaeozoological and archeobotanical remains, as well as a programme of lipid analysis, is necessary in order to shed further light on Viking Age consumption.

11th and 12th centuries

The Viking Age and Early Medieval material is merged into phase I although this is, admittedly, rather coarse phasing. As stressed in the account of the individual site excavations, the material can be divided into stratigraphical phases or subphases, with FHM 4573 Skt. Clemens Stræde and FHM 4278 Rosensgade representing pure Viking Age consumption, while FHM 4881 Studsgade 8-10 contains Viking Age and Early Medieval material. The widest variety of ware types is evident at FHM 4573 Skt. Clemens Stræde, where ceramics from Friesland and Baltic types are seen together with local Viking Age material. The phase from FHM 4225 Guldsmedgade is somewhat later. Here we have a sherd of Pingsdorf ware together with Medieval low-fired coarseware cooking pots. The same 11th century horizon is traceable at FHM 4881 Studsgade 8-10 and Medieval low-fired coarseware cooking pots with out-turned rims are dominant at both sites. Apart from the aforementioned Pingsdorf ware, all the ware types are local – there are so far no traces of imported display vessels, but that may of course change with new excavations.

3.2 Medieval and Post-Medieval material

The Medieval and Post-Medieval material is much more varied than the Viking Age or Early Medieval material and significant differentiation takes place during this period. As will be argued later, the ceramics in phase IV, the 15th century, change profoundly in the course of a short time span, and this brief transitional period is therefore not evident at many sites. As for imports, the Andenne-type ware is the earliest type, followed by the Low Countries highly decorated ware, proto stoneware and Rouen-type ware. Stoneware was generally introduced in the early 14th century, and to a larger number of households. This perhaps marked a shift in contacts or a widening of distribution networks, or perhaps even broader involvement in whatever activities led to the presence of these types within the town.

3.3 Phase II: 13th century

The ceramics material from the 13th century is rather limited and restricted to a few sites. This material comprises greywares with about 15% glazed, locally produced ceramics, i.e. glazed jugs. Only a very few pieces of Andenne-type ware are present, all at FHM 4587 Mejlgade 26. The same site also produced Rheinish proto stoneware, as did another site, FHM 4278 Rosensgade, in the same area. An Andenne-type sherd turned up in the later phases at FHM 4881 Studsgade 8-10 and is probably residual. FHM 4225 is also active at the end of the phase. Sherds of Viking Age low-fired coarseware in FHM 4573 Skt. Clemens Stræde and FHM 4124 Bispetorv are residual, while a few Post-Medieval sherds in FHM 4587 Mejlgade are intrusive (table 26).

3.4 Phase III: The 14th century

Phase III shows little apparent variation (table 27).

All the stratigraphic units in this phase are characterised by relatively large amounts of greywares and virtually all of them appear also to include Medieval well-fired redware jugs (table 29) This latter type is most prominent at FHM 4074 Gammel Moesgaard (34%), FHM 4616 Telefontorvet (30%) and FHM 4587 Mejlggade 26 (29%). But the percentages are never uniformly high: FHM

Town phase II							
Sum of sherd counts							
Ware types	**FHM 3731**	**FHM 4278**	**FHM 4573**	**FHM 4587**	**FHM 4616**	**FHM 5124**	**Total**
Andenne-type ware				2			2
Baltic blackware						11	11
Black pot, early type						6	6
Medieval low-fired coarseware						165	165
Medieval well-fired coarseware	56			59	11	247	373
Medieval well-fired redware	4			7	3	63	77
Other blackware						15	15
Proto stoneware		2		2			4
Post-Medieval well-fired redware				4			4
Viking Age low-fired coarseware			81			208	289
Total	**60**	**2**	**81**	**74**	**14**	**715**	**946**

Table 26. Ware types in town phase II. Number of sherds.

Town phase III										
Sum of sherd counts	**FHM**									
Ware types	**FHM 3474**	**FHM 4074**	**FHM 4225**	**FHM 4278**	**FHM 4587**	**FHM 4616**	**FHM 4730**	**FHM 4881**	**FHM 5124**	**Total**
Baltic burnished greyware			3		19	5				27
Black pot, early type			257					10		267
Black pot, Varde type			19							19
Black pot, Vorup type	14									14
Brügge-type ware			1							1
Langerwehe stoneware			4							4
Medieval low-fired coarseware			114					1	4	119
Medieval well-fired coarseware	161	424	838	318	69	262	119	186	138	2515
Medieval well-fired redware	15	168	282	53	34	157	2	8	15	734
Other blackware	1		5		13			4	1	24
Other whiteware							4			4
Post-Medieval well-fired redware		1	134		5			5	1	146
Proto stoneware			5	3		4				12
Raeren stoneware	1	3	3	1		1			1	10
Rouen-type ware		1	1			2				4
Saintonge polychrome ware						1				1
Siegburg stoneware			20	4	6	2				32
Waldenburg stoneware				5						5
Other	1		10	1				6	42	62
Total	**193**	**597**	**1696**	**385**	**146**	**434**	**125**	**220**	**202**	**3998**

Table 27. Ware types in town phase III. Number of sherds.

4225 Guldsmedgade has about 20% and FHM 4278 Rosensgade only 9%. The lowest proportions are seen at the rural sites, around 2-3%.

If we look at the percentages of imports in phase III, some differences of detail become apparent. The proportion of imports is greatest at FHM 4587 Mejlgade 26, with 11%, which is rather a high value for Aarhus. FHM 4616 Telefontorvet has 3% and FHM 4225 Guldsmedgade has 1%, while imports are barely represented anywhere else in the town, apart from at FHM 5124 Bispetorv, and certainly not at the rural sites, with the exception of FHM 4074 Gammel Moesgaard. Due to the high-resolution phasing at, especially, FHM

4587 Mejlgade 26 and FHM 4225 Guldsmedgade, we do have some insight into events during this phase. FHM 4616 Telefontorvet and FHM 4225 Guldsmedgade, as well as the large FHM 5124 Bispetorv, do contain French and Low Countries wares as well as Rhenish stoneware and Baltic types. The evidence from FHM 4616 Telefontorvet is particularly revealing. In the first phase of the house, dendrochronologically dated to 1300-30, the floors contain fragments of French whiteware jugs and glazed local jugs: nothing more. After 1335 (dendrochronological date), there was use of proto stoneware, Baltic burnished greyware, Saintonge polychrome ware, Siegburg stoneware and French whitewares, all in the form of jugs. The stratigraphically later phase contains only Medieval well-fired redware jugs, greywares and fragments of burnished Baltic greywares. There are no French types in this phase, only stonewares and Baltic types, with no evidence of French or Low Countries imports. Why is this? The three sites were active at the same time, so the chronology does not provide us with an immediate answer. The French types may have been distributed in a way that did not include FHM 4587 Mejlgade 26. Perhaps the North Sea types came to Aarhus through Ribe, while most of the stonewares originated from contacts with the Baltic coast.[157] It therefore seems that the variety of imports evident at specific sites, especially FHM 4616 Telefontorvet and FHM 4225 Guldsmedgade, in the first part of the 14th century, disappears in the middle of the 14th century. Before this time, we see the presence of a range of colourful types, such as Rouen-type ware, Low Countries highly decorated ware and also Saintonge polychrome ware together with Baltic burnished greyware jugs, Siegburger jugs and proto stonewares. However, it seems as if the colourful imports disappear sometime in the later part of 14th century, leaving only the Baltic wares and stoneware types. From then on, utilitarian stoneware and the Baltic well-fired burnished ware are the only imported types. Unfortunately, this change cannot be dated more precisely than to the middle of the 14th century: This question must await further excavations and future scientific dates.

3.5 Phase IV: The 15th century

As we have seen, the colourful types disappear sometime in phase III, and phase IV also shows a rapid development in types. FHM 4616 Telefontorvet appears to show greater similarities with the ceramics inventory in phase III than that in the later parts of phase IV; especially as demonstrated by FHM 4201 Skt. Clemensborg and FHM 4225 Guldsmedgade, both of which are dated by dendrochronology and numismatic evidence, respectively. We now see the use of black pots, early type, and Post-Medieval redware, early type, and the stoneware imports continue. The material from the 15th century is less varied than that of earlier phases (table 28).

Most of it still comprises Medieval well-fired coarseware cooking pots, but Medieval well-fired redware jugs have largely disappeared, as have the colourful imported jugs. Only one example is found here – a Rouen-type ware jug dropped on the floor in the cellar at FHM 5124 Bispetorv. Great care was probably taken of this decorative jug and it was of considerable age when it was smashed on the floor. The Rhenish stoneware now constitutes a significant import type and at least two jugs are present at FHM 4201 Skt. Clemensborg and FHM 4225 Guldsmedgade. The greatest diversity is seen at FHM 5124 Bispetorv, where the finds include a Low Countries tin-glazed ware jug (the first occurrence in Aarhus), Rhenish stoneware jugs, Baltic burnished ware and a very old jug of Rouen-type ware, as mentioned above. FHM 4616 Telefontorvet, which dates from the earliest 15th century, still has glazed jugs, together with Baltic well-fired burnished ware and Rhenish stoneware. By the middle of the 15th century, at the latest, this inventory has disappeared and the only local types now are cooking pots, both glazed and unglazed, and the drinking vessels are now all of Rhenish stoneware. Amounts of imports are low – 3-5%, but they represent a stable commodity at the urban sites. FHM 4225 Guldsmedgade provides a more detailed insight. A smithy here, dated to the second half of the 15th century

Town phase IV									
Sum of sherd counts									
Ware types	**FHM 4201**	**FHM 4225**	**FHM 4573**	**FHM 4587**	**FHM 4616**	**FHM 4881**	**FHM 4999**	**5124**	**Total**
Baltic burnished greyware	1			21	4			4	30
Black pot, early type		515				4		16	535
Black pot, Varde type	11	65						14	90
Cologne stoneware					4				4
Dutch redware					1				1
Frechen stoneware					1			1	2
Langerwehe stoneware	1								1
Low Countries tin-glazed ware								2	2
Medieval well-fired coarseware	45	62		34	269	2	82	132	626
Medieval well-fired redware	6	27		7	107	1	4	12	164
Near-stoneware				1	1			2	4
Other blackware	130	6		85	75	22		11	329
Other whiteware	4	3		13	7			14	41
Post-Medieval well-fired redware	63	87		123	114	34	6	167	594
Raeren stoneware		2		2	2			3	9
Rouen-type ware								4	4
Siegburg stoneware	2	2		3	4			2	13
Residual/other	2	5	0	1	8	5	89	48	158
Total	**265**	**774**		**291**	**596**	**68**	**181**	**432**	**2607**

Table 28. Ware types in town phase IV. Number of sherds. Note the dominance of Post-Medieval redware.

by numismatic evidence, was found to contain local greywares and Late Medieval well-fired redware, early type cooking pots deposited on the floor, together with some Rhenish stoneware. And at FHM 4201 Skt. Clemensborg, Baltic burnished ware and Rhenish stoneware were deposited in the winter of 1452-53: The Late Medieval transition was now over. It is worth noting that the stonewares do not occur at the rural sites, with the exception of the previously mentioned manor FHM 4074 Gammel Moesgaard. The rural sites are rather few in number and the material from them is rather sparse, but it may be worth considering in future excavations whether the imported ceramics generally just did not reach the rural population, or whether the apparent scarcity is an illusion resulting from a low number of finds.

3.6 Phase V: The 16th century

In the 16th century, the material is quite varied, with the greatest variation in ware types being found at FHM 5124 Bispetorv (table 29).

The proportion of black pots clearly varies within and across the urban area and large percentages were found at both FHM 4225 Guldsmedgade and FHM 4201 Skt. Clemensborg. FHM 4201 Skt. Clemensborg has one piece of Low Countries tin-glazed ware, with the other imports here being whitewares, plates and pots – at least two vessels, plus utilitarian Raeren-type and Siegburg stoneware. FHM 4225 Guldsmedgade has a similar range of imports: simple utilitarian wares of Siegburg, Frechen and Raeren-type stoneware. However, FHM 5124 Bispetorv is very different, with a larger proportion of display and serving vessels in whitewares and a smaller proportion of stoneware vessels. The serving and eating vessels here are directed towards display. A Low Countries redware chafing dish is a unique find for Aarhus and adds to the impression of luxury at this site. Another unique vessel is a Low Countries tin-glazed ware vessel that has parallels in Amsterdam.[158] There is little doubt that the urban environment shows considerable variation during the 16th century, with display-related types of ceramics being primarily

Ware types	FHM 3474	FHM 4074	FHM 4201	FHM 4225	FHM 4278	FHM 4573	FHM 4587	FHM 4881	FHM 5124	FHM 5419	Total
Sum of sherd counts											
Baltic Blackware								1	8		9
Baltic Burnished grayware				2					1		3
Black pot, early type				656				190	39	83	968
Black pot, Varde type			67	138	1		5		65		276
Black pot, Vorup type	108										108
Cologne stoneware								7	1		8
Danish slipware			2						2		4
Dutch redware				1				10	2		13
Frechen stoneware				7	1			1			9
Industrial ceramics			1	1				3	1		6
Langerwehe stoneware				1							1
Low Countries tin-glazed ware								2	1		3
Medieval low-fired coarseware								16	32		48
Medieval well-fired coarseware	9		30	31	1		26	41	153		291
Medieval well-fired redware		8	33	8			4	4	5		62
Near stoneware									1		1
Other blackware		6	573	3			46	57	166		851
Other whitewares		17	9	6	1		6	5	40		84
Porcelain									1		1
Post-medieval well-fired redware	28	129	544	224	75	40	82	581	320	26	2049
Post-medieval well-fired redware with slip decoration	4	7	5	9	2		3	31	5	22	88
Raeren stoneware			6	1					15		22
Rouen-type ware				1							1
Siegburg stoneware			4	4			2		1		11
Tin-glazed ceramics			2								2
Viking Age low-fired coarseware						14		29	132		175
Werra								2			2
Weser		1									1
Westerwald stoneware			2	1							3
Total	**149**	**168**	**1278**	**1094**	**81**	**54**	**174**	**980**	**991**	**131**	**5100**

Table 29. Ware types in town phase V. Number of sherds.

found at FHM 5124 Bispetorv. There seems to be a link with the Post-Medieval redware cooking pots. The proportion of the latter is about 30% at all sites except Bispetorv, where these vessels constitute 70%. As for the plate/cooking pot ratio, the emphasis on plates is much greater at Bispetorv than at the other sites: There are 23% plates at FHM 5124 Bispetorv and only 4% at FHM 4225 Guldsmedgade. It is therefore clearly evident that the consumption at Bispetorv was directed towards luxury and display and differed markedly from the rest of the town. As we have seen, this is very evident in the types of stoneware present: Bispetorv contains rich finds of decorated stoneware jugs that have no parallels in other parts of the town.

Ware types	FHM 1978	FHM 4201	FHM 4225	FHM 4278	FHM 4587	FHM 4881	FHM 5124	Total
Town phase VI								
Sum of sherd counts								
Black pot, early type			72			93	2	167
Black pot, Varde type	127	8	82	8	47		19	291
Danish slipware		2	3				1	6
Low Countries redware			1				1	2
Low Countries tin-glazed ware				1	1			2
Other blackware		8	44		173	14	30	269
Other whiteware		25	1		12		16	54
Post-medieval well-fired redware	425	125	75	19	172	125	94	1035
Post-medieval well-fired redware with slip decoration		9	12		7	3	4	35
Raeren stoneware			8				8	16
Siegburg stoneware			5					5
Tin-glazed ware					1			1
Westerwald stoneware	6	1			1		2	10
Unidentified/other		2	32	1		8	47	90
Total	**560**	**180**	**335**	**29**	**414**	**243**	**224**	**1985**

Table 30. Ware types in town phase VI. Number of sherds.

3.7 Phase VI: The 17th century

In the 17th century, the proportion of imports increases (table 30).

Imports are now between 7 and 10%, with Low Countries/German Post-Medieval whitewares being among the dominant wares: These comprise pots and plates with green or bicoloured glaze and the same vessel types are seen at all the sites. The other imports comprise stoneware jugs. The stoneware is very varied: Simple utilitarian Raeren stoneware is seen all over the town, but FHM 5124 Bispetorv is markedly different and has a very varied assemblage of display types. These include four mugs produced in c. 1620, one of which was manufactured by the Rhenish master Jan Beldam. The display vessels include another Raeren-type stoneware jug with a relief decoration depicting Justitia, dated 1583. Also belonging to this phase are fragments of a jug bearing the coat of arms of Julich-Kleve-Berg, which was found in the fill in the demolished houses, and a Low Countries redware strainer.

Low Countries redware is rather rare in Aarhus, but does occasionally occur. At the other sites, the stoneware is primarily utilitarian, for example at FHM 4225 Guldsmedgade, where two jugs of Siegburg stoneware and one of Raeren-type stoneware were used, together with a plate in Low Countries/German Post-Medieval whiteware. Westerwald stoneware was found at FHM 4201 Skt. Clemensborg and Low Countries tin-glazed ware is represented at FHM 4278 Rosensgade. The ratio of black pots to display types and Post-Medieval redware is remarkable. FHM 4225 Guldsmedgade, FHM 4201 Skt. Clemensborg and, to some degree, FHM 4881 Studsgade 8-10 have the lowest proportion of redware pipkins, while the highest is found at FHM 5124 Bispetorv and FHM 4587 Mejlgade 26. The proportion of blackware/tripod pipkins and imports does seem to vary somewhat from phase to phase within the same site: FHM 4201 Skt. Clemensborg shifts from 60 to 34% greyware between phases V and VII, while FHM 4225 Guldsmedgade falls from 78% in phase IV to 52% in phase VI. This may be interpreted in terms of a rapidly changing consumption pattern in the town – or even as an indication of a high turnover of inhabitants on the plots. The more stable consumption is clearly evident at FHM 4881 Studsgade 8-10, FHM 5124 Bispetorv and FHM 4587 Mejlgade 26: All show constant, high proportions of tripod pipkins as well as a wide variety of imports. Since these were some of the wealthier streets in the 17th century, according to the taxation records, it is tempting to suggest that the plots here were more stable in terms of their inhabitants, while the others may have been subject to a greater population turnover.[159]All of this will be addressed in the conclusion.

3.8 Phase VII: The 18th century

The 18th century is only represented at FHM 1978 Wilhelmsborg, FHM 4201 Skt. Clemensborg and FHM 3474 Stavtrup. The very small assemblage from FHM 3474 Stavtrup does not carry much information, but at least it enables us to say that faience was known there. Many industrial types are present at FHM 1978 Vilhelmsborg, among them English industrial types, tin-glazed ceramics, porcelain and stoneware bottles. It is evident that the largest and best-dated site, FHM 4201 Skt. Clemensborg, has a large variety of industrial types from the late 18th century onwards (table 31).

It seems that industrial types had quite an impact in the 18th century and about 90% of the imports are industrial wares during this phase. These include mugs and jars of Raeren-type stoneware and some whiteware pots. The industrial wares are primarily plates, cups and bowls in creamware, i.e. classic tableware. Black pots dominate the local wares. Due to the sparse 18th century material from other sites, the material from FHM 4201 Skt. Clemensborg largely lacks local parallels, although the material from the site FHM 5501 Latin 3/Borggade 6 is promising. As the ceramics report was concluded in January 2016, the material was not included in this project, but will be available for comparison in future work.

3.9 Phase VIII: The 19th century

The 19th century material is only present at FHM 4201 Skt. Clemensborg and as stray finds at FHM 3474 Gammel Moesgaard. As the material from FHM 4201 Skt. Clemensborg has already been presented in detail previously in this book and other publications are being planned, I will only draw attention to the rather large proportion of industrial faiences in the small body of material from this phase.

Summing up, we see a chronological development in consumption in the area, as well as an increasing differentiation between the urban sites. This will be unfolded in a chapter on consumer horizons, after a brief chapter on food, coins, cloth and immigration.

Town phase VII							
Sum of sherd counts							
Ware types	**FHM 1978**	**FHM 4074**	**FHM 4201**	**FHM 4278**	**FHM 4587**	**FHM 5124**	**Total**
Baltic Burnished grayware						2	2
Black pot, early type						1	1
Black pot, Varde type			190	50	3	4	247
Black pot, Vorup type	76						76
Cologne stoneware	151		2				153
Danish slipware			2	2	3		7
Dutch redware			1				1
Frechen stoneware			5				5
Industrial ceramics	6		76	7		6	95
Low Countries tin-glazed ware			1				1
Medieval well-fired coarseware			3		1	58	62
Medieval well-fired redware			4				4
Other blackware			154		4	18	176
Other whitewares			95		4	3	102
Porcelain	22		1		1		24
Post-medieval well-fired redware	295		867		23	106	1291
Post-medieval well-fired redware with slip decoration	73		44		1		118
Raeren stoneware		1	7			2	10
Tinglazed ceramics	95						95
Tin-glazed ceramics					1	1	2
Weser			2				2
Westerwald stoneware			2				2
Total	**718**	**1**	**1456**	**59**	**41**	**201**	**2476**

Table 31. Ware types in town phase VII. Number of sherds.

Figure 143. Opposite page: *Kitchen Scene, Master of the Amsterdam Bodegone, c. 1625. ©Museum Boijmans Van Beuningen, Rotterdam.*

4 Context

4.1 Food and food culture

At this point it is worth taking a closer look at cooking and foodways in the town. As stated above, analyses of animal or botanical material have great potential, but this study will necessarily be largely limited to an analysis of the relevant artefacts and written sources. However, even given the obvious limitations this implies, it is still possible to gain some insight into the subject.

First and foremost, it is relevant to ask what evidence there is of change in ceramics function over time within the town boundaries.

Figure 144 shows that cooking pots were the most commonly used form of ceramic vessel from the 9th to the 19th century, which is hardly surprising in a Danish context. From the 13th century onwards, bowls and jugs form a significant part of the inventory. The 15th century sees the introduction of plates in increasing numbers and in the 16th century the pan appears, while jugs and bowls become less important throughout both these centuries. The 17th century sees the introduction of the jar and in the 18th century cups are added to the repertoire. What we see expressed here are three consumer revolutions: 1. The appearance of ceramic tableware, mainly jugs, in the 13th century, 2. the introduction of pans and plates, indicating the advent of fried food and individual servings, in the 15th/16th centuries and

3. the introduction of cups in the 18th century, pointing to consumption of new beverages: tea, coffee or chocolate. It is then relevant to ask whether a closer look at this rather crude analysis can reveal any traceable difference in consumption between town and countryside, between urban and rural environments, and whether there are any differences between the sites within the urban town centre.

Town and countryside
The assemblages from the rural sites are obviously much smaller than those from the urban sites and are therefore less representative and informative.

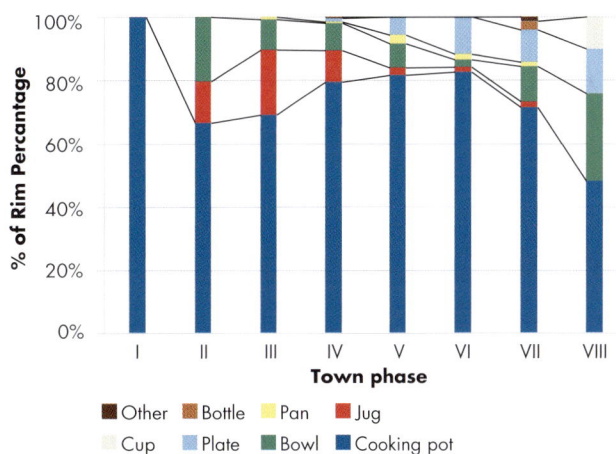

Figure 144. Functional types in the urban centre (no. = 22,199; rim percentages). Note the increasing variety of functional types, with pans and plates occurring from the 15th/16th centuries (phases IV and V), while cups and bottles turn up in the 18th century (phase VII).

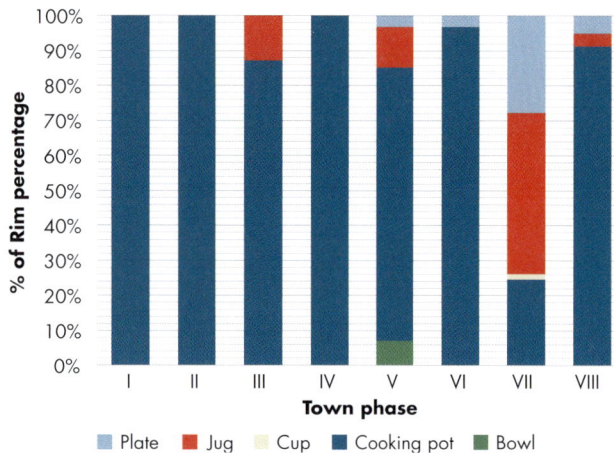

Figure 145. *Functional types at rural sites (no. = 4333; rim percentages). The very high proportion of jugs in phase VII is due to a large number at the manor Vilhelmsborg.*

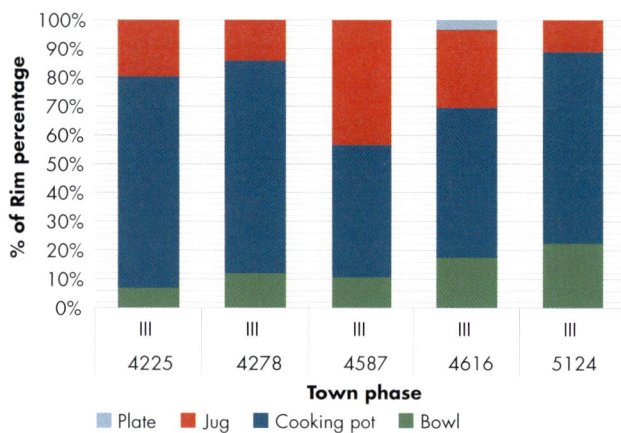

Figure 146. *Functional types at urban sites, 14th century (no. = 3063; rim percentages).*

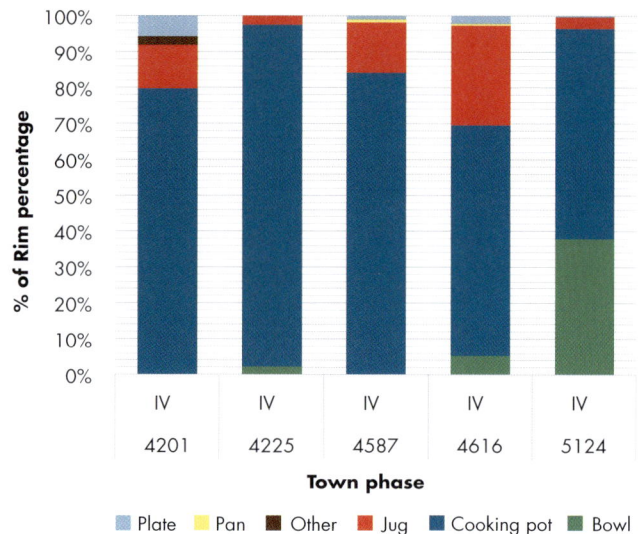

Figure 147. *Functional types at urban sites in the 15th century (no. = 2874; rim percentages).*

Nevertheless, rural inhabitants appear to have used tableware like their urban counterparts in the 14th century, although the amounts may have been different. The material from the 13th century is so limited in size that the absence of jugs here is insignificant. The 16th century sees the introduction of the plate, exactly as was the case in the town a century earlier, so individual servings or special serving vessels were also employed here, although the exact dating of this introduction awaits further date evidence. However, no pans have so far been found at the rural sites, so it could be that the fried food was an urban speciality in this area. It might be of significance that pans were not

present at the farms at Tårnby.[160] Cups are also absent, apart from at the manor, FHM 1978 Vilhelmsborg. Perhaps the spread of tea progressed more slowly in the countryside than in the towns. However, new excavations may well broaden our perspective on rural consumption significantly. It is evident that tea services, especially in English industrial wares, were used at an early 19th century farmstead at Hårup near Silkeborg, and further excavations may well reveal a similar development in the Aarhus area.[161] Leaving aside the possible use of pans, there does seem to have been a somewhat similar consumption pattern on either side of the town gates. But it is worth noting that the occurrence of functional types varies a great deal between the rural sites, with the manor FHM 4074 Gammel Moesgaard being the only site were jugs were used in significant numbers. Likewise, the manor FHM 1978 Vilhelmsborg is the only place where cups and plates were used. This may of course indicate a similarity between consumption in certain parts of urban centre and the manorial lifestyle.[162]

Inter-urban differences in function types

After this brief analysis, it is relevant to ask whether there are any differences between the various sites in the town, i.e. whether the food culture, as reflected in

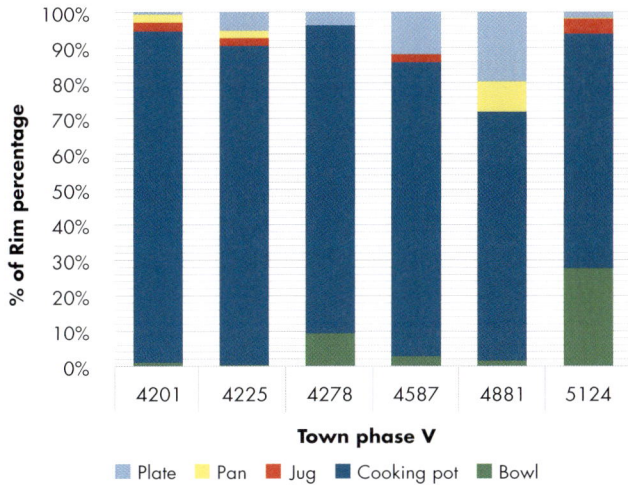

Figure 148. Functional types in the 16th century (no. = 7032; rim percentages).

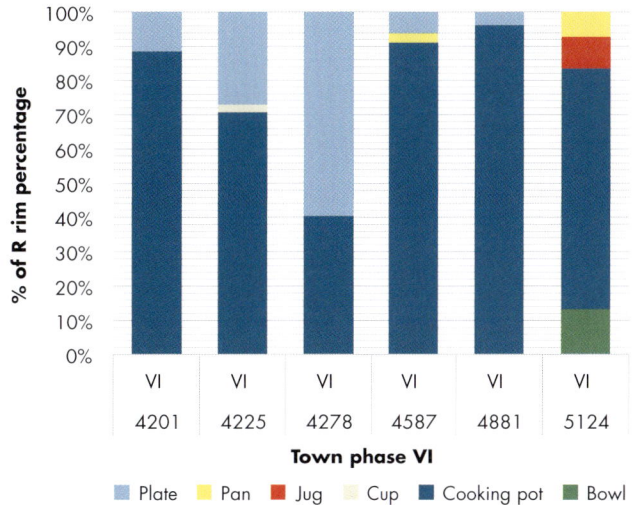

Figure 149. Functional types in the 17th century. Note the common occurrence of plates (no. = 2357; rim percentages).

the ceramics, varied or was the same all over Aarhus. In the 13th century, all active sites show bowls, jugs and cooking pots, but the total number is low and the evidence is therefore inconclusive. If we look at the material from the 14th century, some differences become apparent (figure 146).

Cooking pots are dominant at all the sites, but FHM 4587 Mejlgade 26 seems to have the largest proportion of serving jugs, followed by FHM 4616 Telefontorvet, while FHM 4225 Guldsmedgade and FHM 4278 Rosensgade have the lowest numbers. FHM 4881 Studsgade is omitted due to its limited size.

The 15th century stands out as a transitional period, with the disappearance of the jug being evident at all sites (figure 147).

The people who lived at FHM 4225 Guldsmedgade still used the fewest types, followed by FHM 4881 Studsgade 8-10. Drinking glasses now appear in the town, as is evident at Guldsmedgade, Rosensgade and, primarily, in the ecclesial quarter at Bispetorv, where large numbers of sherds from drinking glasses datable to the Late Medieval and Early Modern period have been found.[163]

The 16th century is characterised by the introduction of the plate and the pan (figure 148).

The distribution of types appears to vary: FHM 4225 Guldsmedgade and FHM 4201 Skt. Clemensborg have the highest proportion of cooking pots, but the new types are found all over the town.

The 17th century sees a marked occurrence of plates at all sites while pans are most frequent at FHM 5124 Bispetorv (figure 149).

The 18th and 19th centuries are hard to compare because numbers of finds are generally low and only FHM 4201 Skt. Clemensborg is available for analysis. The most significant development is an increase in tableware, mainly cups, linked to the use of industrial faiences. This brief analysis of the distribution of functional types on the urban sites shows that the various types are more or less present at all sites, but that the amounts seem to vary. This may indicate that urban households shared a common food culture – at least as reflected in the ceramics – but that the ratio of for example fried food to porridge and gruel varied somewhat within the town. It would be interesting to compare the ceramics' functions in the urban and rural areas over a shorter time span, and on a site by site basis in order to see whether the food culture was shared across the urban boundaries. The best option in this respect is the 14th century, where a manor, Gammel Moesgård, and a village, Stavtrup, are available for study. The number of sherds from these sites is rather low for comparative purposes, but it may be possible to identify a tendency for the manor to have a greater proportion of tableware, mainly jugs, than the farm. In terms of the quality of ceramics material and the ware types present, the manor is comparable with FHM 4587 Mejlgade 26, while the village is better matched with FHM 4225 Guldsmedgade. Likewise, the only two comparable 18th century sites are FHM 4201 Skt. Clemensborg and the manor FHM 1978 Vilhelmsborg. The black pots and the Post-Medieval redwares at the two sites are quite similar. But porcelain cups and plates, tin-glazed ceramics from the Store Kongensgade factory, English industrial ceramics of high quality and stoneware water bottles are only present at the manor. The consequences of this for our perception of the consumption and lifestyle will be discussed later.

Summing up, we can conclude that four changes are evident in the functional types: 1. The introduction of specialised tableware, i.e. jugs, in the 13th century, followed by 2. the introduction of cooking pots with internal glaze in the 15th century, followed by 3. tableware for serving and eating, and 4. pans – interpreted here as frying pans – in the 16th century. There is, accordingly, an increase in tableware until the late 18th century, when new forms – especially cups associated with the drinking of tea and perhaps coffee – are introduced. The rural functional types are more difficult to assess as the ceramics material here is quite sparse. However, pans have not yet been found at rural sites and cups and tea services appear to be absent too in the 18th century, although they are quite common in the 19th century. Bowls have also not been identified as yet, although their presence cannot be discounted. It seems that the ratio between cooking pots and serving vessels varies within the town, with the latter being particularly abundant at FHM 4587 Mejlgade 26, near the coast,

and at FHM 4616 Telefontorvet – both locations on major roads leading into town. On the other hand, FHM 4225 Guldsmedgade and FHM 4278 Rosensgade, both to the northwest, have ratios of cooking/serving vessels approaching those seen reflecting the rural consumption.

Vessel size and function

If we look at the size of the greyware cooking pots, it seems to be possible to divide them into sets of small (10-14 cm), medium (16-20 cm) and large (22-28 cm) diameters. The small and medium-sized pots are present from the Viking Age and throughout the Middle Ages, while larger pots are increasingly common from the 14th century onwards and the smallest pots disappear. This could be interpreted in terms of a changing food culture and food preparation in the 16th century; a point to be elaborated later. The variation in the rim diameter/size of glazed cooking pots mirrors that of greyware, with small (10-14 cm), medium (16-20 cm) and large (>22 cm) examples. The abundance of these does not seem to vary with time.

The obvious question then is how the functional types made in different fabrics relate to each other through the history of the town. It is apparent that the greyware cooking pots and, to some degree, the greyware bowls see decreasing use with time, while redware cooking pots become increasingly widespread from the 14th and 15th centuries onwards. The four consumer revolutions previously mentioned are visible: 1. The introduction of the jug, greyware, redware or imported, in the 13th century. 2. The introduction of the redware cooking pot in the 15th century. 3. The introduction of plates: local decorated and undecorated redware and imported, in the 15th/16th century, and 4. the introduction of porcelain and industrial cups linked to consumption of tea, coffee or cocoa in the 18th century. The first revolution is linked to the introduction of specialised serving – at least in ceramics. The second ceramics revolution is interesting because it could be linked to a change in food culture towards an emphasis on fried food and the third is interesting because of the presence of individual ceramic tableware. The introduction of tea and coffee sets has already been mentioned. This will be dealt with in the following, after a chapter on monetisation.

4.2 Coins and contacts – the numismatic evidence

Coins are an obvious source of information in a study of the people who lived and traded in the town. An overview of the coins found in the Aarhus area was published in 1979, but as the number of coins recovered in the region has increased significantly since then, it is relevant to revisit the numismatic evidence here.[164] An archaeological study of the coins found in the area around Aarhus is at an early stage, but a preliminary overview will be given here in order to clarify the evidence provided by the coins and compare it with that from studies of other aspects of materiality in the area. This chapter is therefore not an attempt to analyse the monetisation process in detail or theorise on economic integration in the Aarhus area, that is best left to numismatists and economic historians, but to present a preliminary overview of the coins as a prerequisite of consumption from an archaeological perspective, as of 2014. The rationale is that the distribution of coins could correlate or contrast with other modes of consumption evident from the other aspects of archaeological materiality examined in this study, and thereby give an insight into how, and under which conditions, this materiality became exchanged and spread.

The available numismatic record comprises both single finds of coins and coin hoards. Many of the single finds result from archaeological excavations and the remainder – mostly earlier finds – were dis-

Figure 150. Burying the Treasure. Consolation of Philosophy, 1476, Harley 4339, f.2. © The British Library Board, London.

covered during construction work. The nine hoards found in the area are also mostly earlier discoveries. Three of them were found within the town area, as defined above, and the rest are from rural areas. It is evident that most of the single finds, and especially those found during an archaeological excavation, have a context – a link between the loss of the coin and the place where it was found – thereby providing an insight into the human handling of coins in day-to-day situations. Hoards, on the other hand, represent quite different situations, such as crises or sudden threats, when fortunes were hidden away.[165] Consequently, single finds with an archaeological context carry valuable evidence on the human handling of coins and may even give information on their daily use, and sometimes even their circulation, that is not easily obtainable by other means. In this sense, a coin can be described as an archaeological artefact with a special function and, for the most, a known date and place of production. This means that coins can be subjected to the same archaeological interpretation with regard to use, discard, post-depositional and recovery processes and even consumption as any other artefact. It is also obvious that coins are now used by archaeologists as a dating instrument and, as with any artefact used for dating purposes, their context has to be interpreted carefully in the research process by both archaeologists and numismatists. Consequently, this interpretation is not unproblematic. At times, a discrepancy arises between the archaeological interpretation of the stratigraphy and the dating and chronological sequencing as viewed by the numismatists. Such a discrepancy is for example apparent in the publication of investigations of a monastery in Randers, where the archaeological

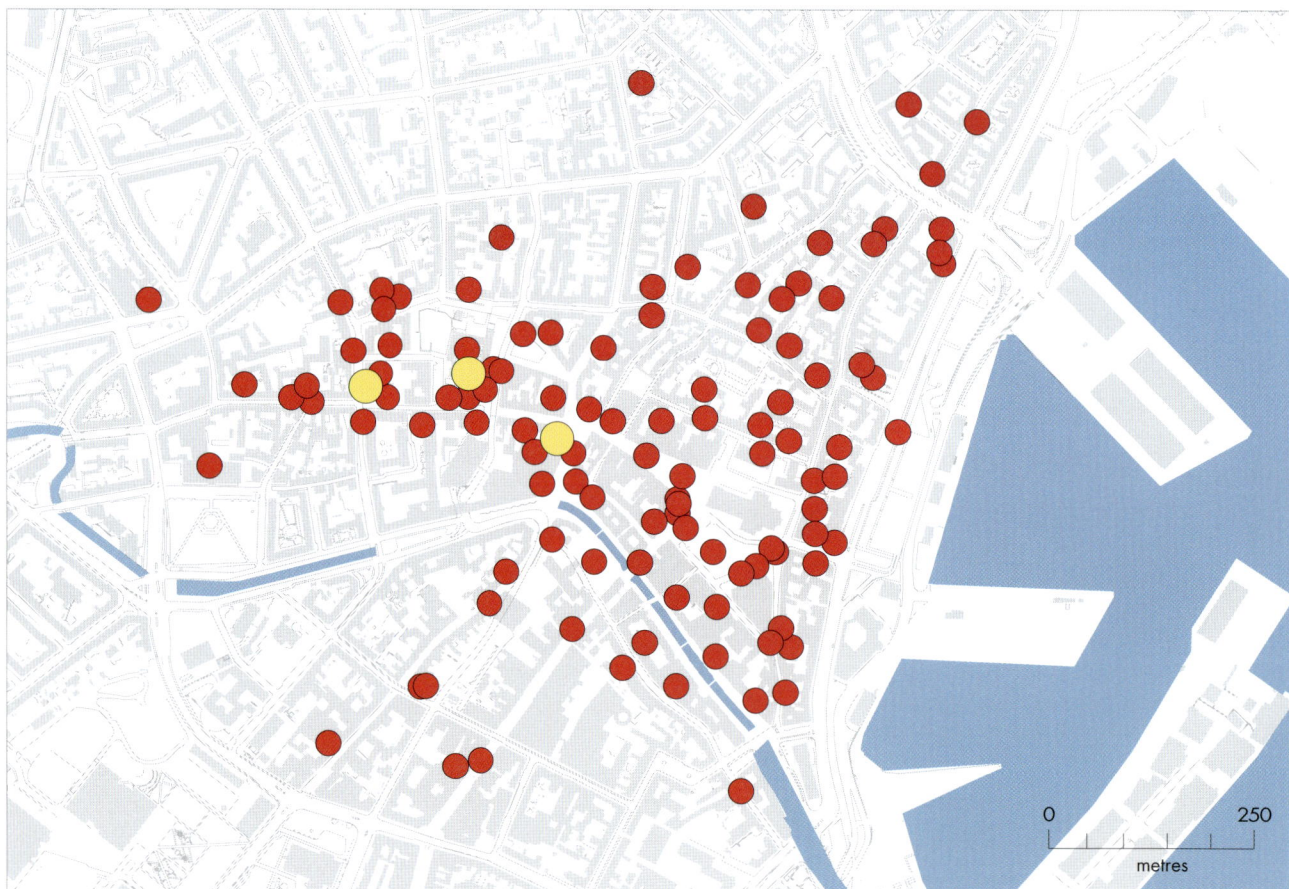

Figure 151. Coins in the town. Yellow dots: coin hoards. Red dots: Single coins.

and numismatic sequencing do not concur. Another example is seen in the excavation findings from a site in Horsens, where coins that were apparently minted in the early 14[166] century appear in contexts that, stratigraphically, are considerably later than this.[166]

The locations of coins found within the urban centre are shown in figure 151.

The total number of Medieval coins found within the study area prior to 2014 is 8046. Their numerical distribution is uneven to say the least: Most of them, 7851 in total, derive from seven coin hoards, while the remainder comprises single finds. Of the latter, the majority, 177 examples, were found within the boundaries of the Early Modern town, while 18 were found outside these. This number is low, very low even, compared to for example Medieval Lund, where c. 1800 coins have been found. The limited number of coins probably reflects special preservation and recovery conditions, and also the fact that Aarhus was a smaller town (than such as Lund) with a different economy, especially in the Early Middle Ages.[167] Although the number of single coins is limited, it is important to note that each of them represents the actual handling of coins and, collectively, they thereby represent a significant number of coin-based transactions. The Aarhus hoards have been found within buildings, but so far none of the single finds of coins has been interpreted as having been deliberately placed during construction works: All of the coins recovered during excavations came from house floors and pavements. Of the single coins, 176 were found in archaeological excavations, while the rest are earlier discoveries. The number of single coins found in any one excavation varies from one to 15, and it is obvious that the location of the excavated area within the town, the size of the excavation and the recovery method – especially the use of metal detectors and sieving – are all important factors with respect to the recovery of coins. The use of sieving and metal-detectors probably explains why coins are more common finds at more recently excavated sites, both inside and outside the town, than at those investigated prior to 1990. Another factor that must

be taken into consideration is refuse collection and disposal. Lost coins may well have been swept up from house floors and yards and deposited in backyards or on streets with the rest of the waste. Refuse containing lost coins may also have been collected and removed entirely from site, i.e. deposited elsewhere. This does not seem to be a major issue in the town of Aarhus, where present evidence suggests that a large-scale publicly organised system of waste disposal was not introduced until the Early Modern period. In the case of other towns and cities such as Aalborg, however, out-of-town waste disposal has resulted in significant finds of Medieval coins being made outside the inhabited area. In the countryside, waste was transported to the outfield as manure and this may explain why coins are very rare finds in excavations of Medieval rural settlements.[168] The preservation conditions for metals are also an important factor with respect to the numismatic record. Thin Late Medieval copper coins may be attacked by acids in the Medieval layers and consequently be in a poor state of preservation when recovered, if they have not been destroyed completely in the ground.

To date, about 75% of the coins have been identified. Many of the remainder are in such a poor state of preservation that precise identification is unlikely ever to be possible. Nevertheless, further investigations of the numismatic material may yet significantly alter what we think we now know.

Looking at the distribution of coins within the boundaries of the town, it is hardly surprising that the largest concentrations coincide with its market places at Lille Torv and Store Torv,[169] where small-scale trade was associated with the loss of low-value coins. A similar link between low-value coins and market places or shops has been demonstrated in Horsens, and also in Dragør and Trondheim.[170] Neither is it surprising that most of the coins are of Late Medieval and Early Modern date, reflecting both the intensification of activities in the town during the later Middle Ages and the spread and increase in the use of coins in society as a whole.[171] The value of the individual

Figure 152. This coin was minted in Aarhus during the reign of Magnus the Good (1042-47). The inscription reads "Lifsig on Arosei", Lifsig in Aarhus. Photo: Hans Skov/Moesgaard Museum.

Figure 153. English gold noble, minted c. 1360 in London. A noble like this was recovered in 1955 during construction works in Skt. Clemens Stræde. ©Trustees of the British Museum.

coins may of course influence their distribution pattern, as low-value coins may not be searched for so vigorously when lost. This aspect of human behaviour could have a significant impact on the distribution of coins found in archaeological excavations, especially in relation to the late 14th century, when low-value coins were abundant.[172]

Very few Viking Age coins have so far been found in Aarhus. The exceptions include a coin minted by Harald Bluetooth that rarely occurs as a single find – three examples of this were recovered during the excavations at FHM 5124 Bispetorv.[173] It seems significant that only one Arabic coin and very few pieces of hack silver have, as yet, been found in the town.[174] The very few Early Medieval coins discovered in the town indicate links with the Rhineland. One is a halfpenny minted in Mainz under Heinrich III (1051-1059) and another is an imitation of a coin minted by Herman III in Nordheim (1089-1099). Both were found near the first cathedral and may reflect contacts associated with the earliest episcopal seat.[175] Of approximately the same age is a penning minted by Svend Estridsen in Viborg between 1047 and 1074, recovered from occupation layers located immediately east of the present cathedral.[176] Coins were also actually minted in Aarhus during the same period, as demonstrated by a coin bearing the inscription "Lifsig in Arosei", struck during the reign of King Magnus the Good (1042-1047).[177] The scant numismatic evidence mirrors the sparse archaeological traces of Early Medieval occupation, which is only evident at a few archaeological sites, primarily those located west of the Priory of Our Lady, in the area around the cathedral and to the north of Lille Torv.[178] No Early Medieval coins have been found in the latter area, which may indicate that coins were used for special purposes at special places and not generally distributed across the town.[179] A similar distribution of coins is evident in Roskilde, so this phenomenon may be typical of Early Medieval towns and cities.[180]

Coins appear as rarely in the 13th century as in earlier times, even though the settlement appears to intensify at this time and extends along the western parts of Vestergade.[181] Very few coins can be dated to this century: One of these is a penny minted by Christopher II (1252-1259), which was recovered from the first pavement on Lille Torv. According to a dendrochronological date, the latter was laid out before 1268.[182] A penny minted by Erik Glipping in the 1260s was recovered from a floor in a house situated directly beside St. Oluf´s Church, near the coast and immediately north of the rampart around the inner town centre.[183] A silver coin minted during the reign of Christopher II (1252-

154

1259) was found at present day Pustervig, north of Lille Torv.[184] The discovery of these coins on a market square and in a dwelling could indicate that they were intended for use in trade, but further work on the coins is required if this possibility is to be explored in more detail. Finds of later Danish debased pennies, dating from c. 1270-1330, are rather frequent from the town centre and the northern part of the town. This may reflect further intensification of economic activities and monetisation of day-to-day economic transactions from the late 13th century onwards. However, the low value of the coins, which means that they may not have been searched for so intently when lost, is also a factor to be taken into consideration.[185] Foreign coins are rare among the single finds from the town and it seems safe to say that the circulation of coinage represents what has been described as "local coins for local use".[186] The few foreign single finds of coins include a svare, minted in Diepholz in 1360-1370, found just north of Lille Torv.[187] The most spectacular coin is a English gold noble, minted in c. 1360, found during construction works in Skt. Clemens Stræde (on land registry title no. 766) in 1955.[188] This is the only gold coin recovered within the study area, either as a stray/single find or in a hoard. Nothing is known about its context, but perhaps it was hidden and never recovered, since a high-value coin such as this, if lost, would have been intensively searched for. It seems likely that it does not reflect the local use of coins in day-to-day activities in the town, but had a function related to long-distance trade, as will be discussed below.

One may wonder how economic transactions were carried out in town in the late 14th century, since the Danish coinage system broke down in the 1330s and Danish minting of coins came to a halt.[189] The use of foreign coins is one possibility but, as previously mentioned, very few of these have so far been securely identified among material from the late 14th century. The precise use of coins in Aarhus in the late 14th century is difficult to investigate, as only a limited number of precise dates are available. Nevertheless, if the apparent lack of foreign coins is a true reflection of the actual situation, this may indicate that most

Figure 154. Post-Medieval redware money box, found in excavation at FHM 5348 Pustervig. Late 15th or early 16th century. Note that the box has been broken open. Photo: Moesgaard Museum.

day-to-day economic transactions were carried out by payment in kind or merchant's credits, as suggested by Bjørn Poulsen.[190] However, it is also possible that low-denomination coins minted in the first half of the 14th century filled the apparent gap. It could be significant that a context dated stratigraphically to the late 14th century contained two coins minted in the first decades of that century.[191] Unfortunately, this context is interpreted as a refuse dump, which includes a mixture of earlier and later material on an open surface, so the possibility that these coins could come from disturbed earlier contexts cannot be ruled out.

Most of the few coins identified from the 15th century are low-denomination sterlings, minted under Erik of Pomerania and Christopher II.[192] These were found in the same areas as those of the previous century, but can now also be seen to have spread south of the river, reflecting the date for the construction of this part of the town, which also accords with the dendrochronological dates.[193] The question is whether the decline in the number of coins recovered reflects an actual monetary contraction or is the result of special circumstances surrounding the loss of coins. Most of the 15th century finds are high-value/high-denomination coins that may well have been searched for more diligently than the abundant low-value/low-denomination coins

Figure 155. Coins in the landscape. Yellow dots: coin hoards. Red dots: single coins.

of the 14[194] century, thereby suggesting an apparent decline in the use of coins, when the archaeological record is considered.[194] The numismatic evidence from Aarhus is much too sparse for any firm conclusions to be drawn at this point, although both the above factors appear to have influenced the record.

Post-Medieval coins are scarce and only coins minted by Christian II and Christian III have been recovered,

together with a few examples from Lübeck: a double shilling minted in 1563 and a coin minted by Christian V in 1697.[195] The decline in the numismatic evidence matches the decrease in the number of archaeological sites with deposits of this age, which in turn probably reflects the disturbance of later occupation layers by the construction activities of the 19th and 20th centuries. For the same reasons, the archaeologically recovered coins cannot be presumed to give a correct representation of the use of coins in the Post-Medieval town.

If we look at the numismatic evidence from rural areas, it is evident that the archaeological record is biased. There have been few excavations of Medieval and Post-Medieval rural sites in the Aarhus area and, despite the use of metal detectors, only two sites, both manor houses, have produced Medieval coins: all debased pennings.[196] However, this does not necessarily mean that coins were not used by the rural population. As a consequence of preservation factors, the cultural layers relating to rural occupation are commonly disturbed. Medieval coins are frequently found in the open fields, where they most likely represent the transporting out of village refuse, as part of the agricultural manuring process.[197] Moreover, written sources clearly relate that smallholders in the Aarhus area paid their rent in coins as early as 1313, which indicates that some coins did circulate, perhaps for special purposes rather than everyday use.[198] The picture from the rather limited number of single finds and coins from churches is supplemented by a number of coin hoards, which provide a valuable insight into the numismatic record, not least because they contain the foreign coins that are so very rare among the single finds. Three coin hoards from within the boundaries of the town provide additional information relative to the urban record. One of these was found on the floor in the crypt of the Priory of Our Lady, while the two others were discovered during construction works in the 19th and early 20th centuries, which explains their lack of a precise archaeological context. The hoards vary greatly in size. The small hoard found in the Priory of Our Lady, dating from around 1350, has already been mentioned above. It contains coins from Hamburg and Lübeck.[199] A hoard dating from the final decades of the 14th century, discovered in the western part of town, mainly contains coins from Mecklenburg (Hamburg, Lübeck, Lüneburg, Salzwedel, Wismar, Rostock, Parchim, Stralsund and Greifswald). There are also a few English sterlings from Durham and London.[200] A very large hoard of about the same date (c. 1392-1400) was found in centre of the town at Lille Torv, the location of the mayor´s residence in the 16th and 17th centuries.[201] This hoard, which was deposited in a large jug of Waldenburg stoneware, contained almost 6000 coins with a wide variety of provenances.

Although coins from many different places are represented, the majority comprise a few types originating in Hamburg, Lüneburg, Lübeck, Wismar and Rostock, which seems to be in accordance with the general circulation of coins in Denmark at the end of the 14th century.[202] Most of the coins date from the final decades of the 14th century, but a few are earlier, being from the early 14th century or even the late 13th century. It is evident that the hoards represent a very different accumulation and use of coins than the single finds found in excavations, which may reflect local circulation. Since the types represented in the hoards appear so far to be largely absent from the general urban area, it is possible they did not circulate in town in any great numbers, but were reserved for long-distance trade, as has been suggested by Bjørn Poulsen. The composition and relative proportions of the coin types in the hoards from Aarhus are not unique. Each is nicely paralleled by examples from elsewhere, such as the four hoards from Stege, which contain a similar distribution of types.[203] As such, the hoards, and especially the very large examples of these, may represent something equivalent to a safety deposit box for people involved in long-distance trade.[204] Of greatest significance is the fact that, in spite of the sparse numismatic record from the town as a whole, at least some people appear to have been able to accumulate a significant amount of capital.

The contrast between single finds and hoards is even greater in rural areas than it is in the town. While rural single finds are very scarce, the evidence from hoards dating from the beginning of the 14th century suggests an abundant presence of coins. There are records of hoards from Spørring,[205] Egå,[206] Sabro,[207] Aakjær,[208] and Tinning Skov.[209]

The Spørring, Sabro and Egå hoards only contain early 14th century coins. They were deposited in open fields and no archaeological link can be made to their former owners, so we do not know whether they were deposited by the local rural population or by people travelling through the area. The circumstances surrounding their deposition cannot therefore be reconstructed, but the presence of these hoards indicates that it was at least possible for some people in rural areas to accumulate moderate to large amounts of capital in the form of coins in the 14th century. Later use of coins is documented by the hoards from Aakjær and Tinning Skov, both of which date from the early 15th century. These hoards appear remarkably similar in their composition to those found in Aarhus, being comprised of foreign coins from Hamburg, Greifswald, Stralsund, Anklam and Wismar, Rostock and Stettin. Both hoards were found in open fields in the immediate vicinity of manors, which makes it possible, but of course not proven, that they reflect an involvement in the manorial economy. It does seem significant that the same northern German coins appear in all the hoards, regardless of their date, suggesting that these hoards reflect a general circulation of coins in the area, rather than coins for special purposes. Even though these high-

value/high-denomination coins do not feature among the single finds from the study area, they may well have been in general use. It could be that their higher value prompted greater efforts to recover lost coins, thereby explaining their absence from the single/stray finds.

Summing up, it can be said that the numismatic record is diverse but rather sparse, and an archaeological analysis is only in its initial stages. Nevertheless, the written evidence does appear to indicate a monetisation of day-to-day transactions in the town, and probably also in surrounding rural areas by at least 1300, and possibly prior to this in the 13th century. The presence of coins in rural areas could reflect monetisation or possibly market integration of the rural population into the urban networks of the same period, meaning that the framework for cultural connections leading to wider integration between town and countryside may well have been fixed in the course of the 13th century at the latest.

4.3 Cloth

Lead cloth seals are one of the best-known sources relative to studies of Medieval consumption. The cloth itself has vanished, but the lead cloth seals once attached to it are sometimes found in towns and cities, most likely reflecting the places where the rolls of cloth were cut up and sold in smaller lengths. The admittedly few identifiable lead cloth seals found in Aarhus originate from Augsburg, Leiden, Brabant and Flanders, while a larger number cannot be identified for preservation reasons.[210] There was an abundance of lead cloth seals at Lille Torv,[211] where 20 examples from Augsburg, Brabant and Flanders were recovered. All of these could be dated to the 17th century, and Lille Torv obviously represented a nodal point in the town's cloth trade. It therefore seems very likely that a merchant trading in cloth had a booth here or a shop in the immediate vicinity. Single lead cloth seals from the 15th century, for example from Ypres, have been found south of the cathedral at Skt. Clemens Torv and Bispetorv,[212] and should probably be interpreted in a similar way. Another seal was discovered in the

Figure 156. Lead cloth seal from FHM 5124 Bispetorv. 15th-16th centuries. Photo: Moesgaard Museum. After Jensen 1992.

northern part of the town and was also datable to the 15th century. An unidentifiable lead cloth seal, dated to the late 18th century, was found on the south side of the river harbour, and an undated example, also unidentifiable, was recovered north of the cathedral, while a number of seals at present in the National Museum and Den Gamle By have no information on where they were found in Aarhus.[213] According to the written evidence, in particular that contained in wills, imported cloth was well known from at least the late 13th century, with an apparent predominance of Flemish products.[214] It seems likely that the cloth trade, at least in Late Medieval times, was conducted via Lübeck, with later trade being directed through the Netherlands.[215] Locally produced cloth and textiles have unfortunately left no traces other than the loom weights that are so abundant in Aarhus' Viking Age sunken-featured buildings. As the technology changed, the loom weights disappeared, but there is no reason to believe that production of cloth in the town came to a halt. The archaeological evidence for trade in cloth is admittedly sparse. Nevertheless, it does seem to indicate the presence of imported cloth in the town by at least the 15th century. It also seems likely that cloth had a special role – part investment and display object, part money substitute.[216] The lead cloth seals found in Aarhus do not reflect direct contact with the cloth-producing areas. They can be interpreted instead as evidence of the decisions made by merchants trading in cloth. The merchants had to consider the wishes of their consumers and secure a large range of cloth types to meet the demand.[217] In this sense, the seals only provide an indirect indication of the town's network of contacts. With respect to the trade in cloth between rural and urban areas, the lead cloth seals may not constitute reliable evidence, as the seals would not have followed the pieces of cloth of finished garments that the peasants bought. Consumption of cloth is well-established in rural areas at least from the 15th century onwards, and we can perhaps presume that a similar practice applied to the peasants in the vicinity of Aarhus, although this is hard to trace archaeologically.[218]

4.4 Immigration

An important part of the study of any town is the role of foreigners and other non-natives with respect to contacts and consumption.[219] An overview of the Danish-German connections has been published recently.[220] As mentioned above, most of the written sources relating to Medieval Aarhus have been lost and there is therefore little documentary evidence regarding the presence of people of foreign descent in the town during this period. The earliest documentary reference to a foreigner in Aarhus – apart from Ketill the Norwegian, named on the runestone in Egå, and the probably English Lifsig, on the coin minted in 1042-1047, is to the merchant Wenemar von Essen, who made his will in Lübeck on 20 May 1322.[221] Wenemar left half a townhouse in Aarhus, which he owned jointly with his relative Hermann. He also donated money to various institutions in Aarhus: the parish church of St. Oluf, St. Clement's Cathedral and the House of the Holy Spirit, the Dominican St. Nicholas' Monastery and the parish church of Our Lady. He mentions a business partner, Gerlach, and states in his will that the money is to be taken from what is owed to him in Aarhus, indicating that he operated within the framework of the German credit system, as known for example from Bergen.[222] In 1331, the same Wenemar von Essen rewrote his will and in this he mentions Herman Witte – another man of German descent, judging from his name – as his host in Aarhus.[223] The will does not reveal where Wenemar von Essen lived in the town, but this reference clearly documents his translocal behaviour. He not only owned property in Aarhus, but had also been to the town, judging from his description of the churches, and he even had a local network comprised of other individuals of German origin. Wenemar von Essen does not mention any people with Danish-sounding names in his will, and this could indicate that Wenemar and his fellows operated within a segregated community in the town. Although we have no information on where exactly Wenemar lived, the fact that he mentions the parish church of St. Oluf first could indicate that this was his local parish church, but this is of course only speculation. The presence of possible immigrants in the town begs the question of how they were accommodated. In Bruges, foreigners who were not citizens were guests in the houses of native burghers or of Germans, who had become burghers in the city, with the hosts acting as middlemen between producers and the German buyers. The Germans thereby formed a trade/purchasing cartel with other guests in order to secure quality and supply.[224]

Wenemar is the earliest individual with a possibly foreign name mentioned in written sources, but others soon follow. In 1356, a letter from the town council of Aarhus to the council of Lübeck regarding the estate of Henrik Blievelt, a citizen of Aarhus, documents both mercantile and family links between citizens in the two cities.[225] This contact continued and in 1406 a citizen of Aarhus, Johan Sveder, mentions an inheritance in Wismar, Rostock and Aarhus, showing that his network encompassed all three.[226] The evidence is sparse but seems to indicate that at least a handful of people of possible German descent had settled in Aarhus by the early 14th century. Moreover, they engaged in trans-local behaviour, maintaining close contacts with their homelands and owning or inheriting property in both Germany and in Aarhus. According to the scant information provided by their wills, their closest networks appear to have included other immigrants in the town, which may in turn indicate the existence of a probably very small, closely-knit immigrant community in Aarhus in the 14th century.

Immigration continued in the 15th and 16th centuries. We can see this from the town registers of 1487-1550, as published by Poul Enemark and Ole Degn, supplemented with information from the work of Hübertz from 1845-1846.[227] These registers give the names, and sometimes the home towns, of the people who applied for citizenship in Aarhus, i.e. they state the name of the applicant and sometimes the place where they had lived previously. The register reveals two groups of immigrants: Those who originated outside Denmark's borders, as they were at any given time, and those who originated within the Danish realm. Moreover, their origin can mostly only be assumed from the sole evidence presented – their names. This leads to obvious source-related problems, as names can be inherited through generations or follow people from one place to another.[228] Furthermore, the registers only allow us to follow the people who applied for citizenship. Other, possibly larger, associated sectors of the population, such as the women, children and servants in the households of these citizens, cannot be followed by these means, but may be traced in detailed historical studies.[229]

A number of people with Dutch or German surnames took up citizenship in the 15th century, beginning with Peder Wilde in 1466 and continuing with Claus, Henrik, Niels, Peter and Valentin, of the same surname, between 1490 and 1505. In this possibly related family group, Valentin Wilde is translocal in his behaviour, being also mentioned as a citizen of Lübeck in 1506.[230] The Wilde family are not the only people with foreign names in Aarhus around 1500. Others include Hans Prusse, Peter Radgiffer Vismer and Jost Pomereling, whose names indicate German descent, and Henrik van Groning, who may have been of Dutch origin – perhaps a Dutchman who relocated to Lübeck.[231] The case of Blasius von Wismar, who took citizenship in 1501, provides an insight into conditions for foreigners who moved to the town.[232] According to the sources, Blasius had to pay eight marks for his citizenship, as well as promise to marry the daughter of a Dane within a year. This is one of the few examples of what we might call an immigration or integration policy, dictated at a local level by the town council. This brief summary of the foreign immigrants in Aarhus gives the impression that the majority of the population was of Danish descent. However, this does not mean that they were all born in the town. The aforementioned town registers, listing citizens of Aarhus from 1471-1550, give a place name as part of their surname in about 10% of cases.[233] Examples included Bernd Hiernø (Hjarnø in Horsens Fjord), mentioned in 1470, and Anders Olufssen Fleestrup (Fløjstrup south of Aarhus), mentioned in 1489. Taking these place names as an indicator of geographical origin is associated with obvious problems, for example when geographical locations become family surnames. However, if we ignore these problems for now and look at the place names the distribution shows distribution shows a distinct clustering within a 60 km radius of the town. Furthermore, more than half the place names lie within 20 km of Aarhus. So even though many of the citizens living in Aarhus were, according to their surnames, not born in the town, they did come from the surrounding villages. It seems the town primarily attracted new citizens from its immediate vicinity and only to a lesser degree from other parts of Denmark. A few citizens were not local, but came from further afield, for example the island of Læsø and the towns of Mariager, Holstebro, and Grenå. The fact that most of the newcomers were of decidedly local origin is not unique to Aarhus, the same can also be said of for example Copenhagen and Aalborg at about the same time.[234]

The town archives also tell of some immigration at this time involving craftsmen from Lübeck, Hessen and Hamburg, who settled in the town, as well as some immigrants from Norway. One example is a barber, Augustinus Lifflænder, who took citizenship in 1593 and possibly came from Livonia, located between present-day Estonia and Latvia.[235] Another is the well-known printer Hans Hansen Skonning from Scania, who came to the town in 1616.[236] A special case is that of sculptor Gert van Groningen, who was possibly Dutch and who obtained citizenship in 1573,[237] while Johan Worm, who became a member of the town council, emigrated from Arnhem around the same time.[238]

This immigration appears to continue into the 18th century, giving the impression of stability in the origin of the immigrants over a longer period, with the majority of the foreign-born citizens coming from areas with ancient contacts with Denmark: Hessen, the area between Schleswig and Rostock, the environs of Hamburg and the southern part of Norway.[239] The number of citizens of foreign descent appears to increase slightly in the 17th century, to around 10% of a total population of about 4000 people, as more people of possible foreign descent migrated to the town.[240] Judging from their names and occupations, these immigrants appear to have been primarily craftsmen from Norway, at that time part of the Danish realm, and what is now Germany, especially the areas around Mecklenburg, Hamburg, Bremen and Lübeck. They included Jakob Heylemand from Hessen

and Jochum Lorents from Lübeck, who took citizenship in 1626 and 1642, respectively.[241] According to their stated occupations, these immigrants were specialist craftsmen, including hatters, dyers, wigmakers and tailors, and their presence resulted in greater craft diversity in the town. They also included a gardener, Johan Friedrich Foss from Güstrow, and a surgeon, Johan Bernhardt Smule from Rostock, who took citizenship in 1713 and 1744, respectively.[242] It is in the same century that Jews are mentioned for the first time, but the citizens of Aarhus apparently did not welcome these newcomers. An example of this is evident in the case of Moses Hinrich from Frederica, who obtained citizenship in 1738. His citizenship was met with protests, although these were not rooted in his religion, but in his contacts with wealthy Jewish communities aboard. It was his financially privileged position that prompted the protests, not the fact that he was Jewish.[243] Just as in the Late Medieval period, not all citizens with Danish names originated in Aarhus. Later sources, from the 17th, 18th and 19th centuries, reveal that approximately 20% of the people who obtained citizenship were born in the town, while around half were from rural parts of Jutland and only around 10% from towns and cities in Jutland, and even fewer from Zealand.[244] Consequently, a large proportion of these new urban citizens appear to have been of rural descent and with origins in the immediate vicinity of Aarhus – exactly the same pattern that was evident in the late 15th century. This indicates a marked geographical mobility within the region. Moreover, many citizens then moved away from the town again. As pointed out by Ole Degn, about half of the citizens appear to have left Aarhus over a period of just seven years, between 1612 and 1619. They were replaced by others, but this high turnover is remarkable. Degn concludes that it was especially the poorer inhabitants who left the town in such large numbers, while the wealthier citizens stayed on. We must therefore imagine a town with a stable group of wealthy families and households and a mobile class of poorer citizens moving in and out.[245] Whether this situation applies to earlier periods is an open question, which I will address in my concluding remarks.

Figure 157. *Three Eating Old Women at a Table, Nicholaes van Haeften, 1694. ©Rijksmuseum, Amsterdam.*

5 Horizons

The analysis of the archaeological material described in the previous chapter has resulted in the identification of seven marked stages of urban consumption. The relatively stable situation in the Viking Age is replaced by the introduction of new western European consumption in the Early Medieval period. Changes are evident in the 13th century with the introduction of German stonewares. A very marked shift occurs in the first decades of the 15th century, when new ways of preparing food are introduced, and another change takes place in the final decades of the 16th century as display becomes profoundly altered. The final change occurs at the end of the 17th century. In the following chapter, the social practice of consumption in each of these stages will be analysed and compared to structural changes during the same period.

5.1 Stages 1-2: The earliest Aarhus c. AD 700-1050 (with Lars Krants)

Aarhus is mentioned for the first time in AD 948 as the seat of the Bishop Reginbrand, who took part in a synod in the German imperial town of Ingelheim on the Rhine.[246] Apart from evidence of Stone Age settlement and a vessel from the Iron Age indicating some activity at this time, the earliest datable traces of occupation in the area later covered by Aarhus appear to be from the 8th or 9th century AD.[247] Pollen analysis reveals the existence of a forested area with beech trees and grassland in the vicinity, indicating that the landscape had become open, perhaps grass-clad, with arable agriculture, some time after AD 200.[248] The earliest securely-dated settlement structure in

Aarhus has been revealed at the site of FHM 4573 Skt. Clemens Stræde. The earliest trace is a shallow ditch, about 2 m wide, running alongside the river, Aarhus Å,[249] which may have acted as a boundary marker for the earliest settlement here. The ditch stood open for a while, being progressively filled up with waste from a settlement for which we as yet have no direct archaeological evidence. The fill included traces of household activities, mainly ceramics and a spindle whorl, as well as faunal remains – cattle, sheep and fish, suggesting the exploitation of coastal resources, i.e. fishing and grazing of livestock. The precise date of the ditch is as yet unknown, but its stratigraphy and the ceramics it contains indicate the 9th century, although an earlier date is possible, as buckles and beads dated to the late 8th century are among the stray finds from the area.[250] After a few years, the ditch was filled in and the area levelled with material containing the same kinds of remains; ceramics, loom weights and the bones of fish and farm animals, indicating household activities of some permanence: cooking and textile production, animal husbandry and fishing. Probably following this, a second ditch of roughly the same dimensions and orientation was dug about 3 m closer to the riverbank.[251] Immediately after levelling of the area, oval sunken-featured buildings were constructed in what appears to have been an intensification and enlargement of the settlement towards Aarhus Å. This may have been connected with an increased emphasis on seafaring in the community, but as the Viking Age harbour has not yet been located, this possibility remains unconfirmed.

The sunken-featured buildings contained exactly the same types of finds as the earlier ditch and the levelling deposits, i.e. traces of household activities of a semi-permanent or permanent nature, mainly ceramics and loom weights, as well as faunal remains from animal husbandry and fishing. Although more work is required before these can be reliably dated, some of the other sunken-featured buildings excavated in Aarhus could also belong to this early settlement phase. This applies to the oval sunken-featured buildings that were excavated in the vicinity of the Dominican friary, to the west, and near the later Studsgade, to the north.[252] In both cases, the houses contained traces of domestic activities: loom weights, ceramics, soapstone vessels etc.[253] Some of the sunken-featured buildings at Bispetorv may belong to this early settlement phase too.[254] The stratigraphically earliest sunken-featured buildings at Bispetorv were oval or circular in outline, and all three of them contained traces of ordinary household activities indicating some permanence, i.e. ceramics, soapstone vessels, loom weights etc., but no evidence of specialised crafts.[255] It is therefore possible that the earliest settlement in Aarhus consisted primarily of oval sunken-featured buildings, and that the activities were directed primarily towards the exploitation of coastal resources and with no significant traces of long-distance exchange and contacts. Whether the settlement was permanent is as yet an open question. The loom weights point towards some form of permanence, and at the Skt. Clemens Stræde site, at least, they indicate continuous occupation from the very earliest activities. The size of the settlement is as yet difficult to estimate, but the archaeological evidence does indicate an occupation along the river and the coast covering a fairly large area, around 11 ha; smaller than Haithabu but larger than Sebbersund near Aalborg.

The activities appear to change during the second settlement phase. The three stratigraphically later sunken-featured buildings at Bispetorv were square in outline and had a hearth. They contained the same traces of household activities as the earlier buildings, but also yielded finds suggestive of specialised crafts, mostly comb-making, while the presence of balance weights appears to indicate trade. A burnt sunken-featured building, dated to the final quarter of the 10th century, contained abundant charred grain, as well as baskets, soapstone vessels, quernstones, a few coins, a weight and a piece of chain-mail, indicating both household activities and a range of more specialised functions related to crafts, trade and warfare. Traces of further crafts: glass bead-making, comb-making and metal production, have been detected in the southern and central parts of town, near Skt. Clemens Stræde, Rosensgade, Kannikegade and Skolebakken.[256] A smithy was located in the eastern part of town near the coast, in what is now Havnegade, and another one in the western part, in what is now Vestergade.[257] Recent research has provided us with an interesting insight into combs and comb-production in town. Studies of the comb-makers' waste show that the raw material used in comb production was almost exclusively red deer antler. On the other hand, most of the complete combs found in the town are of reindeer antler, pointing towards contacts with Norway.[258]

The excavation in Skt. Clemens Stræde revealed a complicated settlement. At this site, close to the river bank, the oval sunken-featured buildings were replaced not by rectangular ones, but by post-built houses with gables facing the river, and of a type that has so far not been seen anywhere else in town. It is possible that this means there was a row of post-built houses along the river, with sunken-featured buildings on the back of the plots. The excavated building had been repaired several times and seems therefore to have had a long lifetime before it was demolished immediately prior to the construction of the earliest rampart. Among the finds from this building are Baltic ceramics of Feldberg type, as well as so-called "teller" – small clay plates, which constitute another distinct type. Both types have been found previously in settlements that clearly predate the town rampart, together with Fresendorf types. The largest proportion of Baltic pottery from town is of Menkendorf type, and of the same date are sherds of Woldgker and/or Bobzin types. Sherds of Warder type are quite frequent in the latest phases in town. The variety of types and their chronological time span indicate the existence of long-term, stable contacts with people on the Baltic coast.[259] The settlement at Skt. Clemens Stræde is particularly enlightening because it was found beneath the oldest rampart and thereby clearly predates the fortified town centre. Other settlement traces that similarly predate the fortification have been recorded at several other locations in the town. To the north, at Mejlgade 8, traces of house floors, hearths etc. were recorded below the earliest rampart, while cultural layers were similarly found below the rampart at Pustervig Torv and oval sunken-featured buildings were discovered below the rampart further to the north at Rosensgade 32-34. We may speculate about who was responsible for fortification of the town, but given the large-scale clearance of the previous occupation, it is clear that this was the work of someone occupying a dominant position. There seems to be some evidence suggesting attacks or unrest. As previously mentioned, a sunken-featured building at Bispetorv, dated to the final quarter of the 10th century, had clearly burned down, as had two similar features excavated at Aarhus Søndervold.[260] Then there is the human skeleton found in the fill of another sunken-hut here.[261] Whether this really constitutes evidence of attacks in the Late Viking Age is an open question that requires further research in future projects.

Returning to the evidence of long-distance contacts, the Norwegian whetstones and soapstone vessels have already been mentioned, as have the Baltic ceramics. Other evidence of the townspeople's contacts is found in the presence of coins minted in Haithabu, a comb marked with the Anglo-Saxon name Hikuin and the mention of Haithabu on a rune stone. Given the evidence of specialised crafts and traces of Baltic contacts, Aarhus can be perceived as a marketplace – or more likely, part production site, with a special focus on coastal resources, part marketplace, at least from the second settlement phase. However, it should be noted that the specialised trade and production took place in the settlement later covered by the rampart. Aarhus was therefore not established as a fortified marketplace, but was an existing marketplace that was reorganised and fortified in the 10th century. Furthermore, the town functioned as an ecclesial centre. Aarhus is mentioned

as the seat of Bishop Reginbrand in AD 948, and by AD 965 the town had a church that is mentioned again in AD 988. The importance of the ecclesial centre for the Viking Age town is unclear, but it is clear that this importance increased in the Early Middle Ages.[262]

5.2 Stage 3: The Early Medieval town c. 1050-1200

The nature and extent of Early Medieval Aarhus is not very well known. At first glance, the activities seem limited compared to the massive evidence from the Viking Age occupation. This could, however, be partly an illusion resulting from the fact that the sunken-featured buildings went out of use and the floor layers and postholes associated with the later occupation were more exposed and suffered greater disturbance and destruction by subsequent building activities. However, this does not provide the full explanation, since the technically advanced excavations undertaken in Aarhus in recent years have not revealed large-scale traces of Early Medieval occupation. At the same time, it would be unfair to describe Aarhus as a town in complete decline. Instead, we see a continuity of function as a centre for trade and craft production, with a revival of the town as an ecclesial centre.

After a period of apparent vacancy, Aarhus again became an episcopal seat, and shortly after this the first cathedral was built west of the ramparts. Over the next century, further ecclesial institutions followed: the churches of Our Lady and St. Oluf are mentioned in 1203. The Church of Our Lady is not known archaeo-logically, although the presence of graves points to a location by the western gate. St. Oluf's Church was built very near the coast, to the north of the Viking Age rampart – a rampart that was still very much a visible feature of the town at this time. The church's graves date from the 13th century, but a grave under its foundations indicates the existence of an earlier, as yet unknown, church on the site.[263] All these churches were built outside the Viking Age rampart. The area inside the rampart may have housed a chapel: A chapel "by the sea" is mentioned in the middle of the 13th century, referring to a late 12th century situation.[264]

Aarhus hosted other institutions too: Coins were minted in the town during the reign of Hardicanute (1035-1042): The mintmaster, Ciadwinw, must have been Anglo-Saxon, as must the mintmaster Lifsig, who struck coins in the town under Hardicanute's predecessor Magnus the Good (1042-1047).[265] Not all meetings were peaceful: According to Adam of Bremen, Aarhus was attacked in 1050 by the Norwegian king Harald Hardrada[266] The town may also have had a military function. Saxo Grammaticus mentions that Prince Magnus used the harbour of Aarhus as a naval base, and that Aarhus was attacked by Slavic Wends in 1158. As yet, however, we have no clear archaeological evidence of warfare in the town.[267]

If we take a look at the archaeological evidence, traces of Early Medieval settlement have been found both inside and outside the rampart that still stood around the town. Most of the excavated Viking Age localities have revealed traces of Early Medieval settlement, i.e. Aarhus Søndervold, Bispetorv and Store Torv.[268] At Bispetorv, the presence of local ceramics from the 11th century indicates a fairly early date for the structures revealed there: A group of furnaces in the eastern part of the site all contain ceramics datable to the Late Viking Age/early 11th century.[269] Unfortunately, any traces of the houses had been disturbed by later building activities. At Søndervold, few traces of the actual houses themselves were found, but a large quantity of Early Medieval ceramics does indicate some activity in this area. Traces of what appears to be Early Medieval settlement, dating at least back to the 12th century, have been found in the vicinity of St. Nicholas, just west of the church,[270] in Guldsmedgade to the northwest[271] and very near Lille Torv, east of the cathedral.[272] Here, the dates seem a little different: The St. Nicholas finds are from the 11th or early 12th century, while the house at Guldsmedgade could be later, from the late 12th or early 13th century. This establishment of settlement outside the rampart may indicate a partial reorganisation of the town in the Early Middle Ages:

No traces of Early Medieval settlement have so far been found near the Viking Age settlement in Studsgade, which indicates a contraction of the town. On the other hand, the rampart does not appear to define the outline or limits of the Early Medieval town. If the settlement contracted when the rampart was constructed, as can be concluded from the site of FHM 4481 Studsgade 8-10 and further sites excavated in Studsgade, people moved outside the ramparts again in the 11th century, and from then on no further contraction of the settlement took place, only expansion.

Traces of involvement in international exchange are few and far between (figure 158).

A small number of sherds of Rhenish ceramics constitute one of the few signs of contact with the Rhineland.[273] Pingsdorf and Paffrath ware, dated to the 12th century, is only found within the fortified part of the settlement and has so far not been seen in the vicinity of the cathedral at that time, St. Nicholas. This situation may indicate a division into an ecclesial centre in the west and a commercial centre in the east.[274] It could constitute the first sign of intensified contacts with what is now Germany, transmitted either from the south, via Lübeck, founded in the middle of the 12th century, or from the west, via the Limfjord. It may have been the demand for salt for the fisheries in the town that prompted these contacts, with the salt in this case coming from Lüneburg. It seems significant that the imported items seen in Aarhus, whether coins or ceramics, have not been found in rural areas. If Aarhus was a centre for wide-scale imports/exports to and from rural areas at this time, we cannot see this clearly in the contemporary archaeological record. On the other hand, there is some evidence of the town's far-reaching contacts in the form of the Anglo-Saxon names of the mintmasters in 11th century Aarhus, as mentioned above.

Foreign coins are very few in number: A pit containing two silver coins dated to the 11th and 12th centuries, together with some ceramics, was found near St. Nicholas Cathedal. The coins are a half dinar from Mainz, minted by Heinrich III (1039-1056), and an

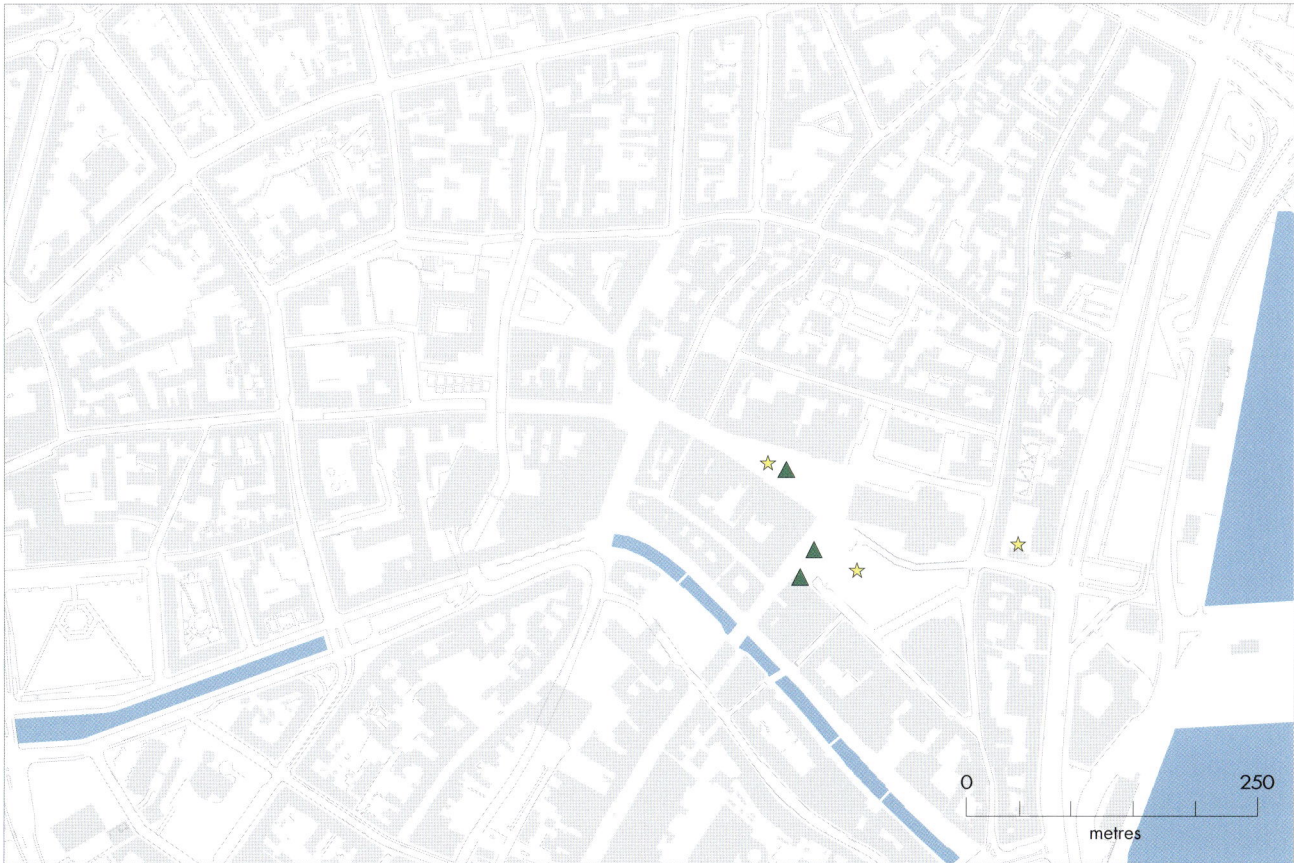

Figure 158. *Finds of Pingsdorf- and Paffrath-type wares in Aarhus. Star: Pingsdorf. Triangle: Paffrath.*

imitation of a coin from Cologne, from the first half of the 12th century. They are the only European coins found in the Early Medieval town and, even though the use of coins was only just beginning at this time, they hardly indicate intense exchange with the Rhineland. Conversely, this situation may indicate ecclesial use of these coins. Local coins are rare too: A coin minted under Svend Estridsen (1047-1075), found near the coast, is so far the only securely identified example.[275] Coins were minted in Aarhus in the middle of the 11th century by Hardicanute (1035-1042) and Magnus (1042-1047) and again during the reigns of the kings Svend, Knut and Valdemar in the middle of the 12th century.[276] However, this may have been just as much to mark royal rights as to meet a need for local coins, since these Aarhus coins have not yet been identified among the numismatic material recovered from

archaeological excavations in the town. Aside from the Rhenish ceramics, very few exotica or other signs of luxury have been found. A shaft carved in Ringerike style, discovered just east of the friary, and gilded mounts from a drinking horn, found by the theatre, are among the very few luxury objects found in the town.[277] The fragmentary traces of settlement that are preserved do not provide much opportunity for functional analysis. However, traces of specialised crafts, blacksmithing, metal-working and comb-making, as well as domestic crafts, such as weaving, have so far been seen at Katedralskolen.[278] Aarhus appears then to have continued relatively unchanged from the Viking Age well into the Early Middle Ages, maintaining its role from the Viking Age, at least in terms of the nature of its foreign contacts. It may be possible to trace a duality of the lifestyle in the town, with high-value

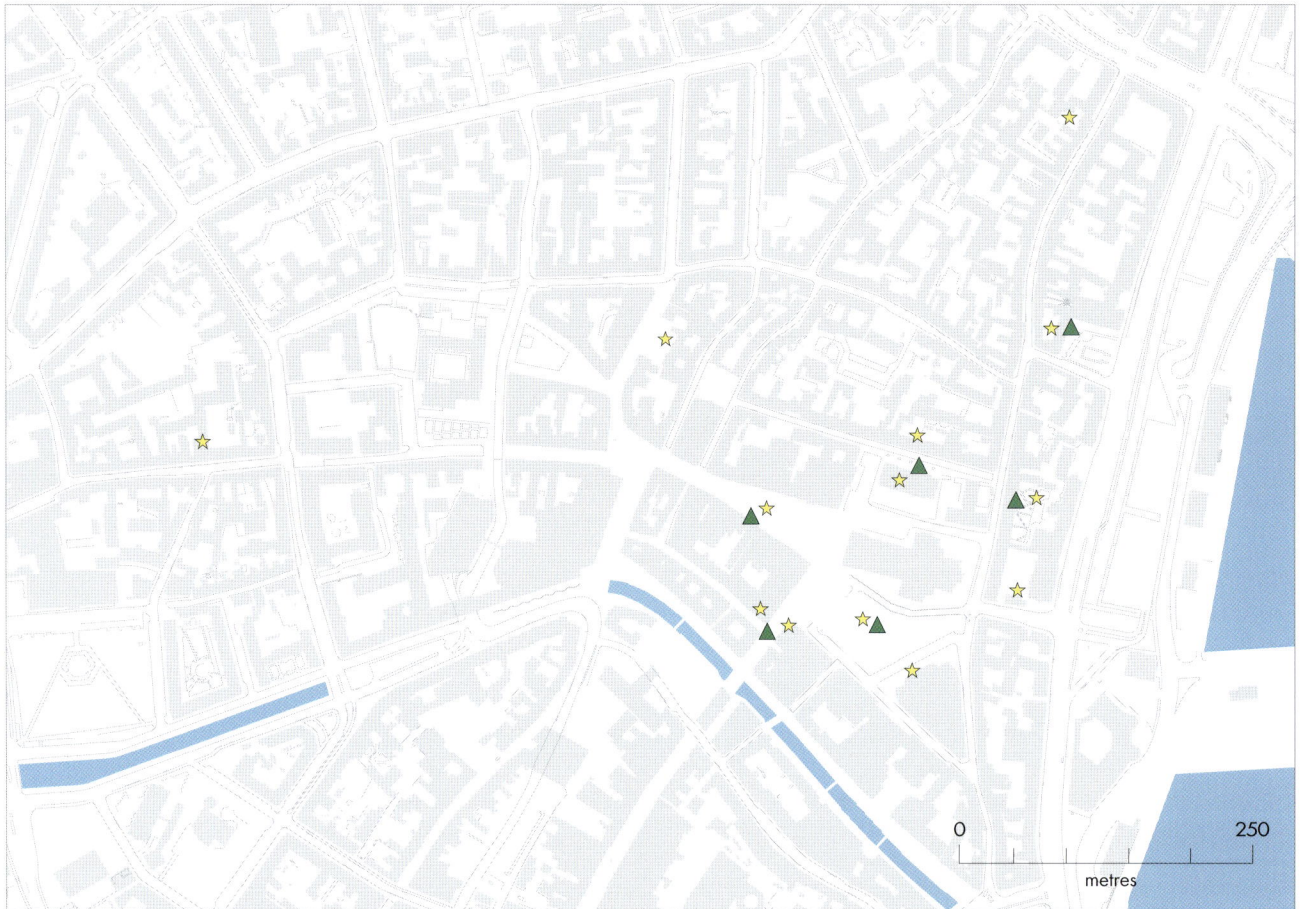

Figure 159. *Location of finds of imports c. 13th century. Star: Proto stoneware. Triangle: Andenne. The areas marked in grey are where evidence of 13th century occupation has been found.*

coins and the very few luxury items being found near the contemporaneous cathedral, west of the rampart, and the few traces of commercial contacts being evident in the area within the rampart.

5.3 Stage 4: The Medieval town c. 1200-1400: Harbour and Hanseatic consumption

The dual consumption pattern evident inside and outside the rampart changed in the late 13th and 14th centuries. Large-scale structural changes, which led to restructuring and reorganisation of the topography, went hand in hand with profound changes in social practice both inside and outside the town, which then

appears to have developed a function as a gateway between the interior and exterior world. From this time onwards, the numismatic evidence increases and it appears as if monetisation of day-to-day activities in urban and perhaps also rural areas then followed (see chapter: Coins and contacts). This is evident in a marked change in the consumption patterns in both town and hinterland, i.e. a spread of artefacts indicating contacts with the wider world.

Of greatest note in the ceramics material is Belgian Andenne-type ware and Rhenish proto stoneware. There is a correlation between the two types in the archaeological record: Andenne-type ware is always found at sites where proto stoneware types are also present. These foreign produced items are the tangible traces of structural changes that led to an increased supply of imported goods in the 13th century. The very presence of the imports may also indicate large-scale changes in production, from household or domestic supply to production aimed at generating a surplus, which could either be capitalised or used directly in exchanges with the people who distributed the imports.[279] The glazed ceramics of Andenne-type ware are profoundly different from anything used in the town before: hard-fired and colourful, with a smooth, hard, glazed surface that must have made handling these items a very different experience. The vessels found in Aarhus are lamps and jugs, both new forms indicating a refinement of the table culture with an emphasis on lighting and pouring. Lamps are only found at Store Torv,[280] while jugs are seen both inside and outside the walled part of the town – at the ecclesial centre: at Nationalbanken north of the cathedral,[281] Bispetorv [282] and just north of the rampart in Mejlgade.[283] The sherds found at Bispetorv were all redeposited, which is unfortunate, but still leave little doubt that they were originally deposited here. The jugs from Mejlgade were found in a house and there is no doubt that they were in use there. This latter location is interesting in the light of the changes in the urban infrastructure at this time, as will be discussed below. First, another ceramics type, Rhenish proto stoneware beakers and jugs, must be considered. These, like Rhenish stoneware as a whole, can be linked to the consumption of German hopped beer, and the spread of these types very probably tells us of a change in social practice connected to the growing consumption in the 13th century of beer brewed in the German tradition. This seems to be precisely the same phenomenon as that evident in legislation introduced by Erik Glipping in 1283, which mentions the selling, importing and consumption of German beer. Both Saxon beer and something called "the new cups" – possibly stoneware vessels, are mentioned in the biography of Bishop Gunnar of Viborg, written around 1250.[284] If we turn to the documentary evidence, this contains very little information on imports to Medieval Aarhus. This may, however, reflect the

nature of the available documentary sources, because imports of beer, wine and cloth are known from other towns and cities, for example Haderslev, from the late 13th century onwards. Consequently, it is possible that these goods could also have been distributed to Aarhus, but there are as yet no written records to confirm this.[285] It is not surprising that imported types have been found in the ecclesial centre of the fortified town.[286] However, they also occur outside the fortifications: in Guldsmedgade,[287] at the far end of Vestergade,[288] at the northern end of Mejlgade and on a stretch of Mejlgade towards the rampart.[289] From this pattern alone, it is clear that consumption in large parts of town, and especially along the main roads leading to the town gates, focussed on tableware and drinking. This change in consumption went hand in hand with a large-scale restructuring of the town centre in the first part of the 13th century. Inside the rampart, a new cathedral, St. Clement's, was constructed, beginning around 1200-50, probably on the site of an earlier chapel mentioned in 1191.[290] The former cathedral, St. Nicholas, was handed over to Dominican monks before 1245, the church was rebuilt and a convent was founded on the site. These large-scale construction activities and the need for transport and resources – building materials, skilled craftsmen, accommodation for workers and supplies, for the ecclesial households, i.e. clerics, the bishop etc., must have had quite an impact, both directly and indirectly, on people in the town. There is no archaeological evidence relating to the settlement structure in the area where the cathedral was built. However, if it was as densely populated as the areas immediately to the west, south and east, a significant number of buildings must have been cleared when the bishop reorganised his town and turned the settlement within the Viking Age rampart into an ecclesial centre that totally dominated the area. In parallel with the construction of the cathedral, the spatial layout of Aarhus was altered, perhaps to make room both for the people who had to abandon the town centre and for a variety of new inhabitants. The reorganisation included a refortification of the old rampart, maybe more for symbolic than military purposes, the clearing and laying out of Store Torv, breaching of the rampart to the west to create Borgporten, the laying out of Lille Torv, Immervad and Vestergade and a large part of the streets to the west and north of the fortification, including the paving of Mejlgade and Studsgade and the laying out of Guldsmedgade, Klostergade etc. A dendrochronological date from Lille Torv dates its layout to between 1253 and 1268.[291] The new organisation of the settlement within the rampart resulted in about a quarter of the settled area being cleared or reused: An undertaking and an impact on the lives of the inhabitants that was just as profound as the construction of the fortification in the Viking Age. The layout of streets to the north and west meant that Aarhus was no longer a fortified town – because the gates lay far to the north of the rampart – but a town with a fortification at its centre: A fortification surrounding the cathedral and the episcopal residence, together with other parts of the town. As mentioned above, the dual consumption pattern changed and the rampart no longer constituted a boundary marking consumption patterns in the town.

The spread of imported wares outside the rampart, especially to the north along the coast, may indicate that people engaged in trade and exchange relocated from within the fortification, where they appear to have been concentrated prior to 1200, to partially new quarters of the town founded outside. These areas were, however, not suburbs, but still very much part of the town. The gates, which are admittedly only known from the later part of the Middle Ages, were located further to the north and the west.[292] The consumption pattern in the town provides a further insight in this respect.

The harbour

The area around Mejlgade and St. Oluf´s Church is of special interest. The concentration of the proto stoneware and Andenne-type ware in these areas is intriguing. We have seen that the site of FHM 4587 Mejlgade 26 had the largest proportions of Medieval well-fired redware and imports in the entire region

in the late 13th century. Of the ceramics found in the large building here, 33% comprise glazed redware and 25% Rhenish and Baltic stoneware types – remarkably high percentages for Aarhus. If we look at the layout of this quarter, things become even more interesting. The excavation revealed evidence of a road leading from Mejlgade to the east, towards the sea; a road that existed at the same time as the outer part of Mejlgade, i.e. in the mid-13th century. Sherds of proto stoneware were found on this road, which may be a coincidence, but these may also reflect the transport of jugs and other goods, such as barrels of beer, from the shore.[293] It is therefore possible that a new merchants' quarter, with alleys running from the street down to the beach, was constructed along Mejlgade sometime in the late 13th century. Unfortunately, most of the area between Mejlgade and the coast was rebuilt in the first decades of the 20th century. Any remaining traces of the Medieval dwellings along the street have therefore been destroyed or are inaccessible; only small plots in the courtyards are still available for archaeological investigation. A sequence of Medieval houses has been excavated recently, in just such a place, at Mejlgade 37, and the earliest of these is dated to the second part of the 13th century.[294] We should also remember here that Medieval cellars and brick buildings have been seen in several places between Mejlgade and the coast (see section: FHM 4587 Mejlgade 26). Early records provide us with a glimpse of what might have been: In 1908, fragments of a brick house dated to the middle of the 14th century were found at Mejlgade 8, about 50 m to the south of Mejlgade 26, while a Late Medieval brick-built cellar was found on the neighbouring plot, Mejlgade 24, in 1922.[295] This area appears therefore to have housed a concentration of brick buildings of a somewhat early date; brick buildings and cellars that have so far not been found in other quarters outside the rampart. It is perhaps significant that St. Oluf's Church was completely rebuilt in the 13th century.[296] We might then suggest that the Mejlgade area accommodated the Medieval harbour, a planned part of the town with small roads leading from the main street to the coast, between the

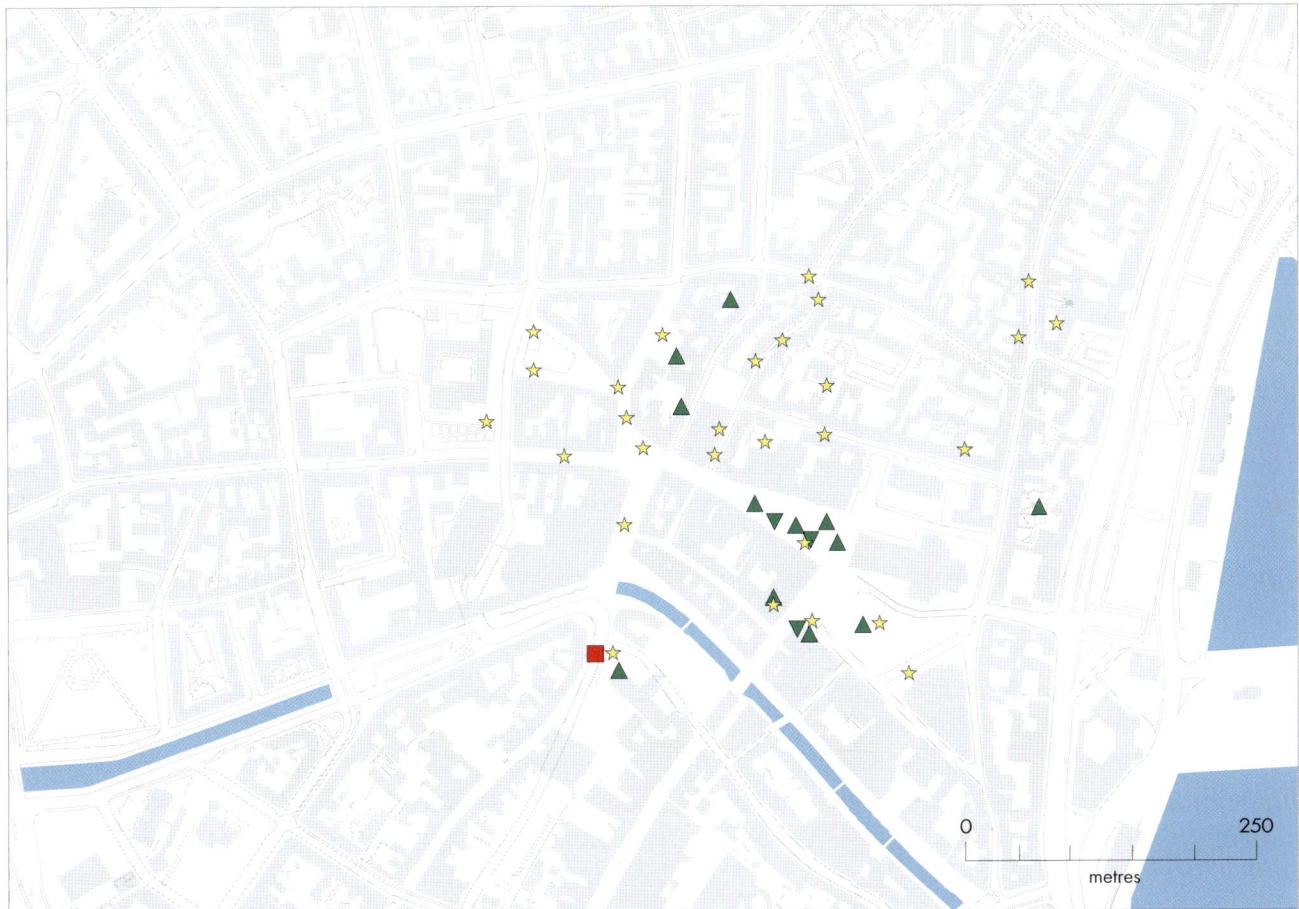

Figure 160. Imports in the 14th century. Star: Siegburg stoneware. Square: Saintonge ware. Inverted triangle: Low Countries highly-decorated ware. Triangle: Rouen type.

merchants' residences and with easy access to storage cellars.[297] This possible reorganisation of Aarhus must be seen in conjunction with the laying out of the streets in the western part of town, the paving of Store Torv and so on. It is tempting to view this spatial reorganisation in the light of the consumption patterns and suggest that people with German-influenced consumption behaviour and German contacts settled here. One might, furthermore, suggest a link with the growth of the Hanseatic towns and cities on the Baltic coast – certainly Lübeck, but also Wismar, Greifswald, Rostock, Stralsund etc. The growth of these towns would certainly have provided Aarhus with contacts and ready access to wider markets.[298]

It could of course be claimed that this Hanseatic influenced practice was shared by all inhabitants of

the urban centre, but the evidence to date does not support this conclusion. Of the 54 sites that have revealed traces of 13th century occupation, 39 contain neither proto stoneware nor Andenne-type ware, only local ceramics. These sites are mainly situated in the northwestern and western parts of the town. Neither did the rural population share this consumption pattern, judging from the evidence available from the sites excavated to date.

The 14th century town followed the lines laid out in the 13th century, with one exception – it now spread south of the river Aarhus Å, along the road leading to the south. The evidence for this is provided by an urban dwelling excavated on the very brink of the river about 50 m south of Immervad. It was constructed in the early 14th century and housed a metal-worker – a metal-worker with a rather interesting consumption pattern, as will be explained below.[299]

The late 13th and early 14th centuries saw the introduction of new types of French, Belgian and German ceramics, indicating the maintenance of previous contacts with a possible further emphasis on Normandy. Belgian Brugge ware is rarest and has only been found at the centre of the town within the rampart, i.e. on Store Torv and Bispetorv, in the Town Hall and in the presumed ecclesial buildings in the immediate vicinity of the cathedral.[300] French Rouen-type ware, which was probably linked to the wine trade, is present in greater quantities. It has been recorded at 12 sites and across a wider area, with the largest amounts again found in the ecclesial centre: around Bispetorv and Store Torv.[301] However, it also occurs in the northern parts within the fortification, directly by the harbour and in the commercial quarter outside the fortification around Guldsmedgade.[302] French Saintonge polychrome ware is more special and has only been seen at one site in the urban area, close to Immervad, south of Aarhus Å. The piece was found on the floor inside a dwelling house, built here in the early 14th century most likely for a specialised metal-worker, and there is no doubt that it was used here and indicates the consumption of wine and other fine beverages. The colourful Saintonge polychrome ware, white with polychrome decoration, mostly depicting birds, must have seemed very exotic. Siegburg stoneware was by far the most common imported type in the 14th century. It has a wider distribution than the others and has so far been found both inside and outside the fortification: In the centre, around the town hall and the ecclesial residences, to the north in the presumed harbour quarter, in the commercial quarter to the west, along Guldsmedgade, Immervad and Vestergade and in the new settlement on the south side of the river.[303] But it is still not seen everywhere: Of the 55 sites covering the 14th century, 27 did not contain imports. The empty areas are again located on the outer northwest perimeter of the town. As in the previous century, these imported wares appear to correlate with each other: The French and Belgian types are found associated with the Rhenish stoneware at all but the smallest sites. There is little doubt that distribution of these imports marks the corresponding distribution of the Hanseatic drinking culture, associated with the consumption of wine and, especially, hopped beer, by some sectors of the population. This distribution may be linked to intensified contacts with Lübeck, as shown by the presence in 1322 of people of German descent with ties to Lübeck – a presence that appears to have been rather stable, with other Germans turning up in the middle of the century. It is therefore striking that the colourful tableware – Low Countries highly-decorated redware, Rouen-type ware and Saintonge polychrome ware – appear to disappear in the middle of the 14th century, while the consumption of Siegburger stoneware intensifies and new Baltic types are introduced. It could be that the Baltic types in part reflect imports of beer from, in particular, Wismar that are visible in the historical records (see chapter: Food and food culture). Consequently, there appears to be a correlation between the presence of imported ceramics and greater numbers of glazed jugs. However, the imports apparently did not replace the local Medieval well-fired redware jugs, but merely supplemented them.

5.4 Stage 5: The Late Medieval town 1400-1550: New food, new harbour

The 15th century saw major structural and behavioural changes going hand in hand with major changes in social practice – it was a century during which the urban landscape became transformed. New foodways were introduced at about the same time as massive programmes of rebuilding and restructuring were implemented. The major and obvious result, or even driving force, as will be discussed later, appears to have been an increase in international contacts and monetary activities. The first traces of this may be evident in the numismatic record. We can see that a number of hoards dating from the late 14th and early 15th

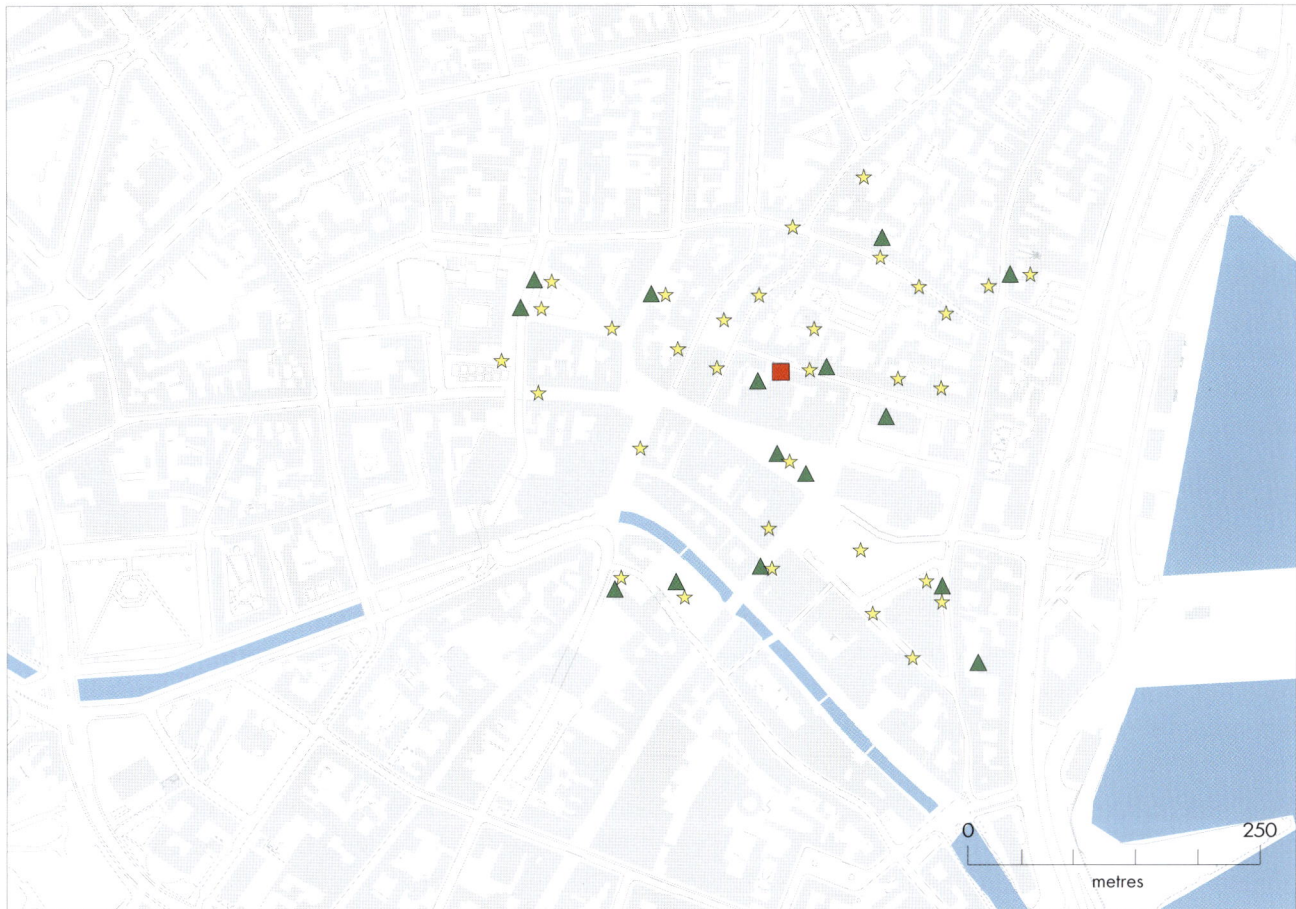

Figure 161. *15th century distribution of stoneware. Star: Siegburg stoneware. Square: Waldenburg stoneware. Triangle: Baltic burnished ware.*

centuries, and containing mainly foreign coins, have been found both in the town and in the country-side (see chapter: Coins and contacts). Although the owners of these hoards are now untraceable, these finds do provide evidence of the economic activities of people from both urban and the rural areas. Moreover, it may have been these activities that lay behind the construction of the new harbour. Initiated shortly before the winter of 1452/53, this harbour marked increased trading activity in Aarhus; perhaps both the cause and the result of intensified contacts with Lübeck and the Hanseatic centres on the Baltic. In the late 15th century, we hear of imports of wine and hops to Aarhus from Lübeck, and foodstuffs were shipped from Aarhus to the Baltic towns.[304] We can also see that St. Clement's Cathedral was rebuilt during the 15th century, with new vaults and a new choir modelled in a clear North German tradition. The bishop, Jens Iversen Lange, initiator of these modifications, even ordered the new altar piece from the workshop of Lübeck craftsman Bernd Notke. An increasingly Hanseatic consumption pattern ensued, as evident from the archaeological record and the written sources.

Of the 71 sites that provide information on the town in the 15th century, half of them contain stoneware (figure 161).

Rhenish stoneware of 15th century type is consequently relatively widespread, but stoneware constitutes a greater proportion of the total number of vessels (measured in number of sherds) in the town centre, around the inner part of Mejlgade and in the

Guldsmedgade quarter, than in the outer parts of town.[305] Other ceramics types of Hanseatic origin are also present: Baltic-type ceramics, burnished jugs from the area between Oder and Weichsel, now turn up in the town in greater numbers, indicating closer contacts with centres in the eastern Baltic from the beginning of the 15th century and a shift from wine to beer. Close parallels to the types found in Aarhus occur at a production site near Güstrow.[306] Decidedly rarer is Waldenburg stoneware, a type that is rather common in the east of Denmark, but has only been found once in Aarhus, in Rosensgade.[307] The distribution of the Baltic types closely follows that of the Rhenish stoneware: They are found in the quarters near the cathedral, along the presumed harbour near Mejlgade, around Guldsmedgade and around the harbour on the south bank of Aarhus Å.[308] This situation appears to match the written evidence with respect to imports to Denmark as a whole. Trave beer is frequently mentioned from the late 13th century, but from the mid-14th century, beer from Rostock, Stralsund and, especially, Wismar appears to dominate the Danish market, while Hamburg becomes increasingly important from the 15th century onwards.[309] It could be these increased imports of beer from the centres east of Lübeck that are reflected in the archaeological record. There is direct evidence of imports to Aarhus from the Late Middle Ages, when customs records from Lübeck supply some information. We know that on 29 August 1492, Dirk Pothoff shipped two small barrels of wine worth 12 marks to the town.[310] That same year, Hans Borchstede exported iron and hops worth 138 marks, and in 1495 Mattes van der Weser exported lead and hops to Aarhus worth 84 marks. Compared with the imports to major ports like Copenhagen, Næstved and Aalborg, imports to Aarhus appear very modest, with no traces of refined consumption and a definite focus on bulk wares and beer.[311]

The 15th century is when domestic ceramics shifted from the glazed jugs and greyware pots to Post-Medieval redware tripod pipkins with internal glaze. It is quite evident that this change was not accompanied by a decline in Hanseatic contacts or even a

break in consumption, as the supply of imported types flowed freely into town both before and after. Nor was it accompanied by a change in the range of imported types. Consequently, this shift appears to have been a domestic phenomenon and not prompted by a general disruption of the town's contact network. The fluid nature of this transition is further underlined by the presence of internally-glazed cooking pots of exactly the same types, and with exactly the same poor glaze, in Lübeck in around 1425-75, i.e. at the same time as their earliest securely-dated occurrence in Aarhus at the mid-15th century.[312] It could very well be that this change in social practice simply followed the Hanseatic lead and was swiftly adopted thereafter.

It is worth noting that the town appears to have grown significantly in the 15th century. As we have already seen, the settlement crossed the river in the 14th century. However, the laying out of the new harbour on its southern bank in the mid-15th century must have had a significant impact on the town and could be a reflection of increased seafaring contacts and probably increased production and exports too. At about the same time, the rampart around the inner town was at least partially demolished and the resulting areas were given by the king to the town or to private individuals. These developments led to large areas being built upon and to several streets being laid out, i.e. Skt. Clemens Stræde and the areas north of Pustervig.[313] At the same time, a convent was constructed at Christiansbjerg, south of the river. This is mentioned in 1462 and it was built on the site of an earlier chapel that was probably located alongside the road leading south from Immervad. [314] The Late Medieval construction works indicate an intensification of activities: The Priory of Our Lady was rebuilt and enlarged, as were the cathedral and the friary to south of the cathedral and the Medieval bishop's residence to the north.[315] All in all, these developments point to significant growth, economically and spatially, in the Late Middle Ages, resulting in both an inner and an outer expansion phase. And this was definitely accompanied by intensification of the Hanseatic influenced consumption in town, something which may also have been the result of increased direct contact (see chapter: Immigrants in Aarhus). Similar Late Medieval urban growth is evident in a number of Danish towns, for example Aalborg and Næstved, so the processes that led to the growth in Aarhus might not be specific to this area, but part of a larger development.[316]

So what do we know about consumption in Aarhus in the Late Middle Ages? The introduction of the tripod cooking pot, followed by the plate, does seem to indicate a change in social practice, including the spread of a more refined cuisine, with an emphasis on fried dishes, as opposed to porridge and gruel, probably made in the greyware cooking pots. Why this practice changed is difficult to say. We know that the tripod pipkin was introduced at around the same time more or less all over Denmark (introduction dates span from before 1433 to shortly after 1452),[317] so it seems that this change was rapid and profound all over the country. It could be that economic growth, especially with respect to international exports, fuelled profound changes, both in the urban place, with the construction of the many religious and secular buildings, and in the urban space, with the introduction of new foodways that led to the dissolution of former practises and the introduction of new ones. As yet, no excavated site has been able to tell us how this affected the rural population in the vicinity of Aarhus. The dated material from rural areas is still much too sparse and many more excavations of precisely-dated settlements are required if this aspect is to be explored. Nevertheless, rural finds of Post-Medieval redware, early type tripod pipkins at a site in the village of Viby near Aarhus, do suggest that at least part of the rural population also participated in this change, even though the available material does not yet allow us to see when in the 15th century this integration occurred.[318]

The introduction of the glazed tripod pipkin appears to be followed by other profound changes in social practice, i.e. the disappearance of Medieval well-fired coarseware and the introduction of black pots. The subject of actual ceramics production lies outside the scope of this volume, but will even so be touched upon briefly here. Unfortunately, no Danish sites provide us with information on the production of the early tripod pipkin, and so far we have no trace of production of this type in our area, so we simply do not know how these types were produced, although the technical and typological similarities direct us toward the well-known 16th century production. But there are several production sites from the 16th century. By that time, production clearly took the form of professional mass-production in large-scale workshops situated on the peripheries of urban centres and run by potters, some of whom at least bore names of Dutch or German extraction.[319] Aarhus itself accommodated at least three potters, as ceramics waste has been excavated at sites in Studsgade, Borggade and Klostergade.[320] We do know that the production of Medieval well-fired redware and Medieval well-fired coarseware was conducted on a smaller scale and primarily at rural locations by potters who may have been tenants or in other ways dependant on landowners, but there are very few technical similarities between this production and the Medieval well-fired redware and production was probably organised differently.[321]

When looking at this consumption, we have to take into account local immigration from nearby rural areas into Aarhus. The written sources allow us to gain some idea of the origin of these people in the years around 1500. It seems that most came from the immediate vicinity of Aarhus and, in particular, from the nearest villages. As already mentioned repeatedly above, the evidence from the countryside is very sparse and further excavations are needed. Nevertheless, the rural consumption, as we are able to trace it, does seem to be characterised by a high proportion of Medieval well-fired coarseware and black pots. As several areas of the town appear to have large quantities of black pots, a topic for further investigation is whether rural immigrants settled in these areas and retained their rural consumption pattern, at least for a while.

Figure 162. The Egg Dance, Pieter Aertsen, 1552. ©Rijksmuseum, Amsterdam.

5.5 Stage 6: The Early Modern Town 1550-1750: Increasing variation

Consumption patterns in the Early Modern town appear to be marked by increased diversity from the 16th century onwards, as well as an increase in the quantity and types of ceramics being brought into the town. New luxury types were introduced in parts of the town: Low Countries tin-glazed ware, stoneware from Cologne, Westerwald, Frechen and Raeren-type stoneware and a range of whitewares. We can link this to imports of specialities like spices, raisins and sugar, of which there are several examples: Søren Olufsen returned from Lübeck in 1652 on a ship carrying dried fruit and spices, paper, soap, cloth and unspecified goods.[322] A ship from Hull brought tobacco and cloth to Aarhus in 1677.[323] A Dutch ship carried salt, raisins and small goods to Aarhus in 1687, and in 1727 another ship departing from Amsterdam had a similar cargo: mainly wine, dried fruit, spices, sugar, salt, cheese and soap.[324] Grain and timber products dominated imports from the Baltic area: A ship carried 200 barrels of oats from Landskrona to Aarhus in 1643.[325] In 1682, we see imports of tar from Gotland[326] and more Baltic grain is imported from Danzig in for example 1685 and 1697.[327] Some of the imports were transported by Danish merchants and shippers, but a curious case shows the direct involvement of immigrants in imports to the town. Antonius Worm, who was of Dutch descent and still had ties with Amsterdam, owed money to an Amsterdam merchant for casks of Rhenish and Spanish wine. The wine ended up in Aarhus, and the merchant had to travel to the town to assert his right.[328] All in all, Aarhus seems mainly to have been an importer of grain and timber products, while consumer goods, primarily salt, but also specialities like almonds, spices and wine, came through Lübeck and the Netherlands, at least from the early 17th century onwards. Some of the goods may have been re-exported: Research by Old Degn into the Aarhus skippers who passed the Oresund around 1640 has demonstrated special contacts with Danzig and Königsberg, Copenhagen and Mariager, Bergen and Newcastle. The goods varied: rye, flax, hemp and wood primarily from Danzig and Königsberg,

Street name/quarter	Year 1612	Year 1636	Year 1683	Year 1728
Torvegade	14	19	129	296
Mejlgade	9	15	80	204
Guldsmedgade	8	16	56	41
Rosensgade	6	8	65	22
Studsgade	6	9	40	22
Skt. Clemensborg	3	9	28	24

Table 33. Average taxation in selected streets in Aarhus (Skilling). After Degn 1996: 247.

fish from Norway, coal and cloth from Newcastle and salt from the Bordeaux area. Many of the goods were on their way from Norway to the Baltic, and Aarhus was the transit point.[329]

It is remarkable that the earliest apparent evidence for luxury consumption – Low Countries tin-glazed ware – was found at Bispetorv, where it seems to pre-date other finds in the town by a good 50 years. We can see this situation as an attempt by the ecclesial elite to retain and consolidate their distinction and elite position at a time of unrest and rapid development in the town.[330] The black pots, however, indicate a very different kind of consumption.

Ole Degn has produced a summary of the taxation of streets in Aarhus in 1612-1728 (table 33). The table shows an apparent correlation between streets with low land taxation and large quantities of black pots recovered from the sites excavated in these streets. It certainly seems that streets with the lowest average taxation (Fiskergade, Studsgade and Rosensgade) have the highest proportion of black pots in the archaeological finds.[331] On the other hand, streets where the average taxation was higher, i.e. Mejlgade and the former Torvegade, covering Store Torv and Bispetorv, have higher proportions of other ceramics types.[332] This pattern appears to continue into the 19th century, when Fiskergade is decidedly poor, while the streets surrounding Lille Torv have wealthy occupants.[333] This brief analysis can only provide a preliminary conclusion – further investigation is required of sites excavated in the future, but there does seem to be a link, whether direct or indirect, between consumption related to black pots and low taxation. The written records allow us to look further into the

situation at Fiskergade. According to the taxation records for 1682, a man by the name of Søren from the village of Spentrup owned the western part of Fiskergade, i.e. the western plot, and rented out five "booths". We do not know whether these booths were dwellings or workshops, or both. The middle plot was owned by Albrecht Nielsen, who lived there in an old house. Niels Andersen Krus owned and lived on the eastern plot. The street was generally rather poor. The five booths were valued at 106 rigsdaler, Albrecht Nielsen's old house at 53 rigsdaler and Niels Andersen Krus' house at 166 rigsdaler. According to the taxation records, the value of the booths was just about average – neither better nor worse than other booths. However, Albrecht Nielsen's old house had one of the lowest valuations in the town, and Niels Andersen Krus' farm, although better than the others in the street, was still below average.[334] Moreover, true to form, the site of FHM 4201 Skt. Clemensborg in Fiskergade shows high proportions of black pots – around 20% – in the middle of the 17th century. Unfortunately, there is a hiatus at the site between 1652 and 1771, so the precise inventories of the persons mentioned here cannot be investigated.

The Early Modern town saw a marked transformation of the urban place, as several ecclesial buildings were demolished, for example the monastery at Christiansbjerg, the House of the Holy Spirit at Immervad and the church of St. Oluf. The Reformation also brought changes to the layout and use of other religious buildings, i.e. the cathedral and the former Dominican priory. A significant development with respect to the ceramics is that the amount and distribution of stoneware appears to decline. Of the 66 sites with evidence from the 16th century, less than half contain stoneware. The consumption at FHM 5124 Bispetorv is markedly different from that in the rest of the town (figure 163).

Here we find a greater proportion of display and serving vessels in whitewares and the most sumptuous stoneware vessels. The serving and eating vessels here are directed towards a type of display we do not see

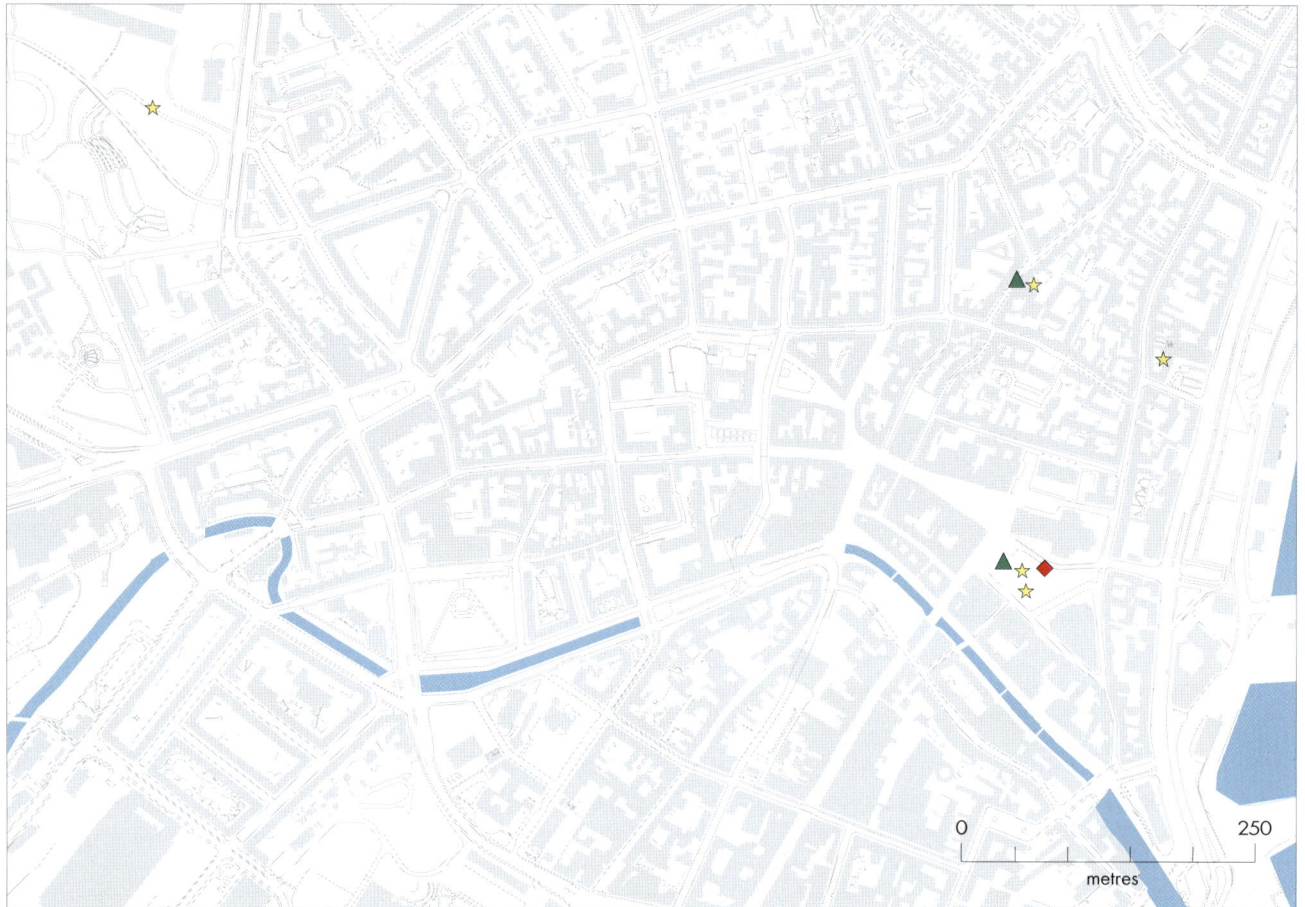

Figure 163. Luxury consumption in the 16th century. Star: Low Countries tin-glazed ware. Triangle: decorated stoneware. Diamond: Low Countries redware.

anywhere else: A Low Countries redware chafing dish is a unique find for Aarhus and adds to the impression of luxury at this site. Among the very exclusive objects is a Low Countries tin-glazed ware vessel with parallels in Amsterdam.[335] The consumption of stoneware is also remarkable, with small apothecary vessels used for medicine being found on the floor of the Chapter House A22. The rest of the stoneware comprises rare tableware. A large tankard of Siegburg stoneware is thought to have been produced in the workshop of Hans Hilgers. It was found in cellar A530, together with another two tankards and at least two plates in whiteware. The most remarkable vessel in this phase is a tankard of Cologne stoneware bearing portraits of princes, which was recovered from the floor in the Chapter House.

There is little doubt that the urban townscape showed considerable variation in consumption in the 16th century, with the display types being primarily used at FHM 5124 Bispetorv. There seems to be a link with the Post-Medieval redware tripod pipkin: The proportion of Post-Medieval redware is about 20-40% at all sites except Bispetorv, where it is as high as 70%. The ratio of plates to cooking pots is also very different at Bispetorv: There are 23% plates at FHM 5124 Bispetorv and only 4% at FHM 4225 Guldsmedgade. It is evident that consumption at Bispetorv was directed towards luxury and display to a much greater degree than in other parts of the town. Since we know that the area accommodated the Post-Medieval episcopal residence, this is hardly a surprise. The archaeological ceramics record

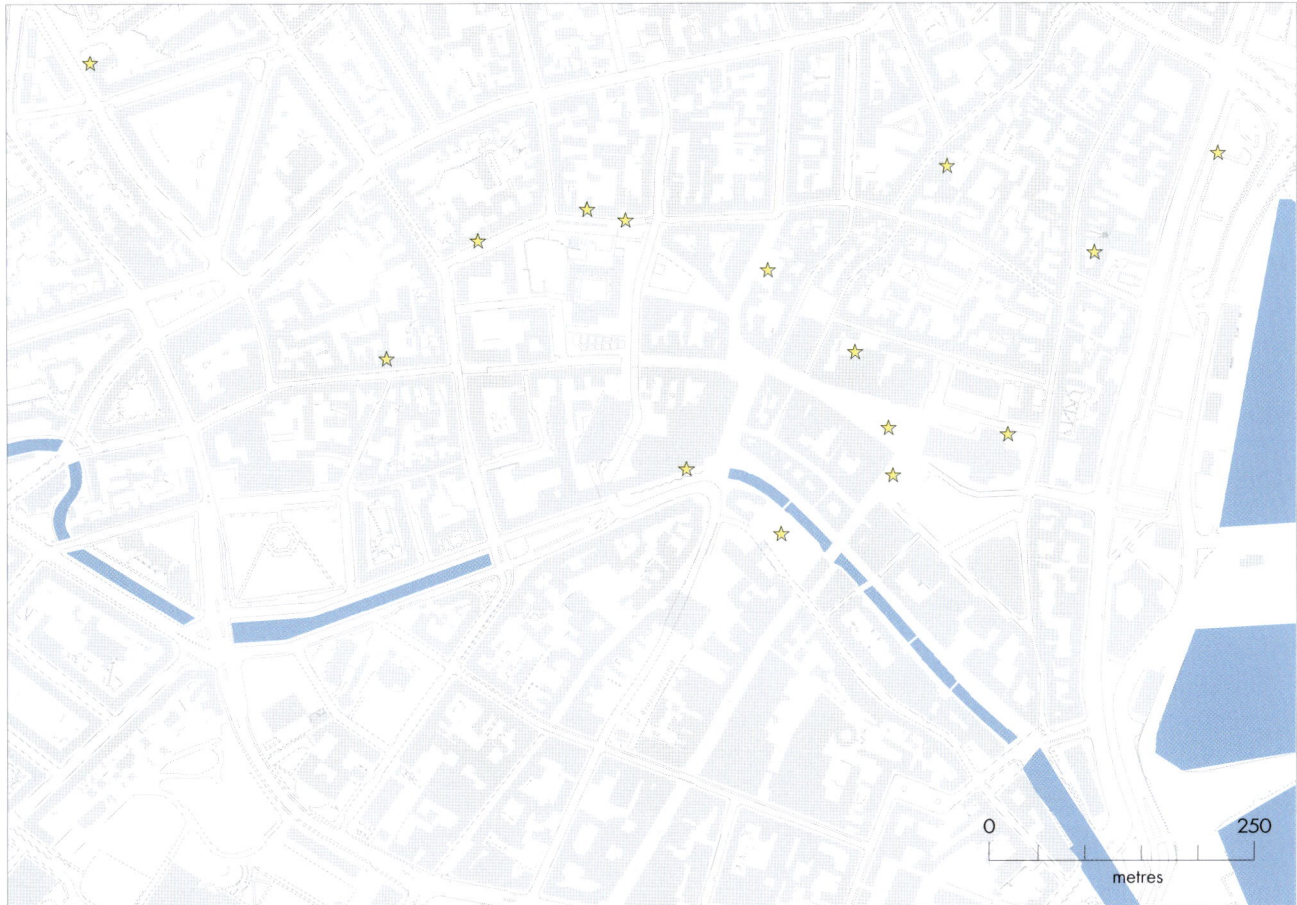

Figure 164. Westerwald in Aarhus. All known sherds.

declines dramatically in the 18th century and little can be concluded about times after that. Nevertheless, fluctuations are evident in the proportion of black pots in Fiskergade in the later phases – from the late 18th century onwards. Unfortunately, no other sites are presently available in the town for comparison, but preliminary excavation results from the site of FHM 5501 Latin 3/Borggade 6 – another poor neighbourhood, indicate a large proportion of black pots here.[336] Fiskergade was one of the poorest streets and, in the light of the marked mobility between town and countryside, the obvious question is whether the large quantities of black pots here are an indication of the food culture of these new citizens.

The 17th century was a time of economic and demographic decline, as documented through studies by Ole Degn. Degn´s research has shown that the wars and the occupation of Jutland 1626-29 took a great toll on the town. In the years 1661-62, 25% of the houses in town were deserted, and the number of new municipal licences to trade declined.[337] And if we look more closely at the archaeological record, the proportion of imports in the 17th century appears to be rather low, as they are only represented at 11 of the 36 sites covering this period. Westerwald stoneware is associated with the later phases of the Early Modern town.

This type has been recovered from quite a few sites covering the 17th century. It is found around the convent, around Vestergade and at a few places in the north of the town[338] (figure 164).

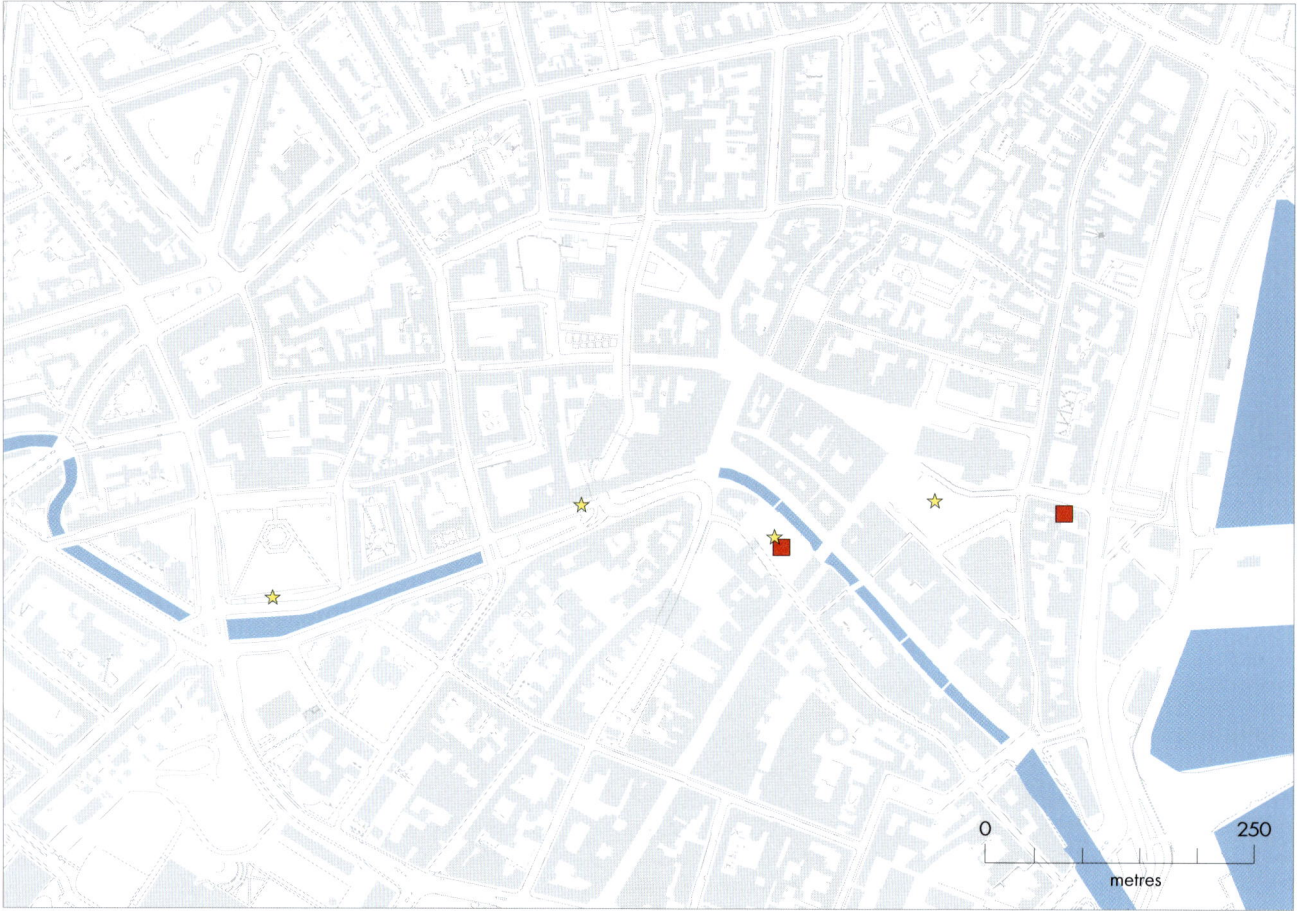

Figure 165. 19th century distribution. Star: Industrial ceramics. Square: Porcelain.

5.6 Stage 7: The onset of modernity

The number of sites with finds from these later times decreases due to preservation circumstances and conditions, i.e. the upper strata have been more exposed to disturbance in the 19th and 20th centuries. For the same reason, preservation of 18th century material is also very random: The 22 sites containing material from the 18th century are all, with the exception of FHM 4201 Skt. Clemensborg, represented by small excavations in the streets. Three of these yielded porcelain[339] and four industrial faience[340] (figure 165).

This random pattern should of course in no way to be seen as a direct reflection of the consumption in the town at this time. Although a general and widely embracing overview of the 18th and 19th centuries cannot, for these reasons, be obtained on the basis of the available archaeological record, the large sites at FHM 4201 Skt. Clemensborg and, to some degree, FHM 5124 Bispetorv do provide us with some degree of insight. Here, there is evidence of the widespread use of early industrial wares, some of them from the United Kingdom, from the late 18th century onwards. Results of a promising excavation conducted in 2015 in Borggade, covering the period c. 1300-1800, have just been processed and cannot be included fully in this study. However, among the ceramics from this site are other industrial wares, among them mochaware bowls or saucers and a creamware plate that has a parallel at the Skt. Clemensborg site.[341] The types represented are plates and cups, i.e. tableware. The porcelain mainly takes the form of cups with transfer print or so-called capuchin ware. Industrial faience is also evident in rural areas, which is no surprise as creamware, mochaware and jackfield ware are found in large quantities in the 19th century phase of the village of Hårup near Silkeborg.[342] Unfortunately, none of the sites here supply further details, for example on when these new wares became integrated into rural consumption. Nevertheless, they do tell us of the integration of a new commodity – tea – and that this commodity, and the social practice it was a part of, transgressed old divisions within the town and also crossed the gulf between town and countryside.

6 Conclusion

So what do we now know about consumption? The analysis undertaken here has resulted in the definition of seven stages or sequences in consumption: Stage 1: Local consumption prior to c. AD 900. Stage 2: Baltic connections c. 900-1000. Stage 3: Stagnation c. 1000-1200. Stage 4: Breakthrough of Hanseatic consumption 1200-1400. Stage 5: New foods c. 1400 to the mid-16th century. Stage 6: Introduction of Modern practice c. 1550-1750. Stage 7: Breakthrough of modernity. In the following, I will look at these stages in more detail.

Stage 1: An analysis of the Viking Age settlement in Aarhus could easily constitute a project of its own, but the work undertaken here indicates that the town's earliest stage lies in the very late 8th or early 9th century AD, when a settlement developed near the mouth of the river. This seems to have been primarily agricultural in character, directed at the exploitation of coastal resources, and appears rather similar to the other minor settlements in the surrounding area.

Stage 2: After some time – perhaps in the early 10th century – the settlement intensified and a Baltic form of consumption becomes visible. The latter was probably a consequence of the inclusion of trade and crafts in local activities and likely associated with the settling of tradesmen of Baltic origin in the area.[343] In the 10th century, this settlement was cleared and a rampart was constructed around part of the previously settled area. The fortified area appears to have been inhabited by the same groups as before. However, this settlement was hardly a large-scale international marketplace, such as that seen at Ribe: There is an almost total absence of Viking Age coins, hack silver and elements of foreign material culture beyond the usual whetstones and soapstone vessels within the urban boundaries. The occupation does though appear to have been intense, relative to that of the subsequent Early Medieval period. However, this could partly be an illusion due to the good preservation conditions prevailing in the Viking Age sunken-featured buildings, whereas the later settlement, mostly comprised of post-built houses, was more exposed to subsequent destruction.

Stage 3: Whatever the reason, following the end of the Viking Age, the town appears almost devoid of traceable functions: Consumption is primarily local with very little evidence of international influence and few finds of coins. Where found, these are concentrated around the cathedral, located to the west of the walled town centre at that time, and probably indicate the main driving force in the town at this time – the ecclesial world, although the scarcity of finds of this date must be taken into consideration.

Stage 4: Only in the late 12th and early 13th centuries does change become apparent, as traces of Hanseatic influenced consumption spread within the fortified area, both in the ecclesial quarter to the south of the present cathedral and in what we perceive as secular dwellings on the periphery of the fortified area. This influence intensified from the 14th century onwards, when Hanseatic consumption, especially visible in the consumption of beer and wine, appears to have been rather widespread in the town. It can be followed through the turn of the 15th century into the next stage.

Stage 5: New food and new types, linked to changing food traditions with a decreased emphasis on porridge and one-pot dishes in favour of a specialised cuisine, spread rapidly along the major streets.

Stage 6: A good way into the 16th century a typical Early Modern consumption pattern, comprising specialised dishes and specialised services, became established.

Stage 7; The final stage is characterised by a range of ceramics types linked to the onset of modernity in the late 18th century – especially types related to the serving of coffee and tea.

6.1 Local, regional and supra-regional ceramics

As we have seen, Aarhus was not a self-sufficient town, but participated in the circulation of goods from the Early Viking Age to the present. We have no evidence for the production of ceramics in town before the late 16th century, and that production involved only one of the many types that circulated in the town and the surrounding rural landscape. If we go deeper into the basic material, the ceramics, we find evidence of wares circulating at different levels and in different ways: local wares, regional wares and supra-regional wares. There is an obvious chronological development.

The local wares are primarily certain types of greywares and blackwares; the Viking Age and Early Medieval greywares and the early and developed black pots are among these. The production sites indicate household production in the rural landscape using simple technology, pit-firing shaping by hand etc., which nevertheless demanded skill and training - skills and training that were suited to being exchanged within the household. Local wares are completely dominant in the Viking Age and Early Middle Ages – stages 1-3. They then disappear, only to be reintroduced in the early 15th century, in stage 5, and from then on used continuously until the late 19th century. In eastern Jutland, local wares seem to disappear around 1200, but finds from western Jutland indicate continuous production of these wares throughout the Middle Ages.[344] These local ware undergo stylistic developments, as new shapes are introduced, together with surface treatments such as burnishing. Nevertheless, we see a remarkable continuation in this ceramics tradition over a very long time span. We have no clear evidence on how these types circulated in our area, but we must see them as part of an urban-rural exchange as seen in Halland.[345] In the 19th century, the black pots were sold by a range of middlemen – small traders who travelled from village to village and from town to town.[346] It seems likely that these local wares were distributed in a similar manner in earlier times.

The supra-regional wares constitute a range of types that were never produced in Denmark prior to industrialisation, i.e. before the end of the 18th century. For example, the various types of stoneware, French and Belgian whiteware glazed jugs, majolica, porcelain and faience. These types were transported to Denmark either as goods in their own right – like majolica, or as by-products of the trade in wine and beer, like the French glazed jugs and the stoneware. Until the end of the 16th century, we have no evidence of how this exchange was organised. At that time at least part of the stoneware was sold by shopkeepers and merchants, as shown in inventories from Elsinore, but it is likely that other types were exchanged in person-to-person relationships, as gifts or as controlled goods. Due to the contacts required, towns and coastal marketplaces are obvious nodal points in this exchange network. The supra-regional wares are present from stage 4, in the 12th century, and the types and proportions of them vary through time.

The regional wares are types that demand highly sophisticated technology and considerable skill in their production: Kilns that produce high, constant firing temperatures, use of the potter's wheel and a knowledge of glazes, all of which points at knowledge obtained through an apprenticeship lasting several years. These types, the hard-fired greywares and the Medieval glazed jugs, are known from many production places, all – or almost all – with the exception being a pottery kiln in Svendborg, located in the rural landscape. Production was probably organised in a tenant-relationship with a landowner. We do not know how these types were distributed, but towns must have acted as nodal points in this exchange, which probably also involved large landowners, such as manors and monasteries. The regional production appears to undergo some dramatic changes. At their introduction in stage 4, in the 13th century, these regional types erase the local ceramics tradition around Aarhus. But in stage 5, around 1400, the regional production is the one to be erased. We see a sudden break in ceramics consumption as the Medieval tradition disappears, to be replaced by a re-introduction of the local ceramics tradition. At the same time new regional types, linked to new culinary traditions, turn up. The inspiration for these types is to be found in Germany area – Rostock, Stettin and Lübeck, to mention but a few. And given the similarities between the types, it does seem likely that the craftsmen were trained here. This production demanded highly-developed technology, large investments and years of training; some form of organisation into guilds also seems likely for this industry. When we find the kilns, they are located in towns, and the products were distributed over long distances. Market trading and trading by order appear to be dominant in the system. This entanglement of local, regional and supra-regional types, with different technologies, distribution systems and levels of training is what characterise the last millennium.

6.2 Urban networks – trade and exchange

As a comprehensive investigation of the written evidence relating to trade and supply in Medieval and Post-Medieval Aarhus is far beyond the resources available for this project, a study of this subject could profitably be pursued and significantly broadened by further research, as has been done for other towns.[347] At this point something should be said with respect to access to materiality. Trade is one of the most oft-used terms in Medieval archaeology, and the presence of finds of non-local origin, such as some building materials, small finds and, most of all, ceramics, are frequently ascribed to patterns of market trade. The question is whether the presence of the foreign objects has such a straightforward explanation. One of the earliest sources that I am aware of mentioning the purchase of ceramics are the accounts of Queen Christine. She purchases ceramics on several occasions, and in one instance it is specifically stated that she orders pottery vessels in Copenhagen.[348] Merchant's accounts and inventories only rarely mention ceramics, mostly Post-Medieval stoneware traded via Cologne, Amsterdam or Bremen – quite a well-known trade. We have to look rather hard at the admittedly meagre written sources relating to consumption in the Middle Ages for any indication that ceramics were subject to trade on the open market. Trade is much too vast a subject to be dealt with here, but I believe that it is fruitful to dig deeper into the forms of Medieval exchange before we conclude too firmly that open access to market trade is the sole explanation for the distributions of Medieval artefacts

That said, we have seen how various imports are evident in the town from the earliest times, for example soapstone vessels, whetstones and quernstones in the Viking Age and Early Medieval period. Later, it is primarily German beer and wine that are, at least indirectly, apparent in the archaeological record, and the lead cloth seals, rare as they are, prove that cloth was also imported, much of it through Lübeck.[349] Other goods are, however, less visible: The bulk trade in grain, hops, salt and similar goods, frequently mentioned in the written sources, is not clearly evident in the archaeological record and further scientific analyses are required in this respect. When written sources become more numerous in the 16th and 17th centuries, we see that imports consisted primarily of fish and timber from Norway, flax, hemp, hops, beer and lead from the Baltic and salt, bricks, spices and wine from Amsterdam.[350] Neither should we forget that Aarhus was given a place at the market involved in the fisheries at Skanør and Falsterbo, at least from 1500.[351]

If we reappraise the archaeological record with this in mind, it seems that stable contacts with Norway and the Baltic countries, especially Mecklenburg-Vorpommern, were established in the 9th century AD. These contacts are visible in the overall archaeological record, and in the written sources, until well into the 18th century. What happened to the goods when they arrived in the town is an open question. The ecclesial elite in town could have accounted for many of them. The town does not appear to have had a clear gateway function until the High Middle Ages, and there is only slight evidence for the spread of foreign culture out into the rural landscape, i.e. in the villages, even after this time. It seems that the integration of town and countryside into a wider economic monetary system in the 13th century demonstrates a clear chronological and chorological correspondence with the integration of a wide range of local and, especially, imported types of materiality into the town. I.e. at least some people in the urban centre experienced integration into a larger system of consumption and larger communities, at the same time as they integrated into a broader monetary system. It must be stressed that, although the numismatic evidence for activity in the 15th century is sparse, especially in the countryside, this does not necessarily mean that economic integration had become reversed. Activity in the town, in the form of construction works, building of religious institutions, dwellings etc., was certainly not in decline, but rapidly on the increase in the late 15th century. Moreover, there is nothing to indicate a

decrease in the integration of consumption during this period either.

6.3 Urban crisis

History and archaeology together tells us of a number of crises through the millennium covered by this book. The main crisis appears to be related to events surrounding the transition from the Viking Age to the Middle Ages, the outbreak of the plague, the so-called Black Death in the 14th century and the wars of the mid-17th century.

We have very little information on what happened in the 11th and 12th centuries. What we do see is a distinct sparseness of traces of settlement in the town, compared to the massive Late Medieval evidence. The aforementioned smithies at Bispetorv and Vestergade, the houses at Guldsmedgade and Studsgade and the wells at Badstuetorv are some the only traces of settlement of this date. On the other hand, the town hosted a cathedral, two churches and a mint in this same period, so it was not devoid of functions – these just appear to have been different from those of the Viking Age. Several dramatic events took place in Aarhus in the Early Middle Ages. The town came under attack in 1050 and 1158, but so far no traces of these attacks have been found.[352] As already mentioned, the lack of finds and evidence may be due to later disturbances, because traces of the post-built houses are easily destroyed and the Early Medieval cultural layers are not easy to spot in narrow trenches. Furthermore, the present cathedral may cover large parts of the Early Medieval town. Nevertheless, this apparent sparseness may give cause to wonder whether Aarhus went through a major transition at the end of the Viking Age as the town transformed from royal stronghold to ecclesial centre. There is no doubt that we need large-scale research focusing on the built environment, as well as trade, exchange and crafts, if we are to dig deeper into the situation in the Early Middle Ages. We might well take our inspiration from Peter Carelli, who has revealed several transformations in consumption in

Early Medieval Lund. Here, consumption appears to have been quite simple in the 11th century, while the 12th century saw the appearance of mass consumption and increasing diversity, which he interprets as the emergence of a new cultural identity related to the emergence of towns.[353]

The second large-scale crisis was the Black Death in the mid-14th century. The effects of the plague were very visible in the countryside, where many villages and several churches were abandoned. Among these are at least two of the villages used in this volume, Todderup and Stavtrup. The plague must have hit just as hard in Aarhus, but we have not been able to trace evidence of desertion and abandonment within the town. There seems to have been a continuity in the 14th century, evident at Telefontorvet (FHM 4616), Guldsmedgade (FHM 4225) and Mejlgade 26 (FHM 4587). It is possible that there was largescale replacement of the urban population with rural newcomers, but if this was the case, we have so far not been able to see it in the archaeological record. What we do see is apparent stagnation or lack of innovation in the 14th century. If we want to penetrate deeper into what happened in the town during the plague, we need a large-scale dating programme focussed on the occupation. This is the only way we will be able to detect periods of stagnation in such a short time span. The excavation in Guldsmedgade may provide further information, as we see a marked variation in the settlement here. During the 14th century, a dwelling was constructed and demolished and a large rubbish pit cut through the remains. After this rubbish pit was filled in and the area levelled, another house was constructed on the spot. This experienced severe stability problems, caused by the soft fill in the large pit, and it was quickly demolished, the area was re-levelled and yet another short-lived house built on the exact same spot. The fact that three houses were built, one after the other, on the plot during the 14th century is remarkable, and it is possible that the lack of continuity in the dwellings reflects a lack of continuity in the dwellers.

The final crisis occurred in the mid-17th century, when plague and war put the town under severe duress, as described in the works of Ole Degn.[354] Again we are not really able to identify deserted plots in town, but this may be because we there are not so many excavations of 17th century dwellings in town, or in the countryside for that matter. It seems the harbour was not, or only very rarely, repaired between the mid-17th century and the end of the 18th century, as shown by the excavation results from Skt. Clemensborg (FHM 4201). This may, of course, be a consequence of commercial stagnation in town in the wake of the Thirty Years' War.

6.4 Urbanity and urbanisation

If we compare the changes in social practice through the seven stages with the changes in the physical layout of the town normally related to urbanisation, there is a remarkable correlation. One of the first physical transformations is evident in the fortification of the earliest Aarhus in the Late Viking Age, when what appears to have been a relatively open settlement became transformed into a small enclosed place behind a rampart. In the 11th-12th centuries, the town became further transformed from fortified marketplace cum coastal resource centre to sparsely occupied, predominately ecclesial centre behind fortifications. The breaching of these fortifications, and the laying out of large new quarters to the west and north, marked the transformation of the ecclesial centre into a thriving Medieval town in the mid-13th century; a town that spread south of Immervad in the 14th century. Aarhus was transformed again around the middle of the 15th century, as the areas south of the river Aarhus Å became incorporated and a new harbour was constructed there. A sixth and major transformation happened in the mid-16th century, when the demolition of ecclesial buildings and the closing of institutions led to a large-scale restructuring of the layout of the town. We are accustomed to seeing these transformations in terms of an organic, linear chronological flow, but it is worth stressing that none of this happened organically. Instead, each transformation should be seen as having been instigated by a central power – either a bishop or monarch, who had the power and the planning apparatus to change the town. Consequently, it makes sense to see Aarhus not as one single town with a single function, gradually developing over time, but essentially as many towns following on, one after the other, on the same site, each with their own special functions and drivers, and with no predetermined or linear developmental pattern.[355] The driving force behind the earliest settlement may have been local landowners who needed a place where coastal resources could be exploited. The power behind the fortified marketplace may have been a monarch who needed to control local trade with the Baltic areas. After the Viking Age, the primary driver may have been the ecclesial institutions, i.e. the town as an ecclesial centre. The restructuring of the town in the late 13th century shows some resemblance to the founding of towns such as Køge. It is possible that it had the same purpose, i.e. an episcopal initiative undertaken in order to exploit the commercial possibilities that came with growing German expansion in the Baltic countries.[356] The construction of the new harbour and the urban expansion southwards in the mid-15th century resemble developments seen in towns such Elsinore about the same time. The prime function here may have been to exploit the commercial opportunities provided by the expansion of the Hansa network. It therefore makes sense to deconstruct the town as a place with a clear linear development and replace it with a sequence of towns with different purposes, functions and prime motivators, not one single development, i.e. to stress sequencing rather than continuity in the urban place.

Returning to patterns of consumption, we have seen that transformations of the urban place are preceded by some changes and superseded by others. Traces of trade and specialised crafts are evident at the settlement which predates the Viking Age fortification. The restructuring of the town in the 14th century is preceded by a spread in Hanseatic consumption in ecclesial and secular parts of the town alike, but is superseded by the introduction of an abundance of new types. Moreover, the expansion of the town to the south around 1443 is predated by the occurrence of the new Hanseatic types.[357] The construction of the new harbour on the south side of the river in the early 15th century is preceded by a change in social practice, i.e. the introduction of new types of primarily Hanseatic origin, but it is followed by the introduction of further new types. Furthermore, the spatial changes that followed the Reformation correlate with an increase in display types and specialisation of tableware. The final stage – the introduction of industrial wares for the drinking of coffee and tea – is not easy to trace in the limited archaeological record, but this material provides what we can refer to as a visible indicator or marker of the onset of modernity and the increased integration of Aarhus into broader markets. It therefore seems that the reorganisations of the urban layout and structures followed social processes and ideas that were already inherent and spreading in town, rather than being the prime cause of them. What we see here are the visible traces of developing opportunities, which lead to changes in social practice and are then followed by planned transformations, in a constant interplay between action and reaction. This may represent the birth of the urban location – the emergence of the idea of a town as a net of streets and market squares, visual axes and easy transport, going hand in hand with the development of urbanity. According to Bjørn Poulsen's studies, the term townsmen – cives, was used for the first time in the mid-12th century.[358] This may mean that an urban identity was being formed at the same time and that prior to this no distinction existed between townspeople and rural population. Of course, this does not mean that towns did not exist before then, but it does mean that the conceptual divide between people living in towns and those in countryside, which we see in Medieval texts, was established at this point.

6.5 Urban strangers and the outer world

The introduction of new practices to the town appears to have involved the breakdown of existing ones. The introduction of the Medieval ceramics tradition was followed by the breakdown of the Baltic ceramics tradition. Similar sequences of introduction/disappearance occurred several times through the Middle Ages, most markedly in the early 15th century, when the Medieval grey pots were replaced by redware cooking pots. As the vessels produced in the two traditions were functionally very different – one linked to porridge, the other to frying, this means that a transfer of knowledge – in this case of ways of cooking, also had to take place in order for the new types to be usable. As they closely resemble the ceramic types found some decades earlier in for example Lübeck, Rostock and Greifswald, it seems possible that the new cooking skills, if not even the cooks and the potters, came to town from that area. This leads us on to the concept of knowledge as an element in social practice. According to Elisabeth Shove's analysis of competence, some everyday tasks are picked up easily, while others demand specialised and extended training and/or have to be transferred outside the immediate household.[359] The guilds represent an obvious formalised community where such knowledge could be transferred. Informal meetings between craftsmen or merchants at markets or in inns are another possible vehicle for this transfer.[360] By now it is probably very clear that I consider meetings between local and foreign actors to have had a potential role in this transfer of knowledge. But are we also able to prove that foreign contacts, mediated through urban centres, played a role in the transfer of knowledge from the Viking Age? A wider variety of sources is needed to prove this, but it is a very good hypothesis.

Looking more closely at this topic, the analysis of the ceramics record has shown that large numbers of non-locally produced artefacts have been recovered from sites in and around Aarhus. The obvious question is why and how did these objects arrive here in the first place, thereby creating opportunities for the formation of new social practices and the disintegration of existing ones. Was this a result of trade or exchange involving the activities of the Danish citizens, or of more direct contacts or even close personal relations with people of non-local origin? The earliest traces of foreigners in Aarhus could be the remains of Baltic ceramics found in the Viking Age settlement and perhaps the people

who used the Norwegian combs. Looking at the written evidence, it is quite clear that the urban community was unstable, marked by foreign visitors, guests or immigrants in stage 4, i.e. from at least the early 14th century onwards, and especially by local immigration from at least the late 15th century, and with a high turnover of poorer inhabitants in stage 6 from at least the 16th century. The sparseness of surviving written sources calls for caution, but nothing so far indicates that Aarhus accommodated large foreign groups in the later Middle Ages.[361] The town did, however, house a few German immigrants, engaged in trans-local practice, probably marrying into Danish families, as shown by the aforementioned case of Blasius von Wismar from the early 14th century. Neither were these the first foreigners in town. Aarhus appears never to have had a German guild, unlike many of the major eastern Danish and Baltic towns such as Malmø and Elsinore, Kalmar and Tallin.[362] The town did though have visitors, guests and citizens of foreign, mostly of German and Norwegian, descent from the Viking Age onwards. Most were probably guests, as in the case of the aforementioned Wenemar von Essen. He was a guest in the house of Herman Witte, who must have been a citizen of the town and was most likely of German descent. These foreigners are well documented in the late 15th and early 16th centuries and appear to have been a constant factor throughout the Early Modern and Modern periods. Such a migration was of course not confined to Aarhus alone, but was a general phenomenon, according to studies by Bjørn Poulsen of Medieval migration across the Baltics.[363] Poulsen highlights the 14th century as the time when this migration became noticeable, and he also stresses the crucial impact it had on Medieval Danish society, for example in administration, the organisation of crafts and guilds and in more worldly matters, such as the importing of beer. Even so, these foreign immigrants do not appear to have constituted any more than a minor group in the town – less than 20 individuals with German names appear to have taken citizenship between 1480 and 1520. Neither do they seem to have formed a closed group, but became integrated into the local population through interpersonal relations and networks, and even marriage, as we have seen. But in the little town of Aarhus even a small number of immigrants must have been noticeable in town life and, as the archaeological record suggests, these cultural encounters resulted in the formation of new social practices. These, in turn, led to the spread of Hanseatic materiality and knowledge in the urban area at the same time that the town developed its role as a nodal point in the exchange between the Baltic area and Norway. This is though not to be seen as a transfer of a Hanseatic cultural package. Instead, there was a progressive entanglement of Hanseatic elements and local culture through the aforementioned interpersonal relations: friendships, family relations, trade relations or a mixture of all of these. The German-born citizens probably acted as spearheads, merging their social practice with that of their networks inside and outside the physical boundaries of the town in a strategy that only partly reflects the strategies of the Hanseatic merchants in Kalmar and Tallin, as presented in Magdalena Naum's analysis of Kalmar and Tallin and Justyna Wubs-Mrozewic's works on Bergen and Stockholm.[364]That the strategy in Aarhus seems to have been different is clear: The institutions that characterise a colony were never founded here, and neither do we see traces of legal distinctions or formalised power relations with the other groups in town. This is in clear contrast to the colonies that developed in for example in Tallin, and in part Kalmar, as revealed by Magdalena Naum's analysis. That a colony never developed in Aarhus, or in other Danish towns, can be seen as the combined effect of a low number of immigrants, a high degree of inter-marriage between Germans and Danes, the strong standing of the town ruler and of the towns in general and, of course, the different position and politics of the Danish state as opposed to Norway, Sweden and Estonia.

While the utilitarian stoneware of the Late Middle Ages and Early Modern period might have been subject to market trade, we have no Danish information on the trading of ceramics before the very end of the 16th century, when such vessels were sold by mer-chants. The more elaborate types – majolica, high-ly-decorated stoneware tankards with metal fittings etc., may have been exchanged within the complex, intertwined networks of clerics, business associates, godparents and the like that made up the communities in the small town. However, this minor group of citizens born outside the realm were not the only non-local elements in Aarhus. Town life was marked by a high, but fluctuating, degree of local and regional mobility from rural to urban areas and back, at least from the Late Middle Ages and continuing up into the Early Modern period.[365] This needs to be taken into account when we reflect upon the materiality of the region. Consequently, the town was not marked by stability, but by instability, and by close relations with surrounding villages, at least in some social circles. It was therefore not a static place, but very much characterised by instability, fluctuations, mobility and contacts with other geographical areas, either rural or urban, in the form of Danish or foreign towns and cities. This does not mean that the townspeople were necessarily culturally open to other traditions, but it does mean that the mobility and the exchange of materiality and skills that followed constitute a factor that must be taken into consideration when dealing with the urban and rural past.

6.6 Localisation of the urban poor

Social topography is not at the centre of this investigation, but the archaeological record does provide some pointers with respect to localisation of the urban poor. The locations of vaulted cellars and brick-built secular buildings are frequently employed as indicators of the social topography of the Medieval town. As mentioned above, remains of four brick-built buildings have been excavated or recorded in Mejlgade, near the coast. Medieval brick houses have also been excavated in the immediate vicinity of the cathedral, and they are interpreted as the remains of possible canonical residences. At least one brick-built cellar from the Early Modern period is preserved at Store Torv 3.[366] In other areas of the town, brick houses or brick cellars are so far notably absent. Imports and large quantities of glazed ceramics, indicating consumption centred on refined display, are conspicuous as early as the 14th century, being evident in the centre of town next to the cathedral, as well as along the major roads, i.e. Frederiksgade, Mejlgade and Guldsmedgade. This pattern appears to be maintained into the 15th and 16th centuries, with Vestergade and Studsgade now visible too. Imports seem to be largely absent or rare in Rosensgade, at Skt. Clemensborg and in the alleys running between the main streets. We can therefore suggest that the wealthy, well-connected and stable elements of the town's population largely occupied the main streets, while less stable elements, including rural newcomers, occupied the areas in between, in smaller streets, alleys and backyards: Marginal spaces for marginalised people. Something similar has been proposed in in Ben Jervis´s studies of Medieval Southampton, where he highlights marginalised people and the heterogeneity of the town. The social and economic diversity of the Late Medieval town has also been described by historian Bjørn Poulsen, who stresses social conflicts and increasing diversity in the 15th and 16th centuries.[367] This spatial organisation appears to have been remarkably stable throughout the centuries. It was probably linked to a class that has not been dealt with in detail in this publication, or anywhere else in our historical archaeology for that matter – the urban outcasts: especially beggars, the poor, criminals and vagrants. Individuals we meet primarily in the court rolls and who are dealt with in historical studies like those of Jørgen Mikkelsen, on the organisation of poor relief.[368]. The fact that they only feature to such a minor degree in this study was not a conscious choice. Instead, it reflects the difficulties inherent in identifying these urban outcasts in the available source material within the framework of this publication. No executioner's house or rake's dwelling has yet been excavated in Aarhus, and neither have the paupers' dwellings in the former Priory of our Lady. Furthermore, eviction cases show that many of these people lived in the households of citizens and,

consequently, their social practice is very difficult to distinguish from that of their hosts in the archaeological record that constitutes the focus of attention in this book. Nevertheless, it may be possible to study these marginal groups in greater details in future works. The fact that three women from the notoriously impoverished street of Fiskergade were accused of witchcraft in the early 17th century may be taken as a sign of the vulnerable position of poor women in the public eye.[369] Old poor women rarely have a high success rate in social practice, and prestige loss may be what made them vulnerable to gossip and rumours. Just as vulnerable were the 128 men, women and children, all non-citizens, who were evicted from the town on 17 January 1588, because they did not possess the necessary travellers' passes from their home towns. The group is referred to as amoral in the court records, and many of them are described as being violent, prostitutes, pimps or previously evicted. Some of them can be placed in town, and of these most lived "behind the convent", i.e. around present Møllestien – a previously notorious poor street, in Rosensgade, Studsgade, Volden, in the vanished streets of Volmers Gyde and Fægyde or in Smediegården, which is near Borggade, all in the northwestern part of town.[370] How these people fared in the midst of winter, following their eviction, we do not know, and such concerns certainly did not stop the town council. This eviction in 1588 was large-scale, but it was not the only attempt by the city council to rid the town of what they perceived as a burden. This was an expression of what is called a process of social disciplining in the field of the history of poverty; a process in which the poorest were increasingly marginalised and criminalised.[371] It is worth noting that the places mentioned in 1588 are precisely the quarters where this investigation has revealed a rural and rather poor lifestyle and consumption. Further research into the court rolls and inventories of estates (probate records) etc. would benefit an investigation into the town's "underworld". Whether such an involuntarily mobile underclass was a Late Medieval/ Early Modern phenomenon, or whether it also existed in earlier periods too, is a ques-

Figure 167. The Drunken Harlot, c. 1255-60. Courtesy of The J. Paul Getty Museum, Los Angeles.

tion that deserves further study. Recent research has shown an increase in the legal measures taken against the urban poor in the early 16th century. This prompts the conclusion that there was an actual increase in the number of poor in the 16th century and it should be noted that this development is visible in the archaeological record analysed in this volume and in previous works based on the same methodologies.[372] According to Carsten Selch Jensen, this attitude towards the urban poor could be a Post-Medieval phenomenon, fuelled by a shift in attitudes towards marginalisation and criminalisation of the poor.[373] He identifies the Middle Ages as a time when mutual help among the inhabitants was of greater importance for the poor than any legislative initiatives from the authorities. But he also highlights the later Middle Ages as the time when a work ethos penetrated society, leading to the authorisation of beggars, with examples in German towns, the repression and criminalisation of those who were unauthorised. There was also division

of the poor into locals and strangers; the honourable and the dishonest, and as we have seen, the town authorities went to great lengths to get rid of the latter group.[374] Bjørn Poulsen has studied the poor too, and he points out references to poor Danes in the court records in Rostock in the mid-14th century, when several Danes were evicted for various crimes. Poulsen sees this phenomenon as evidence of poor Danes looking for better prospects in the emerging Baltic towns.[375] There is no doubt that the urban or rural poor, the strangers, the dishonest and the other marginalised groups have so far received little or no attention from Danish historical archaeology, which appears to be focussed on studies of the norm, rather than the deviant. Some of these questions are though being addressed in the ongoing Urban Diaspora project, but in order to examine even more of them from an archaeological perspective, we need to develop methodologies that are directed towards identifying the materiality of these marginalised urban groups –

and their rural counterparts, for that matter, and we need collaboration with history and science in order to succeed.

6.7 Performing urbanity

As we have seen, the main features that emerge from the consumption analysis are patterns of stability and change. The town's contacts appear remarkably stable from the Early Middle Ages to the 19th century, i.e. contacts with the same region, primarily Lübeck, Hamburg and the towns and cities of the western Baltic. Once established, these contacts appear not to have changed much. The same is true of consumption patterns in the town, where differences emerge between the town centre and the outskirts/surroundings in the 13th century, around the same time as Aarhus appears to become a legal entity.[376] If town and countryside had different consumption patterns prior to this, we need new source material in order to be able to see it. The main Hanseatic influences appears to have been confined to the ecclesial centre and around the possible harbour quarter in Mejlgade, while consumption resembling that of the rural villages mostly took place in Rosensgade, but also to some extent in Guldsmedgade and certainly at Skt. Clemensborg, from the mid-15th century. Later, a clear centre of display becomes evident on Bispetorv, with further display practised in Mejlgade, Studsgade and, judging from the supplementary finds, around Vestergade too. But this was not the case in the notoriously poor street Møllestien, just 50 m south of Vestergade. If we are to interpret this in the light of the information available on immigration and mobility, stable, relatively well-off citizens may have inhabited these places, while the backyards and outskirts were the places for the poor and unstable elements. On this basis, it seems that the relational entanglement as defined by Stockhammer,[377] i.e. implementation of practice centred around consumption of imported goods, does not characterise all of the occupants within the physical boundaries of the town. Instead, it may mark out the topography of complex elite communities, including both ecclesial and secular elites, with complex social practices, some of which only cooperated with fellow townspeople and others who also encompassed the rural elite. If we then look at the rural areas around Aarhus, the distribution of Hanseatic influences is visible at the manors from the 14th century onwards, while the villages appear to have become integrated into the urban consumption pattern at some time in the 15th century.

What we see might rightfully be described as an entanglement or perhaps an ethnogenesis: A creation of new cultures in a complex and multipolar web of interactions between locals, regional immigrants and foreigners settling in the town. This web was underpinned, supported, created or influenced by the special circumstances that have been summarised by Bjørn Poulsen as the special legal framework that characterised towns: the legal rights of the townsmen, the autonomy of the towns and the duties and obligations that followed from this, including the formations of estates and the legal and factual separation of merchants and craftsmen from the early 15th century onwards.[378] I have only been able to touch upon this very briefly within the framework of the present project, and it is clear that, in order to be able to take all of the legal framework into account, archaeologists need to collaborate with historians in interdisciplinary projects.

As previously stated, this book is based on an analysis of the household as a community. Individual identities can only be assessed in archaeology under very rare circumstances, because the household is usually the smallest unit in this respect. It is only under very rare circumstances that materiality can be related to one particular person in our part of the world. The material culture, as represented by the ceramics, has been divided up in three groups: local – i.e. blackwares and greywares, regional – i.e. glazed redwares, and foreign – i.e. imports. If we follow the very simple model set up in the chapter on "Theory", a simple analysis of the relative amounts of foreign, regional and local material culture allows us to draw conclusions on cultural hybridity in households with more than one of these types present. In this analysis, the zones near the coast and around Store Torv certainly stands out as being different, with high percentages of both foreign and regional wares. On the other hand, the northwest part of town appears relatively unaffected by this entangled urbanity, showing strong links to a local/rural culture and some involvement at regional level. An analysis of this kind is of course over-simplistic, but it does nevertheless hold some truth with regard to the obvious entanglement, and even more so as the inclusion of the hinterland permits the investigation of cultural divides both in urban and in rural areas. Crude as it may be, the model allows us to see groups emerge, function and disappear, instead of identifying already known groups in the archaeological record.[379] In such an analysis, "urbanity" comes across as a function of the creation of new social practices, with the exchange of materiality and meaning in networks involving locals and foreigners. Urbanity can therefore be thought of as an entanglement of supra-regional and regional culture – a point I will return to later.

This model allows us to identify cultural heterogeneity within the boundaries of the town. Perhaps more importantly, it allows us to see the cultural entanglement that crosses the physical boundaries of the town and very clearly recognise the shared culture between the northwest part of town and the rural areas. If we then link this hypothesis of urbanity and rural culture with the historical evidence for the presence of people associated with the two areas, i.e. Lübeck and the villages around Aarhus, a link appears to form, whereby the exchange of materiality, knowledge and meaning could have been orchestrated through the informal meeting places that are a central part of town life. Since well-conducted social practice gives access to more of the same, it is possible that this constant positive reinforcement is the reason why Aarhus has been a success as a town while others, like Søborg and Slangerup, were not.

It is worth noting that any model of cultural entanglement has to take into account the social structure of the households, and that this status affects our model of urbanity as a hybrid. Unlike those of the present day, Medieval households were socially unequal, consisting of a married couple, as masters of the household, children, other relatives, hired help and servants, apprentices and lodgers of many kinds. Furthermore, the household was in some respects unstable: the married couple comprised the stable element, while the other members could and did move around between households, thereby acting as channels of exchange of both knowledge, materiality and meaning. We also have to take into account the traditional role of women as guardians and carriers of food culture; culture that could, as suggested by Mary Beaudry, be shared and exchanged in reciprocal hospitality.[380] Returning to the meeting between cultures in the town – and outside, it is historically well-known that many people from rural areas spent a longer or shorter time as servants in town, before they settled back in their villages or took citizenship in the town. We do not, as yet, know much about the composition of households in Aarhus, and certainly not in the Middle Ages, but when the sources do give us some information, they tell of servants from the rural areas working in the households of citizens.[381] If this was common practice, then many of the urban households had members sharing a rural culture in their midst and the household itself then evolved into hybrid: A meeting place between local and regional, urban and rural practice and culture, leading to elements of urban culture being fed back to rural areas when the former servants settled there later in life.[382] This constant exchange between rural and urban and foreign might, as suggested by Mary Beaudry, have been a catalyst for the exchange of food ideas and the rapid adoption of new items.[383] Usually, the household is the smallest detectable unit when an urban dwelling is excavated, and rarely are we able to see which members of the household used or acquired the materiality we find. Nevertheless, this will be an important aspect of future projects, because such an analysis will allow us to penetrate further into the cultural dynamics of the household. Turning it from a reflection on the modern family structure to a meeting point between people of different backgrounds, social and economic standing, age, profession, gender and rank; a meeting point that constantly enacted and

Figure 168. The Temperate and the Intemperate, Master of the Dresden Prayer Book, about 1475-80. Courtesy of The J. Paul Getty Museum, Los Angeles.

re-enacted a group connection. What we see evident here in the materiality can potentially be interpreted as traces of entangled communities marked or separated by networks or a number of economic, social or ethnic differences, or a mixture of all of these, reflected, enacted and re-enacted in consumption and food culture. The disentanglement of this complex situation is no small task, and yet the deep entanglement could be the very heart of the matter in our part of the world.

6.8 Urban consumption – entangled urbanities

If we return to urbanity, we have now established that this comprises a myriad of practices, one replacing the other in an organic flow through generations, from ancestors to descendants. As such, urbanity can be understood as "the rhythm of society", as expressed by Elisabeth Shove, and what we see in archaeological excavations can be perceived as underlying transformations in relations between practices and the way they are entangled.[384] It is time to note that not all practices are equally important. According to Shove, life revolves around a handful of dominant projects – interlinked practices that, in combination, "require that participating individuals expend their labour power or in some other way engage themselves in activity in a given manner, a given time and place". One such bundle of practices for an individual in the past could well be their occupation, which bound participants into communities through involvement in guilds, workshops and congregations gathered around the guild altars in churches. Other examples could be a colony of immigrants, sharing and exchanging practices through formalised or non-formalised communities, or the clerics who lived south of the cathedral.

Expressions of urbanity are related to lifestyle, and now is the time to stress the fact that the lifestyle-related performance of urbanity does not erase the need for analysis of the conscious processes generally included in urbanisation: monetisation, foundation of institutions etc. On the contrary, the two concepts go hand in hand, interacting with each other. According to Shove, living in an urban community is about understanding, conforming and adapting to the routines of the social and the physical space and making them one's own. The town thereby influences personality development, behaviour, values and relations, and creates creativity through leakage zones – market places, taverns, inns and other public places where individuals meet and creativity arise.[385] But as many archaeological excavations have shown, such places are full of the materiality of consumption, demonstrating, in particular, the importance of drinking in such meetings and the role of alcohol as a great mixer of people. This then takes us back to the central position of consumption, not only in urban life, but in life itself, and the stable or short-lived communities of people united through the performance of consumption. Consumption is, for this reason, a very powerful activity: For what is consumption if not a collective ritual aimed at group mobilisation, involving materiality with meaning?

What are the foreign stoneware vessels, the majolica plates and the porcelain dishes if not that?

Is urbanity only performed through social practices surrounding consumption? Certainly not! Many social identities are expressed through other means, such as dress, speech, language, lifestyle etc., which cannot be explored in this study, but are being investigated through other projects project as I write.[386] There are other arenas too: In a true contrast – the Medieval dialectic principle, social practices surrounding waste is another aspect that will be analysed in a later project. There is a certain irony in the contrasts of intake and output, food and bodily waste, as practices in which urbanity is embedded.

From a chronological perspective, some changes seem more profound than others. The marked shift in social practice in stage 4, in the very early 13th century, takes place simultaneously with a large-scale restructuring of the urban landscape – renewal of the fortifications, laying out of the streets and market squares and the expansion of the occupied areas. It might be fair to call this the breakthrough of urbanity, fuelled by contacts with the emerging urban centres in the Baltic, while the previous stages could be referred to as pre- or early urban. The second major change is the one around 1400: new houses, new harbour, new social practices go hand in hand. Then comes the introduction of the individual tableware in the 16th century – at about the same time as the Reformation. The next major break is the onset of modernity in the late 18th century, and we must not forget the many other processes operating during this period: a boom in economy and trade, increasing mobility, social unrest and a rise in population. The question is whether urbanity is, in reality, an expression of cosmopolitanism, with actors possessing multiple citizenships, performing overlapping identities. Nevertheless, the strong division apparent within the boundaries of the town seems to indicate a rigidness and a lack of inclusion that appears to go against cosmopolitan ideals. But following Bell´s example, we can suggest that urbanity is a result of an ethnogenesis, which created a shared "urban" identity uniting the people involved at a regional and supra-regional level, whether natives or foreigners. But this ethnogenesis, if we may call it that, differs from the ethnogenesis which Hu calls "a metaphor for the creativity of oppressed and marginalized peoples birthing a new cultural space for themselves amidst their desperate struggle to survive."[387] That is unless we consider these people marginalised and oppressed in relation to the metropolises on the southern shores of the Baltic: Lübeck, Stettin, Rostock and Danzig, which would be stretching it. In both the ethnogeneses suggested here, in the 13th century, and that in the 15th century, we see a homogenisation of tastes and a preference for certain goods before and during the time when many ethnic, i.e. German, names appear in the written sources. This is exactly the same phenomenon as seen in David Curta´s works on ethnogenesis in the Roman Empire.[388] Urbanity appears very much an elite phenomenon, and perhaps it is actually born out of a struggle for dominance and power in the meetings with the urban and rural poor who reinforced their identity through defining the outcasts in a never-ending circle.[389] We can identify a rather direct parallel to ethnogenesis among whites in Spanish colonies – another elite phenomenon.[390] Yet we cannot see a counterculture – but perhaps the practice of identifying themselves with their ancestral village, which we see among the new inhabitants of rural descent in Aarhus in the 15th and 16th centuries, is one of the few signs we have of persistence, even resistance, against urbanity.[391] The reader will understand that I have difficulty in identifying a common urban identity encompassing all people within the physical boundaries of the town. This is in contrast to historian Bjørn Poulsen, who argues for the existence of what he calls an urban spirit, because "the Danish towns generally managed to act as units and that fighting parties were re-integrated."[392] Poulsen seeks an explanation in the constant battle for town privileges and in factors that stimulated urban unity, such as the oaths sworn to towns and the taxes payed. Poulsen may well be right on these points, but it is important to be aware of differences in scale and sources between archaeology and history when such conclusions are drawn. Many of the written sources

shed light on certain groups of the people who lived in the town and especially on burghers, who were represented by the town council. Archaeology, on the other hand, is a democratic discipline, because our sources relates to everyone who lived and worked in town, burghers or not. That is why this book concentrates on the gaps, power struggles, suppressions and exclusions, divisions between the groups of burghers and the others. The differences between the two approaches stand our clearly when Poulsen mentions that the rosary fraternity in the town of Schleswig had 136 members in the 1480s and correlates this with the approximately 200 houses and 2000 inhabitants in the town, concluding that the guild united a significant part of the population. It may well be that a significant proportion of the burghers were represented, but an archaeologist would focus on the fact that more than 90% of the inhabitants were not members of the guild. Therefore, one of the tasks of archaeology may well be to focus on the voiceless inhabitants.

The reader will have noticed that I have not mentioned state formation, the founding of institutions or the legal framework in this analysis. That is not because the questions are unimportant, but because an analysis would demand efforts that lie beyond the framework of this project. This is a field where interdisciplinary cooperation with the field of history is crucial. At this point, I will only suggest, as maintained by Hu, that the rise of the state may have had a profound effect on urbanity, meaning that it may have led to what Hu calls the "durability of alliances or networks that was previously fluent and temporary, formalizing and instrumentalizing them".[393]According to Hu, this may be visible if we track durability and uniformity of symbols and types of social interaction. In tracing the effects of state formation on the permanence of social groups by such means, we need data relating to a wide range of materiality from the Viking Age and Early Middle Ages. And if we want to trace such effects in the Middle Ages and later periods, we need interdisciplinary cooperation with history. We already know parts of the framework: The sumptuary laws and the social structure based on rank that the state attempted to impose on the people in the Early Modern period. But as yet we do not know the response of the people to this pressure. If we are to address such questions archaeologically, this must be based on large-scale intensive comparative analyses of primary data, not unlike the dataset that forms the basis of this book.

This project is a study of urbanity based on a specific element of the archaeological record, chosen as the best possible option within the framework of the project. It is very clear that this material has limitations, and that we require contributions from other disciplines, specifically science and history, if the issues raised here are to be addressed in more detail. Because of this, it might be that the focus on urbanity instead of on urbanisation raise more questions than it provides answers at this point. As pointed out by Kalmring, when he says that there are questions that we do not yet know how to answer archaeologically – like how do we identify intent in the archaeological record? How do we distinguish between ethnic and social identity, and myriads of other identities that are operating? Kalmring, somewhat sceptically, questions whether the quest for the performative practices of urban dwellers is unfeasible – an intellectual pastime.[394] But here I would like to reply that archaeology is a method as well as a research field, one of many by which we can gain an insight into the past. If the questions we wish to address demand new methodologies or answers from an interdisciplinary field that involves not only archaeology, but also anthropology, history, literature, history of religion and science, to mention but a few, so be it. The more we see of the past, the more entangled it appears to be. I think it would be sensible to accept that the most interesting questions are the complex ones, and that complex questions demand complex answers.

This analysis of urban consumption leads us to question the idea of the town as a homogenous society with a single shared performance of urbanity. In fact, some of the social practices most frequently interpreted as performances of urbanity only includes a limited, perhaps even very small, percentage of the people who actually lived within the physical boundaries of the town. What we see instead appear to be several spaces inhabited by different groups with different performances. The powerful are the ones who are able to define what constitutes urbanity at any given time and make others succumb to their practice, whether they are the ecclesial community, the town council, masters in workshops, masters of the household or informal leaders in the urban community. If we are not very aware of the power relations that formed the past as we see it, we will only write the history of the powerful, and not include the people with engaged deviant, unaccepted practice: The outcasts, the strangers, the queer and the powerless, like the people who were evicted from the town in 1588.[395] That leads us to the penultimate point to be made here, with respect to the connection between social practice and social capital, or as Latour and Woolgar put it "Cycles of credibility", where a well-conducted social practice accumulates social capital – or "honour" to use the Medieval term, thereby leading to increased prestige, inclusion in further practices with new participants and an increase in social standing.[396] On the other hand, a failed practice leads to a downwards spiral of disrepute – expressed in Medieval sources as "evil housekeeping", and subsequent marginalisation and exclusion. This circle of inclusion and exclusion may be what kept the town together: Some groups are marked by stability through generations, able as they are repeatedly to accumulate the social capital that keeps them afloat, while others are the losers marked by instability and frequent substitution. If we do not want only to write the history of the winners, we will benefit from redirecting our focus away from physical urban boundaries, since these tend to homogenise the townscape and estrange the rural landscape to the coexistence of several expressions or levels of urbanity, formed by different communities with different agendas, entangled within the spatial boundaries of the town and beyond. With this in mind, we can say that urbanity is not so much a matter of place, more a state of mind.

If we, finally, try to ask how it felt to live in Aarhus

in the past, the answer is far from simple, and probably far from constant. The various processes described and examined in this book must have been very evident to the inhabitants. The transformation from a Viking Age stronghold to a Medieval town would have been a landmark process, and a hagiocentric world view, the introduction of institutionalised communities in the congregation and the guilds and the institutionalised care in the convents must have made their mark on life in the Medieval town. The changing world view at the Reformation and the large number of urban poor moving from town to town, and similar numbers of urban outcasts, must have been very conspicuous, and these processes would have been reinforced by economic and political disasters such as the decline seen in the wake of the Thirty Years' War. The question is whether we really see an increasing social and cultural gap between the town and countryside, as a consequence of an urbanity. that excluded both the urban and the rural poor. According to Hu, we might ask whether the Age of Enlightenment, with its distaste for folk culture and "superstition" and its penchant for order and neatness, control and education, contributed greatly to the enforcement of social hierarchies and distinctions, not only in Aarhus, but also in Denmark as a whole.[397] If so, we have a classic example of enlightenment as a movement that creates a counterpart in its attempt to eliminate that very element. If we dare to venture into such research questions, I believe that archaeology, with its ability to look beyond the public discourse, has a significant role to play.

After completing this book, it is time to reflect on what we really see in an archaeological excavation – in the myriads of contexts, structures and artefacts we discover every day. To those of us who see the results, produce the spreadsheets, the floor plans, the plans of plots and maps of towns and try to find out what really happened through the many centuries, it may appear to be a rolling, gradual, almost linear development. But in reality, this apparent stability is an illusion, created by our rear-mirror perspective on the past. Because what we see may well be the result of failed attempts, blind alleys and halting development, the myriads of entanglements that constitute human life. To quote Axel Christophersen: "What we see is likely to be a result of unforeseen effects of decisions made with other goals in mind."[398]

This is a book covering 1000 years, which unavoidably leads to a consideration of time and its nature. We sometimes think of the past as a slower, calmer era, but reading this book will expose this as an illusion: The past is characterised by constant change. Some of Aarhus' landmarks have, however, also acted as such in the past, as tools of memory, materialising time in space, uniting past and present in the public eye, creating a mental map of the town in the mind of the newcomer, and acting as welcoming friends in the minds of those us who have our roots in the town. The Priory of Our Lady and St. Clement's Church act as both physical and mental landmarks in the town. The river, Aarhus Å, has re-emerged from beneath the pavement that covered it for decades, and the sound of water once again forms the background for urban life as it has done since the town emerged. The town rampart has long been covered with buildings and pavements, but more than a millennium after its construction it still holds the city centre in a close embrace, visible in the winding streets at its foot. All of these act as points of remembrance, as silent witnesses, as carriers of memories of the town and as barriers to destruction and oblivion for those of us who have our ancestral roots in the town, and for the many newcomers. Yet it is difficult to see the same consistency in the archaeological record resulting from our excavations: All that remains are scraps, bits and pieces that we try to put together to provide glimpses of former lives. But it is what it is; archaeology is after all a discipline built on transient matter. Whether or not you think my efforts have been successful, as you turn the last page of this book, I hope to have been able to convince you that a primary aim of archaeology is to place humans at the heart of history and to see how they coped with life as they knew it in ways that might shed light on our own.

| All sites | | | | | | | | | | | | | | | | |
| Sum of sherd counts | | | | | | | | | | | | | | | | |
Town phase	FHM 1978	FHM 3474	FHM 3731	FHM 4074	FHM 4201	FHM 4225	FHM 4278	FHM 4573	FHM 4587	FHM 4616	FHM 4730	FHM 4881	FHM 4999	FHM 5124	FHM 5419	Total
0					190	412	9		11	19		790		235		1666
I		17				427	178	1761				586		2276		5245
II			60				2	81	74	14				715		946
III		193		597		1696	385		146	434	125	220		202		3998
IV					265	774			291	596		68	181	432		2607
V		149		168	1278	1094	81	54	174			980		991	131	5100
VI	525				180	335	29		414			243		224		1950
VII	718			1	1456		59		41					201		2476
VIII		85			632									1		718
VIIII														80		80
Total	1243	444	60	766	4001	4738	743	1896	1151	1063	125	2887	181	5357	131	24786

Table 32. Ceramics (sherds) in the town phases, site by site.

Fabric code	Ware type	Sum of sherd counts	Sum of RP	Sum of weight
C1	Andenne-type ware	4	0	20
A0b	Baltic blackware	243	412	4024
A2b	Baltic burnished greyware	66	61	652
A1b	Black pot, early type	2049	3073	30817
A1d	Black pot, Varde type	1134	1757	19865
A1c	Black pot, Vorup type	226	309	1933
B1a	Brügge-type ware	1	0	4
G1	Capuchin ware	6	0	20
E3	Cologne stoneware	168	600	208
B2a	Danish slipware	47	255	673
E2	Frechen stoneware	16	120	522
F2	Industrial ware	286	884	3438
E4	Langerwehe stoneware	6	35	71
B2c2	Low Countries redware	19	48	361
C4	Low Countries/German Post-Medieval whiteware	353	891	5158
F1	Low Countries tin-glazed ware	10	8	62
A1a	Medieval low-fired coarseware	1173	790	9934
A2a	Medieval well-fired coarseware	4109	3858	54832
B1c	Medieval well-fired redware	1116	675	13797
A1e	Other blackware	1869	2955	40152
D1	Pingsdorf-type ware	2	0	8
G2	Porcelain	42	81	123
B2c1	Post-Medieval redware	5640	9497	89684
B2b1	Post-Medieval redware with slip decoration	975	2921	8283
D2	Proto stoneware	25	62	325
E5	Raeren stoneware	81	137	1162
C2	Rouen-type ware	9	66	27
C5	Saintonge polychrome	1	0	1
E1	Siegburg stoneware	64	165	548
F3	Other tin-glazed ceramics	121	99	280
A0a	Viking Age low-fired coarseware	4893	1955	42402
E8	Waldenburg stoneware	5	0	32
B2b2	Werra ware	2	14	30
C3	Weser ware	4	13	58
E6	Westerwald stoneware	21	6	165
Total		**24786**	**31747**	**329671**

Table 33. Ceramics classification.

	Site phase/Rim type	Absolute date	504	501	1023	505	307	1010	1014	1019	1021	1012	VJ302	1028	1007	1009	1003	1013
	FHM 4201 phase 15	Winter 1779/80	8									9	1					
IX	FHM 4201 phase 17	After 1779-94 and before 1838	1	5	7							21	15					9
	FHM 4201 phase 14	Winter 1772/73	3			12	13	417	102	57	16	300	153	55	372	12	44	22
	FHM 4201 phase 16	After 1779-94	1									19	18			25		
VII	FHM 4278 phase 5													5		7		
	FHM 1978 phase 1														17	50	68	
	FHM 4201 phase 12	After 1571 and before 1651/52													8		15	
VII	FHM 4201 phase 13	Winter 1651/52																
	FHM 4881 phase 7															8		87
	FHM 4201 phase 11	C. 1571															11	
	FHM 4881 phase 5																	
	FHM 4881 phase 6																	
	FHM 4881 phase 4																	
	FHM 4587 phase 3																	
	FHM 4201 phase 10	Winter 1547/48																
	FHM 4201 phase 6	1480																
	FHM 4201 phase 2	After 1443 before 1452/53																
	FHM 4201 phase 8	1514																
V	FHM 4201 phase 9	Winter 1512/13																
	FHM 4201 phase 7	After 1480 to before 1514																
	FHM 4999																	
	FHM 4225 phase 7																	
	FHM 4201 phase 3																	
	FHM 4201 phase 5																	
	FHM 4225 phase 8	Coin 1422-40																
IV	FHM 4074	Dendro 1396																
	FHM 4225 phase 6																	
	FHM 4587 phase 2																	
	FHM 4278 phase 3																	
	FHM 4225 phase 4																	
	FHM 4225 phase 5	Coin 1310-20																
	FHM 3731	Coin 1230. Hist. date pre 1313																
	FHM 4616 phase II	Dendro 1335																
	FHM 4616 phase III																	
III	FHM 4587 phase 1	Coin 1320-29																
	FHM 4881 phase 2																	
	FHM 4225 phase 3																	
	FHM 4730																	
	FHM 3474 phase 1																	
	FHM 4225 phase 2																	
II	FHM 4616 phase 1																	
	Total		**13**	**5**	**7**	**12**	**13**	**417**	**102**	**57**	**16**	**349**	**187**	**60**	**397**	**102**	**138**	**118**

Table 34. Matrix of seriated data showing 42 stratigraphic phases and 39 rim types. Sum = 8876 RP. Same dataset as the correspondence analysis (CA) shown in figures 134-137. Absolute dates are marked and town phases added.

502	AJ302	1020	1002	1001	1004	1035	1005	1016	309	1017	AJ308	TJ302	608	605	606	611	702	703	601	607	701	B601	Total
																							18
																							58
	119	12		51																			1760
																							63
5																							17
54		73	10																				272
	12		14		16		17																82
	6																						6
		37		18	59		48																257
20	257	51	10	265	199	61	18																892
	25			70	86						20												201
	8			40	118		90			12													268
				5			13																18
		17				63	8				25												113
	58	11		59	12	47				53	171												411
						22		14		8	11												55
								12															12
	46					7	45	22			199												319
						45	6	14		83	105												253
						7	16		13	21	99												156
										8													8
7				8			65			49	628	78	33			24			12				904
											28												28
											53												53
							2			8	369			21		19							419
											145			22	46	6							219
						10	55	6		131	313	15	177	32		90			88				917
											26			36	2	16							80
														52									52
											26								25				51
											79		71	10	18	57	24	9	124	8	12		412
															6	15			7				28
															12	57			71	15			155
														4					9				13
															1	1			8	1			11
														5					57				62
																			34				34
																4			154				158
																			5		10		15
																			7			7	14
																					12		12
86	531	201	34	516	490	262	383	68	13	373	2297	93	390	73	85	289	24	9	601	24	34	7	8876

Table 34 continue.

Ware type	Town phase I	II	III	IV	V	VI	VII	VIII	VIIII	Total
Viking Age low-fired coarseware	4240	289	48	33	175					4785
Baltic blackware	190	11	11	2	9	1		2	4	230
Andenne		2		1		1				4
Pingsdorf type		2								2
Medieval low-fired coarseware		165	119	108	48	10				450
Medieval well-fired coarseware		373	2515	626	291	46	62	18	14	3945
Medieval well-fired redware		77	734	164	62	7	4	5	4	1057
Proto stoneware		4	12	4	1					21
Baltic burnished grayware			27	30	3		2			62
Brügge-type ware			1							1
Black pot, early type			267	535	968	167	1		1	1939
Langerwehe stoneware			4	1	1					6
Post-Medieval well-fired redware			146	594	2049	610	1291	314	21	5025
Raeren stoneware			10	9	22	16	10	5		72
Rouen-type ware			4	4	1					9
Saintonge polychrome			1							1
Siegburg stoneware			32	13	11	5				61
Waldenburg stoneware			5							5
Other blackware				329	851	269	176	23	15	1663
Other whiteware				41	84	54	102	51		332
Dutch redware				1	13	2	1			17
Frechen stoneware				2	9		5			16
Low Countries tin-glazed ware				2	3	2	1		1	9
Black pot, Varde type					276	285	247	50	6	864
Black pot, Vorup type					108		76	28		212
Post-Medieval well-fired redware with slip decoration					88	425	118	45	2	678
Werra					2					2
Weser					1		2			3
Westerwald stoneware					3	8	2	5		18
Danish slipware					4	16	7	14	2	43
Cologne stoneware					8		153	3		164
Tin-glazed ceramics					2	1	97	10	1	111
Porcelain							24	16	1	41
Industrial ceramics							95	129	8	232
Total	**4430**	**923**	**3936**	**2499**	**5093**	**1925**	**2476**	**718**	**80**	**22080**

Table 35. Seriation of ware types in town phases based on sherd count. Intrusive and residual sherds have been excluded from FHM 5124 Bispetorv.

Catalogue of form types

Black pot, early type, Black pot, Varde type:

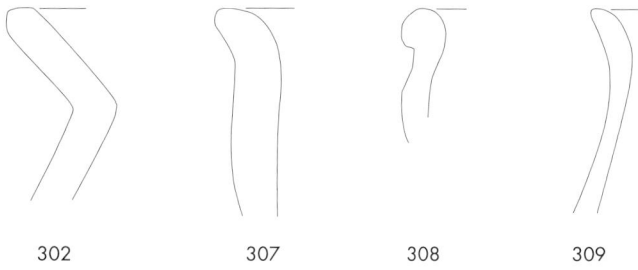

302 307 308 309

Black pot, Vorup type:

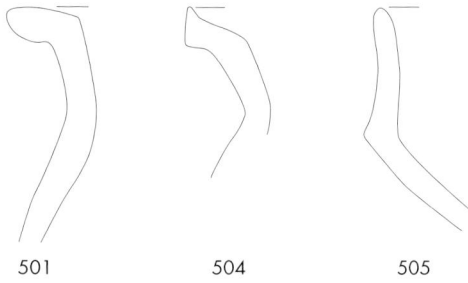

501 504 505

Medieval well-fired coarseware:

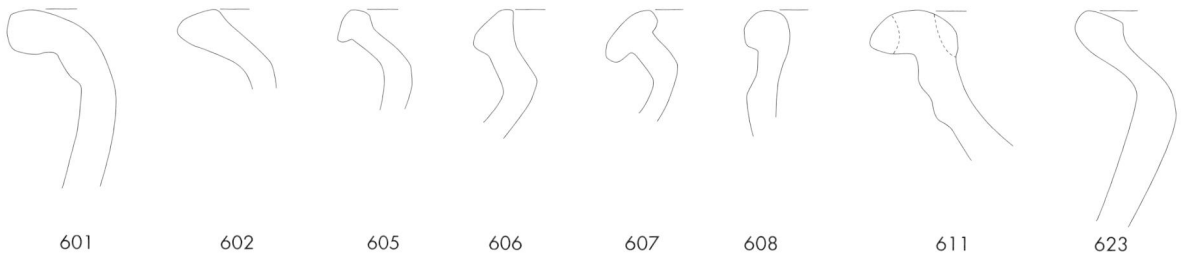

601 602 605 606 607 608 611 623

Medieval well-fired redware:

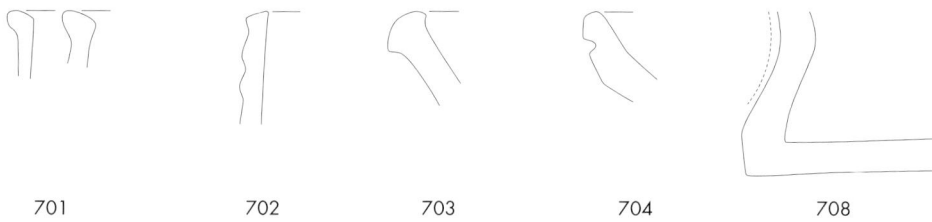

701 702 703 704 708

Figure 169. Rim and handle types.

Post-medieval well-fired redware:

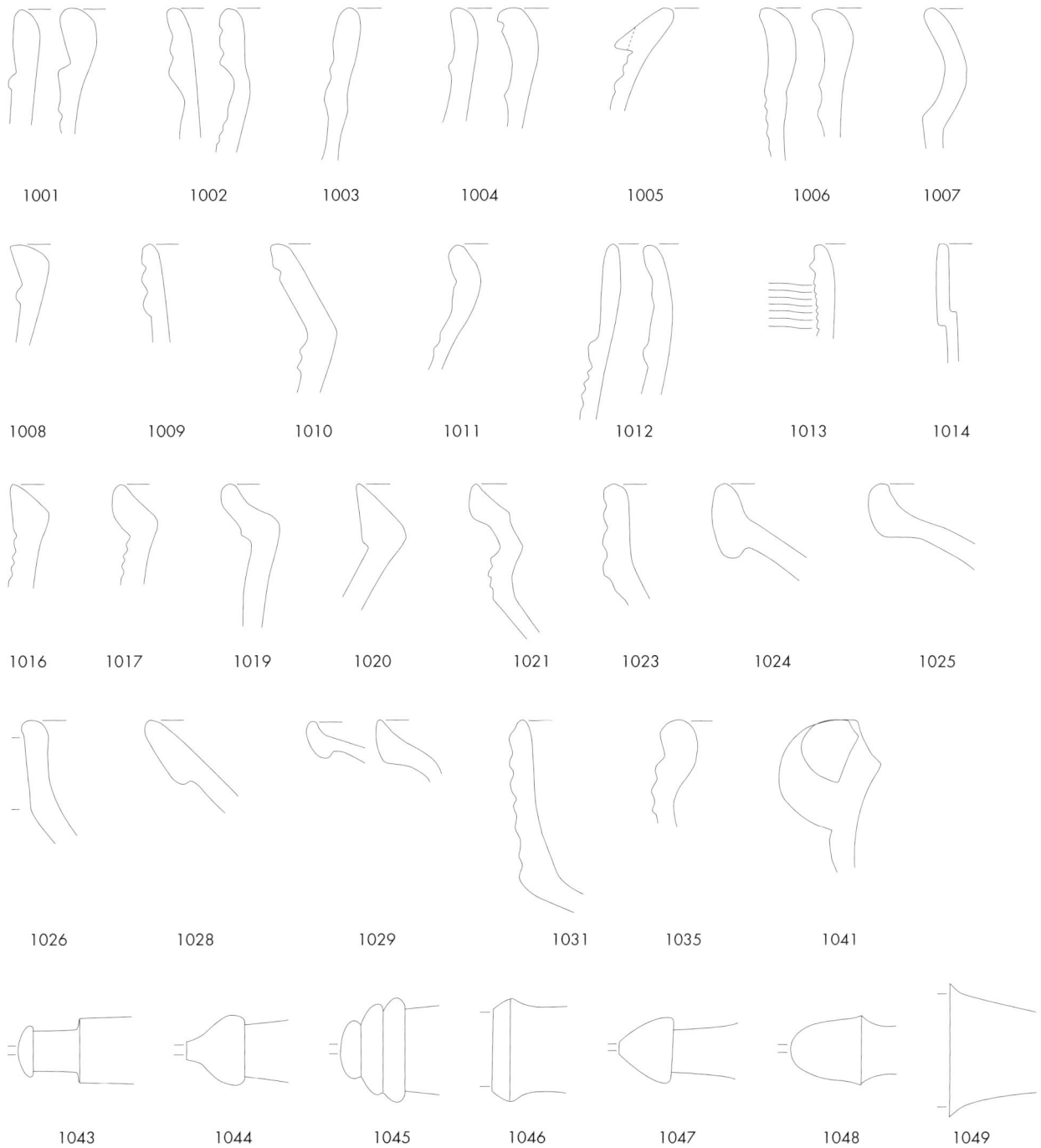

1001 1002 1003 1004 1005 1006 1007

1008 1009 1010 1011 1012 1013 1014

1016 1017 1019 1020 1021 1023 1024 1025

1026 1028 1029 1031 1035 1041

1043 1044 1045 1046 1047 1048 1049

Figure 169 continue. Rim and handle types.

Post-medieval well-fired redware with slip decoration:

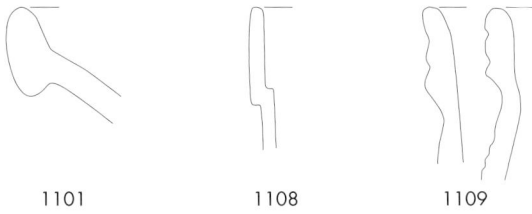

1101   1108   1109

Other whitewares:

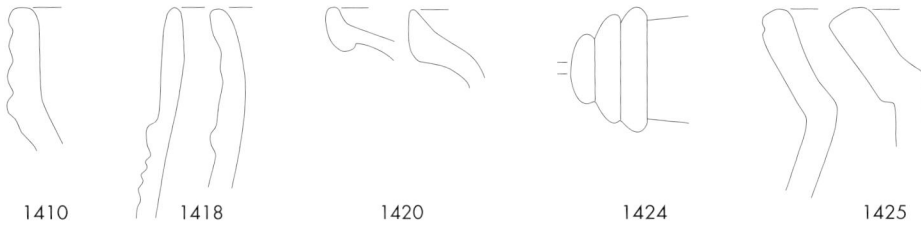

1410   1418   1420   1424   1425

Weser: Werra: Balic Burnished grayware:

1502   1601

1701

Protostoneware:

1902

Tin-glazed ware:

2101   2102

Porcelain:

2201   2203

Figure 169 continue. *Rim and handle types.*

Catalogue of ware types

A0a. Viking Age Low-fired Coarseware

Colour, external margin:	Dark Gray 10YR 4/1
Colour, internal margin:	Dark Gray 10YR 4/1
Colour, external surface:	Dark Gray 10YR 4/1
Colour, internal surface:	Dark Gray 10YR 4/1
Hardness:	Soft
Feel:	Rough
Fracture:	Very coarse
Inclusions:	Quartz, 30%, poorly sorted, 0,5-3mm, sharp grains.
Forming:	Coiled, hammered
Secondary forming:	Smoothed surface

A0b. Baltic Blackware

Colour, core:	Dark Gray 10YR 4/1
Colour, external margin:	Dark Gray 10YR 4/1
Colour, internal margin:	Dark Gray 10YR 4/1
Colour, external surface:	Dark Gray 10YR 4/1
Colour, internal surface:	Dark Gray 10YR 4/1
Hardness:	Soft
Feel:	Smooth
Fracture:	Finee
Inclusions:	Quartz, 10%, good blacking, 0,2-3mm, rounded.
Forming:	Coiled, slow-turning wheel
Secondary forming:	Smoothed surface

A1a. Medieval Low-fired Coarseware

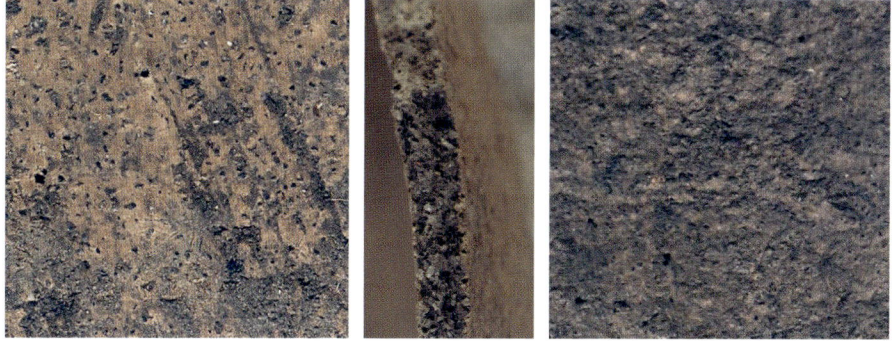

Colour, core:	Dark Gray 10YR 4/1
Colour, external margin:	Dark Gray 10YR 4/1
Colour, internal margin:	Dark Gray 10YR 4/1
Colour, external surface:	Dark Gray 10YR 4/1
Colour, internal surface:	Dark Gray 10YR 4/1
Hardness:	Soft
Feel:	Rough
Fracture:	Rough
Inclusions:	Quartz, 30%, well-sorted, 0,5-1mm, rounded.
Forming:	Coiled, hammered
Secondary forming:	Smoothed surface

A1b. Black pot, early type

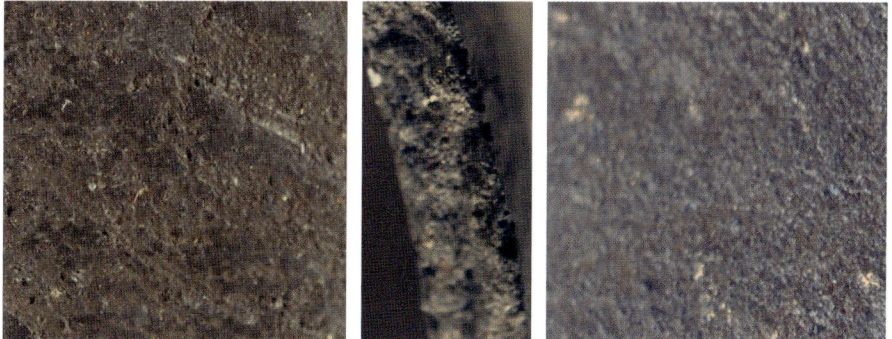

Colour, core:	Light Gray 10YR 7/1
Colour, external margin:	Light Gray 10YR 7/1
Colour, internal margin:	Light Gray 10YR 7/1
Colour, external surface:	Very Dark Gray 7,5YR 5/1
Colour, internal surface:	Very Dark Gray 7,5YR 5/1
Hardness:	Hard
Feel:	Rough
Fracture:	Rough
Inclusions:	Quartz, 30%, poorly sorted, 0,2-0,5mm, sharp
Forming:	Coiled; hammered
Secondary forming:	Scraped
Characteristics:	Burnished external surface, rim and shoulder

A1c. Black pot, Vorup type

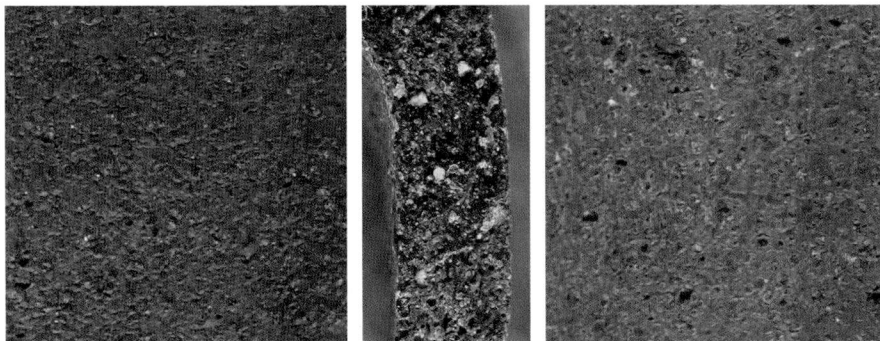

Colour, core:	Very Dark Gray 7,5YR 5/1
Colour, external margin:	Very Dark Gray 7,5YR 5/1
Colour, internal margin:	Very Dark Gray 7,5YR 5/1
Colour, external surface:	Very Dark Gray 7,5YR 5/1
Colour, internal surface:	Very Dark Gray 7,5YR 5/1
Hardness:	Hard
Feel:	Harsh
Fracture:	Harsh
Inclusions:	Quartz, 30-50%, middle sorted, 0,5-1,5mm, sharp-grained
Forming:	Coiled, hammered
Characteristics:	Violet tinge

A1d. Black pot, Varde-type

Colour, core:	Dark Gray 10YR 4/1
Colour, external margin:	Dark Gray 10YR 4/1
Colour, internal margin:	Dark Gray 10YR 4/1
Colour, external surface:	Dark Gray 10YR 4/1
Colour, internal surface:	Very Dark Gray 7,5YR 3/1
Hardness:	Soft
Feel:	Rough
Fracture:	Flakey
Inclusions:	Quartz, 30%, poorly sorted, 0,1-1mm, well-rounded
Forming:	Coiled; coiled
Secondary forming:	hammered body, Scraped rim and external surface
Characteristics:	Burnished

A2a. Medieval Well-fired Coarseware

Colour, core:	Dark Grayish Brown 10YR 4/2; Dark Gray 5YR 4/1
Colour, external margin:	Dark Grayish Brown 10YR 4/2; Dark Gray 5YR 4/1
Colour, internal margin:	Dark Grayish Brown 10YR 4/2; Dark Gray 5YR 4/1
Colour, external surface:	Dark Grayish Brown 10YR 4/2; Dark Gray 5YR 4/1
Colour, internal surface:	Dark Grayish Brown 10YR 4/2; Dark Gray 5YR 4/1
Hardness:	Hard
Feel:	Rough
Fracture:	Rough
Inclusions:	Quartz; 5-40%; well-sorted to poorly sorted, 0,5-0,1mm; sharp to rounded
Forming:	Wheel-thrown, hammered or coiled
Secondary forming:	Scraped

A2b. Baltic Burnished Grayware

Colour, core:	Dark Gray 10YR 4/1
Colour, external margin:	Dark Gray 10YR 4/1
Colour, internal margin:	Dark Gray 10YR 4/1
Colour, external surface:	Dark Gray 10YR 4/1
Colour, internal surface:	Dark Gray 10YR 4/1
Hardness:	Very hard
Feel:	Fine
Fracture:	Fine
Inclusions:	No visible inclusions
Forming:	Wheel-thrown
Burnished:	External surface, decorative
Characteristics	Thin, hard

B1a. Brügge-type ware

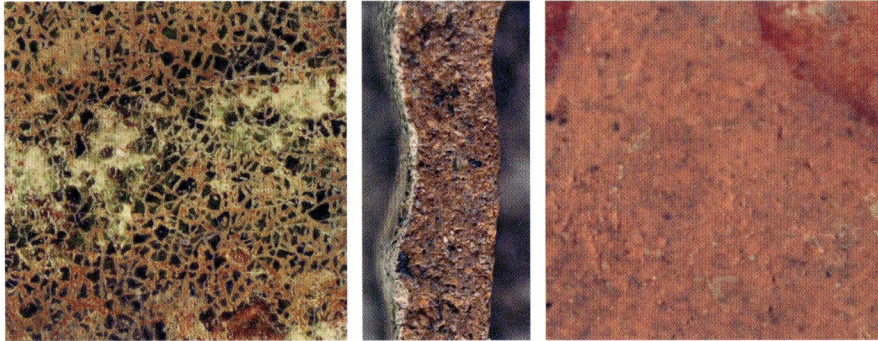

Colour, core:	Red 2,5 YR 4/8
Colour, external margin:	Red 2,5 YR 4/8
Colour, internal margin:	Red 2,5 YR 4/8
Colour, external surface:	Red 2,5 YR 4/8
Colour, internal surface:	Red 2,5 YR 4/6
Hardness:	Hard
Feel:	Rough
Fracture:	Fine
Inclusions:	Quartz; 10%, unsorted, 0,1-0,5mm; sharp
Forming:	Wheel-thrown
Secondary forming:	Stamped
Engobe placering:	External surface
Engobefarve:	White 5 Y 8/1
Placement of glaze:	External surface
Colour of glaze:	Green on slip with yellow spots

B1b. Medieval Well-fired Redware with Slip Decoration

Colour, core:	Red 2,5 YR 5/8-5/6
Colour, external margin:	Red 2,5 YR 5/8-5/6
Colour, internal margin:	Red 2,5 YR 5/8-5/6
Colour, external surface:	Red 2,5 YR 6/8-5/6
Colour, internal surface:	Red 2,5 YR 6/8-5/6
Hardness:	Hard
Feel:	Rough
Fracture:	Medium
Inclusions:	Quartz, 5-10%, well-sorted, 0,5-1mm, well-rounded
Forming:	Wheel-thrown; coiled
Secondary forming:	hammered
Placement of slip:	External surface
Slip colour:	White 10YR 8/2
Placement of glaze:	External surface,
Colour of glaze:	Red 10 R 5-8, Red 2,5 YR 4/6, Dark Yellowish Brown 10YR 4/6

B1c. Medieval Well-fired Redware

Colour, core:	Red 2,5 YR 5/8-5/6
Colour, external margin:	Red 2,5 YR 5/8-5/6
Colour, internal margin:	Red 2,5 YR 5/8-5/6
Colour, external surface:	Red 2,5 YR 6/8-5/6
Colour, internal surface:	Red 2,5 YR 6/8-5/6
Hardness:	Hard
Feel:	Rough
Fracture:	Medium
Inclusions:	Quartz, 5-10%, well-sorted, 0,5-1mm, well-rounded
Forming:	Wheel-thrown; coiled
Secondary forming:	hammered
Placement of glaze:	External surface,
Colour of glaze:	Red 10 R 5-8, Red 2,5 YR 4/6, Dark Yellowish Brown 10 YR 4/6

B2a. Danish Slipware

Colour, core:	Red 2,5 YR 4/6 – Red 2,5 YR 5/8 – Light Red 2,5 YR 6/8 – Light Red 2,5 YR 6/6
Colour, external margin:	Red 2,5 YR 4/6 – Red,5 YR 5/6
Colour, internal margin:	Reddish Brown 2,5 YR 4/4 –Light Red 2,5 YR 6/8
Colour, external surface:	Reddish Brown 2,5 YR 4/4 – Red 2,5 YR 4/6
Colour, internal surface:	Reddish Brown 2,5 YR 4/4 – Red 2,5 YR 4/6
Hardness:	Hard
Feel:	Smooth
Fracture:	Fine
Inclusions:	Quartz, 5%, poorly sorted, 0,05-0,1mm, rounded grains
Forming:	Wheel-thrown
Placement of slip:	Internal, external or both surface
Slip colour	White 10 YR 8/2,
Placement of glaze:	Internal or external surface
Colour of glaze:	Yellow 2,5 YR 7/6, Bright Green.

B2b1. Post-medieval Redware with slip decoration

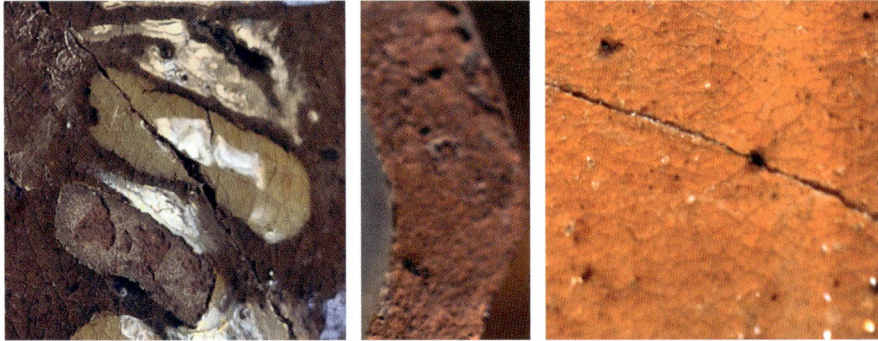

Colour, core:	Red 2,5YR 4/6 – Red 2,5YR 5/8 – Light Red 2,5YR 6/8 – Light Red 2,5YR 6/6
Colour, external margin:	Red 2,5YR 4/6 – Red,5YR 5/6
Colour, internal margin:	Reddish Brown 2,5YR 4/4 –Light Red 2,5YR 6/8
Colour, external surface:	Reddish Brown 2,5YR 4/4 – Red 2,5YR 4/6
Colour, internal surface:	Reddish Brown 2,5YR 4/4 – Red 2,5YR 4/6
Hardness:	Hard
Feel:	Smooth
Fracture:	Fine
Inclusions:	Quartz, 5%, poorly sorted, 0,05-0,1mm, rounded grains
Forming:	Wheel-thrown
Placement of slip:	Internal surface
Slip:	Horn-painted
Engobefarve	White 10YR 8/2, Yellow 2,5YR 7/6, Bright Green
Placement of glaze:	Internal or external surface
Colour of glaze:	Dark Red 2,5YR 3/6; Yellowish Red 5YR 5/6.

B2b2. Werra ware

Colour, core:	Pink 5YR 7/4
Colour, external margin:	Pink 5YR 7/4
Colour, internal margin:	Pink 5YR 7/4
Colour, external surface:	Pink 5YR 7/4
Colour, internal surface:	Pink 5YR 7/4
Hardness:	Hard
Feel:	Smooth
Fracture:	Smooth
Inclusions:	Quartz,1%, poorly sorted, 0,01-0,5mm, well-rounded; grog, 1%
Forming:	Wheel-thrown
Placement of slip:	Internal surface
Colour of slip:	Bleg Yellow 5Y 8/4
Placement of glaze:	Internal surface
Colour of glaze:	Reddish Brown 5YR 5/3

B2c1. Post-medieval Redware

Colour, core:	Red 2,5 YR 4/6 – Red 2,5 YR 5/8 – Light Red 2,5 YR 6/8 – Light Red 2,5 YR 6/6
Colour, external margin:	Red 2,5 YR 4/6 – Red,5 YR 5/6
Colour, internal margin:	Reddish Brown 2,5 YR 4/4 –Light Red 2,5 YR 6/8
Colour, external surface:	Reddish Brown 2,5 YR 4/4 – Red 2,5 YR 4/6
Colour, internal surface:	Reddish Brown 2,5 YR 4/4 – Red 2,5 YR 4/6
Hardness:	Hard
Feel:	Rough
Fracture:	Hackly
Inclusions:	Quartz, 5-10-20%, well-sorted, 0,05-1mm, rounded
Forming:	Wheel-thrown
Secondary forming:	Cut, smoothed
Placement of glaze:	Internal, smooth
Colour of glaze:	Dark Red 2,5 YR 4/6 – Red 2,5 YR 4/8; Dark Yellowish Brown 10 YR 3/6; Dark Reddish Gray 5 YR 4/2.

B2c1a. Post-medieval Redware, early type

Colour, core:	Red 2,5 YR 4/6 – Red 2,5 YR 5/8 – Light Red 2,5 YR 6/8 – Light Red 2,5 YR 6/6
Colour, external margin:	Red 2,5 YR 4/6 – Red,5 YR 5/6
Colour, internal margin:	Reddish Brown 2,5 YR 4/4 –Light Red 2,5 YR 6/8
Colour, external surface:	Reddish Brown 2,5 YR 4/4 – Red 2,5 YR 4/6
Colour, internal surface:	Reddish Brown 2,5 YR 4/4 – Red 2,5 YR 4/6
Hardness:	Hard
Feel:	Rough
Fracture:	Hackly
Inclusions:	Quartz, 5-10-20%, well-sorted, 0,05-1mm, rounded
Forming:	Wheel-thrown
Secondary forming:	Cut, smoothed
Placement of glaze:	Internal, patchy
Colour of glaze:	Dark Red 2,5 YR 4/6 – Red 2,5 YR 4/8; Dark Yellowish Brown 10 YR 3/6; Dark Reddish Gray 5 YR 4/2.

B2c2. Low Countries Redware

Colour, core:	Red 2,5 YR 5/8
Colour, external margin:	Red 2,5 YR 5/8
Colour, internal margin:	Red 2,5 YR 5/8
Colour, external surface:	Red 2,5 YR 5/8
Colour, internal surface:	Red 2,5 YR 5/8
Hardness:	Hard
Feel:	Rough
Fracture:	Fine
Inclusions:	Quartz; 5%, well-sorted; 0,1-1mm, rounded
Forming:	Wheel-thrown
Placement of glaze:	Internal surface
Colour of glaze:	Red 2,5 YR 4/8

C1. Andenn- type ware

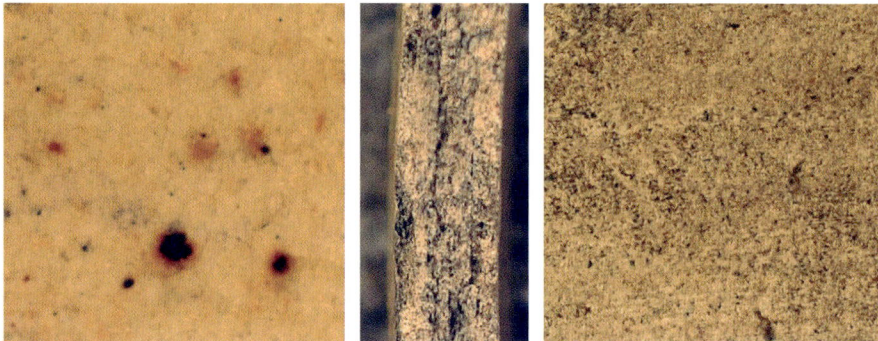

Colour, core:	Yellow 2,5 Y 8/6
Colour, external margin:	Yellow 2,5 Y 8/6
Colour, internal margin:	Yellow 2,5 Y 8/6
Colour, external surface:	Yellow 2,5 Y 7/8
Colour, internal surface:	Yellow 2,5 Y 7/8
Hardness:	Hard
Feel:	Rough
Fracture:	Medium
Inclusions:	Quartz, 10%, well-sorted, 0,05-0,1mm, rounded.
Forming:	Wheel-thrown
Placement of glaze:	External surface
Colour of glaze:	Olive Yellow 2,5 YR 6/6

C2. Rouen-type ware

Colour, core:	White 2,5 Y 8/1
Colour, external margin:	White 2,5Y 8/1
Colour, internal margin:	White 2,5Y 8/1
Colour, internal surface:	White 2,5Y 8/1
Hardness:	Hard
Feel:	Rough/chalky
Fracture:	Middle
Inclusions:	Quartz, 5%, sorted, 0,1-0,5mm, sharp-grained; black rock, 1%
Forming:	Wheel-thrown
Placement of glaze:	External surface
Colour of glaze:	Mottled Green

C3. Weser ware

Colour, core:	Reddish Yellow 5 YR 6/6 - 5YR 7/6; Very Pale Brown 10 YR 7/4-8/4
Colour, external margin:	Reddish Yellow 5 YR 6/6 ; Very Pale Brown 10 YR 7/4
Colour, internal margin:	Reddish Yellow 5 YR 6/6 ; Very Pale Brown 10 YR 7/4
Colour, external surface:	Reddish Yellow 5 YR 6/6 ; Very Pale Brown 10 YR 8/4
Colour, internal surface:	Reddish Yellow 5 YR 6/6 ; Very Pale Brown 10 YR 8/4
Hardness:	Hard
Feel:	Smooth/chalky
Fracture:	Fine
Inclusions:	Quartz, 2-5%, middle sorted, 0,05-0,1mm, rounded; quarzite, 1%; black iron ore 1%
Forming:	Wheel-thrown
Secondary forming:	Stamped.
Placement of glaze:	Internal surface
Colour of glaze:	Light Yellowish Brown 2,5Y 6/4; Bright Green; Olive Yellow 2,5 Y 6/8; Dark Red 2,5YR 3/6; Yellowish Red 5 YR 5/6; Olive Yellow 2,5 Y 6/6; Brownish Yellow 10YR 6/6; Yellow 10YR 7/8; Brown 7,5YR 4/4
Characteristics:	Green and Brown paint.

C4. Low Countries/German Post-medieval whiteware

Colour, core:	Reddish Yellow 5 YR 6/6 - 5 YR 7/6; Very Pale Brown 10 YR 7/4-8/4
Colour, external margin:	Reddish Yellow 5 YR 6/6 ; Very Pale Brown 10 YR 7/4
Colour, internal margin:	Reddish Yellow 5 YR 6/6 ; Very Pale Brown 10 YR 7/4
Colour, external surface:	Reddish Yellow 5 YR 6/6 ; Very Pale Brown 10 YR 8/4
Colour, internal surface:	Reddish Yellow 5 YR 6/6 ; Very Pale Brown 10 YR 8/4
Hardness:	Hard
Feel:	Smooth/chalky
Fracture:	Fine
Inclusions:	Quartz, 2-5%, middle sorted, 0,05-0,1mm, rounded; quarzite, 1%; black iron ore 1%
Forming:	Wheel-thrown
Secondary forming:	Stamped.
Placement of glaze:	Internal surface
Colour of glaze:	Lys Yellowish Brown 2,5 Y 6/4; Bright Green; Olive Yellow 2,5 Y 6/8
Characteristics:	Green and Brown paint.

C5. Saintonge Polychrome ware

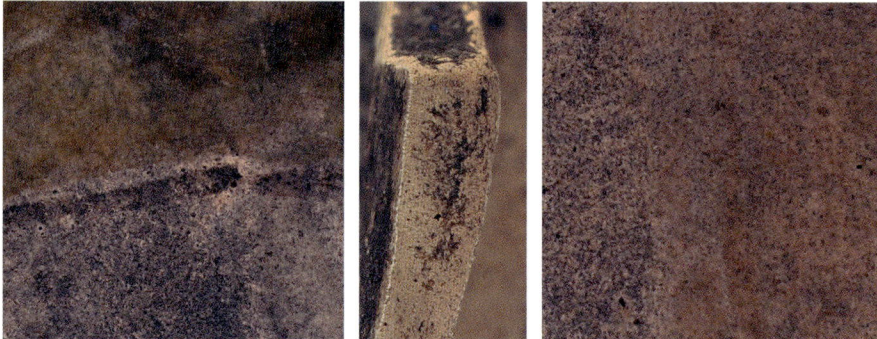

Colour, core:	White 2,5 Y 8/1
Colour, external margin:	White 2,5 Y 8/1
Colour, internal margin:	White 2,5 Y 8/1
Colour, external surface:	Yellow 2,5 Y 7/8
Colour, internal surface:	Yellow 2,5 Y 7/8
Hardness:	Hard
Feel:	Smooth
Fracture:	Fine
Inclusions:	Quartz, 10%, well-sorted, 0,05-0,1mm, rounded
Forming:	Wheel-thrown
Placement of glaze:	External surface
Colour of glaze:	Olive Yellow 2,5 YR 6/6, Olive Yellow 2,5 Y 6/8

D1.Pingsdorf-type ware

Colour, core:	White 5Y 8/8
Colour, external margin:	White 5Y 8/8
Colour, internal margin:	White 5Y 8/8
Colour, external surface:	Dark Gray 5Y 4/1
Colour, internal surface:	Dark Gray 5Y 4/1
Hardness:	Hard
Feel:	Rough
Fracture:	Rough
Inclusions:	Quartz, 10-15%, well-sorted, 0,2-0,5mm, rounded
Forming:	Coiled
Characteristics:	Occasional paint

D2. Proto Stoneware

Colour, core:	Dark Olive Gray 5Y 3/2
Colour, external margin:	Dark Olive Gray 5Y 3/2
Colour, internal margin:	Dark Olive Gray 5Y 3/2
Colour, external surface:	Olive Brown 2,5Y 4/4
Colour, internal surface:	Olive Brown 2,5Y 4/4
Hardness:	Very hard
Feel:	Rough
Fracture:	Rough; Hackly
Inclusions:	Rock, 10%, well-sorted, 0,2mm, sharp
Forming:	Wheel-thrown
Characteristics:	Melting inclusions

E.1. Siegburg Stoneware

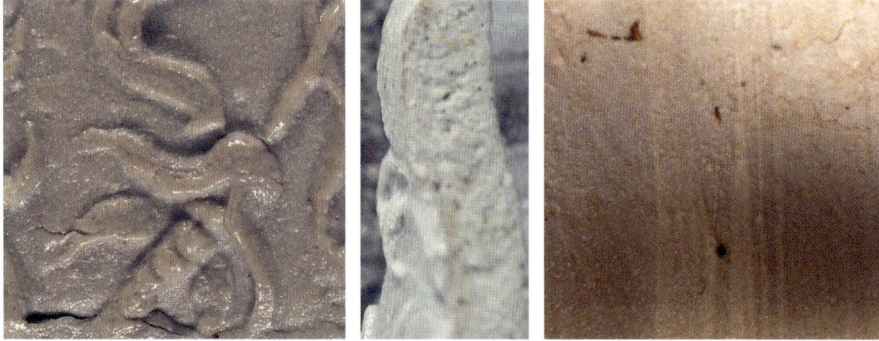

Colour, core:	Yellow 5 Y 8/8
Colour, external margin:	Yellow 5 Y 8/8
Colour, internal margin:	Yellow 5 Y 8/8
Colour, external surface:	Yellow 5 Y 8/8
Colour, internal surface:	Yellow 5 Y 8/8
Hardness:	Very hard
Feel:	Smooth
Fracture:	Flintlike
Inclusions:	No visible inclusions
Forming:	Wheel-thrown
Placement of glaze:	External surface
Colour of glaze:	Yellowish Brown 2,5 YR 4/4, Red 2,5 Y 5/8 - 6/8
Characteristics:	Spotty glaze,, ashglaze

E2. Frechen Stoneware

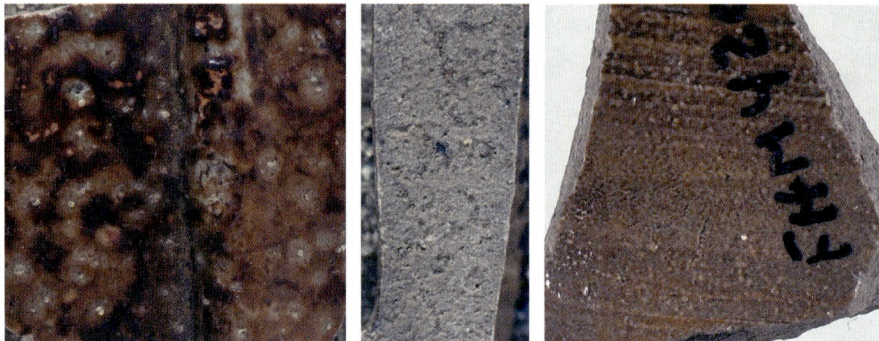

Colour, core:	Gray 5 YR 5/1
Colour, external margin:	Gray 5 YR 5/1
Colour, internal margin:	Gray 5 YR 5/1
Colour, external surface:	Gray 5 YR 5/1
Colour, internal surface:	Reddish Gray YR 5/2
Hardness:	Very hard
Feel:	Smooth
Fracture:	Fine
Forming:	Wheel-thrown
Secondary forming:	Moulded
Placement of glaze:	External surface
Colour of glaze:	Motttled Yellow and Brown
Characteristics:	Thick mottled salt glaze

E3. Cologne Stoneware

Colour, core:	Light Brownish Gray10YR 6/2- 10YR 7/2
Colour, external margin:	Light Brownish Gray10YR 6/2
Colour, internal margin:	Light Brownish Gray10YR 6/2
Colour, external surface:	Light Brownish Gray10YR 6/2
Colour, internal surface:	Light Gray10YR 7/2; pink 7,5YR 7/4
Hardness:	Very hard
Feel:	Smooth
Fracture:	Fine
Forming:	Wheel-thrown
Secondary forming:	Moulded
Engobefarve:	Brown
Placement of slip:	External surface, Internal surface
Placement of glaze:	External surface
Colour of glaze:	Strong Brown 7,5YR 5/6; Dark Brown 7,5YR 3/4; Light Gray 10YR 7/1
Characteristics:	Moulded decorations

E5. Raeren-type Stoneware

Colour, core:	Light Gray 10YR 7/1;
Colour, external margin:	Light Gray 10YR 7/1;
Colour, internal margin:	Light Gray 10YR 7/1
Colour, external surface:	Light Gray 10YR 7/1;
Colour, internal surface:	Yellowish Brown 10YR 5/4
Hardness:	Very hard
Feel:	Smooth
Fracture:	Like flint
Inclusions:	No visible inclusions
Forming:	Wheel-thrown
Placement of glaze:	External surface, internal surface
Colour of glaze:	Dark Yellowish Brown 10YR 4/4; Dark Yellowish Brown 10YR 4/6; Light Reddish Brown 2,5Y6/4
Characteristics:	Salt glaze

E6. Westerwald Stoneware

Colour, core:	Gray 10YR 6/1	
Colour, external margin:	Gray 10YR 6/1	
Colour, internal margin:	Gray 10YR 6/1	
Colour, external surface:	Gray 10YR 6/1	
Colour, internal surface:	White 10YR 8/1	
Hardness:	Very hard	
Feel:	Smooth	
Fracture:	Like flint	
Inclusions:	No visible inclusions	
Forming:	Wheel-thrown	
Secondary forming:	Stamped	
Colour of glaze:	White 10YR 8/1; blue	
Characteristics:	Salt glaze	

E4. Langerwehe Stoneware

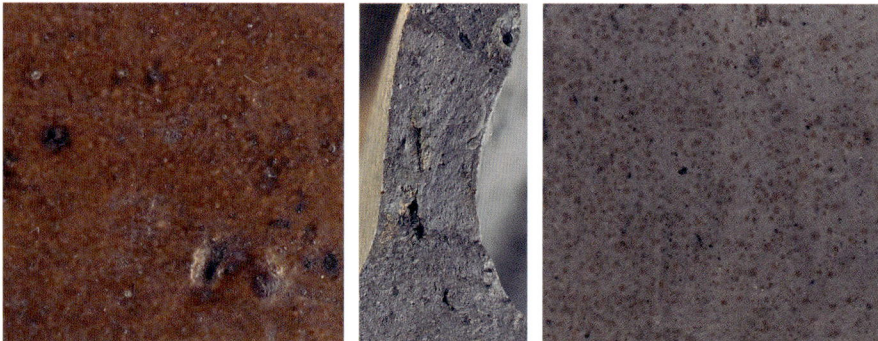

Colour, core:	Reddish Gray 10R 6/1	
Colour, external margin:	Reddish Gray 10R 6/1	
Colour, internal margin:	Reddish Yellow 5 YR 7/6	
Colour, external surface:	Reddish Yellow 5 YR 7/6	
Colour, internal surface:	Reddish Yellow 5 YR 7/6	
Hardness:	Very hard	
Feel:	Smooth	
Fracture:	Like flint	
Inclusions:	Few grains of quartz, 0,1 mm, rounded	
Forming:	Wheel-thrown	
Placement of slip:	Reddish Brown 2,5YR 4/4	
Colour of glaze:	Brown	

E9. Waldenburg Stoneware

Colour, core:	Yellow 5Y 8/8
Colour, external margin:	Yellow 5Y 8/8
Colour, internal margin:	Yellow 5Y 8/8
Colour, external surface:	Yellow 5Y 8/8
Colour, internal surface:	Yellow 5Y 8/8
Hardness:	Very hard
Feel:	Smooth
Fracture:	Like flint
Inclusions:	No visible inclusions
Forming:	Wheel-thrown
Placement of glaze:	External surface
Colour of glaze:	Yellowish Brown 2,5YR 4/4, Red 2,5Y 5/8 - 6/8
Characteristics:	Wire marks. Cordons on body

F1. Low Countries Tin-glazed ware

Colour, core:	Pink 7,5YR 8/4
Colour, external margin:	Pink 7,5YR 8/4-8/2
Colour, internal margin:	Pink 7,5YR 8/4-8/2
Colour, external surface:	Pink 7,5YR 8/4-8/2
Colour, internal surface:	Pink 7,5YR 8/4-8/2
Hardness:	Hard
Feel:	Smooth
Fracture:	Fine
Inclusions:	Quartz, 5%, well-sorted, 0,01-0,5, rounded, black iron ore;
Forming:	Wheel-thrown
Placement of glaze:	Internal and external surface
Glaze:	Tin glaze internal surface; lead glaze external surface
Colour of glaze: on external sur face.	White, bright blue, Yellow 5Y 7/8 on Internal surface; Pale Green

F2. Industrial ware

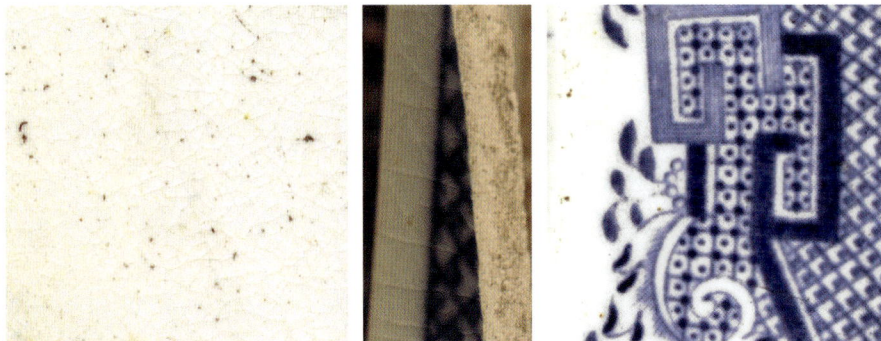

Colour, core:	Pink 7,5 YR 8/4
Colour, external margin:	Pink 7,5 YR 8/4-8/2
Colour, internal margin:	Pink 7,5 YR 8/4-8/2
Colour, external surface:	Pink 7,5 YR 8/4-8/2
Colour, internal surface:	Pink 7,5 YR 8/4-8/2
Hardness:	Hard
Feel:	Smooth
Fracture:	Fine
Inclusions:	Quartz, 5%, well-sorted, 0,01-0,5, rounded, black iron ore;
Forming:	Wheel-thrown, moulded
Placement of glaze:	Internal and external surface
Glaze:	Tin glaze internal surface and external surface
Colour of glaze: on exter nal surface.	White, Bright Blue, Yellow 5 Y 7/8 on internal surface; Pale Green
Decoration:	Transfer print

G1. Capuchin ware

Colour, core:	White
Colour, external margin:	White
Colour, internal margin:	White
Colour, external surface:	White
Colour, internal surface:	White
Hardness:	Very hard
Feel:	Smooth
Fracture:	Like flint
Inclusions:	No visible inclusions
Forming:	Wheel-thrown. Moulded
Placement of glaze:	External surface and Internal surface
Colour of glaze:	White inside. Dark Reddish Brown 5 YR 3/2 outside

G2. Other Porcelain

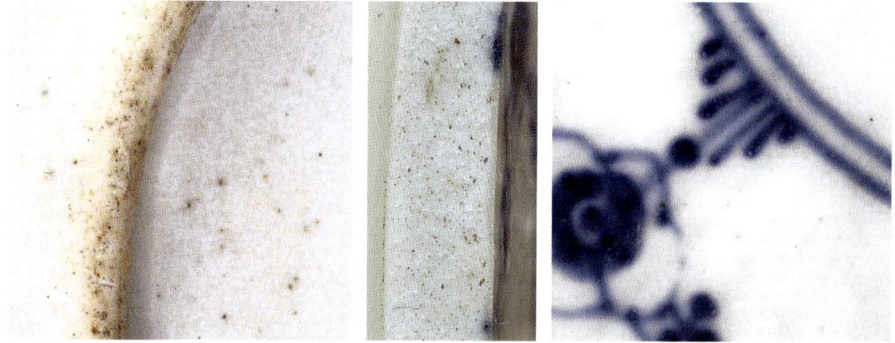

Colour, core:	White
Colour, external margin:	White
Colour, internal margin:	White
Colour, external surface:	White
Colour, internal surface:	White
Hardness:	Very hard
Feel:	Smooth
Fracture:	Like flint
Inclusions:	No visible inclusions
Forming:	Wheel-thrown, formpresset
Placement of glaze:	External surface and Internal surface
Colour of glaze:	White

Notes

1. Dietler 2010: 209-210.
2. Herva 2009; Immonen 2007; Jervis 2014; Naum 2013; Naum & Nordin 2013; Naum 2015.
3. Beaudry & Parno 2013: 287-289.
4. Barthes 2013; Beaudry & Parno 2013; Brickell & Datta 2011; Scholliers 2001.
5. Isaksson 2000; Mulryne 2004; Poulsen 2010; Wade 1996.
6. Wandsnider 2015: 15.
7. Christophersen 2015: 113; Smith 2015: 146.
8. Christophersen 2015: 112.
9. Christophersen 2015: 109.
10. I would like to thank Professor Axel Christophersen, NTNU University Museum, for discussing this term.
11. Mullins 2011: 142.
12. FHM 4225 Guldsmedgade; FHM 4201 Skt. Clemensborg; FHM 4573 Skt. Clemens Stræde; FHM 4616 Telefontorvet and FHM 5124 Bispetorv.
13. Jantzen 2013: 122.
14. Dietler 2010.
15. Karg 2007.
16. Bartels 1999; Burke 1994; Gaimster 1997; Gaimster & Stamper 1997; Scholliers 2001; Simon-Muscheid 2000.
17. Bynum 1987; Bynum 2011; Dyer 1989; Poulsen 2004a-b; Poulsen 1999; Unger 2004; Woolgar 1999; Woolgar 2006; Woolgar 2010.
18. Linaa 2006.
19. Jervis 2014: 2-9.
20. Svart Kristiansen 2005.
21. Linaa 2015a.
22. Linaa 2003.
23. Linaa 2006.
24. Naum & Nordin 2013.
25. Linaa 2015a; Linaa 2012. Papers under preparation in collaboration with Associate Professor Jaquelline van Gent, ARC Centre of Excellence for the History of Emotions, Melbourne.
26. Madsen 1999.
27. Gaimster 1997: 418; Brown 1997.
28. Brown 2002.
29. Jervis 2014.
30. Aken-Fehmers et al. 2013; Bartels 1999; Clayes, Jaspers & Ostkamp [should be Clayes et al.]2010, Gawronski 2012; Jaspers 2007.
31. E.g. Gaimster 1997; Roehmer and Schöne 2014; Schäfer 2004; Stephan 1992.
32. Naum & Nordin 2013.
33. Naum 2013, 2015.
34. Immonen 2007.
35. Herva 2009.
36. Karlsson et al. 2003.
37. Andrén 1985; Carelli 2001; Roslund 2001; Wienberg 1993.
38. Linaa 2011.
39. Aspects currently under investigation in the Urban Diaspora project, funded by The Council for Independent Research/ Humanities.
40. Poulsen 2000, 2009a-b, 2013a.
41. Linaa 2015.
42. My heartfelt thanks to Axel Christophersen for discussions of this theoretical standpoint.
43. Latour 2005.
44. Bourdieu 1977; Hodder 2003; Jenkins 2004; Jones 1997; Tilley 1999.
45. Hu 2013: 371.
46. Christophersen 2015: 114.
47. Bhabha 2003; Stockhammer 2012.
48. Stockhammer 2012: 16.
49. Dietler 2010: 217.
50. Immonen 2007; Naum 2013, 2015.
51. Hu 2013: 374; Roslund 2001: 64.
52. Hu 2013: 378. Tilly 2005: 144.
53. Kalmring 2015.
54. Hu 2013: 373; Curta 2011: 541.
55. Jones 1997: XIII.
56. Hu 2013:372; Voss 2015: 657.
57. Roslund 2001; Naum 2012, 2013, 2014, 2015a+b.
58. Voss 2015: 655.
59. Naum 2015; Wallerström 1997.
60. Christophersen 2015. I am grateful to Axel Christophersen for discussing this point with me during the writing of this book.
61. I would like to thank Axel Christophersen for discussing this term with me.
62. Shove et al 2012: 48-53.
63. Shove et al 2012: 52.
64. Bourdieu 1977: 223; Shove et al. 2012: 53-54.
65. Shove et al. 2012: 100.
66. Latour & Woolgar 1979; Shove et al. 2012: 104.
67. Shove et al 2012: 35
68. Shove et al. 2012: 64-65.
69. Shove et al. 2012; s. 66-67.

70. Jervis 2014: 21.
71. Shove *et.al.* 2012: 72.
72. Thanks to curator Hans Skov, Moesgaard Museum, for comments on this and the following chapters.
73. Jantzen 2013.
74. Skov 1996, 1997, 1998, 1999, 2004, 2005a-c, 2009, 2010.
75. Poulsen 2011.
76. Toftgaard Jensen & Norskov 2005.
77. Bitsch Christensen 2011.
78. Bitsch Christensen & Mikkelsen 2008.
79. Gejl 1996.
80. Skamby Madsen 2005; Skamby Madsen & Vinner 2005a-b.
81. Jantzen 2013: 22-23.
82. Skov 2005c: 40-41.
83. Jesch 2011; Roesdahl & Wilson 2006; Øbye Nielsen 2005a-b and www.runer.ku.dk.
84. Sindbæk 2011: 97-99.
85. Dam 2009: 67.
86. Jeppesen 2000, 2003. Jeppesen & Adamsen 2005.
87. Jantzen 2013: 125; Madsen 1996: 18-20.
88. Jeppesen 2011.
89. Jeppesen 2005: 2011.
90. FHM 4588 Egå Gymnasium
91. Gammeltoft 2012; Bjerrum 1964: IX-XII.
92. Sindbæk 2011: 105-106.
93. Jantzen 2013: figs. 4.1 and 27.
94. Hybel & Poulsen 2007: 8-10.
95. Sindbæk 2007; Sindbæk 2009.
96. Madsen 2006: 103.
97. Jantzen 2013: 51.
98. Jantzen 2013: 37.
99. Jantzen 2013:121.
100. Jantzen 2013: 63. Skov 2010: 891-892.
101. Skov 2009: 6-10; Madsen 1996: 107-118.
102. Jantzen 2013: 37-39.
103. Jantzen 2013: 84; Skov 2004, 1998.
104. Grau Møller 1997.
105. Jensen 1992; Orduna 1995: nos. 247-252.
106. Brown 2002; Linaa 2006.
107. Linaa 2006: 65-67.
108. Orton *et al.* 1993.
109. Blake & Davy 1983; Brown 2002: 3-4; Erdmann 1984.
110. Orton *et al.* 1993: 7.
111. Elaborated in Linaa 2006: 58-59 with references.
112. Brown 2002: 6. More in Linaa 2006: 65-66.
113. Hoffmeyer 1904-06 II: 130.
114. Linaa 2006: 99-105; Schulz 1990.
115. Linaa 2006: 85; Jensen 1988.
116. Linaa 2006: 101 with references.
117. Linaa 2006: 96-96; Schmidt 1996.
118. Linaa 2006: 119-120.
119. Linaa 2006: 10; Rostholm 1980.
120. Guldberg 1999; Linaa 2006; Madsen 1991.
121. Madsen 1991.
122. Jantzen 2013: 86.
123. Linaa 1995: 98.
124. Jantzen 2013: 79.
125. Degn 1996: 247.
126. Andersen *et al.* 1971.
127. Jantzen 2013: 92-95.
128. Andersen *et al.* 1971.
129. Jantzen 2013: 99-100.
130. Jantzen 2013: 102-103.
131. Jantzen 2013: 80-81.
132. Jantzen 2013: 81-82.
133. Jantzen 2013: 95.
134. Haugsted 1923.
135. FHM 5124 Bispetorv (land reg. title no. 7000ac).
136. Jantzen 2013: 100-103.
137. Christensen *et al.* 1994.
138. Gawronski 2012 no. 478: 199.
139. Gaimster 1997 no. 40: 30-31; plate 11.
140. FHM 5124 Bispetorv x442; A15.
141. Hildyard 1999: 72-75, figs. 117-118.
142. Hoff & Jeppesen 1992.
143. Excavation report FHM 4074 Gammel Moesgaard. Ceramics report by Jette Linaa 1999 in case file.
144. Excavation report FHM 4739 Elev.
145. Excavation report FHM 4999 Kattrup III; Moesgaard Museum. Ceramics report by Jette Linaa 2012 in case file.
146. Thanks to Associate Professor Jens Andresen, University of Aarhus, for comments on the correspondence analysis in this book.
147. E.g. Brown 2002: 88-93.
148. Linaa 2006: 57-58.
149. CAPCA version 2.2 developed by Associate Professor Torsten Madsen, Institute of Archaeology; University of Aarhus; 2005-12.
150. Linaa 2006: 55-56.
151. Linaa 2003; Linaa 2010.
152. Linaa 1995.
153. Linaa 2006: 75-76.
154. Linaa 2006: 135; fig. 51.
155. Thanks to Curator Hans Skov, Moesgaard Museum, for comments on this and the following chapters.
156. Krants forthcoming.
157. Thanks to Head of Archaeology, Curator Morten Søvsø, Museum of South-West Jutland, for enlightening me on the possible transfer from Ribe.
158. Gawronski 2012: no. 478: 179.
159. Degn 1996: 247.
160. Linaa 2006: 260-264.
161. SIM 104/2014 Neptunvej; Thanks to Curator Kirsten Nellemann Nielsen, Museum Silkeborg, for access to the

material. Ceramics report by Jette Linaa 2015 in case file.

162. Linaa 2006: 134-136; Linaa 2014.

163. FHM 4225 Guldsmedgade (land reg. title no. 633) X ARW, context ALM, house 9, phase 1; FHM 4278 Rosensgade (land reg. title no. 733a) AZ, DB; FHM 5124 Bispetorv (land reg. title no. 7000ac).

164. Poulsen 1979, supplemented by unpublished information gathered from the records and correspondence in the archives of Moesgaard Museum. The hoards from the Aarhus area are published in Jensen 1992. Thanks to Senior Researcher Jens Christian Moesgaard, The National Museum of Denmark, for comments on this chapter.

165. Moesgaard 2006; Guntzelnick Poulsen 2008.

166. Mikkelsen 2002; Mikkelsen & Smidt Jensen 1995: 9; Linaa 1995: 220. Grinder-Hansen 2000.

167. Carelli 2001: 189.

168. Moesgaard 2006: 242-243.

169. FHM 2033 Store Torv (land reg. title no. 7000ad).

170. Moesgaard 2006: 240.

171. Moesgaard 2006: 235; Guntzelnick Poulsen; 2008: 151.

172. Moesgaard 2006: 252-253.

173. Moesgaard 2009. Moesgaard 2011. FHM 5124 Store Torv (land reg. title no. 7000 ad).

174. FHM 5124 Bispetorv (land reg. title no. 7000ac); FHM 1600 Mejlgade 8 (land reg. title no. 859a).

175. FHM 1485 Nygade (land reg. title no. 542c-e). Correspondence archive, Moesgaard Museum.

176. FHM 3833 Katedralskolen (land reg. title no. 859a). Hauberg 1906: no. 57.

177. Skov 2006: 653; Skov 2009: 9-10.

178. FHM 1485 Nygade (land reg. title no. 542c-e); FHM 3880 Store Torv (land reg. title no. 7000ad); FHM 5124 Bispetorv (land reg. title no. 7000c); FHM 4661 Rosensgade 18-20 (land reg. title no.707); FHM 4225 Guldsmedgade (land reg. title no. 633). See Jantzen 2013: 95.

179. Carelli 2001: 196.

180. Nielsen & Schiørring 1976.

181. As seen at FHM 4324 Vestergade 58 (land reg. title no. 504a); FHM 3997 Guldsmedgade 4-6 (land reg. title no. 640a); FHM 4258 Vestergade 49 (land reg. title no. 473); FHM 2714. Jantzen 2013: 97.

182. FHM 3907 Lille Torv (land reg. title no. 7000v.) EK and CS.

183. FHM 4587 Mejlgade 26 (land reg. title no. 869a) A200 x325: MB 214-220.

184. FHM 3992 Pustervig Torv (land reg. title no. 7000cy).

185. Poulsen 2002a: 319-20; Moesgaard 2006: 252-253.

186. Poulsen 2002a: 319.

187. FHM 3992 Pustervig Torv (land reg. title no. 7000cy); AUD 2001: 247.

188. Edward III gold noble from the treaty period (1361-1369) found at Skt. Clemens Stræde 5 (land reg. title no. 743) DGB 363:54.

189. Poulsen 2002a: 320.

190. Poulsen 2002a: 330.

191. FHM 4225 Guldsmedgade (land reg. title no. 633) AFG (MB 425-427; Roskilde; 1300-1310) and AJM (MB 552.553; Nørrejylland 1320).

192. FHM 4225 Guldsmedgade (land reg. title no. 633) ARH; FHM 1393 Skt. Clemens Torv 6; land reg. title no. 774a); FHM 4587 Mejlgade 26 (land reg. title no. 869a); FHM 4222 Graven/Studsgade (land reg. title no. 7000db/ay).

193. FHM 4201 Skt. Clemensborg (land reg. title no. 166a).

194. Poulsen 2002a: 321.

195. FHM 4300 Mejlgade 18B (land reg. title no. 865a) W; FHM 4340 Domkirkeplads (land reg. title no. 7000ad) X17; FHM 4074 Gammel Moesgaard xAH; XI.

196. FHM 4074 Gammel Moesgaard AJ, BE, BD, EA, R. Fensten Hovgaard, Lars Krants personal information.

197. Moesgaard & Thornbjerg 2008.

198. Poulsen 1979: 228, 1985, 2002a; Rasmussen & Christensen 1975; Ulsig 2004.

199. Jensen 1992 II: 134 (No. 189).

200. Jensen 1992 II: 209 (No. 239).

201. Jensen 1992 II: 203-208 (No. 238).

202. Jensen 1992 I: 97.

203. Jensen 1992 II: 138 (No. 198): 199-200 (No. 235): 225-226 (No. 254): 227 (No. 255).

204. Poulsen 1979: 281-285.

205. Jensen 1992 II: 66-67 (No. 131).

206. Jensen 1992 II: 116 (No. 175).

207. Jensen 1992 II: 28 (No. 91).

208. Jensen 1992 I: 218 (No. 249).

209. Jensen 1992 II: 215 (No. 246).

210. Cloth seals found at FHM 4481 Studsgade 8-10 (land reg. title no. 1046c) nX294; FHM 3907 Lille Torv (land reg. title no. 7000v); FHM 1393 Skt Clemens Torv 6 (land reg. title no. 774a); FHM 5124 Bispetorv (land reg. title no. 7000ac); FHM 2858 Frederiksgade 76 (land reg. title no. 355a). Andersen *et al.* 1971: 63.

211. FHM 3907 Lille Torv (land reg. title no. 7000v); FHM 5124 Bispetorv (land reg. title no. 7000ac); FHM 4881 Studsgade 8-10 (land reg. title no. 1046c).

212. FHM 1393 Skt. Clemens Torv 6 (land reg. title no. 774a); FHM 5124 Bispetorv (land reg. title no. 7000c).

213. FHM 4201 Skt. Clemensborg (land registry title no. 166a) DB and FHM 4496 Mejlgade (land reg. title no. 860a)(x015). DGB 80; 115:87; 647:82; 195:15; NM F1743.

214. Poulsen 2002b: 37-39.

215. Roodenburg 2004.

216. Poulsen 2002a: 329-330; Poulsen 2004b: 65.

217. Jahnke 2009b: 77.

218. Poulsen 2004b: 60-65.

219. Heartfelt thanks to Archivist Ole Degn for ongoing help and discussions on Late- and Post- Medieval migrants in

Aarhus.

220. Poulsen 2013b.

221. Brandt *et al.* 1964: 70.

222. Wubs-Mrozewicz 2005: 224.

223. Brandt *et al.* 1973: 113.

224. Jahnke 2009b: 75-76.

225. Diplomatarium Danicum ser. 3; vol. 4 – http://diplomatarium.dk/drb/supplement/1356-11-24.html).

226. Diplomatarium Danicum ser. 4; vol. 10; no. 551.

227. Enemark 1971; Hübertz 1845-1846 I; Degn 1996.

228. Enemark 1971: 283-295.

229. Poulsen 2008.

230. Enemark 1971 I: 287; II: 259.

231. Enemark 1971 I: 282; 1971 II: 32-36, 258-259.

232. Hubertz 1845-1846 I: 256.

233. Enemark 1971 I: 274.

234. Poulsen 2004a: 218; Enemark 1971 I; 274.

235. Hübertz 1845: 279.

236. Vellev 2008.

237. Hübertz 1845: 224.

238. Fabricius *et al.* 1945: 365-366.

239. Toftgaard Jensen & Norskov 2008: 136-138.

240. Degn 1996: 261-263.

241. Hübertz 1845: 629.

242. Hübertz 1845: 636.

243. Hübertz 1846: 27.

244. Degn 1996: 263; Toftgaard Jensen & Norskov 2005: 136-138.

245. Degn 1996: 265.

246. Thanks to Professor Søren Sindbæk, Centre for Urban Network Evolutions, for comments on this chapter. Madsen 2006: 103.

247. Iron Age vessel ÅBM 48/02X1 at Moesgaard Museum.

248. Andersen *et al.* 1971: 296.

249. FHM 4433 Skt. Clemens Stræde 12 (land reg. title no. 767a); FHM 4573 Skt. Clemens Stræde 10 (land reg. title no. 766).

250. Skov 1997; 2009: 12-3; Skov 2005a: 16, 2005b.

251. FHM 4573 Skt. Clemens Stræde 10 (land reg. title no. 766) B53.

252. Jantzen 2013: 93-94. FHM 5050 Christiansgade (land reg. title no. 7000f) 1485; FHM 1844 Frue Kirkeplads (land reg. title no. 586) 1772 and 1966. FHM 4881 Studsgade 8-10 (land reg. title no. 1046); FHM 4513 Studsgade 32-36 (land reg. title no. 1055)

253. FHM 5050 Christiansgade (land reg. title no. 7000f) A91 A92; A93; A115; A116.

254. Andersen *et al.* 1971. FHM 5124 Bispetorv (land reg. title no. 7000ac). Skov 2009: 11-13.

255. FHM 5124 Bispetorv (land reg. title no. 7000ac) A 685/810; A707; A850.

256. Jantzen 2013: 132; Skov 1998: 280-281; Skov 2006: 655.

257. Jantzen 2013: 113. FHM 4488 Havnegade 2A (land reg. title no. 855a); FHM 4278 Rosensgade 17-19 (land reg. title no.

258. Ashby; Coutu & Sindbæk 2015.

259. FHM 4573 Skt. Clemens Stræde (land reg. title no. 766) x325; X595-596; X453; X462; X860 of Feldberger type.

260. CME and FAR; Andersen *et al* 1971: 42, 48.

261. Skeleton CTR found in DAQ; Andersen *et al* 1971: 46.

262. Moesgaard & Hilberg 2010.

263. Jantzen 2013: 51.

264. Jantzen 2013: 37.

265. Jantzen 2013:121.

266. Jantzen 2013: 63.

267. Skov 2009: 6-10; Madsen 1996: 107-118.

268. FHM 1393 Skt. Clemens Torv 6 (land reg. title no. 774a); FHM 2033 Store Torv (land reg. title no. 7000ad); FHM 4278 Rosensgade (land reg. title no. 733a); FHM 5124 Bispetorv (land reg. title no. 7000ac).

269. FHM 5214 Bispetorv (land reg. title no. 7000ac) A82; A 803; A 818; 910 and A95.

270. FHM 1890 Vestergade (land reg. title no. 581a); FHM 1485 Nygade (land reg. title no. 542c-e); FHM 4689 Vestergade 48 (land reg. title no. 510a) A-B. Andersen & Madsen 1986: 97; Jantzen 2013: 95-97.

271. FHM 4225 Guldsmedgade (land reg. title no. 633).

272. FHM 3833 Katedralskolen (land reg. title no. 859a). Skov 1996, 2009: 14-15.

273. FHM 3833 Katedralskolen (land reg. title no. 859a) no. FB.

274. Pingsdorf: FHM 2633 Store Torv (land reg. title no. 7000ad); FHM 3833 Katedralskolen (land reg. title no. 859a); FHM 2633 Store Torv (land reg. title no. 7000ad) FB; FHM 3880 Store Torv (land reg. title no. 7000ad); FHM 1600 Mejlgade 8 (land reg. title no. 859a). Paffrath: FHM 3959 Skt. Clemens Torv (land reg. title no. 7000ab) DG; FHM 3880 Store Torv (land reg. title no. 7000ad) MI; FHM 4067 Skt. Clemens Torv 9 (land reg. title no. 776).

275. FHM 3833 Katedralskolen (land reg. title no. 859a) AH. Andersen & Madsen 1985: 35.

276. Jantzen 2013: 121.

277. FHM 1485 Nygade (land reg. title no. 542c-e) field II; pits AC; AD; AE; AF; field VI: floor layer BL; field VIII; pit DQ with coins EE; EF. Shaft from FHM 1844 Frue Kirkeplads (land reg. title no. 586) 1844 A.

278. FHM 3833 Katedralskolen (land reg. title no. 859a) field II.

279. Mullins 2011: 137.

280. FHM 2633 Store Torv (land reg. title no. 7000ad) LO.

281. FHM 2738 Nationalbanken II (land reg. title no. 726b).

282. FHM 5124 Bispetorv (land reg. title no. 7000ac) X520; X3533.

283. FHM 4526 Mejlgade 26 (land reg. title no. 869a) X310; X421

284. Poulsen 2002b: 31-32.

285. Poulsen 2002b: 33.

286. FHM 2633 Store Torv (land reg. title no. 7000ad) VC; FHM 2738 Nationalbanken II (land reg. title no. 726b); FHM 1393 Skt. Clemens Torv 6; (land reg. title no. 774a); FHM

4944 Skt. Clemens Torv 9 (land reg. title no. 753b); FHM 3833 Katedralskolen (land reg. title no. 859a); FHM 5124 Bispetorv (land reg. title no. 7000c); FHM 4159 Skolegyde og Bispetorv (land reg. title no. 7000aq); FHM 4262 Aarhus Teater (land reg. title no. 755a).

287. FHM 4225 Guldsmedgade (land reg. title no. 633).
288. FHM 4689 Vestergade 48 A+B (land reg. title no. 510a).
289. FHM 5297 Mejlgade 53 (land reg. title no. 1015); FHM 4587 Mejlgade 26 (land reg. title no. 869a) X357; X390; FHM 4384 Katedralskolen (land reg. title no. 859a).
290. Jantzen 2013: 37-39.
291. Jantzen 2013: 78; Skov 1998, 2004..
292. Jantzen 2013: 69.
293. FHM 4587 Mejlgade 26 (land reg. title no. 869a) A123 X357; A247 X390.
294. FHM 5308 (land reg. title no. 1023). Ceramics report by Jette Linaa 2015 in case file.
295. Jantzen 2013: 103.
296. Jantzen 2013: 50.
297. I would like to thank Lars Krants for suggesting this interpretation.
298. Jahnke 2000, 2009 a-b, 2012, 2013, 2014.
299. FHM 4616 Telefontorvet (land reg. title no. 217b).
300. FHM 3880 Store Torv (land reg. title no. 7000ad) FY; FHM 4067 St. Clemens Torv (land reg. title no. 776) FHM; FHM 4721 Bispetorv (land reg. title no. 7000ac).
301. FHM 4067 Skt. Clemens Torv (land reg. title no. 776) AN; AO; AP; AQ; FHM 1393 Skt. Clemens Torv 6 (land reg. title no. 774a); FHM 4182 Badstuegade 1b (land reg. title no. 643c).
302. FHM 4225 Guldsmedgade (land reg. title no. 633) X321; X559; FHM 4202 Badstuegade 19 (land reg. title no.) FHM 4661 Rosensgade 18-20 (land reg. title no. 707) X89; X190; FHM 1660 Mejlgade 8 (land reg. title no. 648) LY. Schiørring 1988.
303. FHM 1393 Skt. Clemens Torv 6 (land reg. title no. 774a); FHM 1844 Frue Kirkeplads (land reg. title no. 586); FHM 1861 Rosensgade 32-34 (land reg. title no. 698a); FHM 3907 Lille Torv (land reg. title no. 7000v); FHM 3992 Pustervig Torv (land reg. title no. 7000cy); FHM 4007 Badstuegade 21 (land reg. title no. 655); FHM 4157 Klostertorv (land reg. title no. 7000ae); FHM 4159 Skolegyde og Bispetorv (land reg. title no. 7000aq); FHM 4198 Volden (land reg. title no. 7000af); FHM 4204 Klostergade/Graven (land reg. title no. 7000ax/db); FHM 4225 Guldsmedgade (land reg. title no. 633); FHM 4231 Mejlgade 23 (land reg. title no. 1028); FHM 4262 Aarhus Teater (land reg. title no. 755a); FHM 4278 Rosensgade (land reg. title no. 633a); FHM 4324 Vestergade 58 (land reg. title no. 504a); FHM 4616 Telefontorvet (land reg. title no. 217b); FHM 4944 Skt. Clemens Torv 9 (land reg. title no. 753b); FHM 5037 Vestergade 11 (land reg. title no. 396a); FHM 4200 Rosensgade (land reg. title no. 7000af);

FHM 4661 Rosensgade 18-20 (land reg. title no. 707); FHM 4696 Frederiksgade Nord (land reg. title no. 7000bz); FHM 5183 Bispetorvet (land reg. title no. 7000ac).

304. Bill et al. 1997.
305. FHM 1393 Skt. Clemens Torv 6 (land reg. title no. 774a); FHM 1861 Rosensgade 32-34 (land reg. title no. 698a); FHM 3350 Graven 3c (land reg. title no. 712c); FHM 3880 Store Torv (land reg. title no. 7000ad); FHM 3907 ; FHM 4157 Klostertorv (land reg. title no. 7000ae); FHM 4198 Volden (land reg. title no. 7000af); FHM 4201 Skt. Clemensborg (land reg. title no. 166a); FHM 4204 Klostergade/Graven (land reg. title no. 7000ax/db); FHM 4225 Guldsmedgade (land reg. title no. 633); FHM 4231 Mejlgade 23 (land reg. title no. 1028); FHM 4262 Aarhus Teater (land reg. title no. 755a) 4461; 4485; 4587; FHM 4616 Telefontorvet (land reg. title no. 217b); FHM 4881 Studsgade 8-10 (land reg. title no. 1046); FHM 4944 Skt. Clemens Torv 9 (land reg. title no. 753b).
306. Schäfer 2004: 108.
307. FHM 4278 Rosensgade (land reg. title no. 633a) ET; KC.
308. FHM 3880 Store Torv (land reg. title no. 7000ad) 4156; FHM 4157 Klostertorv (land reg. title no. 7000ae); FHM 4200 Rosensgade (land reg. title no. 7000af); FHM 4201 Skt. Clemensborg (land reg. title no. 166a); FHM 4222 Graven/Studsgade (land reg. title no. 7000db/ay); FHM 4225 Guldsmedgade (land reg. title no. 633); FHM 4278 Rosensgade (land reg. title no. 633a); FHM 4587 Mejlgade 26 (land reg. title no. 869a); FHM 4616 Telefontorvet (land reg. title no. 217b); FHM 5037 Vestergade 11 (land reg. title no. 396a); FHM 4721 Bispetorv (land reg. title no. 7000ac); FHM 4944 St. Clemens Torv 9 (land reg. title no. 753b); FHM 5124 Bispetorv (land reg. title no. 7000c).
309. Poulsen 2002b: 43.
310. Vogtherr 1996: no. 1161.
311. Poulsen 2000: 67.
312. Schulz 1990: 200-205. For Denmark: Linaa 2006 and FHM 4201 Skt. Clemensborg (land reg. title no. 166a).
313. Jantzen 2013: 140.
314. Jantzen 2013: 54.
315. Jantzen 2013: 45-46.
316. Andersen 1987: 56; Johansen et al 1992: 222-236.
317. Linaa 2006.
318. FHM 5419 Damagervej 2.
319. Linaa 2006: 124-125.
320. FHM 4306 Klostergade 36 (land reg. title no. 1090a); FHM 5501 Latin 3/Borggade 6 (land.reg. title no. 1074a).
321. Linaa 2006.
322. Hübertz 1846: 543.
323. Recordid 693996 www.soundtoll.nl.
324. Recordid 563488 www.soundtoll.nl.
325. Recordid 810209 www.soundtoll.nl.
326. Recordid 748817 www.soundtoll.nl.

327. Recordid 722187; 690473 www.soundtoll.nl.
328. Adams 2011: KBB 1591: 613.
329. Degn 1986.
330. FHM 5124 Bispetorv (land reg. title no. 7000ac); Mullins 2011: 139-140.
331. FHM 4201 Skt. Clemensborg (land reg. title no. 166a); FHM 4881 Studsgade (land reg. title no. 1046c); FHM 4278 Rosensgade (land reg. title no. 733a).
332. FHM 4785 Mejlgade 26 (land reg. title no. 869a); FHM 4881 Studsgade (land reg. title no. 1046); FHM 5124 Bispetorv (land reg. title no. 7000ac).
333. Toftgaard Jensen & Norskov 2005: 82-89.
334. Thomsen 1933-1940.
335. Gawronski 2012: 199 no. 478.
336. FHM 5501 Latin 3/Borggade 6. Ceramics report in case file at Moesgaard Museum.
337. Degn 2008: 110-113.
338. FHM 2633 Store Torv (land reg. title no. 7000ad); FHM 3959 Skt. Clemens Torv (land reg. title no. 7000ab); FHM 4006 Aaboulevarden Øst (land reg. title no. 700bx); FHM 4306 Klostergade 36 (land reg. title no. 1090a); FHM 4325 Klostergade (land reg. title no. 7000ax); FHM 4340 Domkirkeplads (land reg. title no. 7000ad); FHM 4689 Vestergade 48 (land reg. title no. 510a); FHM 4694 Aaboulevarden Nord (land reg. title no. 7000i); FHM 4881 Studsgade 8-10 (land reg. title no. 1046); FHM 5306 Klostergade (land reg. title no. 7000ax).
339. FHM 4695 Mølleparken (land reg. title no. 2003c); FHM 4667 Aaboulevarden (land reg. title no. 7000i); FHM 4727 Borggade (land reg. title no. 7000cf).
340. FHM 4230 Aaboulevarden 28-30 (land reg. title nos. 779c and 791); FHM 4336 Borggade 6 (land reg. title no. 1074a); FHM 4480 Havnegade 2 A (land reg. title no. 855a); FHM 4667 Aaboulevarden (land reg. title no. 7000i).
341. FHM 5501 Latin 3 Borggade 6. Ceramics report by Jette Linaa in case file.
342. SIM 104 /2014 Neptunvej. Ceramics report by Jette Linaa 2015 in case file. I wish to thank archaeologist Kirsten Nellemann Nielsen, Museum Silkeborg, for access to the material.
343. Thanks to Lars Krants for discussing this point.
344. Linaa 2006: 52.
345. Rosén 2004.
346. Guldberg 1999: 135.
347. Pajung & Poulsen 2014.
348. Christensen 1904: 274.
349. Rodenberg 2011.
350. Degn 1996: 299-306.
351. Bill 1997: 197.
352. Madsen 1996: 118-119.
353. Carelli 2001: 208.
354. Degn 1996: 289-294.
355. I would like to thank Søren Sindbæk for information on this point.
356. Jahnke 2009a: 27-30.
357. Andrén 1985; Poulsen 2002b: 49-51.
358. Poulsen 2013a: 121.
359. Shove et al 2012: 48-53.
360. Christophersen 2015: 130.
361. Poulsen 2013b: 45-46.
362. Poulsen 2013b: 47; Naum 2015: 74.
363. Poulsen 2013b.
364. Naum 2015; Wubs-Mrozewicz 2004, 2011.
365. Degn 1996: 264.
366. Land reg, title no. 748a Store Torv 3. Jantzen 2012.
367. Jervis 2014: 22; Poulsen 2013a: 126.
368. Mikkelsen 2008.
369. Degn 1996: 286.
370. Hübertz 1845-46 vol I: 217-218.
371. Selch Jensen 2008: 300.
372. Selch Jensen 2008: 296; Linaa 2006: 172.
373. Selch Jensen 2008: 300.
374. Hübertz 1845-1846 vol I: 217-218; Selch Jensen 2008: 306.
375. Poulsen 2013b: 51-52.
376. Jantzen 2013: 122.
377. Stockhammer 2012: 23.
378. Poulsen 2013a: 122.
379. Jarvis 2014: 32.
380. Beaudry & Parno 2013: 291.
381. Degn 1996: 263.
382. Voss 2015: 659.
383. Beaudry & Parno 2013: 291
384. Shove et al. 2012: 96.
385. Shove et al. 2012.
386. See also Poulsen & Fonnesbech-Wulff 2000.
387. Voss 2025: 36; Hu 2013: 385.
388. Curta 2005: 201; Hu 2013: 390.
389. Bell 2005; Voss 2015: 665.
390. Voss 2015; Hu 2013: 388.
391. Voss 2015: 660.
392. Poulsen 2013a: 127-128.
393. Hu 2012: 392.
394. Kalmring 2015.
395. Hübertz 1945-1946 vol I: 217-219.
396. Latour & Woolgar 1979; Shove et al. 2012: 104.
397. Hu 2013: 394.
398. Christophersen 2015: 131.

Bibliography

Aken-Fehmers, M.v., Burghout, F., Jaspers, N.L., Lambooy, S., Megens, L., Ostkamp, S., Verhaar, G., Eliëns, T. & Tucker, J. 2013, *Delfts aardewerk: geschiedenis van een nationaal product.* Gemeentemuseum; Waanders Uitgevers, Den Haag; Zwolle.

Andersen, A. 1987, *Middelalderbyen Næstved,* Centrum, Viby J.

Andersen, H.H., Crabb, P.J. & Madsen, H.J. 1971, *Århus Søndervold: en byarkæologisk undersøgelse,* Gyldendal, København.

Andersen, H.H. & Madsen, H.J. 1985, "Byudgravning ved Århus Katedralskole", *Kuml,* vol. 1985, pp. 35-95.

Andrén, A. 1985, *Den urbana scenen: Städer och samhälle i det medeltida Danmark,* Habelt, Bonn.

Ashby, S.P., Coutu, A.N. & Sindbæk, S.M. 2015, "Urban networks and Arctic outlands: Craft specialists and reindeer antler in Viking towns", *European Journal of Archaeology,* pp. 1-26.

Asingh, P. & Engberg, N. (eds) 2002, *Marsk Stig og de fredløse på Hjelm,* Ebeltoft Museum, Ebeltoft.

Bartels, M. 1999, *Steden in Scherven: Vondsten uit beerputten in Deventer, Dordrecht, Nijmegen en Tiel (1250-1900),* Stechting Promotie Archeologie, Zwolle.

Barth, F. 1998, *Ethnic groups and boundaries: the social organization of culture difference,* Reissued edn, Waveland, Prospect Heights, Ill.

Barthes, R. 2013, *Mythologies,* 1. American pbk. ed. edn, Hill and Wang, New York.

Beaudry, M.C. & Parno, T.G. 2013, *Archaeologies of mobility and movement,* Springer, New York.

Bell, A. 2005, "White Ethnogenesis and Gradual Capitalism: Perspectives from Colonial Archaeological Sites in the Chesapeake", *American Anthropologist,* vol. 107, no. 3, pp. 446-460.

Bhabha, H.K. 2003, *The location of culture,* Reprint edn, Routledge, London.

Bill, J., Poulsen, B., Rieck, F. & Ventegodt, O. 1997, *Fra stammebåd til skib. Dansk søfarts historie 1,* Gyldendal, Kbh.

Bitsch Christensen, S. (ed) 2011, *Renæssancens befæstede byer,* Dansk Center for Byhistorie, Aarhus.

Bitsch Christensen, S. & Mikkelsen, J. (eds) 2008, *Danish towns during absolutism: urbanisation and urban life 1660-1848,* Aarhus University Press, Aarhus.

Bjerrum, A. 1964, *Danmarks stednavne. Stednavne i Århus och Skanderborg amter,* Kbh.

Blake, H. & Davey, P. 1983, *Guidelines for the processing and publication of medieval pottery from excavations: report by a working party of the Medieval Pottery Research Group and the Department of the Environment,* Department of the Environment, London.

Bourdieu, P., 1977, *Outline of a theory of practice,* Cambridge University Press, Cambridge.

Brandt, A.v. & Hach, E. 1973, *Regesten der Lübecker Bürgertestamente des Mittelalters. 1351-1363.*

Bricka, C.F., Laursen, L., Marquard, E., Olsen, G.; Jørgensen, J.; Holmgaard, J. & Degn,O., 1885-2005, *Kancelliets brevbøger vedrørende Danmarks indre forhold: i uddrag. A. Reitzel, Kbh.* (KBB)

Brickell, K. & Datta, A. 2011, *Translocal geographies: spaces, places, connections,* Ashgate, Burlington, VT.

Brown, D. 1997, "Pots from Houses", *Medieval Ceramics,* vol. 21, pp. 83-94.

Brown, D.H. 2002, *Pottery in medieval Southampton, c 1066-1510,* Council for British Archaeology.

Burke, P. 1994, *Popular culture in early modern Europe,* Scolar Press.

Bynum, C.W. 1987, *Holy feast and holy fast: the religious significance of food to medieval women,* University of California Press Berkeley.

Bynum, C.W. 2011, *Christian materiality: an essay on religion in late medieval Europe,* Zone Books.

Bøgh, A., Henningsen, H. & Dalsgaard, K. (eds) 2014, *Nørre Vosborg i tid og rum,* Aarhus Universitetsforlag, Aarhus.

Carelli, P. 2001, *En kapitalistisk anda: kulturella förändringar i 1100-talets Danmark,* Almqvist & Wiksell International, Stockholm.

Christensen, T., Larsen, A., Larsson, S. & Vince, A. 1994, "Early Glazed ware from medieval Denmark", *Medieval Ceramics,* vol. 18, pp. 76-79.

Christensen, W. 1904, *Dronning Christines hofholdningsregnskaber,* Gyldendal, Kbh.

Christophersen, A. 2015, "Performing towns. Steps towards an understanding of medieval urban connumties as social practice.", *Archaeological Dialogues,* vol. 22, pp. 109-132.

Claeys, Johan., Jaspers, N.L., Ostkamp, Sebastiaan,, Gemeente Vlissingen.,ADC ArcheoProjecten., 2010, *Vier eeuwen leven en sterven aan de Dokkershaven: een archeologische opgraving van een postmiddeleeuwse stadswijk in het Scheldekwartier in Vlissingen,* ADC ArcheoProjecten, Amersfoort.

Clausen, J. 1939-41, *Aarhus gennem Tiderne 1-4,* Kbh. (tr. Aarhus).

Curta, F. 2011, "Medieval Archaeology and Ethnicity: Where are We?", *History Compass,* vol. 9, no. 7, pp. 537-548.

Curta, F. 2005, *Borders, barriers, and ethnogenesis: frontiers in late Antiquity and the Middle Ages,* Brepols, Turnhout.

Dam, P. 2009, "Skovenes udbredelse før landboreformerne", *Landbohistorisk Tidsskrift,* pp. 51-88.

Degn, O. 1986, "Århus-skippere gennem Øresund: Århus' handelsflåde og skibsfart omkring 1640", *Erhvervshistorisk årbog,* vol. Bd. 36 (1986), pp. 77-91.

Degn, O. 1996, "Borgernes by" in *Aarhus Byens historie-1720,* ed. I. Gejl, Århus Byhistoriske Udvalg, Aarhus, pp. 243-341.

Degn, O. 2008, "Town development and urban population in the Danish Kingdom, ca. 1620-1680 - From prosperity to crisis" in eds. S. Bitsch Christensen & J. Mikkelsen Aarhus University Press, Aarhus, pp. 97-132.

Dietler, M. 2010, "Consumption" in *The Oxford handbook of material culture studies,* eds. D. Hicks & M.C. Beaudry, Oxford University Press, Oxford, pp. 208-228.

Dinshaw, C., 1999, *Getting medieval: sexualities and communities, pre- and postmodern,* Duke University Press, Durham, NC.

Diplomatarium Danicum: 5. række (1413-1450). http://dd5rk.dsl.dk

Duerr, H.P. 1994, *Nakenhet och skam,* Brutus Östlings Bokförlag Symposion, Stockholm.

Dyer, C. 1989, *Standards of living in the later Middle Ages: social change in England, c. 1200-1520,* Cambridge Univ. Press, Cambridge.

Enemark, P. 1971, *Studier i toldregnskabsmateriale i begyndelsen af 16. århundrede: med særligt henblik på dansk okseeksport,* Aarhus.

Erdmann, W., 1984, "Rahmenterminologie zur mittelalterlichen Keramik in Norddeutschland", *Archäologisches Korrespondenzblatt,* pp. 417-436.

Etting, V., Hvass, L. & Boje Andersen, C. 2003, *Gurre slot: kongeborg og sagnskat,* Sesam, Kbh.

Fabricius, K., Hammerich, L.L. & Lorenzen, V. 1945, *Holland-Danmark: Forbindelserne mellem de to Lande gennem Tiderne,* Jespersen og Pio, Kbh.

Franciere, A. 2002, *Gennemgang af knoglemateriale fra fire lokaliteter,* 2nd edn, Moesgaard Naturvidenskabelige Undersøgelser rapport, Højbjerg.

Gaimster, D. 1997, *German stoneware 1200-1900: archaeology and cultural history: containing a guide to the collections of the British Museum, Victoria & Albert Museum and Museum of London,* British Museum Press, London.

Gaimster, D. & Stamper, P. 1997, *The age of transition: the archaeology of English culture 1400-1600: proceedings of a conference hosted by the Society for Medieval Archaeology and the Society for Post-Medieval Archaeology at the British Museum, London 14-15th November 1996,* Oxbow, Oxford.

Gammeltoft, P. 2012, "Ældre sønderjyske stednavne", *Sønderjysk månedsskrift,* vol. 2012, nr. 1, pp. 3-9.

Gawronski, J. 2012, *Amsterdam ceramics: a city's history and an archaeological ceramics catalogue 1175-2011,* Lubberhuizen, Amsterdam.

Gejl, I. 1996, "Borgernes by", *Aarhus; Byens Historie 1 -1720, Århus Byhistoriske Udvalg,* Aarhus, pp. 124-320.

Grau Møller, P. 1997, *Kulturhistorisk inddeling af landskabet: Kulturhistorien i Planlægningen,* Miljø- og Energiministeriet, Skov- og Naturstyrelsen, Kbh.

Grinder-Hansen, K. 2000, *Kongemagtens krise: det danske møntvæsen 1241-ca. 1340: den pengebaserede økonomi og møntcirkulation i Danmark i perioden 1241-ca. 1340,* Nationalmuseet, Kbh.

Guldberg, M. 1999, *Jydepotter fra Varde-egnen: produktion og handel ca. 1650-1850,* Landbohistorisk Selskab, Kerteminde.

Guntzelnick Poulsen, T. 2008, "Tolkning af enkeltfundne mønter: hvor meget er mange mønter?", *Nordisk Numismatisk Unions medlemsblad,* vol. 2008, nr. 4, pp. 151-163.

Hauberg, P. 1906, *Danmarks Myntvæsen i Tidsrummet 1146-1241,* Bianco Lunos Bogtrykkeri, Kbh.

Haugsted, E. 1923, *Udgravningerne paa Bispetorvet i Aarhus Efteraaret 1921,* De forenede Bogtrykkerier, Aarhus.

Herva, V. 2009, "Living (with) Things: Relational Ontology and Material Culture in Early Modern Northern Finland", *Cambridge Archaeological Journal,* vol. 19, no. 3, pp. 388-397.

Hildyard, R. 1999, *European ceramics,* V&A Publications, London.

Hodder, I., 2003, *Reading the past: current approaches to interpretation in archaeology,* 3rd ed. edn, Cambridge University Press, Cambridge.

Hoff, A. 2015, *Den danske kaffehistorie,* 1. udgave edn, Wormianum, Højbjerg.

Hoff, A. 2015, *Den danske tehistorie,* 1. udgave edn, Wormianum, Højbjerg.

Hoff, A. & Jeppesen, J. 1991, "Todderup: en udgravet torpbebyggelse og torperne historisk belyst", *Kuml,* vol. 1991/92, pp. 165-188.

Hoff, A. & Jeppesen, J. 1992, "Thorbjørns torp", *Skalk,* vol. 1992, nr. 1, pp. 9-13.

Hoffmeyer, J. 1904-1906, *Blade af Aarhus Bys Historie I-II,* Hagerup, Kbh.

Høyem Andreasen, M. 2014, *Kursorisk gennemsyn af arkæobotanisk materiale fra latriner fra FHM 4225 Guldsmedgade (FHM 4296/1427).*

Hu, D. 2013, "Approaches to the Archaeology of Ethnogenesis: Past and Emergent Perspectives", *Journal of Archaeological Research,* vol. 21, no. 4, pp. 371-402.

Hübertz, J.R. 1845-46, *Aktstykker vedkommende Staden og Stiftet Aarhus I-III,* Kbh.

Hybel, N. & Poulsen, B. 2007, *Danish resources c. 1000-1550: growth and recession,* Brill, Leiden.

Immonen, V. 2007, "Defining a culture: the meaning of Hanseatic in medieval Turku", *Antiquity,* vol. 81, no. 313, pp. 720-732.

Isaksson, S. 2000, *Food and rank in early medieval time,* Archaeological Research Laboratory, Stockholm University, Stockholm.

Jahnke, C. 2000, *Das Silber des Meeres: Fang und Vertrieb von Ostseehering zwischen Norwegen und Italian 12.-16. Jahrhundert,* Böhlau, Köln.

Jahnke, C. 2009 (2009a), "Der Aufstieg Lübecks und die Neuordnung des südlichen Ostseeraumes im 13. Jahrhundert. Czaja, Roman, Städtelandschaften im Ostseeraum im Mittelalter und in der Frühen Neuzeit" in

Tow. Naukowe, Torun, pp. 29-72.

Jahnke, C. 2009 (2009b), "Some aspects of Medieval Cloth Trade in the Baltic Sea Area" in *The Medieval Broadclot. Changing Trends in Fashion, Manufacturing and Consumption*, eds. K. Vestergård Pedersen & M.-. Nosch, Oxbow, Oxford, pp. 74-89.

Jahnke, C. 2012, "The city of Lübeck and the Internationality of Early Hanseatic Trade" in *The Hanse in Medieval and Early Modern Europe*, eds. J. Wubs-Mrozewics & S. Jenks, Brill Adademic Publishers, pp. 37-58.

Jahnke, C. 2014, "The Sea: Challenge and Stimulus in the Middle Ages" in *The Medieval Broadcloth. Changing trends in fashion, Manufacturing and consumption*, eds. K. Vestergård Pedersen & M.-. Nosch, Cambridge University Press, pp. 64-71.

Jantzen, C. 2013, *Middelalderbyen Aarhus*, Den Gamle By, Aarhus.

Jaspers, N.L., 2007, *Schoon en werkelijk aangenaam: Italiaanse importkeramiek uit de 16de en 17de eeuw in Nederlandse bodem*, [eigen uitgave].

Jenkins, R. 2004, *Social identity*, 2. edition edn, Routledge, London.

Jensen, J.S. 1992, *Danmarks middelalderlige skattefund, c. 1050 - c. 1550 I-II*, Det Kongelige nordiske Oldskriftselskab, Kbh.

Jensen, V. 1988, "Kakler, keramik og glas ældre end 1550", *Hikuin*, vol. Nr. 14 (1988), pp. 109-120.

Jeppesen, J. & Adamsen, C. 2005, "Randlev. Landsby og gravplads" in *Vikingernes Aros*, ed. A. Damm, pp. 62-71.

Jeppesen, J. 1992, "Nybyggere i middelalderen", *Århus-årbog*, vol. 1992, pp. 48-54.

Jeppesen, J. 2000, "Randlevs vikinger", *Østjysk hjemstavn*, vol. Årg. 65 (2000), pp. 9-20.

Jeppesen, J. 2003, "Over Randlev-skatten i arkæologisk sammenhæng", *Nordisk Numismatisk Unions medlemsblad*, vol. 2003, nr. 3/4, pp. 39-44.

Jeppesen, J. 2005, "Egå" in *Vikingernes Aros*, ed. A. Damm, Moesgård, Højbjerg pp. 76-79.

Jeppesen, J. 2005, "Lisbjerg" in *Vikingernes Aros*, ed. A. Damm, Moesgård, Højbjerg, pp. 52-61.

Jeppesen, J. 2005, "Vikingernes Aros" in *Vikingernes Aros*, ed. A. Damm, Moesgård, Højbjerg, pp. 76-79.

Jeppesen, J. 2010, "Voldbækgravpladsen: yngre jernalder, vikingetid og middelalder ved Brabrand Sø", *Kuml*, vol. 2010, pp. 49-84.

Jeppesen, J. 2011 (2011a), "Magnate Farms and Lordship from the Viking Age to the Medieval Period in Eastern Jutland" in *Settlement and Lordship in Viking and Early Medieval Scandinavia*, eds. B. Poulsen & S.M. Sindbæk, Turnhout, pp. 137-145.

Jeppesen, J. 2011 (2011b), "Randlev" in *Aros and the world of the vikings: the stories and travelogues of seven Vikings from Aros*, eds. H. Skov & J. Varberg, 1. edition edn, Moesgård Museum, Højbjerg, pp. 84-86.

Jervis, B. 2014 (2014a), "Middens, memory and the effect of waste. Beyond symbolic meaning in archaeological deposits. An early medieval case study", *Archaeological Dialogues*, vol. 21, no. 2, pp. 175-196.

Jervis, B. 2014 (2014b), *Pottery and social life in medieval England: towards a relational approach*, Oxbow Books, Oxford.

Jesch, J. 2011, "Runic Inscriptions and the Vocabulary of Land" in *Settlement and Lordship in Viking and Early Medieval Scandinavia*, eds. B. Poulsen & S.M. Sindbæk, Turnhout, pp. 31-44.

Johansen, E., Møller Knudsen, B. & Kock, J. 1992, *Fra Aalborgs fødsel til Grevens Fejde 1534. Aalborgs Historie 1*, Aalborg kommune, Aalborg.

Jones, S. 1997, *The archaeology of ethnicity: constructing identities in the past and present*, Routledge, London.

Kalmring, S. 2015, "Urbanity by its 'smallest units'. Comments on 'performing towns'", *Archaeological Dialogues*, vol. 22, no. 2, pp. 137.

Kancelliets brevbøger vedrørende Danmarks indre forhold: i uddrag. 1885-2005, A. Reitzel, Kbh.

Karg, S. 2007, *Medieval food traditions in Northern Europe*, National Museum of Denmark, Copenhagen.

Karlsson, P., Tagesson, G., Ersgård, L., Holmgren, R., 2003, *I Tyskebacken: hus, människor och industri i stormaktstidens Norrköping*, Riksantikvarieämbetet, Stockholm.

Krants, L. 2005, "Århus åhavn – særligt om bolværkerne ved Fiskergade" in *Bolværker fra middelalderen og nyere tid*, ed. T. Roland, pp. 61-72.

Latour, B. 2005, *Reassembling the social: an introduction to actor-network-theory*, Oxford University Press, Oxford.

Latour, B. & Woolgar, S. 1979, *Laboratory life: the social construction of scientific facts*, Sage Publications, Beverly Hills.

Linaa Larsen, J. 1995, *Keramik fra torvet i Horsens: typologi, proveniensbestemmelse og datering*, Afd. for Middelalderarkæologi og Middelalder-arkæologisk Nyhedsbrev, Højbjerg.

Linaa Larsen, J. 1999, "Skrædderens hus: inventar fra en hustomt i renæssancens Sønderside", *Mark og montre*, vol. Årg. 35 (1999), pp. 11-28.

Linaa Larsen, J. 2003, "Til bords med Marsk Stig: en oversigt over keramikken fra Hjelm", *Kuml*, vol. 2003, pp. 227-246.

Linaa Larsen, J. 2005, "Sønderside revisited: på sporet af et marinarkæologisk problemkompleks", *Mark og montre*, vol. Årg. 41 (2005), pp. 93-106.

Linaa Larsen, J. 2006, *Keramik, kultur og kontakter: køkken- og bordtøjets brug og betydning i Jylland 1350-1650*, Jysk Arkæologisk Selskab, Højbjerg.

Linaa, J. 2010, "Genstandsfundene" in *Tønderhus: en købstadsborg i hertugdømmet Slesvig*, eds. L. Krants Larsen, J. Linaa, J. Herts & I. Lauridsen, Museum Sønderjylland, Tønder, pp. 80-120.

Linaa, J. 2011, "Mester Trebing fra Hessen. Livet i glashytten Stenhule ved Silkeborg 1604-1610", *Hikuin*, vol. 37, pp. 189-207.

Linaa, J. 2012, "In Memory of Merchants. The Consumption and

Cultural Meetings of a Dutch Immigrant in Early Modern Elsinore. Odense 2012" in *Later Historical Archaeology in Britain and Denmark, c. 1500-2000 AD* eds. D. Cranstone, P. Belford & L. Høst-Madsen, Syddansk Universitetsforlag, Odense, pp. 91-104.

Linaa, J. 2014, "Mad på tre af 1300-tallets borge." in *Dansk Madhistorie. Mad i krig og krise,* ed. I. Hellvik, Dansk Landbrugsmuseum, Højbjerg, pp. 4-17.

Linaa, J. 2015, "Consumption. Meals, Miracles, and Material Culture in the Later Middle Ages" in *The Saturated Sensorium: Principles of Perception and Mediation in the Middle Ages,* ed. H.-H. Lohfert Jørgensen, H. Laugerud & K. Skinnebach, Aarhus University press, Aarhus, pp. 229-246.

Linaa Larsen, J. & Skov, H. 2003, "Boligmiljø på byernes parceller-især i Århus" in *Bolig og Familie i Danmarks Middelalder,* ed. E. Roesdahl, Højbjerg, pp. 119-128.

Madsen, H.J. 1991, "Skumstrup - Vilhelmsborg: en herregård-stomt fra renæssancen", *Hikuin,* vol. Nr. 18 (1991), pp. 197-224.

Madsen, H.J. 1996, "Vikingernes By 900-1100" in *Aarhus Byens historie-1720,* ed. I. Gejl, Århus Byhistoriske Udvalg, Aarhus, pp. 13-123.

Madsen, P.K. 1999, *Middelalderkeramik fra Ribe: byarkæologiske undersøgelser 1980-87,* Jysk Arkæologisk Selskab, Højbjerg.

Mikkelsen, H. 2002, *Vor Frue Kloster: et benediktinernonnekloster i Randers,* Kulturhistorisk Museum, Randers.

Mikkelsen, J. 2008, "Poor relief in provincial towns in the Kingdom of Denmark and the Duchy of Schleswig, ca. 1700-1850" in *Danish Towns during Absolutism. Urbanisation and Urban Life 1660-1848,* eds. S. Bitsch Christensen & J. Mikkelsen, Aarhus, pp. 365-410.

Mikkelsen, H. & Smidt-Jensen, J.; 1995, *En smuk lille by,* Skalk 5, p. 5-10.

Moesgaard, J.C. 2006, "Single finds as evidence for coin circulation in the Middle Ages – status and perspectives", *Nordisk Numismatisk Årsskrift,* pp. 228-275.

Moesgaard, J.C. 2009, "Hvorfor er der så få enkeltfund af Harald Blåtands mønter?", *Nordisk Numismatisk Unions medlemsblad,* vol. 2009, nr. 4, pp. 135-139.

Moesgaard, J.C. 2011, "Cross-motif coins from Aarhus" in *Aros and the world of the vikings: the stories and travelogues of seven Vikings from Aros,* eds. H. Skov & J. Varberg, 1. edition edn, Moesgård Museum, Højbjerg, pp. 67-69.

Moesgaard, J.C. & Hilberg, V. 2010, "Opsigtsvækkende fund af korsmønter: er hypotesen om "Tyskervældet" i Hedeby 974-983 forkert?", *Nordisk Numismatisk Unions medlemsblad,* vol. 2010, nr. 4, pp. 143-150.

Moesgaard, J.C. & Tornbjerg, S.Å. 2008, "Møntbrug på lan-det i middelalderen: de enkeltfundne mønter fra mid-delaldergården i Bjæverskov", *Aarbøger for nordisk oldkyn-dighed og historie,* vol. 2008, pp. 195-212.

Mullins, P.R. 2011, "The Archaeology of Consumption", *Annual Review of Anthropology,* vol. 40, pp. 133-144.

Mulryne, J.R. 2004, *Europa triumphans: court and civic festivals in early modern Europe,* Ashgate, Aldershot, Hants, England.

Naum, M. 2008, *Homelands lost and gained: Slavic migration and settlement on Bornholm in the early Middle Ages,* Lunds uni-versitet, Lund.

Naum, M. 2012, "Ambiguous pots: Everyday practice, migration and materiality. The case of medieval Baltic ware on the island of Bornholm (Denmark)", *Journal of Social Archaeology,* vol. 12, no. 1, pp. 92.

Naum, M. 2013, "Premodern Translocals: German Merchant Diaspora Between Kalmar and Northern German Towns (1250–1500)", *International Journal of Historical Archaeology,* vol. 17, no. 2, pp. 376-400.

Naum, M. 2015, "Material Culture and Diasporic Experiences: A Case of Medieval Hanse Merchants in the Baltic", *Archeological papers of the American Anthropological Association,* vol. 26, no. 1, pp. 72.

Naum, M. & Nordin, J.M. 2013, *Scandinavian colonialism and the rise of modernity: small time agents in a global arena,* Springer, New York.

Nielsen, I. & Schiørring, O. 1976, "Roskildes middelalder på kort" in *13 bidrag til Roskilde by og Egns historie,* ed. F. Birkebæk, Roskilde, pp. 94-110.

Nielsen, J.N. 2015, *Glargårde: dansk glasfremstilling i renæssancen,* Nordjyllands Historiske Museum, Aalborg.

Orduna, J.R. 1995, *Middelalderlige klædeplomber: blyplomber fra klæ-de importeret til Danmark indtil 1600,* Afd. for Middelalder-arkæologi, Højbjerg.

Orton, C., Tyers, P. & Vince, A. 1993, *Pottery in archaeology,* Cambridge University Press, Cambridge.

Pajung, S. & Poulsen, B. 2014, "Et senmiddeladerligt handelsnet-værk: Flenborgkøbmanden Namen jansens købmandsbog 1528-49", *Temp,* vol. Nr. 9 (2014), pp. 23-42.

Paludan, H. (ed) 1985, *Århus bys historie: fra vikingetid til nutid,* Husets Forlag, Aarhus.

Paludan, H. 1996, "Bispestaden 1100-1500" in *Aarhus Byens historie-1720,* ed. I. Gejl, Århus Byhistoriske Udvalg, Aarhus, pp. 123-242.

Poulsen, B. 1979, "Møntbrug i Danmark 1100-1300", *Fortid og Nutid,* vol. 28, pp. 281-285.

Poulsen, B. 1985, "Mønter i den senmiddelalderlige danske agrarøkonomi", *Hikuin,* vol. 11 (1985), pp. 227-236.

Poulsen, B. 1994, "Land og by i senmiddelalderen", in *Danmark i Senmiddelalderen,* eds. P. Ingesman & J.V. Jensen, Aarhus Universitetsforlag, Aarhus, pp. 214-217

Poulsen, B. 1999, "Daglivets fællesskaber" in *Middelalderens Danmark,* eds. P. Ingesman, U. Kjær, P.K. Madsen & J. Vellev, Gad, Kbh, pp. 188-207.

Poulsen, B. 2000, "Krydderier og klæde. Statusforbrug i sen-middelalderens Danmark" in *Danmark og Europe i senmid-delalderen,* eds. P. Ingesman & B. Poulsen, Aarhus, pp. 64-94.

Poulsen, B. 2002 (2002a), "A monetary contraction in late medieval Denmark?", *Nordisk Numismatisk Årsskrift,* vol. 2000-2002, pp. 319-334.

Poulsen, B. 2002 (2002b), "The Widening of Import Trade and Consumption around 1200 A.D., a Danish Perspective" in *Cogs, Cargoes and Commerce: Maritime Bulk Trade in Northern Europe,* eds. L. Berggren, N. Hybel & A. Landen, Toronto, pp. 31-52.

Poulsen, B. 2004 (2004a), "Tilbagegang og vækst i senmiddelalderens danske by (2004a)" in *Middelalderbyen. Danske Bystudier 1,* ed. S. Bitsch Christenen, pp. 191-248.

Poulsen, B. 2004 (2004b), "Trade and consumption among late medieval and early modern Danish peasants", *Scandinavian Economic History Review,* vol. 52, no. 1, pp. 52-68.

Poulsen, B. 2008, "Aarslevs ældste historie", *Årsskrift / Lokalhistorisk Forening for Sønderhald,* vol. 2008, pp. 6-17.

Poulsen, B. 2009 (2009a), "Forholdet mellem land og by i dansk middelalder", *Historisk tidsskrift,* vol. 109, h. 1 (2009), pp. 1-20.

Poulsen, B. 2010, "Meeting the king in late medieval Denmark" in *Power and persuasion: essays on the art of state building in honour of W.P. Blockmans,* eds. P.C.M. Hoppenbrouwers, A. Janse, R. Stein & W. BLockmans, Brepols Publ., Turnhout, Belgium, pp. 141-156.

Poulsen, B. 2013 (2013a), "Identities in the Danish Medieval Town: Les identités dans la ville danoise au Moyen Âge (2013a)", *Revue d'historie Nordique,* vol. 16, pp. 115-131.

Poulsen, B. 2013 (2013b), "Late Medieval Migration across the Baltic: The Movement of People between Northern Germany and Denmark" in *Guilds, Towns and Cultural Transmissions in the North 1300-1500,* eds. L. Bisgaard, L. Boje Morgensen & T. Petitt, Odense, pp. 31-56.

Poulsen, B., Bjørn, C. & Fonnesbech-Wulf, B. 2000, "Samfundet set af en 1500-tals borger: Om typer og social mobilitet i Hans Christensen Sthens "Kort Vending"" in *Mark og menneske. Studier i Danmarks historie 1500-1800,* pp. 123-139.

Poulsen, K. 2011, *Den middelalderlige bydel nord for volden i Århus,* Middelalder-arkæologisk Nyhedsbrev, Højbjerg.

Rasmussen, P. & Christensen, C.A. 1972-1975, *Århus domkapitels jordebøger,* Landbohistorisk Selskab, Kbh.

Rodenberg, M. 2011, "The city of Lübeck and the Internationality of Early Hanseatic Trade" in *The Hanse in Medieval and Early Modern Europe* eds. J. Wubs-Mrozewicz & J. Jenks, Brill Adademic Publishers, Leiden, Lund, pp. 37-58.

Roehmer, M., Schöne, S., 2014, *Formenkosmos Siegburger Steinzeug: die Sammlung im Hetjens-Museum,* Nünnerich-Asmus, Mainz am Rhein.

Roesdahl, E. & Kock, J. (eds) 2005, *Boringholm: en østjysk træborg fra 1300-årene,* Jysk Arkæologisk Selskab, Højbjerg.

Roodenburg, H. 2007, *Forging European Identities. Cultural exchange in early modern Europe vol 4.* Cambridge University Press, Cambridge.

Roslund, M. 2001, *Gäster i huset ; kulturell överföring mellan slaver och skandinaver 900 till 1300,* Vetenskapssocieteten i Lund, Lund.

Rostholm, H. 1980, "Herningsholm: udgravninger 1975-1980", *Antikvariske studier,* vol. Bd. 4 (1980), pp. 199-240.

Schäfer, H. 2004, "Töpfereiabfall des frühen 15. Jahrhunderts aus Güstrow", *Archäologische Berichte aus Mecklenburg-Vorpommern,* vol. 11, pp. 108-121.

Schiørring, O. 1988, "Byens hus: - udgravning af det middelalderlige rådhus i Århus", *Hikuin,* vol. Nr. 14 (1988), pp. 39-48 348.

Schmidt, G. 1996, "Der frühneuzeitliche "Moor- oder Dreckwall" von 1554 bis 1560 in Lübeck", *Lübecker Schriften zur Archäologie und Kulturgeschichte,* vol. 24, pp. 265-308.

Scholliers, P. 2001, *Food, drink and identity: cooking, eating and drinking in Europe since the Middle Ages,* Berg, Oxford.

Schulz, C. 1990, "Keramik des 14. Bis 16. Jahrhunderts aus der Fronerei in Lübeck", *Lübecker Schriften zur Archäologie und Kulturgeschichte,* vol. 19, pp. 163-203.

Selch Jensen, C. 2004, "Byerne og de fattige - den internationalle baggrund for den danske udvikling" in *Middelalderbyen. Danske bystudier ; 1,* ed. S. Bitsch Christensen, Aarhus Universitetsforlag, Aarhus, pp. 295-324.

Shove, E., Pantzar, M. & Wattson, M. 2012, *The dynamics of social practice,* Sage, London.

Simon-Muscheid, K. 2000, "Der Umgang mit Alkohol: Männliche Soziabilität und weibliche Tugend" in *Kontraste im Alltag des Mittelalters,* ed. G. Jaritz, Verlag der Österreichischen Akademie der Wissenschaften, Wien, pp. 35-60.

Sindbæk, S.M. 2007, "The Small World of the Vikings: Networks in Early Medieval Communication and Exchange", *Norwegian Archaeological Review,* vol. 40, no. 1, pp. 59-74.

Sindbæk, S.M. 2009, "Open access, nodal points, and central places: Maritime communication and locational principles for coastal sites in south Scandinavia, c. AD 400-1200 / Avatud ligipaas, solmpunktid ja keskused: veeteed ja Louna-Skandinaavia rannaasulate paiknemisloogika aastail 400-1200 pKr", *Estonian Journal of Archaeology,* vol. 13, no. 2, pp. 96.

Sindbæk, S.M. 2011, "Social Power and Outland Use in Viking Age Settlement" in *Settlement and Lordship in Viking and Early Medieval Scandinavia,* eds. Bjørn Poulsen & S.M. Sindbæk, Brepols, Turnhout, pp. 97-111.

Sindbæk, S.M. & Poulsen, B. 2011, *Settlement and lordship in Viking and early medieval Scandinavia,* Brepols, Turnhout.

Skaarup, B. 2006, *Renæssancemad: opskrifter og køkkenhistorie fra Christian 4.'s tid,* Gyldendal, Kbh.

Skaarup, J. 2005, *Øhavets middelalderlige borge og voldsteder,* Langelands Museum, Rudkøbing.

Skamby Madsen, J. 2005, "Søvejen til Aros" in *Vikingernes Aros,* ed. A. Damm, Moesgaard, Højbjerg, pp. 98-105.

Skamby Madsen, J. & Vinner, M. 2005, "Skibe, navigation og havne" in *Vikingernes Aros,* ed. A. Damm, Moesgaard,

Højbjerg, pp. 80-97.

Skov, H. 1996, "Dominikanerklosteret i Århus", *Hikuin,* vol. 23, pp. 135-148.

Skov, H. 1997, "Udgravningerne ved Aarhus Katedralskole i 1994-95", *Kuml 1995/1996,* pp. 189-206.

Skov, H. 1998, "Udgravningerne i Århus Midtby 1994-97", *Kuml,* vol. 1997/98, pp. 227-294.

Skov, H. 1999, "Brønde i Århus fra vikingetid til nyere tid" in *Menneskelivets mangfoldighed. Arkæologisk og antropologisk forskning på Moesgård,* ed. O. Højriis, Højbjerg, pp. 269-280.

Skov, H. 2004, "The infrastructure in Århus betweem 900 and 1600 AD", *Lübecker Kolloquium zur Stadtarchäologie im Hanseraum,* vol. IV, pp. 551-566.

Skov, H. 2005 (2005a), "Aros 700-1100" in *Vikingernes Aros,* ed. A. Damm, Moesgaard, Højbjerg, pp. 15-39.

Skov, H. 2005 (2005b), "Udgravningerne i vikingernes Aros" in *Vikingernes Aros,* ed. A. Damm, Moesgaard, Højbjerg, pp. 118-119.

Skov, H. 2005 (2005c), "Viby" in *Vikingernes Aros,* ed. A. Damm, Moesgaard, Højbjerg, pp. 40-45.

Skov, H. 2009, "Det ældste Århus (ca. 770-1200)", *Århus Stifts Årbøger,* vol. 92, pp. 5-20.

Skov, H. 2010, "The defense and town fortifications of Aarhus from the 8th to the 15th century", *Lübecker Kolloquium zur Stadtarchäologie im Hanseraum,* vol. VII, Lübeck, pp. 883-897.

Skov, H. 2014, "The monasteries in Aarhus", *Lübecker Kolloquium zur Stadtarchäologie im Hanseraum,* vol. IX, Lübeck, pp. 697-715.

Skriver, J.B. 2008, *Moesgård: historien om en herregård,* Moesgård Museum, Højbjerg.

Smith, M.L. 2015, "Towns and cities. A commentary on 'performing towns'", *Archaeological Dialogues,* vol. 22, no. 2, pp. 146.

Søgaard, H. 1961, *Det ældste Århus,* Universitetsforlaget i Aarhus, Aarhus.

Stephan, H. 1992, *Keramik der Renaissance im Oberweserraum und an der unteren Werra: Beiträge der Archäologie zur Erforschung der Sachkultur der frühen Neuzeit,* Rheinland-Verlag, Köln.

Stockhammer, P.W. 2012, *Conceptualizing Cultural Hybridization: A Transdisciplinary Approach,* Springer Berlin Heidelberg, Berlin, Heidelberg.

Svart Kristiansen, M. (ed) 2006, *Tårnby: gård og landsby gennem 1000 år,* Jysk Arkæologisk Selskab, Højbjerg.

Thomsen, C.J.T. 1933-40, *Realregister til Aarhus Bys Skøde- og Panteprotokoller 1683-93: Udarb. paa Grundlag af Skøde- og Panteprotokollerne og beslægtede Arkivalier,* Aarhus.

Tilley, C. 1999, *Metaphor and material culture,* Blackwell Publishers, Oxford, UK.

Tilly, C. 2005, *Identities, boundaries, and social ties,* Paradigm Publishers, Boulder, Colo.

Toftgaard Jensen, J. & Norskov, J. 2005, *Købstadens metamorfose: byudvikling og byplanlægning i Århus 1800-1920,* Dansk Center for Byhistorie, Aarhus.

Ulsig, E. 2004, *Århusundersøgelsen - under Det nordiske Ødegårdsprojekt: samt Ødegårdene - en datering,* Aarhus Universitetsforlag, Aarhus.

Unger, R.W. 2004, *Beer in the Middle Ages and the Renaissance,* University of Pennsylvania Press, Philadelphia.

Vellev, J. 2008, "Hans Hansen Skonning: Forfatter, klokker, bogtrykker og papirmager: - starten på industrien i Århus" in *Det skjulte Århus,* ed. P. Pedersen, L. Hannestad, J. Steensig, H. Krongaard Kristensen, Aarhus Universitetsforlag, pp. 23-46.

Venborg Pedersen, M. 2013, *Luksus: forbrug og kolonier i Danmark i det 18. århundrede,* Museum Tusculanum, Kbh.

Vogtherr, H. 1996, *Die Lübecker Pfundzollbücher 14921-1496,* Böhlau, Köln.

Voss, B.L. 2015, "What's New? Rethinking Ethnogenesis in the Archaeology of Colonialism", *American Antiquity,* vol. 80, no. 4, pp. 655-670.

Wade, M.R. 1996, *Triumphus nuptialis danicus: German court culture and Denmark: the "great wedding" of 1634,* Otto Harrassowitz, Wiesbaden.

Wallerström, T. 1997, "On Ethnicity as a Methodological Problem in Historical Archaeology. A Northern Fennoscandian Perspective." in *Visions of the past: trends and traditions in Swedish medieval archaeology. Lund studies in medieval archaeology; 19; Skrifter; 24,* eds. H. Andersson, P. Carelli & L. Ersgård, Central Board of National Antiquities, Stockholm, pp. 299-352.

Wandsnider, L. 2015, "On complementarity of practice, scale and structure. Scalar aspects of social/material space in Anatolian peri-urban contexts in antiquity", *Archaeological Dialogues,* vol. 22, no. 2, pp. 149.

Wienberg, J. 1993, *Den gotiske labyrint: middelalderen og kirkerne i Danmark,* Almqvist & Wiksell International, Lund.

Wille-Jørgensen, D. 2014, *Kongens borg: 123 års arkæologi på Vordingborg,* Danmarks Borgcenter - Museum Sydøstdanmark, Vordingborg.

Woolgar, C.M, 2006, *The Senses in Late Medieval England,* Yale University Press, New Haven

Woolgar, C.M. 2010, "Food and the middle ages", *Journal of Medieval History,* vol. 36, no. 1, pp. 1-19.

Woolgar, C.M. 1999, *The great household in late medieval England,* Yale University Press, New Haven, CT.

Wubs-Mrozewicz, J. 2005, "The Bergenfahrer and the Bergenvaarders: Lübeck und Amsterdam in a Study of Rivalry c. 1440-1560" in *Das Hansische Kontor zu Bergen und die Lübecker Bergenfahrer: International Workshop Lübeck 2003,* ed. A. Grassmann, Schmidt-Römhild, pp. 206-230.

Øeby Nielsen, G. 2005 (2005a), "De danske runestens oprindelige plads", *Kuml,* vol. 2005, pp. 121-144.

Øeby Nielsen, G. 2005, "Runesten og magt i Østjylland", *Hikuin,* vol. Nr. 32 (2005), pp. 105-124 129.